PHILOSOPHY
An Introduction

PHILOSOPHY
An Introduction

ARCHIE J. BAHM
UNIVERSITY OF NEW MEXICO
ALBUQUERQUE

JOHN WILEY & SONS, INC.
440 Fourth Avenue, New York

CHAPMAN & HALL, LTD.
London

To my parents
JOHN and LENA

Preface

This textbook is designed for students interested in a general introduction to philosophy. Its primary aims are two: first, to provoke careful thought, and second, to provide acquaintance with the main philosophical problems and their traditional methods of solution.

In pursuing the first objective, I have sought to nurture open-mindedness and broader appreciations by presenting a sympathetic, but critical, examination of accepted beliefs. My second purpose is a dual one: to interpret for the reader the great philosophical issues, ideals, and outlooks, an understanding of which is essential to a liberal education, and to supply the minimum vocabulary needed by the enlightened reader. In contrast both with the view that philosophy is properly studied only by reading original sources and with the view that the student of philosophy should merely reflect on his own experiences and immediate interests, the view taken here is that individual development is better served when these two tendencies interact. That is, personal insight is facilitated by appreciation of, and criticism of, mankind's principal systems of thought. Without some guidance, the beginner is lost. Without thinking for himself, the student cannot make philosophy his own.

Problems are arranged in three groups, which pertain to knowledge, reality, and values. Different types of philosophy are contrasted with respect to each problem. Since some students will prefer to begin with reality or values, rather than with knowledge, the book is written in such a way that one may select to suit varying needs. However, there are advantages to be gained from following the chapters in the order of their presentation. Although the book is not primarily historical, the selection of types in Part I may serve as a summary account of modern European and American philosophy.

Part I, *Knowledge*, is introduced by examining naive realism, the common-sense view, and presenting detailed and effective criticisms aimed at stirring beginners out of a normal complacency. Ten modern alternatives are then summarized, compared with naive realism, and criticized. Thinkers whose views are stated here include Locke, Berkeley, Hume, Kant, Hegel, Comte, Feigl, Russell, Sellars, Santayana, Bergson, James, and Dewey. Numerous quotations from original sources, selected for succinctness and intelligibility, capture some of the spirit of these thinkers themselves. A history of modern philosophies of science may be found, by those who care to look for it, embedded in the treatments of knowledge.

Part II, *Reality*, begins with the dualism of Descartes, because in it is to be found the clearest statement of the interactionistic view of mind-body relationships, a view closest to the established prejudices of a majority of unreflective students. Contradictions inherent in dualism, which set the course of modern metaphysical thinking, provided this doctrine with its main paradoxical muddles, and endowed students with much of their personal confusion, are laid bare. Then eight attempts to deal with these paradoxes are explained, compared, and criticized. The views of Spinoza, Leibniz, Newton, Plotinus, Morgan, Boodin, and Whitehead, among others, are contrasted in such a way as to show a pattern of development which, although not strictly chronological, clarifies the issues, the opposing stands, and the trends in metaphysical thinking that contend for our allegiance today. In addition to discussing the general problem of the place of mind and body, or of spirit and matter, in ultimate reality, Part II serves as a summary of views on more specific problems, such as causation, relations, space, time, change, novelty, substance, freedom, values, and God.

Part III, *Values*, pertains to goodness, beauty, rightness, religion, society, government, wealth, and education. Since, if each of these received as extensive treatment as knowledge and reality, the book would be far too long, consideration of each is limited to a chapter. The same method used in dealing with knowledge and reality, in Parts I and II, is used within each chapter in Part III, except on a smaller scale. The chapter on ethics treats of rightness, intentions, responsibility, freedom, rights, justice, punishment, virtue, ideals, and wisdom.

The book begins with a description and definition of philosophy, and it ends with suggestions for evaluating the success of the introductory course, advice regarding the possibilities for continuing a study of philosophy, and hints concerning uses which students may make of philosophical societies. Since it is normal for some beginners to be disappointed with their first course, because they had anticipated values different from those to be found, it seems helpful to point out that they may gain advantages even greater than those they had expected. Advice, which must be given and received with caution, ranges, for various types of readers, from quitting immediately to lifelong devotion. Although the book is not written primarily for majors in philosophy, and although philosophical pursuits do not aim primarily at financial rewards, I have not hesitated to survey the varieties of professional possibilities. Pointers for further reading include references to current journals and dictionaries, as well as to usual sourcebooks in various fields.

Inclusion of organicism, my own view, serves four purposes. First of all, the reader has a right to know where I stand. It seems fairer for me to state my views clearly than to pretend neutrality and then to permit my opinions to permeate the book unannounced. Second, I have made use of an opportunity, inherent in a customary privilege, for expressing a personal viewpoint. Since my opinions are systematically summarized here for the first time, this is a sourcebook of organicism as well as a textbook on philosophy. Third, I believe my view to be especially useful for introductory purposes, since it is not only a distinct contemporary type but one peculiarly fitted for clarifying significant contrasts in other views. Such fitness is due to the fact that it was developed largely out of the processes of teaching about conflicting philosophies. It fills a gap in a pattern of opposing outlooks, and at the same time serves as a philosophy about philosophies, which may prove helpful to those seeking perspective. Apparent similarities exist between organicism and Whitehead's philosophy of organism. Therefore, after Whitehead's attempt to develop a dynamic metaphysics is summarized sympathetically, differences as well as similarities between organism and organicism are pointed out. My concluding challenge to Whitehead's views provides the student with a sample of an up-to-date conflict. Finally, my attempt to solve philosophical problems is intended as an example for students. Although not all students will be willing or able to construct a system, I hope to instill in some of my readers the courage to do so. Philosophical synthesis is a job that needs doing again and again, not only by each individual for himself, but for mankind which, it seems, can have its problems solved, not all at once by one mind, but piecemeal, by many different minds, at many different times, each mind contributing a uniquely valuable insight.

The greatest shortcoming of this book, in my opinion, is its neglect of Oriental philosophies. Doubtless this will not be felt by those who share current Western prejudices concerning introductions to philosophy. Many will wish the book had made fuller reference to early Western philosophers, such as Plato, Aristotle, Augustine, and Aquinas, and some will observe that it contains no chapters devoted to philosophy of history or philosophy of language. It is not a textbook in logic, although certain theories of logic are discussed, and, as is usual with introductory textbooks, it needs to be supplemented by a course in logic.

ARCHIE J. BAHM

University of New Mexico
March, 1953

Acknowledgments

The writer wishes that he could express adequately his gratitude to all persons who have contributed to making this book possible. Robert Williams, his first teacher of philosophy, inspired open-mindedness and his teaching provided an example of what an introductory course should be. The purposes and structure of Roy Wood Sellars' *The Principles and Problems of Philosophy,* which served the author as an early model, are doubtless reflected in the present work. The students who, during the author's twenty years of teaching, have responded in varying ways to opportunities for philosophic inquiry, have played an important part in shaping the book.

Joseph Katz' constructive comments on Plotinus, Gustav Mueller's recommendations concerning Hegel, and William Bernhardt's critical reading of the chapter on philosophy of religion deserve grateful recognition. University of New Mexico professors who have offered suggestions regarding specific chapters include Paul Walter on social philosophy; Frederick Irion, A. L. Gausewitz, and Robert E. Clark on political philosophy and law; Julian Duncan, David Hamilton, and Mervyn Crobaugh on economic philosophy; and Leighton H. Johnson and Wilson H. Ivins on philosophy of education. Finally, the author is indebted especially to Hubert G. Alexander, his friend and department head, for encouragement, and to Luna, his wife, for many valuable suggestions.

Acknowledgment to publishers for permission to quote from copyrighted materials is given in the footnotes. However, particular mention of appreciation for permission to use numerous quotations is given to The Macmillan Company, Harper and Brothers, the Philosophical Library, Appleton-Century-Crofts, Houghton Mifflin Company, the Ronald Press, and Henry Holt and Company.

Contents

CONCLUSION

· I ·
What Is Philosophy?

Philosophy is seen differently through different eyes. Some persons see it as good, some as bad, and still others as mysterious. The good view comes, naturally, from its appreciators; the bad and the mysterious from those who fail to understand it. The blame for these adverse views rests partly upon the inherent nature of philosophy, its impenetrability to the uninitiated, partly upon those professors of philosophy who glorify themselves by appearing in a cloak of mystery or who are unwilling to lead the novice step by step, but most of all upon those impatient seekers who wish to have in a moment what can be had only in an hour. The darker side of the estimation of philosophy is well worth viewing. A student informs us: "The term 'philosophy' conveys to most people a vagueness and uncertainty. The layman is ignorant of its aims and the popular impression is that it is a collection of high-flown, meaningless words and phrases on useless subjects." Such a view is not without foundation, but the foundation is one of failure. The grapes are sour to those who cannot reach them. Mysterious? "Philosophy is a mysterious subject," says C. J. Ducasse. Yet it is no more mysterious than agronomy, astrophysics, ethnography, seismology, or any other subject with which one is not familiar. The unknown appears mysterious. So, although philosophy does deal with the unknown, its mystery comes mainly from ignorance and unfamiliarity. Appreciation of philosophy will follow understanding.

One of the most difficult questions which a teacher of philosophy has to answer is: What is philosophy? "The word," another student tells us, "is one of those elusive abstractions which, rabbit-like, always barely escapes capture and definition. It means a variety of things to different persons. Each man you questioned would stop, meditate, and give you another definition." A perusal of current attempts to define philosophy would confirm this student's view. The differences between definitions offered by contemporary specialists are not merely verbal; they are real. Yet each seizes something essential.

Six distinguishable components are present in philosophy. Examination of all six seems necessary for a complete description, although many definers neglect, and others deny, the importance of some of them. What are they? Problems, attitudes, methods, activities, conclusions, and effects. Philosophy as an attitude and method is emphasized by Brightman and Barrett. Says Brightman: "Philosophy is essentially a spirit or method of approaching experience, rather than a body of conclusions about experience." [1] Rejoins Barrett: "It is not the specific content of these conclusions, but the spirit and method by which they were reached, which entitles them to be described as philosophical." [2] Ducasse says: "Were I limited to one line for my answer to it, I should say that philosophy is general theory of criticism." [3]

Emphasis upon philosophy as problems or theories, on the other hand, appears in Leighton's definition: "Philosophy, like science, consists of theories or insights arrived at as a result of systematic reflection." [4] For Maritain, as for Herbert Spencer, "Philosophy is concerned with everything, is a 'universal science.'" [5] To this Sellars adds: "Our subject is a 'collection of sciences,' such as theory of knowledge, logic, cosmology, ethics, and aesthetics, as well as a unified survey." [6] Any student of the history of philosophy will testify that problems and, especially, theories, are what one seeks in philosophy. William James, on the other hand, stresses activity: "Philosophy in the full sense is only man thinking. . . ." [7] For others, philosophy is what philosophy does, how it functions, its results in the lives of people influenced by it. Regardless of the varying emphases, and in spite of genuine differences, in contemporary definitions, philosophy can be described as being constituted of all six components, not merely of any one or two. Let us consider each in turn.

[1] Edgar S. Brightman, *Introduction to Philosophy*, p. 7. Henry Holt and Co., New York, 1925.

[2] Clifford Barrett, *Philosophy*, p. v. The Macmillan Co., New York, 1935.

[3] Curt J. Ducasse, *Philosophy of Art*, p. 3. Dial Press, New York, 1929.

[4] Joseph A. Leighton, *The Field of Philosophy*, fourth edition, p. 4. Appleton-Century-Crofts, Inc., New York, 1930.

[5] Jacques Maritain, *An Introduction to Philosophy*, p. 103. Sheed and Ward, New York, 1930.

[6] Roy Wood Sellars, *The Principles and Problems of Philosophy*, p. 3. The Macmillan Co., New York, 1926.

[7] William James, *Some Problems of Philosophy*, p. 15. Longmans, Green and Co., New York, 1911.

Problems

What problems are philosophical? Philosophers usually consider their task as that of understanding man and the universe. This is a large order and is difficult to deal with all at once. Consequently, the large problem is broken down into many smaller ones. Although there has been some disagreement among philosophers as to which problems are the more important, a certain general agreement has been reached concerning which are philosophical—all of them, however, being questions concerning which "we have assumed answers . . . before we even thought of asking them." [8] If not all problems are philosophical, which ones are? To ask: How far is it from New York to London? is not to ask a philosophical question. But to ask: What is distance? or What is space? is philosophical. Do you know whether it will rain tomorrow? This is of no philosophical importance. But What is knowledge? is a basic philosophical inquiry. Is it true that all swans are white? This may trouble the zoologist, but not the philosopher. But with What is truth? the philosopher is deeply concerned. Is it a fact that Caesar is dead? or Is it a fact that 2 plus 2 equals 4? These are concerns of the historian and mathematician. The philosopher wants to know What is a fact? What time is it? is not, but What is time? is, a philosophical question. Is the shirt you are wearing the same one that you sent to the laundry? Philosophers ignore such questions. But What is sameness? the philosopher would like to know. Are the Niagara Falls beautiful? is a question for sightseers; the philosopher wonders: What is beauty? Is it wrong to commit bigamy in the United States? This is a problem for jurists, whereas philosophers inquire: What is the nature of rightness and wrongness? The foregoing samples, pairs of related questions, the one philosophical, the other not, should reveal that philosophical questions are always general. Questions concerning particular things do not ordinarily constitute philosophical problems. When a philosopher seems to be puzzling about a particular, he is really seeking a general principle exhibited therein. If we are to survey with any degree of completeness the problems included in philosophy, we shall have to go beyond mere examples and to classify them systematically. For purposes of classification, they may be divided into two important

[8] W. A. Sinclair, *An Introduction to Philosophy*, p. 12. Oxford University Press, London, 1944.

groups: those that constitute the so-called philosophical sciences and those comprising philosophy as a comprehensive science.

THE PHILOSOPHICAL SCIENCES

Within its broad domain philosophy contains several more or less well-defined subject matters which may properly be called sciences, although they have not been received by everyone as sciences of full stature. Each probes a basic question, the answer to which is essential to a complete account of the world and of life. Each examines a phase of experience as distinct and as fundamental as those investigated by the non-philosophical sciences. What, then, are the philosophical sciences, and with what problems is each concerned?

Epistemology is an inquiry into the nature of knowledge and truth and certainty. Close to psychology in some of its phases, epistemology digs into the problem of the relation of knowing to that which is known. Is an idea of a mountain like a mountain? It is not like it in size; for the idea is within one's head while the mountain is larger than the head. It is not like it in stuff, for the mountain is made of granite and soil and sand and snow; but these are not the ingredients of the normal head. It is not like it in shape, for the mountain has three dimensions, though seen only in two, and the mountain has numerous ridges and ravines, which are not elements of an idea. It is not like it in duration, for the mountain endures for thousands of years, the idea for a second. How, then, is knowledge like its object? Epistemology is concerned, also, with whether objects known can exist independently of their being known, with what limits there are to knowing, with different ways of knowing, with origins of knowledge, and with consequences of solutions to the foregoing for dealing with all other problems. If what is true of knowledge in general is true also of the particular knowledge which anyone seeks, then, if the epistemologist can prove, in general, that certain kinds of knowledge are impossible, he can save much vain searching, in particular, for such impossible types of knowledge.

Logic is the science of the methods of reflection. It is usually considered the basic discipline in all philosophy and in all science, even more than mathematics, which rests upon logical foundations. It is concerned with problem-solving and with understanding and evaluating the various methods of solution. Thus, it needs to consider many questions: What is the structure of thought, and how is it related to the structure of the world? How does the mind function in solving problems? What biases and limitations of thinking precondition reasoning? What principles are presupposed in valid inference? What fallacies commonly occur in thinking, and how may they be avoided? What deductions are possible from any given statement? How trustworthy are inductions from any specific set of data? What are ambiguity and definiteness, and how much of each should be expected in reasonable interpretation?

Philosophy of science attempts to define the nature of science. Thus, it is concerned with, or presupposes, epistemological and logical conclusions. Its special task is to consider the limitations involved in applying these conclusions in the various fields of science, as these develop from time to time, and to assist critically in integrating their results into a world view. Thus, part of its job is to assist in constant reconsideration of newer scientific and metaphysical conclusions in the light of each other. In particular, philosophy of science concerns itself with understanding and evaluating so-called scientific methods, including conditions for reliable observation, classification, generalization, and verification. Still more particularly, it deals with the nature of experimentation, with probability in trial-and-error situations, and with the relative stability, and necessary tentativity, of scientific conclusions.

Semantics pertains to meanings and their relations to words, thoughts, and things. Philosophers have always been concerned with meanings, but recent critical examination of language has resulted in fuller analyses of the functions of symbols, signs, signals, etc., in helping to create both experienced objects and the experiencing mind. If symbolizing is "essential to thought, and prior to it," [9] then important clues, not only to man's problems, predicaments, perplexities, and purposes, but also to the nature of mind itself, may be found by studying the process of symbolization. If mind is partly a product of its symbolic faiths, if "mind is itself an act of faith," [10] then philosophers must seek to understand the symbolical.

Metaphysics investigates many problems, all related to the general question: What is the nature of existence? Let us review some of the typical metaphysical problems: What is reality? How many kinds of being are there? Can a universe be both one and many? What are the basic characteristics of existence? What is time? What is space? What is substance? What are relations? What is a

[9] Susanne K. Langer, *Philosophy in a New Key*, p. 33. Harvard Univ. Press, Cambridge, 1942.

[10] Hartley Burr Alexander, *Truth and the Faith*, p. 8. Henry Holt and Co., New York, 1929.

cause? What is a fact? What is sameness? What is purpose? What is change? What is novelty? What am I? Is the world determined? Is the universe purposive? Does the world progress? Is there a God?

Axiology, or theory of value, examines values. What are goodness and badness? What are the kinds of value? Naively the child thinks the candy bar good, but later, when he is sated, thinks it bad. Are goodness and badness in candy bars, or in the thinking? When a baker makes a loaf of bread, he says it is good for health; health is good for steady work; work is good for making money; money is good for lots of things. But is there something that is good for nothing except itself? That is, is there something which is just good, without being good for something else?

Aesthetics asks two questions: What is beauty? and What is art? That these two questions, often confused, are distinct is obvious. For, some beauty is beauty of nature, not of art, and some art is ugly, not beautiful. Both these questions demand an answer. A picture may be beautiful to one, ugly to another. Where then is beauty? In the eye of the beholder? On the canvas? Or somewhere else? Having once settled these questions, the aesthetician is troubled by a another one: What are the essential characteristics of beauty? There is beauty in music, painting, poetry, drama, sculpture, architecture, costumes, the dance, sunsets, and women. All have something in common. What is it? Likewise, he wants to know what are the necessary qualities of art. Finally, he inquires into the bases for judging beauty and art, and seeks to establish, in so far as he can, a set of standards, both a comprehensive one for all beauties and arts as well as one for each distinctive type of beauty or art. Some aestheticians find beauty almost all-pervasive (i.e., including little beauties as well as great beauties) and thus consider an understanding of beauty one of the most important and most practical of everyday needs.

Ethics examines the right and the wrong. Popular notions identify ethics with the commandments: Thou shalt and Thou shalt not. But no science ever commanded or preached. Being a science, ethics investigates. It wants to know how to determine when an act is right. What is obligation? What is duty? Responsibility? Conscience? Justice? Happiness? Wisdom?

Philosophy of religion is a branch of philosophy which inquires into religion. Philosophy of religion is not religion. Rather, it is a science which seeks to understand religion, and it is the philosopher, mainly, who grapples with the question of religion. There are many great religions: Christianity, Brahmanism, Buddhism, Confucianism, Taoism, Shintoism, Mohammedanism, Judaism. If all these are religions, do they not have something in common? Is there an essence of religion which is to be found in all? If so, what is it? If part of the essence of religion is found to be a concern for "the good life" and how to achieve it, this concern becomes a major problem for philosophical investigation.

To this array of philosophical sciences, many more might be added. *Social philosophy, political philosophy,* and *economic philosophy* are relatively important, but with the development of sociology, political science, and economics as separate sciences, questions concerning these particular fields are being left more and more to them. *Philosophy of education,* which investigates the ultimate purposes of education, is being handled at present largely by educational specialists. *Philosophy of history,* which attempts to interpret history, not merely in terms of social, political, and economic processes, but also as a significant part of cosmic processes (what is the place of the history of man in the drama of the universe?), is a field yet relatively undeveloped. The multitudes of other specialized fields of philosophical problems, such as *philosophy of physics, philosophy of business, philosophy of marriage, philosophy of physical education,* etc., must not detain us here.

It has become customary to group philosophical problems, and, thus, the philosophical sciences, into three groups, as we have done in this text, namely, those centering about the problem of knowledge or experience (epistemology, logic, philosophy of science, semantics); reality or existence (metaphysics, including ontology, cosmology, and theology); and values, together with their social manifestations (axiology, aesthetics, ethics, philosophy of religion, social, political, and economic philosophy, and philosophy of education). Such groupings of philosophical sciences, and even the gathering of problems under each of the specific sciences, may seem hard to justify, since there is so much overlapping. Yet, if each science and each grouping is taken as a focus of problems rather than as an area with well-defined boundaries, philosophical communication is provided with great convenience.

PHILOSOPHY AS A COMPREHENSIVE SCIENCE

The many specialized philosophical sciences do not appropriate all the problems which confront the philosopher. The best known, and perhaps the most important, problems of philosophy are still to be considered. In at least three ways, philosophy functions as a comprehensive science: it criticizes the sciences, synthesizes the sciences, and is the mother of the sciences.

All sciences, such as biology, psychology, sociology, astronomy, aesthetics, semantics, physics, etc., stand in need of *criticism*. Such criticism is of two sorts; namely, that directed toward premises and that toward conclusions. Each science makes presuppositions which, if examined carefully enough, may be found to be untenable or at least unprovable. To philosophy falls the task of careful examination. Again, each science makes presuppositions that may be found to contradict the presuppositions of other sciences. Also, each science eventually arrives at results which may appear to conflict with the conclusions of other sciences. To philosophy falls this task of comparing assumptions and conclusions.

Some examples of the many presuppositions which scientists today naturally and normally make are: Things exist in space and time; the objects of science are independent of their being known; relations and facts exist; true belief is possible; things are really separate. Assumptions as obvious as these commonly pass unquestioned. But, at times, trouble appears because of them. The job of examining them for the sciences then becomes the concern of philosophy. So, whenever different sciences make contradictory assumptions, philosophical problems arise. So long as a scientist keeps within his own field, he encounters little difficulty. Being occupied with his own troubling details, he usually overlooks what his assumptions imply for other fields. An illustration should make this clear: Today, physicists, biologists, and psychologists generally assume that every effect must have a cause, that is, that nothing can happen without being caused to happen in the way that it does happen. A body falls toward the earth instead of away from it because of gravitation. One's eyes are blue instead of yellow because they result from definite hereditary structures. A child is afraid of cats because he has been negatively conditioned by previous experience. For these sciences, the "law of cause and effect" holds universally.

Jurisprudence, ethics, and religion, on the other hand, seem to presuppose the contrary. That is, not everything must have happened in the way that it did. People are free to choose. They are presented with alternatives. They may select the one or the other without inevitable compulsion. Punishment is inflicted on the assumption that the law violator deliberately chose to violate. The young and the insane are exempt because they are not normal ethical beings. Normal men, however, are free to choose. If this were not a basic assumption, surely our laws would be written differently. Ethical codes are founded on the belief that a man can choose to follow them or not. He can act rightly or wrongly. If it were not so, no one could be held blameworthy, and no one could be immoral. Few are the followers of Socrates, who said, "No man can do wrong voluntarily." Religious salvation is often considered a matter of willing. The sinner must choose. But which alternative he chooses is a matter for him alone to decide. If his will is not determined, then, here, the law of cause and effect is neglected, ignored, and even denied. Allowing for exceptions, which will occur to alert readers, it is still true, in general, that these two apparently contradictory assumptions are basic to different fields of explanation. Surely, such apparent contradictions cannot stand in a final picture of the world. No science is complete which does not fit itself into the conclusions of other sciences. To make this clear is one of the difficult tasks of philosophy.

Conclusions of science, like their assumptions, also occasionally contradict. In mathematics it is an accepted principle that $1 + 1 = 2$ and that $(1)x + (1)x = (2)x$. By reflection alone, some say, the mathematician reached this conclusion. Physicists have chosen an experimental method to determine the speed of light and have concluded that approximately 186,300 miles per second is the fastest possible speed. Now, if light waves are traveling in two opposite directions from a source, at what speed are they separating? At the speed of light, or at twice the speed of light? Whenever such apparent contradictions arise, they must be resolved. If they involve only one science, the difficulty may be called scientific, and if they involve more than one, it may be termed philosophical. Thus, both with regard to assumptions and conclusions, philosophy functions as a criticizer of the sciences.

Synthesis is a second function that philosophy performs for the sciences. Each science dwells on one aspect, or phase, of experience. Each does its part. But, wherever there is a part, there is a whole. To know only a part is to have an incomplete or distorted view. The final goal of science should be to understand the whole, to see the picture complete. Philosophy, as a science of sciences, as a supreme science, or as a comprehensive science, seeks constantly to perform this function. "The object of philosophy," says Broad, "is to take over the results of the various sciences, add to them the results of religious and ethical experiences of mankind, and then reflect upon the whole, hoping to be able to reach some general conclusions as to the nature of the universe and as to our position and prospects in it." [11] "Philosophy," for Whitehead, "is not one among the sciences with its own little scheme of abstractions which it works away at perfecting and improving. It is the survey of sciences, with the special object of their harmony and of their completion." [12]

Who has not heard the story of the blind men of Burma who visited the elephant? Upon returning from their venture, they compared views about the nature of the beast. Said one, who had felt of the elephant's leg, an elephant is like a tree. Another had grasped the tail, and reported him to be like a rope. The trunk was traced by a third, who insisted it was much like a serpent. A fourth, who had stretched himself on the elephant's side, likened him to a barn. Whenever a scientist insists that the whole universe is like the part which he investigates, he may be compared with a Burmese blind man. We might have the separate reports of all the sciences and yet not see the whole elephant. In order to comprehend the total scheme, the function of synthesis is necessary.

As *mother of the sciences,* philosophy has had a long and interesting history. At one time, no distinction was made between philosophy and science. Gradually, as reflections upon problems became increasingly complex and as special techniques were developed, specialists limited the range of their inquiries, and the particular sciences were born. Among the first were mechanics, mathematics, and astronomy. Among the latest were psychology and sociology. The romance of the maturing of these offspring of the fecund mother must be left to the history of science. Deeper concern is felt for those yet unborn, especially about the philosophical sciences that have not yet been granted independence. Wonder about these new children gives rise to speculation about philosophy's future. Will the philosophical sciences become, one day, sciences in their own right? If so, will philosophy's task be done? Will she become barren? Or will there be new conceptions now unsuspected? Optimism about her future is expressed by Perry:

> As the sciences have settled area after area of his original domain, the philosopher has pushed on to the outer edge of things. The

[11] C. D. Broad, *Scientific Thought,* p. 20. Harcourt, Brace and Co., New York, 1923.

[12] Alfred North Whitehead, *Science and the Modern World,* pp. 126–127. The Macmillan Co., New York, 1926.

physical frontier, we are told, has ceased to exist—so far, at any rate, as America is concerned. There is no more free land. But the passing of the intellectual frontier is not in sight. There is plenty of free land beyond the areas which religion and the sciences have fenced and cultivated, and brought under the rule of law and order. The philosopher lives on this frontier and makes crude charts of the region which lies beyond. In the nature of the case, the mass of mankind must remain in the settled communities, while the pioneers must be few and sparsely distributed. But it has always been true in America that some flavor of the frontier spirit has pervaded even the settled communities—some love of freedom, some boldness of action, some primitive sense of fair play. So it is not unreasonable to suggest that the great body of normal, sane, practical, respectable people, the people with whom philosophy is not a vocation, will, especially if they be American and have the blood of frontiersmen in their veins, nevertheless find the essential spirit of philosophy congenial. They will, perhaps, wish to make occasional excursions for themselves; but in any case, they will respect those qualities of mind that prompt other men to plunge into the deep waters and roam the trackless forests of the great intellectual adventure.[13]

But philosophy's future promises more than intellectual pioneering. The job of synthesizing partially incoherent sciences will become more and more difficult as greater numbers of sciences develop and demand their places in the larger picture. Each new science presents another challenge to the hope for wholeness and total coherence. Thus does philosophy's task become greater rather than smaller. As a comprehensive science, then, philosophy has the functions of, first, giving birth, secondly, settling quarrels, and, finally, harmonizing in one house the several somewhat self-centered sciences. And, especially since births and quarrels continue, "a mother's work is never done."

It would be a mistake to leave the impression that philosophy's comprehensive function is limited to criticizing and synthesizing only the sciences, for its function is involved also in the activities of all persons who are philosophical. Not only do professional philosophers criticize each other's assumptions and conclusions as each tries to achieve a broader synthesis, but also each man's search for a wholesome outlook, for the meaning of life, is a manifestation of this function.

[13] Ralph Barton Perry, *A Defence of Philosophy*, pp. 55–56. Harvard University Press, Cambridge, 1931.

The beginner in philosophy often finds himself disconcerted by puzzling paradoxes. Many beginners say, "Philosophy is confusing." The truth is that a study of philosophy usually reveals an already existing confusion of which the thinker is almost entirely unaware. Since he is not aware of it, he tends to attribute it to the philosophy which he begins to study, rather than to himself. It is in the interest of larger and more stable comprehension that teachers of philosophy raise "confusing" questions. He must make his students conscious of their conflicting ideas for, as Lucretius said, "A person cannot begin to learn what he thinks he already knows." Once a person discovers his predicament (and that his predicament is his own) he will seek a way out, and this seeking is philosophy performing its comprehensive function. In times of rapid cultural transition and of increasingly larger intellectual melting pots, the need for assisting people to obtain philosophical inclusiveness becomes greater. The problem of achieving comprehensiveness of viewpoint faces each individual, as well as scientists, philosophers, and whole societies.

By way of summary, we may recall that philosophy is a group of problems. Some of these are relatively specialized and have come to constitute the philosophical sciences of epistemology, logic, philosophy of science, semantics, metaphysics, axiology, aesthetics, ethics, political and social philosophy, and others. Some of its problems are relatively general, such as criticizing assumptions and conclusions and synthesizing the results of scientists, philosophers, and of every man who discovers, and seeks his way out of, confusion.

Attitude

What is the philosophical attitude? Certainly not all attitudes are philosophical. For example, attitudes of jealousy, terror, or intolerance are not philosophical. Persons who are at times philosophical may also have these attitudes, but on these occasions they are not philosophical. The philosophical attitude may best be characterized by nine words or phrases: *Troubled, perplexed, wondering.* Philosophy begins in wonder. It starts in perplexity. It originates in curiosity. There must be a problem, for an untroubled attitude is not philosophical. *Reflective.* Merely being confronted with a difficulty does not constitute a philosophical attitude. The problem must be thought about, pondered over, and a solution attempted. *Doubting, undogmatic.* He who would be philosophical must be able to entertain doubts about his own beliefs. Reflection without willingness to doubt one's own or others' accepted beliefs can hardly be considered philosophical. "Philosophy is an attitude of mind towards doctrines ignorantly entertained" and "it refuses to be satisfied by the conventional presupposition that every sensible person knows the answer." [14] O. K. Bowsma stresses, perhaps overstresses, this, when he says, "The function of philosophy is not to answer questions but to question answers."

Open-minded, tolerant. One with a philosophical attitude will be not merely undogmatic about his own beliefs, but open-minded and tolerant about the beliefs of others. He will give every opinion a hearing, and will not condemn without reason. He shares the spirit expressed by someone: "Whenever two intelligent people disagree, each has something to learn from the other." *Willing to be guided by experience and reason.* Since, with regard to most fundamental problems, the facts are not all in, the philosophical attitude is characterized by a willingness to discard present beliefs and to accept new ones if new facts of experience demand a change. By reasoning logically about problems, we often find that certain of our beliefs must be given up if others are to be held. The philosophical attitude is willing to accept the guidance of logical reasoning.

Uncertainty, suspended judgment. There must be a willingness to remain uncertain about any and every question concerning which not all the evidence is available. When philosophical, one is willing to suspend judgment as long as conclusions are not warranted. *Speculative.* Believing as well as doubting characterizes the philosophical attitude. Even though not all the facts are in, there is always an attempt to arrive at a solution in the light of the facts available. Tentative solutions are sought. It is a believing attitude, without being a dogmatic attitude; that is, it is speculative. "Extreme scepticism and extreme dogmatism are equally unacceptable." [15]

Persistent. Philosophy is a persistent attempt to solve problems. A momentary doubt or speculation does not make one a philosopher. The philosophical attitude is usually an outgrowth of a long period of reflective thinking. Philosophy is a quest for understanding, which refuses to be discouraged by difficulties; it is "an obstinate effort to think clearly." It is not so much lack of intelligence, as impatience, that prevents the average person from becoming philosophi-

[14] Alfred North Whitehead, *Modes of Thought*, pp. 233–234. The Macmillan Co., New York, 1938.

[15] James Burnham and Philip Wheelwright, *An Introduction to Philosophical Analysis*, p. 451. Henry Holt and Co., New York, 1932.

cal. *Unemotional.* The philosopher is noted for his "cool calm reflection." As a philosopher, he neither loves nor hates, likes nor dislikes, but simply seeks to comprehend or understand. Ideally, he wants reason at a maximum, emotion at a minimum. However, it may be disputed whether any attitude can be completely unemotional, and it is debatable to what extent the philosophical attitude should be without emotion. Some Oriental thinkers, deploring the sharpness with which Westerners separate reason from emotion (and philosophy from life), point out that, at least in its original Greek meaning, philosophy (love of wisdom) involves an emotional attitude toward an emotionally lived life. The philosophical attitude, then, instead of being completely unemotional, aims to be an impartial emotion, a disinterested interest, or what contemporary scientists like to call a willingness to be objective.

Method

What is the philosophical method? It consists primarily in reflection, or reflective thinking. "Philosophical reflection is not something that only rare men called philosophers engage in. Just as each man in his own life practices to some extent medicine, engineering, finance, art, and so on, so does he practice philosophical reflection." [16] This is a very natural method, one naturally used by everyone, including children and primitive peoples, in certain problem-solving situations. To undertake it requires neither genius nor long training. But from its beginnings it often develops into habits of insight which seem profound, subtle, astounding and, to superficial observers, a bit silly at times. Even as it is but a step from the sublime to the ridiculous, so the philosophical method in the hands of the merely clever or of intellectual clowns may be misused to turn philosophy into sophistry, wisdom into folly, profundity into mere fun. Whoever mistakes sophistry for philosophy misunderstands not only philosophy but also himself as philosopher.

Since the philosopher's job is problem-solving, that is, investigation of general problems to which we presuppose some answer, his method must be suited to his task. To the extent that philosophical problems are like those in the sciences, scientific method and philosophic method are the same. In two ways, they are exactly the same: Both use inductive and deductive methods.

[16] Brand Blanshard and others, *Philosophy in American Education*, p. 140. Harper & Bros., New York, 1945.

Induction pertains to drawing general conclusions from many different particular experiences. For example, if food is good because it is desired, and if friendship is good because it is desired, and if life is good because it is desired, then may it not be that all that is good is good because it is desired? Like other scientists, philosophers formulate hypotheses suggested by observations, which they then test by appeals to further experiences. They experiment with ideas, with general ideas, even with whole systems of ideas, such as Spiritualism, Materialism, Emanationism, etc.,[17] each of which may be tried out to see whether, or to what extent, it serves as a satisfactory interpretation of experience in its larger aspects.

The fact that philosophers still recognize many alternative systems signifies that philosophical experimentation is still going on. Whoever is irritated because philosophers have not yet "made up their minds" overlooks the fact that philosophy, as a finished product, and philosophical experimentation are not entirely compatible. Whoever refuses to be willing to pursue philosophical solutions experimentally lacks something of what it takes to be a good philosopher. Some, who mistakenly believe that experiments take place only in laboratories, think that philosophers are not experimental. A scientific specialist, though obviously manipulating test tubes or telescopes, is also conducting a thought experiment. His laboratory instruments are essential aids to experimentation, but they cannot constitute the whole experiment. They are only supplementary to the larger process which goes on in his mind, for laboratory equipment, no matter how intricate and precise and useful, does not do the scientist's thinking and concluding for him. No experimenter can escape mental experimentation, and no mental experiment ceases to be an experiment simply because it utilizes no obviously specialized instruments.

Deduction consists in discovering implications and drawing inferences. No one can test a hypothesis without finding what it implies, especially with regard to other experiences, and then seeing whether what is inferred can actually bear the test of experience. Both single ideas and whole systems of ideas involve implications. If an idea or system is true, then whatever is implied by it is also true and may be used as a guide to the goals of living. However, though everyone knows, in a general way, what implication is, those who have become, or who have remained, experimental about the nature of logic continue to be open-minded concerning implication itself.

[17] See outline of chapters for Parts I and II for further examples.

Although at one period of Western thought it was believed that man's final conclusions concerning the nature of logical implication had been reached, more critical examinations of the nature of logic have recently reopened questions once considered closed. We are no longer sure just what is meant by "being logical." Beginners disappointed with the discovery that there are many logics may take comfort in the thought that, with regard to logic, philosophers' minds are still open on this subject. Each student may, then, feel free to conduct his own experiments concerning the nature of logic, instead of feeling forced to accept dogmatic canons and fixed forms of reasoning. However, it is a mistake to jump hastily to the conclusion that, therefore, each person may follow his own whim and fancy without logical penalty. Only if one is willing to be objective about logic will he succeed in arriving at a workable hypothesis about what logic really is.

Even though the basis of implication is in one's own mind, its nature is what it is, and it is not, apparently, given to fickleness. Furthermore, a systematic study of all logics reveals them to have certain common characteristics, or first principles. For example, all include some principle of consistency or non-contradiction. When two assertions are contradictory, obviously one of them must be false. However, since various logics may presuppose different solutions to metaphysical, epistemological, and axiological questions, just as various metaphysical, epistemological, and axiological theories involve different logics, the question of the ultimate nature of logical consistency and contradiction cannot be settled in isolation from still unsettled problems in these other fields. It may well be that each of the many logics reveals the structure of a different perspective, all of which perspectives may be partly true because each discloses part of the complicated whole of experience. It may be true that "the more perspectives we have, supplementing and augmenting each other, the better will be our true understanding of the universe." [18] Therefore, "let us regard each as experimental." [19] Even though we have not drawn final conclusions concerning the nature of logic, still we can hardly employ the philosophical or scientific method without using deduction.

In addition to induction and deduction as aspects of its method, philosophy, if pursued very far, involves a third aspect called *dialectic*.

[18] Hubert G. Alexander, *Time as Dimension and History*, p. 118. Univ. of New Mexico Press, Albuquerque, 1945.
[19] *Ibid.*, p. 119.

The more profoundly we penetrate to an understanding of ourselves, the more fully we become aware of both the necessity and nature of making presuppositions. A presupposition is any assumption which we make, or must make, whenever we hold a certain view. That is, a presupposition is an implied assumption. For example, "I think" implies an "I" which thinks. Or, "That is false" implies that "It is true that that is false." Or, "No consistency" means "Consistently without consistency." Dialectic, although it takes many forms, is simply the discovery that, no matter what standpoint we take, there is always another standpoint to be discovered which we had not previously recognized and which is, in a sense, other than or opposed to the stand which we have just taken. This discovery, then, constitutes a third perspective which comprehends both, and which also presupposes its being different from whatever is opposed to it. Dialectic progresses until either the thinker becomes fatigued, distracted, or comes to the conclusion that dialectic is itself a methodological standpoint which has its own non-dialectical opposite, a conclusion which accepts both as part of what must be seen.

Since dialecticians differ regarding whether dialectic ends ultimately in a dialectical impasse, in which one cannot escape the toils and tensions of constant dialectical involvement, or in dialectical peace, an absolute peace in which process and presupposition are utterly dead, each student may come to his own conclusion. However, the difference between an end of change and an ending in change may not be so great as at first appears. One example of dialectic recurs whenever one becomes aware that, since knowing is directed from one who knows to the object known, the knower, although he can never be fully aware of himself at the moment of knowing, can nevertheless deduce by implication that he as knower must have been there. Dialectic, in this example, is the mind turning back upon itself, rather than turning its back upon itself. Reflective thinking, then, consists not merely in thinking something through again and again, but also in thought thinking about itself. One cannot become wholly critical without becoming dialectical, and no one fully understands the philosophical method until he begins to feel at home with dialectic.

The philosophical method, then, is really several methods or is a method with many aspects. Unfortunately, some of these aspects have been singled out as superior, and have been over-stressed to the neglect or denial of others. But, despite outstanding historical examples of methodological extremists and their contemporary disciples (today we over-idealize induction), whoever neglects or denies any one of them fails to become fully philosophical.

In reflecting upon any predicament, philosophers commonly press their explorations in two directions, which may be called analytic and synthetic. By way of analysis, they "divide up their difficulties," in the words of Descartes, and tackle each concept separately, pressing it down to its many ultimate premises. So important is this procedure that C. H. Langford has ventured to say that "philosophy consists in ostentation," i.e., philosophy is the clarification of concepts to their minutest detail. It is the method of Socrates, who went about humbly asking questions, seeking simply to get a clear answer. The quest for analysis presupposes a faith, or a hope, that analysis, which begins with the whole, will result in discovery of some ultimate elements. Synthesis, on the other hand, is pursuit of the whole through its parts. Parts never stand alone. They are always parts of a whole. Thus, in order to comprehend a part completely, one must comprehend its whole. He cannot understand a spoke, who has never seen a wheel. The quest for synthesis presupposes a faith, or a hope, that the synthetic method will discover some ultimate whole. But how can one rightly hold both these opposing faiths, or hopes, unless there actually are both ultimate elements and an ultimate whole? This problem of reconciling these faiths constantly plagues the philosopher, as they are inherent in the methodological assumptions he uses in dealing with every problem, including everyday problems.

As a method, then, philosophy is not an acceptance of what first seems obvious, is not satisfied with mere hunches, is not wishful thinking, is not an appeal to authority, is not acceptance of what is customarily held, if this is based merely on past evidence, and is not escape into despair about ever solving problems in the face of apparently insurmountable difficulties. Whatever else philosophy is, it is a method of dealing with problems by thinking reflectively.

Activity

What is philosophical activity? Philosophy exists actually only in the activity of philosophizing and in the resulting living, or way of life. The latter will be dealt with under "Effects." By "philosophizing" is meant whatever goes on in the minds of individuals, or groups of individuals, when they are thinking, reflecting, or pondering about philosophical problems.

The activity which constitutes philosophizing includes the wondering and questioning of the curious child, the sceptical figure-it-out-for-myself reflectings of rebellious youth, the wary decisions of those who have learned to calculate prudently under the responsibilities of maturity, parenthood, and lengthening old age, as well as the more ponderous probings of professional philosophers. Some philosophical activity is relatively light and trivial, and some of the seemingly simplest wits have been among the world's wisest philosophers. Chinese sayings are short and usually simple enough for everyone to understand. But other philosophical activity consumes a lifetime of subtle dialectic, intricate chains of reasoning, meticulous systematic scrutiny, and the careful construction of a technical jargon which requires specialized professional preparation to understand. Philosophy is to be identified not merely with the simplest or the most complex activity, but may be of any kind, and may result in true or false conclusions, useful or not to anyone. Bad philosophy is still philosophy, even as bad medicine is still medicine, and as bad business is still business.

How much philosophical activity takes place subconsciously remains an open question. But surely there is no such activity without some prior awareness of a problem, and without some concern about it. Philosophical activity does not begin until one's routine habits of thinking have been broken by some perplexity, and it does not continue without some undercurrent of intellectual restlessness. It involves a feeling of challenge and some responding to such challenge. It is characterized by the inner tensions of a troubled conscience which feels uneasy until it resolves somehow what appear to be conflicting truths. Thus, although the philosophical attitude is relatively unemotional, philosophical activity cannot escape being entangled in the whole gamut of human emotions, fears, hopes, frustrations, weariness, elation, and anger. But such involvement, though natural and wholesome in many ways, results too often in bad philosophy if the philosophy is not critically refined on calmer occasions. Philosophical activity which fails to embody philosophical attitudes and methods falls short of philosophy in the fullest sense.

Especially significant for most beginners is the activity required for maturing intellectually. Each person goes through, or should go through, a process of philosophical infancy (simply acquiring beliefs and faiths), philosophical adolescence (revolting against inherited conclusions and seeking freedom of thought by doubting and rethinking one's own beliefs), and philosophical maturity (arriving at beliefs which are his own for reasons of his own—beliefs which are satisfactory to himself for reasons which he considers satisfactory to himself). Although intellectual rebellion makes adolescence seem unreasonable to elders, it is really an "impulse toward rationality," [20] an impulse toward the kind of intellectual independence in which one achieves stature by becoming responsible for making up his own mind. Not all adolescent distrust of parental opinions is philosophical activity, but some of it is, and, such as is, is healthy when guided by the philosophical attitude. The maturing process, intellectual aging, is characterized, first, by uncertainties; next, by hope of discovery; then, by a glimpse of the goal in sight, and, finally, by a growing satisfaction and peace of mind. Although not all persons mature fully, some who do mature fully do gradually cease their philosophical activity, and thus philosophy with them tends to pass beyond philosophy. But as long as one can enjoy his mental peace open-mindedly he can remain philosophical.

Philosophical activity is not merely individual and solitary, however. It is also social. It consists of what goes on in philosophy classes (and, thus, is conditioned by curriculum requirements, hours when classes are scheduled, size of classes, teaching skill, class morale), what goes on in "bull sessions," in the various privacies where people "let down their hair," as well as in public forums where philosophical issues are at stake. More professionally, philosophical activity is what happens in annual conferences of philosophical associations (and thus is conditioned by the number of such associations, the numbers of members participating, and the particular papers read and how stimulating they are) and in the philosophical journals (which often depend on subsidies as well as on considerable circulation in order to exist).

Although philosophical activity aims at wholeness, until that wholeness is achieved, philosophy is characterized by partisan movements which seem to the beginner to add up to an amazing confusion. But philosophers themselves are hopeful that, even as an individual can work his way out of inner conflicts, so can societies free themselves eventually from intellectual perplexity. Today's rapid industrialization and metropolitanization keep our philosophical melting pots bubbling high. The uniformity for which beginners hope can hardly be expected until the world's cultures merge into a world culture that has achieved a stability—a new world-wide medievalism—from which

[20] William E. Hocking, "Philosophy—The Business of Everyman," *Journal of the American Association of University Women*, June, 1937, p. 213.

it will be harder to break away than from nationalistic medievalisms which were forced to reckon with the modernisms of other nationalistic cultures. Professional philosophers are hopeful, but somewhat wary in their hope. Today's philosophers direct their activities primarily toward seeking unity. If that unity is ever achieved, the most fertile minds will then be occupied in searching for new diversities.

If today we are impatient about our progress, we should consider certain facts. Societies, being groups, usually take longer to straighten out their conflicts than individuals. Societies today do not take philosophical progress seriously enough to make the pursuit of philosophy financially attractive to many persons. So long as we practice a philosophy of life which recommends tinkering with gadgets instead of philosophizing about happiness, we cannot expect much success in finding a final philosophy of the good life. The reader may take these statements as a personal challenge to accept his share of the responsibility which his society has for its own philosophical condition. "The function of philosophy in universities is properly the same as its function in the cultural development of a society: to be the intellectual conscience of the community. . . ." [21] But the individual who is willing to represent responsibly the community's intellectual conscience runs a risk, if he takes his responsibilities too seriously, of being poisoned, like Socrates, lynched, like Jesus, or burned, like Bruno. Many contemporary societies, however, are much more tolerant of those who "corrupt the minds of youth" than more settled philosophical communities were, or will be.

Societies and cultures, too, go through their periods of philosophical infancy, adolescence, and maturity. Western civilization today is still adolescent. Consequently, generations of its people suffer from uncertainties in its philosophical conflicts. But youth is a time for healthy growth, so now is a time when individual philosophers can assist such growth and enjoy some success in promoting this development. "It is to the best that can be achieved in this continuing process, not to the particular results which have been at any time its accredited outcome, that the philosopher is ultimately committed, and it is in this commitment that philosophers of different schools unite and in its name that they can work together. It is not, like the alleged finalities of the dogmatist, an intellectual excuse to stop thinking about matters held to be too important for further critical inspection. It is a way in which men go on thinking, and hence are able to

[21] Blanshard and others, *op. cit.*, p. 80.

learn all that a growing experience and maturing wisdom can teach them. This way of going on and growing up is what it means to be a philosopher." [22]

Philosophy, then, is activity, people at work on their problems, or perhaps their problems working on them. It is futile to speculate as to whether there is some sum total of activity, occurring at odd moments or persistently in persons all over the globe and during all historical times, which constitutes philosophy. But, certainly, apart from activity there is no philosophy in the fullest sense of the term.

Conclusions

Which conclusions are philosophical? Perhaps the simplest, even though somewhat inaccurate, answer is that philosophical conclusions are those which have been reached by philosophers. This leaves the problem of deciding who were and who are philosophers. Some agreement has been reached about great thinkers of the past. We now point without question to Socrates, Plato, Aristotle, Plotinus, Augustine, Aquinas, Bacon, Hobbes, Descartes, Locke, Berkeley, Hume, Spinoza, Leibniz, Kant, Hegel, Schopenhauer, Nietzsche, Bradley, Bosanquet, Royce, Bergson, and James. But there are many others, and who shall decide which others? As for contemporaries, how shall their status be decided? Dewey, Whitehead, Russell, most will agree, are philosophers. But who else? Hundreds, if not thousands, deserve the name. Further, not every theory proposed by each of these famous men can be considered philosophical—Berkeley's essay on tarwater, for example. Yet such an answer may be useful to the novice at the beginning of his philosophical investigations. The student will conceive philosophy too narrowly, however, if he fails to recognize that the conclusions, true or false, of amateurs as well as of specialists, are also part of what constitutes philosophy.

Another way to answer our question is this: A conclusion can hardly be philosophical unless it is a conclusion to a philosophical problem. If one has determined which problems are philosophical, then it becomes comparatively easy to decide which conclusions are philosophical. In epistemology, for example, realism, subjectivism, and scepticism are properly regarded as philosophical theories. But also the nebulous and unnamed hypotheses resulting from the faltering attempts of newcomers must be included. Still another answer

[22] *Ibid.*, pp. 84–85.

may be given: Here attitude and method are deciding factors. If a conclusion is not reached by reflective methods and pursued with open-mindedness, it can hardly be considered philosophical. Conclusions arrived at by appeal to authority, oracle, or magic are not philosophical, except in so far as the authority, oracle, or magician is also a philosopher. Conclusions accepted from custom, as well as on authority, are philosophical only either when they have been arrived at philosophically before having been accepted, or when they have been open-mindedly reflected upon by those who accept them from custom. He who receives his views from other philosophers without having deliberated upon them himself is not a philosopher, and his conclusions, as his, are not philosophical.

Beginners look first for conclusions. The quest is always for the goal. Not the attitudes, methods, activities, but the conclusions are what people want from philosophy. This is the most important part of philosophy, especially for the beginner. He wants and, unfortunately, expects to find answers ready and waiting for him. When he does not find them immediately, he is disappointed and often despairs. Many beginners give up too easily because they expect wisdom to come too easily, like something that can be purchased over the counter rather than like something which must be grown from the soil by toiling, fretting, and favorable climate. In popular thinking, the philosopher is mistakenly believed to be an oracle, a wise man who knows all the answers to deeper questions. He thinks of himself, however, as a workman, an intellectual craftsman, who often values more highly his method and attitude than he does his conclusions. Thus, he will seek to convey what he considers most valuable. But his pupils often feel that they are not getting what they came for, and consequently fail to take away what the philosopher has to give, namely, a more reliable way of seeking truth for himself. Like other scientists, philosophers seek to acquaint their pupils with the important conclusions of the past and with something of the historical flounderings by which they were reached, but also to impart the skills with which to progress, falteringly, if necessary, beyond the conclusions which others have arrived at heretofore.

The popular attitude toward philosophy is, however, not without some justification, not so much because some philosophers have claimed that they have the answers, as because some conclusions seem to be arrived at of necessity. Some, though not all, philosophers believe that they have discovered certain apparently inescapable results. Whether or not they are inescapable depends partly upon what one is willing to assume as certain, and so long as there are variations in willingness there are differences as to what may be considered inescapable.

All this is provoking to the beginner. He wants to know: Why can't philosophers agree? Must philosophy end in confusion? Must the result be every man for himself and each man's view is as good as any other's? Those who ask these questions have been reared with the ideal that truth is single and that there ought to be only one single view of it. But truth may be such that no single view of it can be wholly adequate. Conger [23] contends that each view is like one band of a spectrum and whoever appreciates only one view is like a person with monochromatic vision who misses the richness (and greater trueness) of the whole spectrum. "If the structure of the universe were revealed all at once and in all its aspects to all men in the same way, we might be expected to share a single all-inclusive philosophy. . . . The variety of philosophical systems is due, in part, to the inexhaustibility of knowledge and to the necessarily partial viewpoint of any one philosopher or generation of philosophers. Such variety, far from signifying a sad state of affairs needing correction, as some are suggesting today, is only a natural and desirable consequence of the subtlety of nature, and of freedom of the mind and fertility of the imagination—the fountainhead of all genuine philosophy." [24]

In spite of lack of assurance of certainty in conclusions, one cannot be philosophical, as pointed out earlier, without some optimism and some willingness to pursue such conclusions as can be reached. "A man may pursue philosophy half-heartedly and rest content with half-formed and inadequate ideas." [25] Too many have done so in the past. But such failure is not so much failure of philosophy as failure of those who pursue, or fail to pursue, philosophy to those ends which are achievable. Philosophy will fail those who fail philosophy. Saddest of failures are those persons who claim to have accepted from others conclusions which are really unacceptable to them. "Everybody has a philosophy, and the differences between man and man are chiefly philosophical differences. I will say more than that: the difference between a man and himself is a philosophical difference,

[23] G. P. Conger, *The Ideologies of Religion,* p. 1.   Round Table Press, Inc., New York, 1940.

[24] J. D. Bronstein, Yervant H. Krikorian, and Philip P. Wiener, *Basic Problems of Philosophy,* p. 686.   Prentice-Hall, Inc., New York, 1947.   Reprinted by permission of the publisher.

[25] Paul Weiss, "Adventurous Humility," *Ethics,* April, 1941, p. 339.

by which I mean that people frequently fall into a philosophy which does not belong to them, and leads them away from themselves because they borrow a philosophy from somebody else. It is a misfit philosophy." [26] People who acclaim one philosophy while obviously living another do not understand themselves, and appear hypocritical to others. They claim conclusions which are not their own and live conclusions which they do not acclaim. Those who are thus in conflict with themselves have much to gain from a study of philosophy, but will suffer much trouble when they are forced to face their own conflicts and work their own ways out. They, especially, are the ones who "find philosophy confusing" when led to a discovery of their own confusion.

Conclusions, then, are part of philosophy, and the most important part, if the goal of an endeavor is what makes it worth while. By "conclusions" is meant not only tentative solutions and present goals already achieved, and there are some, but also goals yet unachieved. Philosophical conclusions, as unachieved goals, are what make us consider philosophical activity important. But once they have been reached, philosophical activity becomes no longer so worthy, for one does not work for that which he already has. If philosophical goals are ever achieved completely, philosophy will pass beyond philosophy into a state in which either there is no striving or the striving is for something other than understanding. If there were no conclusions, tentative or otherwise, there would be no philosophy.

Effects

Not only does philosophy consist in what philosophers do, but also philosophy is what philosophy does. "By their fruits ye shall know them." If one knows what is done, then he knows this much about the doer, namely, that the doer is the kind of thing which does that which is done. Thus, in order to understand philosophy completely, one must have some acquaintance with its consequences. Not all of these can be understood, and thus philosophy can never be understood completely, partly because we do not know even all of the effects of past philosophies upon past societies and we have an indefinite future in which still undeveloped philosophies will have their yet undeterminable effects. Even as philosophical activity is a continuing process, so the effects of intermingling lines of philosophical

[26] Hocking, *op. cit.*, p. 212.

influence upon, and from, millions of people constitute, at any one time, an indeterminable quantity and, throughout the passages of many times, include unimaginable dynamic conglomerations. Any definition of philosophy which seeks to include its effects must remain a dated document. Nevertheless, some of the results of philosophy are obvious to anyone who will look at them. These may be observed in the lives of individuals, in the behavior of groups, and in the courses of civilizations.

Individuals are affected by their philosophies in their day-to-day lives. One's choices are motivated, not only by his hunger and weariness, heredity and glands, habit and stimuli, but also by his philosophy, by his beliefs about what is good or best or bad or worst. Sometimes he is conscious of the wisdom of his choices. More often he is a victim of the subconscious conflicts of partially absorbed and incompletely accepted viewpoints influencing his decisions. Even his occasional refusal "to be philosophical" is itself a consequence either of philosophical conflicts which torment him into rebellion against "philosophy," or of a philosophical conclusion that he ought not to be philosophical. Philosophy, as consequences, depends for its fate upon how it affects the lives of particular people who act, or refuse to act, upon particular beliefs and at particular times. Thus, philosophy is partly responsible for the optimisms and pessimisms and meliorisms which pervade each person's pursuit of his life's goals. And philosophy results, ultimately, in something which is not philosophy. For if one ever succeeds completely in his quest, he will get answers which he does not doubt, and thus he closes his mind. The better his conclusions, the less his doubt, the greater his dogmatism, and the more closed-minded he becomes. One wants to be open-minded so that he may become closed-minded, so that he can know with certainty. Thus philosophy is not an end in itself, but ends, or seeks to end, in certain knowledge.

Groups, too, are influenced by philosophy, even as they have their origin, nature, course of development, and future prospects determined partly by the ideologies of their effective members. Wars "to make the world safe for democracy" are made possible only by the effectiveness of appeals to those who feel their philosophies are worth fighting for. "The difference between life in the democratic and fascist countries was not a difference in the technology or in science or even in general education; it was a difference in ideas, ideals, and loyalties. Changes in people, in ways of doing things, and in history begin in persons who are convinced of the worth of some idea or who are captured by some vision of a different scheme of things." [27] Philosophy is not a luxury subject to those who are aware of the different effects of philosophies on politics and business. The wise man of action knows that if he is to be successful in leading people he must first discover their basic philosophy and appeal to it in order to motivate them. If this philosophy will not yield the ends he desires, then he must either fool the people or convert them to a new philosophy which will result in the desired action.

Finally, civilization itself is a product of philosophy, even as it, in turn, produces philosophy. Some even contend that "there is no specifiable difference between philosophy and its role in the history of civilization. Discover and define some characteristic, some unique function in civilization, and you have defined philosophy itself." [28] "Thus philosophy marks a change of culture. In forming patterns to be conformed to in future thought and action, it is additive and transforming in its role in the history of civilization. Man states anything at his peril; once stated, it occupies a place in a new perspective; it attains a permanence which does not belong to its existence; it enters provokingly into want and use; it points in a troubling way to need for new endeavors." [29] Without philosophy, then, there would be no civilization, and civilizations differ from one another as romantic, rationalistic, pacific, aggressive, mystical, and mundane, partly because of their philosophical differences.

The effects which constitute philosophy, then, are those which make a difference in the civilizations of the world. If a particular philosophy makes a particular difference, one can understand something of the nature of that philosophy by noting the resulting differences. However, it is not the total consequence of any activity that constitutes a particular philosophy's effects, but only that in the result which is different from what it would have been if this philosophy had not participated in producing the result.

Resummarizing this description of philosophy, we may recall that philosophy involves certain problems, attitudes, methods, activities, conclusions, and effects. This is what philosophy is today.

[27] Harold H. Titus, *Living Issues in Philosophy*, p. 3. American Book Co., New York, 1946.

[28] John Dewey, *Philosophy and Civilization*, p. 6. G. P. Putnam's Sons, New York, 1931.

[29] *Ibid.*, p. 8.

Philosophy and Science

How are philosophy and science related? We have described philosophy as a science or group of sciences. Yet it is also customary to differentiate between philosophy and science. In this section, we turn our aim, and, consequently, our language, from "science" as inclusive of both philosophical and non-philosophical sciences to "science" as referring primarily to non-philosophical sciences. Although no absolute boundaries exist between them, for their differences are differences in degree, we shall speak here of comparing philosophy (philosophical sciences) and science (non-philosophical sciences). Since philosophy was described as consisting of six components, philosophy and science may be compared with respect to each of the six.

The problems of scientists and philosophers are different, though the difference may not be as great as some claim. For, on the one hand, both aim, ultimately, at understanding life and the universe, but, on the other, each pursues this aim by attacking different problems. Science, or, less misleadingly, the sciences, deal with a variety of problems: astronomy with heavenly bodies, physics and chemistry with material elements, biology with life, sociology with groups, and so on. Each of these problems is subdivided into many others, constituting the subsciences, which seem to be increasing endlessly. Each science or sub-science tackles a particular problem or set of problems. To a certain extent, each of the philosophical sciences does the same. But, in addition, philosophy as a comprehensive science has the unique problem of synthesizing the results of all other sciences into some kind of whole. This problem turns out to be one of the most difficult and, apparently, one of the most interesting. For, ". . . the astronomer has become somewhat restive and refuses to be bound longer by such restrictions and prohibitions [from philosophizing]. He has defined a philosopher, somewhat ungraciously, as an individual who claims for his own and arrogates to himself all the really interesting parts of all other sciences." [30]

Some persons would summarize the difference between scientific and philosophical problems by saying that science aims always at analysis, philosophy at synthesis. Although this interpretation is not entirely correct, it contains an element of truth. Scientists do devote

[30] Heber D. Curtis, "Receding Horizons," *The Scientific Monthly*, August, 1938, p. 245.

themselves mainly to analysis and, therefore, tend to interpret their problems in terms of taking things apart to see what they are made of. Yet, of course, they do this because they want, in the end, to understand how things function as wholes; so the task of the scientist is not finished until his results contribute to some larger synthesis. Philosophers do concern themselves with synthesis and see their problems in terms of understanding how things are related to larger wholes. But, of course, this cannot be done adequately until analysis has shown just what the internal nature of the thing is which allows it to function in the larger whole. Thus, although scientists are inclined to analyze and to specialize, and philosophers to synthesize and to generalize, neither can escape the opposite tendency. Something of the importance in which this distinction is held may be gathered from the half-serious, half-cynical, and now trite, saying: "A scientist is one who knows more and more about less and less until he knows everything about nothing, whereas a philosopher is one who knows less and less about more and more until he knows nothing about everything."

In attitude, philosophy and science are essentially alike: wonder, reflection, doubt, tolerance, willingness to abide by experience and reason, suspended judgment, speculativeness, persistence, and relative freedom from the biasing effects of emotion all belong to the scientific attitude. If there is any difference in emphasis, it arises from the philosophical need for doubting even doubt or for criticizing criticism. Scientists often start with uncritical assumptions, such as, for example, assuming that one can be completely objective about data. Philosophers, when they recognize that willingness to be objective is itself one kind of subjective attitude, conclude that a person is not as completely objective as he can be, unless he recognizes the impossibility of being completely objective. This willingness to be thoroughly self-critical is merely an extension of the willingness to be objective, though to scientists who do not engage in such self-criticism it may seem different in kind.

The methods of philosophy and science also are much alike. However, there is a tendency among certain sciences to emphasize laboratory experimentation and the use of manipulative devices in gathering data, whereas philosophy, like mathematics ("the most exact science"), makes little use of laboratory instruments because they are of no immediate use in handling its problems. Both science and philosophy involve observation of data, formulation of hypotheses, and verification, in seeking their goals. Although there is a tendency for philosophers to be preoccupied with intellectual experimentation and to be unusually handy with their most used experimental tool, i.e., the principle of consistency, no philosopher is really satisfied, nor can he satisfy others, until he has tried out his theories in actual practice. For example, a metaphysical conclusion that "to exist is to be both one and many" may be tested by observing numerous things to see whether they are actually both one and many. Despite similarities between philosophy and science, "the nature of philosophy is widely misconceived. The strictures on philosophy some scientists voice, for example, are usually based on the false assumption that philosophy is but the fossilized guesswork of prescientific ages; whereas the truth is that philosophy deals with questions other than those the sciences study, but strives to study them scientifically too." [31]

There is one difference in stress, however, regarding dialectic. Whereas scientists can escape the dialectical implications involved in their problems no more than philosophers can, today, at least, scientists tend to define science in light of ideals of rationality from which dialectic is largely omitted. Science itself, conceived differently in different ages, is now usually pictured, perhaps somewhat incongruously, in terms of rationalistic ideals regarding conclusions, but with empirical ideals with respect to method. A philosopher, with a larger and longer look at man's methodology, feels he must remain open-minded relative to the usefulness of intuitive, mystical, and dialectical, as well as of deductive and inductive, methods. But there is no reason for defining science in such a way as to exclude the use of these methods, just because contemporary scientists habitually neglect them.

The activities of the philosopher and of the scientific researcher are as much alike and different as the particular problems with which the particular men deal. Each type of problem requires its own specific means of dealing with it and consequent appropriate activities. But, common to both philosophers and scientists is persistent, painstaking, patient endeavor, guided by alert, honest, earnest interest in gaining as much truth about the problem as possible.

Science aims at conclusions and consists partly in conclusions, just as philosophy does. Both are commonly misunderstood to consist entirely of conclusions. But both also have still more conclusions unreached than reached. Hypotheses which have worked successfully or satisfactorily for a long time are usually called "laws," whether they be philosophical or scientific. Some people consider

[31] Blanshard and others, *op. cit.*, p. 140.

scientific conclusions more practical, but one's judgment here will depend upon his interests. For there are multitudes of scientific laws concerning which only a few persons are interested, and which are of no practical value at all to most people. Differences in the usefulness of philosophical and scientific theories will depend upon which theories momentarily lie closer to the needs of the interested person.

Who knows what the differences in effects of philosophy and science are? Today more than ever before we are becoming aware of the influences of scientific discoveries upon life and the world, through such institutional agencies as school, government, business, and recreational media. But, strangely enough, each of these influences is an effect of philosophy as well as of science, for inherent in each scientific effect is the result of that philosophy which contends that it is good to investigate scientifically.

Science and philosophy supplement each other, then, and depend upon each other for such supplementation. The aim of each science is to know the truth about a part, but the whole truth about a part cannot be known completely apart from the truth about the whole. One does not know all there is to know about atoms until he knows that atoms make men and until he knows the kinds of men atoms make. A knowledge of psychology presupposes a knowledge of chemistry, but a knowledge of chemistry is not, in the end, complete, until the psychological effects of chemicals are known. So, too, knowledge of chemicals is incomplete until their causative chains are traced to the stars, to beauty, to love, and to God. In the end, the chemist and every other scientist wants to become a philosopher. So long as human limitations do not permit such achievement, the scientist and the philosopher are mutually dependent. Philosophy is dependent upon the sciences for their conclusions and for all the drudgery required for deriving them. Without the parts of the puzzle available, philosophy cannot picture the whole. Although we have been speaking as if philosopher and scientist were always different men, according to popular misconceptions, the reader will recognize that the traits of the scientist and the philosopher are simply two different aspects of his own nature, distinguishable for convenience, but inseparable in fact.

Philosophy and Religion

Although philosophy is very much like science, especially in aim, attitude, and method, both philosophy and science differ greatly from religion. The aim of philosophy and science is to understand the universe. The aim of religion is not so much to understand the universe as to remove fear of the mysteriously harmful and to conserve whatever is deemed most precious or valuable. It is often said that philosophy seeks a unified view of the world, while religion seeks unity with the world, or with the beneficent powers in it. Differences in aim result in differences in problems, attitude, method, activities, conclusions, and effects.

The problems of religion, unlike those of philosophy and science, are primarily practical, not theoretical. Religion seeks to achieve the good life. Philosophy and science aim to understand life. As we succeed better in understanding the good life, we should become more successful in achieving it; as our science and philosophy improve, our religion should improve. As we come to know more about the unknown, we hope to become less fearful. Since one's attempts to deal with practical problems will depend upon his understanding, his efforts to deal with religious problems will be conditioned by how he has dealt with his philosophical problems. His religion depends upon his philosophy. Too many people contrast religion and philosophy as if they were separate and independent things. But the truth is that they, too, are interdependent. Religion depends upon science and philosophy for its theoretical foundations and its theoretical progress. Science and philosophy depend upon religion for both their beginning and end. They began, and begin, in the religious demand for insight. For, if there were no felt need for security in the universe, the need for seeking to understand the universe would, doubtless, never arise. Philosophy and science aim at and will reach their goal only in religious living, i.e., happy living, secure living, satisfying living. Unlived philosophy is sterile, useless, false. If philosophy is thought and religion is action, then one's religion is one's philosophy in action. Then the problems of religion are not primarily problems of understanding, intellectually, for these are philosophy's problems, but rather of "understanding" emotionally, i.e., of making oneself at home in the universe in light of the understanding provided by one's science and philosophy.

Like the philosophical attitude, the religious attitude is persistent. Men naturally seek security persistently. But, unlike the philosophical attitude, the religious attitude may be highly emotional. Fear or faith, panic or hopefulness, despair or confidence—these are common religious attitudes. But open-mindedness, suspended judgment, doubting, and reasoning are not essential, though they may be present. Conviction is desirable and dogmatism is permissible, especially concerning vital issues.

When problems differ, methods usually differ. Faith versus reason, trust in tradition versus experimentation, acceptance of authoritative revelation versus acceptance of experience—these claimed differences between philosophy and religion are only partially true. Philosophy and science also rest on faith, faith in the validity of principles of reasoning, faith in the usefulness of experimentation, faith in the reliability of experience. They also rest on tradition, for there are traditions in philosophy and science which are quite compelling in their actual effects upon contemporary thinking. In addition, they rest upon revelation—upon the insights which lead to countless discoveries. Further, religion does not exclude reasoning, experience, and experimentation from its methods, but it uses them whenever they seem serviceable. The methods of religion tend to suit its problems, and if prayer or worship, intuition or mystical revelation, sacrifice or service, are relied upon, probably they are well fitted to the immediate demands of religious practice. Again, philosophy and religion are but different aspects of each person's nature, though in each person one of the aspects may be predominant.

The activities of scientists differ markedly from the work of priests and preachers, for the methods involved in developing habits of exact critical analysis differ from the methods necessary for instilling unshakable acquiescent faith. But the obviousness of these differences, heightened by bitter conflicts which have been abetted by ignorance and by parties likely to gain from such strife, has obscured the fact that philosophy and religion are essentially supplementary rather than contradictory. Philosophy and religion do not long exist apart from each other. Religion is aimless without some understanding (philosophy and science). Philosophy is useless unless used. Though to a narrower viewpoint our definition may seem too broad, let us say that religion is one's philosophy in action. That is, one's philosophy consists primarily in his understanding and evaluation of life, or in his ideas of and attitude toward life; whereas his religion is his quest for the best in life as he understands it.

Philosophy involves activities, as pointed out previously, not only those of philosophizing but also those of daily living in which one's philosophical conclusions are effective. This means, then, that philosophy, by its very nature, involves religion. Religion, likewise, cannot be described accurately without including religious beliefs, and what are such beliefs if not philosophy? Of course, it is true that not all religious beliefs are philosophical in the sense that they have been reached by means of philosophical attitudes and methods, but they are philosophical in the sense that they constitute conclusions which represent whatever philosophical understanding the religious person has. Recognition of this supplementariness and mutual involvement should make us seek to be more philosophical and scientific with respect to our religious beliefs and should lead us toward more practical efforts to employ our philosophical and scientific conclusions in our religious questing for the good life. The difficulty of understanding how philosophy and religion can be opposites and still supplements has led simpler minds to consider them merely as antagonistic. Awareness of their mutual dependence should bring us to realize that in philosophizing we are examining the intellectual foundations of our religion. A little philosophizing tends to make one atheistic, for philosophy criticizes all, including theological assumptions; but a lot of philosophy tends to make one more fully religious, not in the sense of inducing closer conformity to local sectarian mores, but in aiding one to live his philosophy by helping him to find a philosophy which more fully fits his living.

The conclusions of religion, if thought of as merely intellectual, may be the same as those of philosophy; but when understood as wholesome (or holy) living, they are the convictions with which we pursue the purposes of life. Religion finds its final conclusions in happy living, not in perfection of doctrine. Whenever men have had neither the time nor ability to reach conclusions scientifically or philosophically, they have had to resort to quicker means of getting needed assurance. Appeals to oracles, astrology, divination, ecstatic revelation, authority, and "reasons of the heart," have proved mandatory in some crisis situations. When these appeals resulted in their being saved from disaster in such crises, it was natural (even, in a measure, scientific) for men to accept the useful conclusions as true.

Today, many ancient views are taught under the name of religion after contrary evidence has become overwhelming. This has prompted many hasty thinkers to conclude that religious views are false while only the scientific are true. Although false conclusions may often be used to serve religious needs, it does not follow that false beliefs are essential to religion. Cultural lag characterizes all institutions normally. The fact that religious institutions have been particularly slow in readjusting themselves should not blind us to the fact that philosophical and scientific institutions may also lag. If one's religion suffers from backward conclusions, he should get rid of them and replace them with better ones. But one cannot, simply by ridding himself of backward beliefs, put an end to religion. Whatever one does with his newer convictions will then be his religion.

The effects of religion are, partly, effects of philosophy. But they are more than that. For there is much in religious practice which is not thought out, much that grows out of fear and agony of pain and humiliation, and much that proceeds naturally from the stupidity or selfishness of petty clergy as well as from the ecstatic joyfulness, confidence, courage, and visions of those we call saints. At some of the religious practices in the past, human sacrifices, inquisitions, penances, crucifixion of the flesh, strict ceremonial observance, we may well feel aghast. But we should not judge others too harshly until we have first tried to put our own intellectual house in order and have then seen what consequences actually follow from our own religious convictions. Although, as we have observed, religion ends in its effects in living itself, nevertheless, such living persists in being unpeaceful and in giving rise to new problems, difficulties, and perplexities. Religion therefore produces need for further philosophical reflection. As always, theory and practice, philosophy and religion, influence each other. Any new religious insecurity may, then, result in further intellectual questing for philosophical certainty.[32]

[32] Portions of this chapter appeared previously as an article, "What is Philosophy?" in *The Scientific Monthly*, June, 1941, pp. 553–560.

· 2 ·
Naïve
Realism

The Problem of Knowledge

What is knowledge? Can there be knowing without that which is known? If not, then what is it that is known? An object? What is an object? Can an object exist without being known? Or do objects depend upon subjects for their existence? Is all knowledge true? or may there be false knowledge? What is meant by true and false? What are facts? Is it proper to speak of unknown knowledge waiting to be discovered? How does knowledge originate? What happens to knowledge after it has been forgotten? What differentiates knowledge from belief? When are beliefs reliable? What is error? Is certainty a matter of feeling, conviction, faith, or do necessary truths exist regardless of our attitudes? Why are some beliefs considered certain while others only probable? What is the difference between sensation, perception, feeling, judgment, experience, reasoning, thought, and appreciation? Is all science knowledge and all knowledge science?

Questions such as the foregoing constitute the epistemologist's problems, and each person is an epistemologist to the extent that he accepts them as his own and seeks to solve them by means of the philosophical attitude and methods. Most readers of this book will previously have been confronted by, and somewhat troubled by, these questions. Most may even already have partial answers to them. If one is not fully satisfied with his conclusions, it may be that he has never seriously and systematically grappled with these questions. The purpose of this book is to help the reader to comprehend the significance of the problems of knowledge, reality, and values, by surveying some of the major types of solution which have arisen to challenge us to accept or reject them.

36

Common Sense

What is common sense? Some say it is something common to all men or that it consists in those beliefs which all commonly accept. Others point out that the term refers to whatever seems obvious. No matter which view we take, philosophy begins in common sense. In fact, philosophy is nothing but common sense persistently and self-critically applied. Philosophical criticisms are simply common-sense criticisms of common sense. In its beginnings, philosophy is neither abstract nor abstruse, for it starts with the simplest, clearest, and most obvious questions. Only when simple answers conflict with each other are we forced to look for more complex solutions. When perplexities arise in previously settled areas of belief, we naturally feel that what was obvious now is obviously not obvious. Thus, for common-sense reasons alone, one is led to abandon common sense. The complexities into which one is drawn inhere in the very questions which he asks himself when he begins to wonder. Whoever pursues his questions, even with a matter-of-fact attitude, soon finds himself demanding insights which agree neither with the viewpoints which he shares with others nor with his own past opinions. But the problems of philosophy are, first of all, common-sense problems.

Tackling first the inquiry into the nature of knowledge, let us consider just what common sense tells us about a table in our room. It is colored. It is solid. It has size and shape. It is heavy and it endures. If we left the room and came back later, it would still be there and would have been there all of the time, unless, of course, someone had moved it in our absence. Our looking at it does not affect it, does not change its nature, does not modify it in the least. Its color, size, and shape really are just as we see them. We could feel its weight if we lifted it. When many of us look at it, we can all see the same thing. If anyone doubts the foregoing statements, he is usually judged a bit queer. Yet, as we shall see, common sense itself gives rise to doubts which lead us eventually to deny many of these assumptions.

In order to name the view held more or less commonly by unreflective people, for purposes of comparing it with more reflective views, epistemologists have come to adopt certain fairly standardized terms. The view just described is sometimes called the "Common-

Sense View," or "Common-Sense Realism." [1] Since it is a view which we acquire and hold naturally, it has been called "Natural Realism." [2] Because such natural acquisition occurs without much reflection, or naively, it may be referred to as "Naive Realism." [3] Since the latter term has become more widely adopted, we shall use it here.

Naive Realism

Philosophers are reflective, whereas naive realists are unreflective. Therefore, this account is a reflective account of an unreflective view. For, strictly speaking, the moment a naive realist reflects upon his view he is no longer completely naive. Thus, the naive realist is something of a straw man set up by epistemologists to represent us in our unreflective moments. This straw man may not be quite like any of us, for most of us have reflected somewhat. Yet we can recognize that it represents a view we hold much of the time.

Six statements summarize this doctrine: 1. Objects which are known exist independently of their being known. They can endure or continue to exist without being experienced by anyone. Knowing the objects does not create them. 2. Objects have qualities, or, if one prefers, properties, characteristics, or attributes, which are parts of the objects. As qualities of objects, they do not derive their existence or nature from the knower. 3. Objects, including their qualities, are not affected merely by being known. Knowledge of objects in no way changes their nature. 4. Objects seem as they are and are as they seem. Or, as we sometimes say, appearances are realities. What seems obviously so is so. 5. Objects are known directly; that is, there is nothing between them and our knowledge of them. They occur in our experience. We experience them exactly as they are without distortion by any intervening medium. 6. Objects are public; that is, they can be known by more than one person. Several people can see the same object and see it exactly as it is.

Criticisms of Naive Realism

Trouble arises for the naive realist when attention is called to the fact that the first and fifth statements are incompatible. Objects are

[1] See R. W. Sellars, *Principles and Problems of Philosophy,* Ch. 3. The Macmillan Co., New York, 1926.

[2] *Ibid.*

[3] See Durant Drake, *Invitation to Philosophy,* Ch. 6. Houghton Mifflin Co., Boston, 1933.

independent of experience and yet are in experience. Upon reflection, we realize our experiences, knowledge, ideas, etc., are located somewhere inside our heads. But objects appear to be located outside of our heads. How can objects which are outside of one's head be in experience which is inside of one's head? How can objects which are known to be some distance away still be known directly when one's knowledge is somewhere within him? How can objects be "out there" and ideas of objects be "in here" unless they are somehow separated? If separated, how can they be known directly? Trouble arises for the naive realist also when he faces the fact of error. Errors occur quite commonly. When they are called to our attention, we are happy to recognize them because, by doing so, we then arrive at the truth. But if asked what assurance is there that the new view is true, we reply that it seems true. But this is the same assurance which we had about the error before it seemed to be an error. The naive realist, then, has no satisfactory account of error, for if things are as they seem and seem as they are, then whatever seems so is so. Error, on such a view, is impossible, theoretically, because an error is something which seems so but is not so.

Recall the common experience of seeing a stick partially submerged in water. Upon first sight, the stick appears bent or broken. If naive realism is to be taken at its face value, then if it seems to be bent it is bent. When the stick is pulled from the water, it appears straight. Does the stick bend as it submerges in the water? Our previous experience with sticks and water usually suggests "No." But since the stick appears to bend as it goes in, what can we do to determine whether it is really bent or really straight? For the moment, it seems both bent and straight. Since it cannot be both, one of the two appearances must be erroneous. Note, here, how common sense rejects common sense. That is, it is a matter of common sense that when two contradictory appearances appear, one of them must be rejected. The next step often taken is to slide a hand along the stick down into the water. To the hand the stick seems straight, even though to the eye it seems bent. Most naive realists are satisfied by this experiment. They accept the stick as straight. The bent appearance is dismissed as error or illusion and the matter is dropped. But, we may ask, what are illusions? They consist in being objects which are not as they seem. If objects are not as they seem, then what makes seeming sometimes so and sometimes not so? In what follows, we shall cite many examples in support of the contention that the common dismissal of errors as "exceptions to the rule" is itself an error. Error is more common than commonly supposed.

Since psychologists distinguish many kinds of perception in accordance with the types of sensation involved, we may conveniently select representative examples. Although some objects are perceived through the functioning of only one kind of sensory end organ, e.g., through seeing, hearing, tasting, or smelling, many others involve more than one. Examples of single-sensory error will be considered first and those of multisensory error later. Error in visual perception is illustrated by railroad tracks, which appear to converge at a point in the distance but which, nevertheless, seem to remain equidistant no matter how far we travel on them. Blood appears blue in veins, red when shed, pale pink or white under a microscope. When plainsmen first venture into high mountains they misjudge distances, traveling miles and miles toward a nearby peak without getting closer. Here, too, mountain streams sometimes seem to run uphill. Mirages so common on western plains lure the novice to lakes that evaporate upon approach. Mirrors baffle infants just achieving competence in reaching for objects in their world. Rainbows puzzle children who see them "right over there." In movies we see shooting, falling, and galloping away, but later the lights reveal only a solid wall or canvas. When western movies were first shown in the West, naive cowboys attending their first movies reacted so realistically, we are told, as to join personally in shooting the villain.

Error in auditory perception is exemplified by first experiences with ringing ears, echoes, striking two keys and hearing only one sound. Gustatory error may be encountered when one eats a large amount of candy. The first piece is sweet and delicious, the fiftieth sour and sickening. Coffee, tobacco, and beer, which seem bitter at first, become agreeable later. Some foods taste different when we have a cold. Olfactory error can occur, as when the stifling smell, obvious upon entering a closed room, seems to disappear even without its being ventilated, after we have remained there a while. Tactile error perplexes one who, having lost a limb, continues to locate pain or itching in the leg region. We notice pressure of our chair against our skin, whereas only our clothes directly touch us. Kinaesthetic errors are well known to meat-market shoppers, as butchers obviously overweigh some packages. The same objects appear heavy and light at different times. An empty basket pops up lightly if we had expected it to be full, yet the same basket feels extremely heavy if full when thought to be empty. Errors of equilibrium result from our twirling the body rapidly enough to become dizzy and then stopping suddenly. The world keeps turning in the opposite direction, or the floor comes up with a bang. Thermal error affects us when we have warmed our hands at different degrees of temperature, and have then plunged them into water of even temperature. To the hot hand the water feels cold and to the cooler hand it feels warm. Torrid bath water and frigid swimming pools are judged to change their temperatures as we become adjusted to them.

Such examples of error trouble the naive realist, but they trouble him very little. He goes from conviction to new conviction, confident in the reliability of each new view. When pressed with the query, "But how can you tell that your new conviction is more reliable than the view given up as erroneous?" he often answers, "Well, I just know." Or, if he is cornered and prodded for an explanation, five kinds of replies eventually come out: He appeals to his other senses for corroboration. He compares his opinion with past experiences. He repeats the experiment. He invokes the testimony of others. He appeals to instruments.

1. If appearances derived through one sensory channel appear contradictory, it is natural to appeal to other senses for corroboration. When one's ears ring unexpectedly, he naturally glances around for the source, but the visual surroundings remain still while the sound seems to move with his head. When one who has lost a leg first experiences an itching as if from this limb, he is impelled to look and to feel whether his leg is still there. The dizzy whirler reaches out toward objects to ascertain whether they whirl as they seem to, and he listens to sounds to determine whether they too revolve. But sometimes different senses contradict each other, though at other times they erroneously corroborate each other. When they contradict, which sense shall we accept as reliable? The half-submerged stick looks bent but feels straight. We hear the distant carpenter's hammer strike once after we see it stop striking. We see lightning flashes now, but hear thunder later. The steam of a distant whistle stops while the sound continues. How do we decide between conflicting senses? Are some senses more reliable than others? The naive realist never quite gets around to answering these questions. If we observe him closely, we will find that at some times he relies principally on his eyes and, at other times, on his ears.

When different senses corroborate an error, we are still more baffled. Who has not had the experience of being on a train as it started moving in the railway terminal. First one feels the rumble of wheels over tracks, hears the movement of the wheels under him, and looks out to see that he is, apparently, at last moving. His eyes corroborate his ears and kinaesthetic sensations. Then he is startled to find that not his but the next train is moving. In movies we both see and hear gaiety, or suffering, or excitement, although nothing is really there but light reflected from a canvas. At times we even smell the fragrance of springtime blossoms, shudder at rumbling earthquakes, sway to the swing of music. The marvels of movies remain for the naive realist merely marvels. For, first he is absorbed by the entrancing realities of screen activities and then he devotes himself to the grimmer realities of his own life. But each is real in its turn and while it lasts. So long as he can distinguish one from the other he does not bother about explaining why. Not only do many of his senses corroborate the reality of movie heroism, but his emotions also lend support through his shedding tears. He is unaware, for the moment, that he has no test of the unreality of the objects of his attention. And he wants none. The same is true of his own life. He is unaware that he has no criterion of the reality or unreality of objects experienced. He has faith in the reality of movie action while it lasts, otherwise he could not really enjoy it. He has faith in his own action, otherwise how could he really enjoy life. But how reliable is such faith?

2. Comparison of present paradoxes with past experiences simply involves greater possibilities of error and greater paradoxes. For past experiences, to be compared, must be remembered. But memory often fails us. What assurance do we have that it is not failing us again? Also, the past experiences themselves may have been erroneous. Can the possibility of erroneous recollection, added to the possibility of erroneous past experience, be used to deny evidence at hand? Perhaps, however, the recollection of experiences repeated many times in the past may be considered more reliable than a single present experience. Yet, past experiences may have been erroneous consistently. We may have seen a movie several times and each time the hero married the heroine. Thus, a plurality of past experiences may consistently corroborate a marriage which does not in fact exist. Still greater paradoxes arise when we stop to realize that past experiences themselves no longer exist, and therefore cannot be recalled. Present recollections are present experiences, not past experiences, so what test does one have that his present recollection is like experiences he has had previously? He cannot compare them, because past experiences do not exist to be compared with present recollections of

them. This fact the naive realist neglects entirely. He thinks he sees directly back into an existing past which in reality has ceased to exist.

3. Doubts sometimes lead to experimentation. Is the bent stick really straight? The naive realist pulls it out, puts it back into the water, and feels it several times to prove that it is really straight. But how can he discount the fact that it also appears bent repeatedly? Also, if past experiences can have been consistently in error, why not present and future experiences? Twirl around again and again and the world will also whirl again and again. The conditions which produce error can themselves be repeated. How can one ever be sure that he is not in error?

4. When doubts become serious, we naturally consult others. Somehow we have come to trust the counsel of others, at least about some things. "Does the stick look bent to you? Feel it and see if it isn't straight." Gregarious naive realists derive much satisfaction from social corroboration, but they fail to realize two things. First, perception of other people as objects to be consulted is itself also liable to error. Most of us have mistaken manikins, mirror images, and movie motions for real men. Or, in dreams we have consulted our friends and have gained their agreement. What proof do we have that there are real people to consult? Secondly, even if we actually consult real people, are they not subject to the same errors as we? Cannot people be in agreement and yet in error? For centuries people agreed that the earth is flat. People having the same kinds of color blindness agree in their discrimination of color. If others share our error, how can we profit by consulting them for proof?

5. The last resort of the naive realist is an appeal to instruments. An immovable half-submerged log is tested by pushing another stick, which is known to be straight, down beside it. Real weight of market purchases is measured on scales. Real heat is measured by thermometers. The real size and shape of the table are tested by ruler and square. But this appeal to instruments is the final blow to naive realism. For an appeal to instruments, like the appeal to other senses, to past experiences, to repetition, and to other persons, is a confession of failure. For it is a confession that apparently obvious objects are not self-evident. An appeal to instruments is an appeal to reflection, and to the extent that we are reflective we cease to be naive.

Before we let the naive realist out of his corner, let us ask him one more question: "How can you tell when you are not dreaming?"

He replies, "I can pinch myself to see if I am awake." "But can you not dream of pinching yourself and of convincing yourself that you are awake?" "Yes, but I can ask others if I am awake, and I can walk and run and read." "But can you not dream of doing these also?" He is forced to admit this, but he persists in discovering additional suggestions, including that of waking up. But people sometimes dream of waking up and of arousing their friends to settle cooperatively their dreaming doubts. If there is nothing in waking moments about which we cannot dream, and if dreams seem real, then what assurance does one have that he is not now dreaming? The Chinese Taoist philosopher, Chuang Tsu (c. 369–268 B.C.), is often quoted as saying: "Once upon a time, I, Chuang Tsu, dreamt I was a butterfly. . . . Suddenly I awaked, and there I lay, myself again. Now I do not know whether I was then a man dreaming I was a butterfly, or whether I am now a butterfly dreaming I am a man." [4]

When confronted with the unsatisfactory conclusion that one cannot be sure of the obvious, it is natural for one to seek some way out of his unpleasant predicament. Nowadays, when some scientific conclusions are taught to beginners with an air of considerable certainty, students commonly appeal to what they have learned in physical, physiological, and psychological sciences as being evidence upon which they can rely in determining the truth of their conclusions. To be sure, the reflective surrender of naive realism in favor of scientific obviousness has considerable merit. Yet, one may have adopted his new convictions too hastily, overlooking the fact that certain doubts and difficulties involved in naive realism reappear in scientific perception, if we but stop to look for them. A scientist must, like the naive realist, begin his empirical quest by perceiving data and accepting what appears just as it appears. If he seeks to be thoroughly objective about his perceptual data, he will accept as obvious whatever appears. But what justification is there for accepting the obvious as reliable when one is a scientist, if he has had to reject it as a naive realist? Price's way of stating this warning is worth repeating.

> Every man entertains a great number of beliefs concerning material things, e.g., that there is a square-topped table in this room, that the earth is spheroid, that water is composed of hydrogen and oxygen. It is plain that all these beliefs are based upon sight and on touch (from which organic sensation can not be separated): based on them in the sense that if we had not had certain particular experiences

---

[4] Quoted in R. O. Ballou, *The Bible of the World*, pp. 512–513. The Viking Press, New York, 1939.

of seeing and touching, it would be neither possible nor reasonable to entertain such beliefs. Beliefs about imperceptibles such as molecules or electrons or x-rays are no exception to this. Only they are based not directly on sight and touch, but indirectly. Their direct basis consists of certain other beliefs concerning scientific instruments, photographic plates, and the like. Thus, over and above any intrinsic uncertainty that they themselves may have, whatever uncertainty attaches to these more basic beliefs is communicated to them. It follows that in any attempt either to analyze or to justify our beliefs concerning material things, the primary task is to consider beliefs concerning perceptible or "macroscopic" objects such as chairs and tables, cats and rocks. It follows, too, that no theory concerning "microscopic" objects can possibly be used to throw doubt upon our beliefs concerning chairs or cats or rocks, so long as these are based directly upon sight and touch. Empirical science can never be more trustworthy than perception, upon which it is based; and it can hardly fail to be less so, since among its non-perceptual premises there can hardly fail to be some which are neither self-evident nor demonstrable. Thus the not uncommon view that the world which we perceive is an illusion and only the "scientific" world of protons and electrons is real, is based upon a gross fallacy, and would destroy the very premises upon which science itself depends.[5]

Furthermore, scientists, too, have no better tests than dreamers. This charge at first strikes scientists as absurd. But for every test that a scientist can propose for his being awake or for the reliability of his conclusions, one may ask, "Is it impossible for him to dream that this is so?" Surely he must answer "No," and thereby admit that he cannot prove his position any better than a dreamer might.[6]

Even if one disregards such shortcomings and uncritically accepts scientific conclusions, he can easily discover further evidence to refute naive realism. Three additional types of criticism may be worth noting.[7]

1. It fails to take into account the extraorganic and intraorganic conditions of knowing. Some scientists describe the human body as an organism and distinguish for convenience between extraorganic and intraorganic factors, i.e., factors outside the body and factors inside the body. If many factors between the thing causing the idea

[5] Henry H. Price, *Perception*, p. 1. Methuen and Co., Ltd., London, 1932.

[6] Part of the foregoing paragraph and most of the following nine paragraphs appeared in an article, "What is Knowledge?" in *The Scientific Monthly*, March, 1943, pp. 269–271.

[7] Suggested by Sellars, *op. cit.*, Ch. 4.

and the idea itself affect the idea, then the idea may be different from what it would be if it were influenced by the thing alone. Let us consider a few such factors.

Extraorganic conditions of visual perception include light sources, pigments, atmospheric conditions, and glasses. Light sources are of many sorts, and what one sees may be stimulated by a single source or by many sources, by light of a single frequency or of mixed frequencies, by light of a single intensity or of many intensities, shining from one angle or from many angles. All these make a difference. Some pigments absorb all rays, others none, others some. Atmospheric conditions, exemplified by fog, snow, dust, rain, and heat waves, affect visibility. Glasses, telescopes, microscopes, their accuracy, their adjustment, their color, all affect perception. Does the real nature of things change as these conditions intervene? Furthermore, the distance which light waves travel is a factor which naive realists neglect. If light travels at a rate of 186,000 miles per second, some fraction of a second is required for transmission from table to eye. So we see the table, not as it is when the light wave reaches the eye, but as it was when the light wave left the table. A fraction of a second seems so insignificant in the total reaction involved in perception that it may be ignored for practical purposes. When distances become great, however, the significance changes. Astronomers astound naive realists with assertions that stars which seem to be in the sky have long since ceased to be there.

Visual perception is conditioned intraorganically by the complicated nature of the eye. Before a colored table can be perceived, light waves reflected from the table's surface must travel through some medium to the surface of the eye, penetrate the skin, travel through the aqueous humor, the lens, the vitreous humor, to the retina and its rods, which react to variations in light intensities, and to its cones, which react to variations in wave frequencies. These cells behave like little chemical batteries or photoelectric cells. When stimulated by light they generate electric currents or nervous impulses which are sent through neurones to the brain. Somehow the brain functions in such a way as to produce attention to, and consciousness of, the object being experienced.

How can color, which the naive realist supposes the table to have, travel on light waves that are merely high-frequency vibrations, penetrate skin, liquid, and lens, then undergo chemical transformation, travel through neurones as electrical impulses, and enter consciousness unchanged?

How can shape, which the naive realist supposes the table to have, be transmitted into conscious experience? Rays traveling simultaneously reach different parts of the curved cornea at slightly different times, travel through a mobile doubly concaved lens and reach the curved, rear inner surface of the eyeball only after having been inverted. Then, the rays stimulate chemical reactions in the rods and cones; but these may react at slightly different rates, if they are variously fatigued, or some may not react at all. What happens to the supposed shape of the table during these chemical reactions? The nervous impulses travel through the optic neurones of different lengths, which twist mazelike on their way to and in the brain. Since we see with two eyes, we really get two sets of patterns of rays. Impulses through the optic nerve split in such a way that those coming from the right half of each eye terminate in the left rear lobe of the brain, and those from the left half of each eye in the right lobe of the brain. These lobes seem to be separated from each other by a longitudinal fissure. How can the supposed shape of the table stand such distortion, transformation, duplication, and separation without affecting its appearance?

How can size, which the naive realist supposes the table to have, be transmitted into one's mind? The table top is three by five feet. But that size cannot really be contained within a head wearing a size seven hat. Size, too, must be transferred through a tiny hole called the pupil and meander through twisting brain-paths. Not size but, at best, relative size can be perceived.

2. It fails to take into account differences in public knowing. To the previously mentioned extraorganic and intraorganic conditions we may add some which emphasize differences between people. Naive realists believe that two or more persons can see an object at the same time and all see it as it is. Thus, all these observers should have exactly the same experiences. But disputes about objects illustrate variations in perceptions. Also, scientific tests have been devised to demonstrate these differences, as, for example, the color-blind tests and the anomaloscope. The anomaloscope is a system of prisms and lenses mounted in a tube such that one can see, through an eyepiece, two halves of a lighted circular field, the color and intensity of which are controlled by screw-adjusted slits permitting monochromatic yellow light (589 millimicrons) to reflect from one half, and a mixture of monochromatic green light (536 mm) and monochromatic red light (670 mm), in any proportion, to reflect from the other half. Tests show that when one person has adjusted the anomaloscope so

that both halves of the visual field appear equal in color and intensity, another person who looks will assert that they appear different and will require readjustment to make the halves appear equal. Thus is demonstrated reported differences in experience when extraorganic conditions of stimulation remain constant. Thus, obviously, different people may not see the same object as it is, but may perceive different objects when confronted by the same stimulus source.

3. It fails to take into account the constructed character of knowing. The term "constructed character" [8] of knowing may be used to name the synthesizing process that goes on in the brain before experiences are produced. The various nervous impulses do not appear in consciousness to be knowingly assembled or constructed into an object. Objects appear in consciousness as wholes, or "gestalts." [9] They enter experience already made. Some unconscious or subconscious process determines our conscious experiences for us, even though we can never become aware of it. The mystery of consciousness may never be explained satisfactorily, but it is obvious, to those who reflect, that something happens within us to make us see things the way we do. This something must be taken into account in explaining the nature of knowledge.

Perhaps the most startling construction is that of consciousness itself. Consciousness seems to be continuous, at least from the time one wakes in the morning until he goes to sleep at night. But psychologists nowadays are inclined to think that consciousness is not a continuum but a series of pulsations, each lasting some fraction of a second. The durations of periods of impulses relative to the durations of periods between impulses vary from person to person and from time to time. Measurement of the length of these pulsating periods of consciousness is difficult and must be done by indirect means. Pulsations of consciousness sometimes correspond to eye-jerks of one who is reading. One sees the line of printed words he is reading as a continuous line, but if he observes another reader's eyes he will note that eyes do not move continuously but stop, flick, stop, and flick.

If consciousness is a series of impulses, why do we seem to be conscious continuously? In order to be conscious of the period between moments of consciousness we would have to be conscious when we are not conscious. This is impossible. We can experience neither

---

[8] *Ibid.*, p. 52.
[9] See Wolfgang Köhler, *Gestalt Psychology*. Horace Liveright, Inc., New York, 1929.

the period between, nor the ending, nor the beginning of a flash of consciousness. In order to experience the end of a flash, we should have to be conscious long enough to include the end within consciousness, which again is impossible. In order to experience the beginning of a flash of consciousness, we should have to be conscious already and to include the beginning of the flash of consciousness within consciousness. Thus the illusion of continuity of consciousness is a basic illusion without which experience could not be. The naive realist cannot believe this.

What Then?

If naive realism is untenable, what view shall we hold? Philosophers have been struggling with this problem for a long time. No easy answer can be expected. Yet the problem is persistent, and some solution to it is presupposed by satisfactory solutions to most other problems. Perhaps the best way to develop further insight concerning knowledge is to follow the progress of famous philosophers. Without going back to early Greek beginnings of Western philosophy, we shall begin with the views of John Locke who lived early in the modern period. Although the problem of empirical knowledge bothered even the earliest thinkers, not until the seventeenth century did it become philosophy's central concern. Ten typical examples have been selected to illustrate major steps in mankind's epistemological achievement. The reader should consult a history of philosophy [10] for fuller details. But enough of each of the ten has been presented to provide some understanding of its viewpoint and something of its significance to contemporary perspectives. From this survey of types should come some acquaintance with philosophy's great minds and their influence upon each other, as well as some awareness of the romance of philosophy's development. One should make acquaintance with some of the great men, the great books, and the great issues that form essential parts of the language and ideology of a liberal education today.

[10] See pp. 427–429 for bibliographical suggestions.

· 3 ·

Representative
Realism

Although the Englishman John Locke (1632–1704) was not acquainted with all the foregoing criticisms of naive realism, he was sufficiently aware of the problem to be accredited by historians as being one of the founders of modern philosophy. Political and religious intolerances of his time, with which he had firsthand acquaintance, convinced him of the need for pointing out the fallacies due to our naive "enthusiasms" [1] and for re-examining the nature of knowledge to discover its limitations and possibilities of certainty. When naive men become enthusiastic about obvious things, "they are sure because they are sure, and their persuasions are right because they are strong in them. For, when what they say is stripped . . . , this is all it amounts to." [2] Responding to his own challenge to re-examine knowledge, Locke wrote his *Essay Concerning Human Understanding* "(1) to discover what is the origin of our ideas, (2) to show what is the certainty, the evidence, and the extent of our knowledge, (3) to compel philosophy to abandon what surpasses human comprehension by marking the limits of its capacity." [3] Men have always sought certainty as part of their quest for security, but with Locke mankind achieved a new depth of awareness of the importance of knowledge in this quest. If there are actual limits to our certain knowledge, we should want to know exactly what these limits are so we will claim as sure only what is warranted.

[1] See Sterling P. Lamprecht, *Locke, Selections,* pp. xxi, 16ff. Charles Scribner's Sons, New York, 1928.

[2] *Ibid.,* p. 18.

[3] Alfred Weber, *History of Philosophy,* p. 298. Charles Scribner's Sons, New York, 1925.

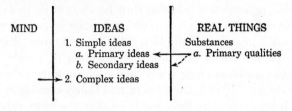

Locke distinguished, as we all do at times, between our minds, our ideas, and the things which cause our ideas. Our minds, at birth, are like blank tablets, having no innate ideas, but getting all ideas from sensations stimulated by real things. Minds are suited to receiving impressions made on them, for storing these impressions, and for using them to think with. Those ideas first impressed upon the mind through the senses are "simple ideas," e.g., those of color, shape, solidity, extension, size, number, motion, and the like. When one experiences several of these simple ideas together in the same way repeatedly, he develops a "complex idea," e.g., of a large, long, brown, solid object called a table. Complex ideas, being partly products of our minds, may not be so true as those simple ideas received directly through the senses without the mind working on them. Thus, our knowledge of real things, through complex ideas, is liable to error. But if the mind is liable to error regarding complex ideas, how can we be sure that even our simple ideas are true representations of real things and their real qualities?

Locke seeks a way out of the difficulties due to disagreements about colors, for example, by distinguishing between two kinds of qualities of real things and, correspondingly, two kinds of ideas caused by those qualities. The qualities which belong to real things themselves apart from their being known, such as size, shape, length, solidity, number, and mobility, he called real or "primary" qualities. "Secondary" qualities, i.e., those that produce in us ideas of color, sound, taste, odor, which vary from person to person and time to time, do not exist in real things except as powers of primary qualities to cause these ideas in us. "The ideas of primary qualities of bodies are resemblances of them, and their patterns do really exist in the bodies themselves; but the ideas, produced in us by secondary qualities, have no resemblance of them at all." [4]

However, even though primary ideas do, and secondary ideas do not, copy, conform to, or agree with, reality, simple ideas are neither

[4] Lamprecht, *op. cit.*, p. 207.

true nor false, regardless of whether they be ideas of shape (primary) or color (secondary). One is in error, not when he perceives a blue color, but when he judges that a blue table is a red table. Knowledge consists in perception of the proper connection of simple ideas in complex ideas which are true when they conform to real things, false when they do not. If all knowledge of real things consists in complex ideas which are derived by the mind from simple sensory experiences, what, then, is the nature of these real things, or "substances," which have the qualities we perceive? We can never know, says Locke, for all our complex ideas are constructed by the mind out of the very limited number of simple ideas which it is capable of receiving. This is a predicament in which human knowing finds itself. We should seek to make the best of our situation, not by condemning others as having false ideas, just because theirs differ from ours, but by being tolerant of others even as we would have them be of us. We should be careful to note more precisely how our complex ideas are derived from our simple ones and then to claim for them no more than is warranted.

Locke's chief contribution to the problem of knowledge is this insistence that we should recognize the sensory origin of all our ideas. He contributed to philosophy its first systematic presentation of "empiricism," the view that all knowledge originates in experience, or, more specifically, in sensory experience. Empiricism is usually contrasted with "rationalism," the theory that reality itself is rational, or reasonable, and that the nature of reality is to be discovered through reasoning rather than through sensory experience. Locke's conclusions appear all the more significant when it is recognized that philosophers before his time had rather uncritically accepted reason as the proper tool for getting knowledge. During the medieval period, the chief controversy raged over whether reason or revelation provided us with the most certain knowledge. With Locke, the most debated issue became that of reason versus experience. Thus was ushered in the modern period and the modern problem: If knowledge originates in sensory experience, how can we derive reliable, true, certain, and universal knowledge? Or, how is science possible?

Since, for Locke, knowledge is not completely reliable, we should constantly make allowances for possibilities of error. "Ideas, instead of being tools for obtaining knowledge of objects, tend to become an obstacle in the way of obtaining knowledge." [5] Science is capable

[5] *Ibid.,* p. xlii.

only of speculative, "tentative and uncertain hypotheses about the nature of these objects." [6] "We are so far from being admitted into the secrets of nature that we scarce so much as ever approach the first entrance towards them." [7] "But our knowledge is even narrower than our ideas; not only can we not go beyond what we experience, but we neither have nor shall have the knowledge of our ideas we desire to have. We do not experience everything we are capable of experiencing. . . . Our ignorance is due to want of ideas. . . ." [8]

So much for a brief summary of Locke's theory of knowledge. Such brevity seems dictated by space and the aim of selecting only enough from the thought of certain men to state the type of solution. Representative realism is a view that accepts a distinction between ideas and real things such that ideas represent the real things in knowledge. The possibility of error is explicitly recognized, warned against, and explained as due to the mind's mistaking complex ideas, which it has constructed, for accurate representations of real things. Error may be avoided only to the extent that we do not confuse primary and secondary qualities, and intolerantly insist that our own constructions are necessarily true. By redefining truth as fidelity of our complex ideas to their sensory originals, we can have a completely empirical theory and test of truth, but this leaves us agnostic about the nature of real things.

In comparing representative realism and naive realism with respect to the six statements (see p. 38), we may note again that, while naive realism holds that things are as they seem and seem as they are, representative realism accepts as fundamental a distinction between experienced ideas and real things.

1. Real things exist, independent of their being known. They can endure or continue to exist without being experienced by anyone. Ideas, on the other hand, depend on minds for their existence, even though they are caused in our minds by real things.

2. Real things have qualities which do not derive their existence or nature from any knower. But ideas representing these things and qualities in the mind are dependent upon such a mind. Since the mind depends completely for its primary ideas upon the primary qualities in things, and since these qualities do not depend on the mind, such qualities are regarded as real. But since there are no

[6] *Ibid.*, p. xliii.
[7] *Ibid.*
[8] Frank Thilly, *A History of Philosophy*, p. 315. Henry Holt and Co., New York, 1914.

qualities in real things corresponding to our secondary ideas, these secondary qualities may be thought of as mind-dependent, or as subjective.

3. Real things and their qualities are not influenced merely by being known, but ideas may be so influenced. Primary ideas are received simply as given; the mind does not make them over but accepts them as they are. Secondary ideas depend upon, and are affected by, the sensory channels which receive them. Complex ideas are produced by the mind out of simple ideas and are thus molded by the creative powers of the mind.

4. Real things do not exist exactly as they appear in complex ideas, but only as they appear in primary ideas. Secondary ideas do not resemble real things. Also, since the mind's construction of complex ideas may differ greatly from the actual structure of real things, all knowledge of such ideas is liable to error and, thus, is unsure.

5. Real things are known indirectly, i.e., through ideas which represent them, although their inner nature (an unknown x) remains forever a mystery. Ideas themselves are known directly, being imprinted on the mind, either by the senses or by the activity of the mind itself.

6. Real things may be public. The same thing may cause different ideas in several people. When two persons see the same thing, their primary ideas should be alike, because both copy the same real qualities, but their secondary ideas can be quite different and their complex ideas may be expected to differ greatly. All ideas are private.

Criticisms

Despite its success in meeting the difficulties most troublesome to naive realism, i.e., how to account for error and the constructive functioning of the mind in knowing, by distinguishing between primary and secondary qualities, representative realism nevertheless fails to be fully satisfactory. Ignoring the fact that Locke was unsystematic in his writing, that he used words loosely, that he was not fully aware of his own biases, and that his ideas were not wholly consistent—shortcomings which might attach to any writer—we may nevertheless point out some troubles inherent in even a consistently presented representative realism.

Locke sought to develop a theory of knowledge, but ended with little more than a theory of ignorance. His virtuous attempt to free men from error by exposing the limits of knowledge led to the conclusion that men have little if any sure knowledge. The distinction between ideas and real things created such a rift between knowledge and its object that no means could be found to bridge the gap. He ends with two worlds, the subjective world of ideas and the real world of things. "Knowledge is nothing but the perception of the connection and agreement or disagreement and repugnancy of any of our ideas." [9] It has nothing to do, except indirectly, with the real world. Our ideas represent real things (hence "representative realism"), but how well they represent them we have no way of knowing, even though we do know that they do not always represent them well.

His theory of truth remains confused and unsatisfactory. On the one hand, he seeks to use the correspondence, or copy theory, of truth. Ideas are true when they copy real things. But, on the other hand, he ends by denying that any of our ideas, except primary ideas, can be copies of real things. Thus, he feels that he cannot define the truth of these ideas in terms of copying, but rather in terms of their agreement with, or lack of repugnancy to, each other. Although he had hoped that true ideas would give us knowledge of real things, he concluded that truth is merely subjective. This conclusion gave great impetus to the development of idealistic philosophies which, in effect, refuted the type of realism Locke sought to maintain.

His ingenious distinction between primary and secondary qualities proved, in the hands of his critics, to be a means to his downfall. For, once he had admitted that some qualities, i.e., secondary qualities, were subjective and not real, it turned out to be rather easy to demonstrate that all qualities are subjective and not real, and that, therefore, there may be no real things at all. Locke's critics ask, "If knowledge is nothing but the perception of agreement or disagreement between ideas and if he is so agnostic about the nature of real things, what reason does he have in the first place for assuming that there are any real things?" Locke gave no satisfactory answer.

Despite his repudiation of innate ideas and rationalism generally, in favor of empiricism, Locke never fully succeeded in shaking off habits of thinking rationalistically. In fact, some critics point out, the motive which Locke had for choosing solidity, extension, figure, motion, and number as primary qualities was that they were more exact, definite, measurable, and thus more rational, whereas tastes,

[9] *Ibid.*, p. 313.

odors, colors, tones, and the like, were secondary because they were inexact, indefinite, immeasurable. Like a typical rationalist, Locke thought primary qualities to be more real because they were more rational. Thus Locke, the great founder of empiricism, failed to be completely empirical, and, we might add, it seems doubtful whether anyone can ever be completely or merely empirical, in Locke's sense.

The dualistic distinction between ideas and real things in knowledge entails a very troublesome dualism of mind and body, or of spirit and matter, in metaphysics. But we shall leave to Chapter 13 our consideration of these criticisms. It may seem, as indeed it should, that Locke has created more problems than he has solved. But is this not to be expected, especially at the beginning of an inquiry? Each new conclusion which we reach that is more complex than the ones we held previously has to make complicated adjustments in our world of thought. We should not condemn Locke too hastily, for he has at least done what all of us have to do in thinking about knowledge, namely, to make a distinction between ideas and real things. If he has made some mistakes, we may welcome them as a warning not to fall into the same errors. Locke was courageous in tackling the problem, constructive in formulating a theory, and provocative in stimulating others to pursue the problem further along the lines which he had begun.

· 4 ·

Subjective
Idealism

George Berkeley (1685–1753), Anglican Bishop of Cloyne, Ireland, in seeking to refute the atheism and freethinking of his time, ingeniously devised an outlook to which philosophy has been indebted ever since. His attack upon materialistic atheism included in its scope a fight against those dualists who attributed to matter an existence equal to that of spirit; and, although Locke was himself a theist, the implications of Locke's theory of knowledge became the focal point of his criticism.

Berkeley, too, was critical of naive realists, of "the illiterate bulk of mankind, that walk the highroad of plain common sense, and are governed by the dictates of nature, for the most part easy and undisputed. To them nothing that is familiar appears unaccountable or difficult to comprehend. They complain not of any want of evidence in their senses, and are out of all danger of becoming sceptics. But no sooner do we depart from sense and instinct to follow the light of a superior principle—to reason, meditate and reflect upon the nature of things, but a thousand scruples spring up in our minds, concerning those things which before we seemed fully to comprehend. Prejudices and errors of sense do from all parts discover themselves to our view; and, endeavoring to correct these by reason, we are insensibly drawn into uncouth paradoxes, difficulties, and inconsistencies, which multiply and grow upon us as we advance in speculation; till at length, having wandered through many intricate mazes, we find ourselves just where we were, or, which is worse, sit down in a forlorn scepticism." [1]

"Upon the whole, I am inclined to think that the far greater part, if not all, of those difficulties which have hitherto amused philoso-

[1] Mary W. Calkins, *Berkeley: Essay, Principles, Dialogues*, pp. 103–104. Charles Scribner's Sons, New York, 1929.

phers, and blocked up the way to knowledge, are entirely owing to ourselves. We have first raised a dust [e.g., Locke's distinction between primary and secondary qualities] and then complain we cannot see. My purpose therefore is to try if I can to discover what those principles are which have introduced all that doubtfulness and uncertainty, . . . to sift and examine them on all sides. How difficult and discouraging soever this attempt may seem, when I consider what a number of great and extraordinary men have gone before me in like designs, yet I am not without some hopes; upon the consideration that the largest views are not always the clearest, and that he who is short-sighted will be obliged to draw the object nearer, and may, perhaps, by a close and narrow survey, discern that which had escaped far better eyes." [2]

Berkeley agreed with Locke in rejecting naive realism, in believing that we can discover a better theory of knowledge, in subscribing to the empiricist doctrine that all our ideas of real things originate in sensory experience and that none are innate, in inferring that our sensations are caused by something external to our minds, in making a distinction between ideas and real things, and in recognizing the subjectivity of secondary qualities. But he sharply differed regarding the distinction between primary and secondary qualities and what is the proper explanation of the cause of our ideas of real things.

"Some there are who make a distinction betwixt primary and secondary qualities. By the former they mean extension, figure, motion, rest, solidity or impenetrability, and number; by the latter they denote all other sensible qualities, as colors, sounds, tastes, and so forth. The ideas we have of these last they acknowledge not to be resemblances of anything existing without the mind, or unperceived; but they will have our ideas of primary qualities to be patterns or images of things which exist without the mind, in an unthinking substance which they call matter." [3] But if we examine an object of our knowledge, our table, for example, we do not find that its shape is "out there" while its color is "in here." Rather, primary and secondary qualities are "inseparably united in the physical object. What we see is not the colored and the extended but the colored extended object." [4] We do not walk away from a table and take its color with us while leaving its shape there. The color and shape of the table come or stay together. If we accept the subjec-

[2] *Ibid.,* pp. 104–105.
[3] *Ibid.,* p. 128.
[4] *Ibid.,* p. xxii.

tivity or mind-dependence of secondary qualities, as Locke does, and "if it be certain that those original [primary] qualities are inseparably united with the other [secondary] sensible qualities, and not, even in thought, capable of being abstracted from them, it plainly follows that they exist only in the mind." [5]

Berkeley has turned Locke's own criticisms of naive realism's belief in real colors against Locke's belief in real shapes. In his own words, "I shall farther add that, after the same manner as modern philosophers prove certain sensible qualities to have no existence in matter, or without the mind, the same thing may be likewise proved of all other sensible qualities whatsoever." [6] "In short, let any one consider those arguments which are thought manifestly to prove that colors and tastes exist only in the mind, and he shall find they may with equal force be brought to prove the same thing of extension, figure and motion." [7]

As a clinching argument, Berkeley points out that, strictly speaking, "an idea can be like nothing but an idea," [8] and so, when Locke and other realists say that ideas and real things are different (ideas being mental, real things being material, and mental and material being unlike in nature) and that primary ideas resemble (i.e., are like and not different from) real qualities, they are involved in contradiction. If mind and matter are unlike, and if knowledge depends upon likeness of mental ideas and material things, then knowledge depends upon the likeness of the unlike, which is absurd, according to Berkeley. If my ideas are like anything outside my mind, it must be another idea in another mind. Since he has refuted Locke's distinction between primary and secondary qualities, which is the very core of Locke's view, he has, in effect, refuted the whole system of representative realism. Now we shall have to look elsewhere for a satisfactory answer, as Berkeley does.

"It is indeed an opinion strangely prevailing amongst men, that houses, mountains, rivers, and in a word all sensible objects, have an existence natural or real, distinct from their being perceived by the understanding." [9] "I say it is granted on all hands (and what happens in dreams, frenzies, and the like, puts it beyond dispute) that it is possible we might be affected with all the ideas we have now, though

[5] *Ibid.*, p. 129.
[6] *Ibid.*, p. 131.
[7] *Ibid.*, p. 132.
[8] *Ibid.*, p. 128.
[9] *Ibid.*, p. 126.

no bodies existed without resembling them. Hence it is evident the supposition of external bodies is not necessary for the producing our ideas; since it is granted that they are produced sometimes, and might possibly be produced always, in the same order we see them in at present, without their concurrence." [10]   "In short, if there were external bodies, it is impossible we should ever come to know it; and if there were not, we might have the very same reasons to think there were that we have now." [11]

But if no real material things exist, how shall we account for the distinction which we seem naturally forced to make between ideas and real things? Berkeley agrees that there are different kinds of ideas, some true and others false, some real and others imaginary, some caused by our own minds while others appear to have causes external to our minds. In brief, for Berkeley, there are two kinds of ideas: those which I cause at will and those which are caused in me whether I will them or not. "I find I can excite ideas in my mind at pleasure and vary and shift the scene as often as I think fit. It is no more than willing and straightway this or that idea arises in my fancy; and by the same power it is obliterated and makes way for another." [12] "But, whatever power I may have over my own thoughts, I find the ideas actually perceived by sense having not a like dependence upon my will. When in broad daylight I open my eyes, it is not in my power to choose whether I shall see or no, or to determine what particular objects shall present themselves to my view." [13]

How does Berkeley account for the production of these ideas which we do not will? We cannot infer that they are caused by material things, for "causes must be held to resemble their effects; and accordingly a material, that is, a non-mental, thing cannot in the nature of the case be conceived as cause of a percept which is mental." [14]   Therefore, only that which is mental can cause that which is mental. If some of our ideas are caused by something outside our minds, they must be caused by other minds. This conclusion is not strange, especially for a good Christian bishop. For, after all, if God, the Great Spirit or Great Mind, is the cause of everything, and if his will continues to operate everywhere, what need is there to interject a supposed material world into the causal

[10] *Ibid.*, p. 134.
[11] *Ibid.*
[12] *Ibid.*, p. 139.
[13] *Ibid.*
[14] *Ibid.*, p. xxiii.

process? An omnipotent God is powerful enough not only to produce in us such ideas as he wishes but also to withhold from us whichever ones he desires. "The ideas imprinted on the senses by the Author of nature are called 'real things'; and those excited in the imagination, being less regular, vivid, and constant, are more properly termed 'ideas' or 'images' of things, which they copy and represent. But our sensations, be they never so vivid and distinct, are nevertheless ideas; that is, they exist in the mind, or are perceived by it, as truly as the ideas of its own framing. The ideas of sense are allowed to have more reality in them, that is, to be more strong, orderly, and coherent than the creatures of the mind; but this is no argument that they exist without the mind." [15] Berkeley's explanation, then, of the usual distinction between ideas and real things is that, although both are in the mind, and thus are ideas, strictly speaking, some appear to be caused in our minds whether we want them or not, and these we call "real things." But their seeming reality is due to their being caused by other minds, especially God's, rather than by material substances.

"To be," says Berkeley, "is to be perceived." If I see an object, then it exists as I see it. If I do not see an object, then I do not know whether it exists or not. How, then, shall we account for the seeming reality of objects when they are not attended to? First of all, they seem to have an independent existence because God wants us to see them this way. Secondly, if God continues to perceive them even though we do not, then they continue to exist as objects in God's mind. "The ideas of sense . . . have a steadiness, order, coherence . . .—the admirable connection whereof sufficiently testifies the wisdom and benevolence of its Author. Now the set rules, or established methods, whereby the Mind we depend on excites in us the ideas of sense, are called 'the laws of nature'; and these we learn by experience, which teaches us that such and such ideas are attended with such other ideas, in the ordinary course of things." [16]

In other words, God is regular in the way in which he causes ideas in us. God does not have to be regular. He could perform miracles. But we would not understand a God who produced nothing but miracles. We would not know what to expect next, and would be completely bewildered. We need regularity. We can trust regularity more than irregularity. God's being regular makes

[15] *Ibid.*, p. 141.
[16] *Ibid.*, p. 140.

God seem more trustworthy than if he were irregular. The so-called laws of nature testify to the trustworthiness of God, and they are not, as atheists, materialists, dualists, and the like, claim, evidence against the existence of God. Berkeley was an enthusiastic promoter of empirical science, since the purpose of science is to discover the laws of nature which are the regularities in the ways in which God causes ideas in us. The scientist, then, is really seeking to know God's will; that is, he wishes to know what ideas God wills us to have. How shall he find them? By examining his experiences. Berkeley gave added impetus to the modern philosophy of science by giving it a theological sanction and a somewhat logic-tight set of arguments which critics have found hard to refute.

Berkeley's view is called "subjective idealism," first because he concludes that all objects of knowledge are subjective, or mind-dependent, and secondly because all existing beings are either ideas or the minds which have these ideas. He believed, in sum, that there are two kinds of beings, minds and their ideas, two kinds of minds, the Infinite Mind (God) and finite minds (persons), and two kinds of ideas, those resulting from a person's will (images) and those originating in God's will (real things). Ideas caused through the senses are true. Images are neither true nor false unless mistaken for ideas caused by God, in which case we are in error (for then we substitute our will for God's will or the ideas which we will for those which God wills). Remembrances of past sensations or of ideas abstracted from sensations are true only in so far as they are faithful to the sensations which they recall or from which they were abstracted. Whoever desires to know the truth will, as a good scientist, seek to derive his knowledge originally from his senses and will continually retest his hypotheses by the test of sensory experience. True knowledge, then, not only is possible, but we cannot escape having it in our sensory experiences. It is here that we make direct contact with that ultimate reality which is God. But true knowledge does not give us assurance that there are real material things.

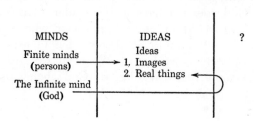

In contrast with naive realism (see p. 38) and representative realism (p. 53), subjective idealism's corresponding six statements are:

1. To be is to be perceived. Objects known, whether "images" or "real things," depend for their existence upon being known. They can continue to exist when unknown by one person, if only they are known by another person or by God.

2. Qualities of objects are parts of the objects, and so, like the objects, they depend upon being known in order to exist. The distinction between primary and secondary qualities is useless, for obviously all known qualities depend upon being known, and we do not know whether there are any unknown qualities.

3. Since objects do depend upon their being "perceived," both their existence and nature depend upon the way in which they are known. Images are wholly dependent on persons, whereas "real things" are dependent also on God.

4. Objects seem as they are and are as they seem. Berkeley believes that the naive realist is correct in this, at least so far as our sensory experiences are concerned. Of course, if we mistook something imaginary for something real we would be in error, but only abnormally naive realists would do this. Naive realists are not materialists, for realism means merely that something has an independent existence, not that it has independent material existence. Ideas caused in us by God do exist independently of our minds, because they continue to exist in God's mind.

5. All objects are known directly; that is, there is nothing between them and our knowledge of them. Again Berkeley accepts the naive realist as right. We know objects themselves, for they are presented wholly, fully, and undistortedly in our minds.

6. Objects are private. Minds do not overlap. Each man has his own ideas or his own private experiences of objects. But, if God chooses to cause exactly the same ideas in two different minds, there is nothing to prevent him from doing so. If he presents ideas to different minds as regularly as he presents them through the laws of nature to single minds, then doubtless we can trust that we have considerable knowledge in common.

Criticisms

Berkeley's system appears logic-tight only to those who accept his theistic premises. Many critics claim that he has not shown how we know that God exists, that he is all-powerful, all-knowing, all-good, all-willing, and that he causes ideas regularly. Berkeley has stated a possibility, but has given no proof. Other theists, who grant his assumptions, arrive at different conclusions. Predestinarians, for example, sometimes assert that God wills everything without exception, even our imaginations. If so, the basis for Berkeley's distinction between images and real things breaks down even on theistic grounds. Still other theists, such as Descartes, believe that God necessarily uses matter in producing ideas; Descartes reasons that a good God would not deceive us about the existence of matter when he causes us to have ideas of real material things.[17] Even on Berkeley's grounds, should we not conclude that, if objects exist as they appear in perception, then if they appear as real material things, as some testify, they exist as real material things?

Berkeley's argument that, since primary and secondary qualities appear inseparable they are necessarily subjective, (a) proves only that those which appear are subjective, but does not prove that there cannot also be real qualities which are unknown, and (b) may as well be used to prove that both are real, as neo-realists, whom we shall study later, do.

Another argument, at first apparently obvious, wilts upon examination. The assumption that an idea can be like nothing but another idea, and that what is mental can be caused only by what is mental, involves the hasty conclusion that if two things are alike they are entirely alike. If this argument were carried out consistently, then every cause must exactly equal its effect, and God, as the cause of my present sensation, must be nothing but (equal to) a present sensation; and my mind which wills my present image must itself be nothing but a present image. Thus, this assumption, when carried out perfectly, leads to absurdities which even Berkeley would not accept.

Finally, if we know only what appears in our sensory experiences, how do we know that our minds themselves exist? My mind is not perceived, but is that which perceives. Since I cannot perceive my mind, but must infer its existence, either I must conclude that it does not exist (by the same argument that material things do not exist because they are not perceived) or I must abandon empiricism in employing the rationalistic argument that "perception implies a perceiver." This and other difficulties troubled Berkeley (almost a third of his essay on *Principles of Human Knowledge* is devoted to

[17] See René Descartes, *Meditations on First Philosophy*, Meditation VI (quoted in Ralph M. Eaton, *Descartes; Selections*, pp. 145–165).

replying to thirteen objections),[18] but he never lost faith in the general soundness of his system.

In evaluating the significance of Berkeley's contributions to modern philosophy, we may too hastily reject his conclusions. We do not have to take them either as the whole truth or as nothing. Rather, in the spirit of modern science itself, many subjective idealists since his time have taken much of his system as an hypothesis to be tried out and tested against alternative hypotheses concerning the nature of knowledge and existence. Since some of them continue to think that it stands up well in comparison, we, too, perhaps, should not reject it hastily. To his credit, we must say that he found a weak spot in Locke, that his system is ingenious and fits well with assumptions commonly made by Christians and other theists, that he promoted empiricism, that he provoked further thought and investigation into the problem of knowledge, and that he inspired many later thinkers. Modern idealists, almost without exception, pay their respects to Berkeley.

[18] See Calkins, *op. cit.*, pp. 141–169.

·5·

Agnosticism

The critical attitude now so habitual to the contemporary scientific mind owes, if not its birth, at least some important steps in its development, to Scotland's David Hume (1711–1776). Hume was aroused by Berkeley's arguments concerning the subjectivity of our ideas of real things. He agreed with Berkeley that the objects of our knowledge are not independently real things, but are ideas, or, as he preferred to call them, "perceptions." "Now since nothing is ever present to the mind but perceptions, and since all ideas are derived from something antecedently present to the mind, it follows that it is impossible for us so much as to conceive or form an idea of anything specifically different from ideas and impressions." [1] If there be any real things, we cannot know them because all we can know are our ideas ("perceptions") of real things, and ideas of real things are ideas. But if we cannot know about real things, either whether there are any or, if there are, what they are like, why is it that human beings have a natural tendency to believe that real things exist? To this question Hume can find no answer, except that such beliefs are "a species of natural instincts" [2] or "original qualities of human nature, which I do not pretend to explain." [3]

The reason why people believe that real things exist independently of their ideas is that they presume that ideas must have external causes. Even Berkeley, who rejected real things as causes of our ideas, still argued that some ideas must have external causes, and therefore concluded that there must be a God to cause them. But, asks Hume, what is the basis of this belief that ideas must have causes? It is true that all people naturally believe in causality, or

[1] Charles W. Hendel, *Hume, Selections*, p. 21. Charles Scribner's Sons, New York, 1927.
[2] *Ibid.*, p. 137.
[3] *Ibid.*, p. 14.

that nothing can come into existence unless it is caused to do so. If nothing can happen without a cause, it follows that when we have ideas, our ideas must have a cause. But, Hume persists, where did we get this natural belief in causality?

Hume's explanation of the origin of our faith in causality led him to a conclusion that is mainly responsible for his lasting fame. He had already agreed with the empirical philosophy of Locke and Berkeley that "all our simple ideas in their first appearance are derived from sense impressions." [4] If so, the idea of causality also originates in sensory impressions. "Knowledge of this relation is not, in any instance, attained by reasoning a priori but arises entirely from experience." [5] But how does it arise from experience? It cannot come from a single impression, because "every effect is a distinct event from its cause," [6] and thus at least two impressions are required to give an impression of cause and effect.

Not every pair of impressions, however, gives us the idea of cause and effect, for we often associate two things without thinking that one causes the other. Even if we see two things recurring constantly together we do not always infer that one causes the other. If we say that causality exists only where "the production of one object by another implies a power," [7] Hume reminds us that "the power lies not in the sensible qualities of the cause, and there are nothing but the sensible qualities present to us." [8] Therefore, we have no direct impression of power, and so have no genuine empirical basis for our idea of cause and effect. Hume's point is this: our faith that nothing can happen without a cause is based upon an inference which itself has not been and cannot be derived directly from our sensory experiences. If the idea of causality cannot originate in sensory experience, and if there are no innate ideas, how does it happen that we have such faith in this idea? Hume's answer is "custom or habit." [9] "All inferences from experience, therefore, are effects of custom, not of reasoning." [10] Consequently, just as other customs and habits that are not based upon necessity are unreliable, so our habit of thinking that nothing can happen without a cause is itself unreliable.

This conclusion has some most startling consequences. Both the whole history of past theology and the whole future of realistic science seem, to many persons, to entail faith in the principle of causal-

[4] Ibid., p. 12.
[5] Ibid., p. 118.
[6] Ibid., p. 121.
[7] Ibid., p. 37.
[8] Ibid.
[9] Ibid., p. 134.
[10] Ibid., p. 135.

ity. The most common argument for the existence of God, that since
the world could not exist unless something caused it to exist, there
must be a first cause or God, is hereby undermined. The faith that
there must be atoms and molecules, because our ideas of chemicals
and objects compounded from them could not exist unless caused
by them, is likewise badly shaken. For, if there can be no certainty
of causality, and if science rests upon causality, then there can be
no certainty in science. If there can be no certainty in theology and
no certainty in science, then of what can we be certain? Nothing,
says Hume, except that we do have the impressions and ideas which
we now actually experience.

Few willingly accept Hume's conclusion. People desire certainty
and want it so much that they cling to the faith that it can be
attained. So, whether as naive realists, as theologians, or as scientists,
men turn against Hume in search for a weak link in his argument.
Fellow empiricists, such as Locke and Berkeley, have no good re-
buttal, for Hume has clearly shown that one cannot conclude that
the idea of causality is a necessary idea if based upon sensory experience alone. Berkeley is no more warranted in claiming that a God
must exist to cause our ideas of real things than Locke is in holding
that real things and their primary qualities cause our ideas of real
things.

Yet, how about those critics who are not empiricists? Rationalists,
who were in a majority in Hume's day, persist even today. If they
assert that the mind is born, not an empty vessel or a blank tablet,
but an active agency with a full set of capacities for reasoning according to necessary laws of thought, then is not Hume helpless before them? No. Hume attacks also the view that we must infer the
existence of minds which have or hold ideas. Both Locke and Berkeley largely overlooked the fact that they had uncritically accepted,
from their rationalistic inheritance, the view that minds exist. They
never doubted that a mind was needed, either to manufacture complex ideas out of simple ones, as Locke said, or to will images, as
Berkeley held.

But, doubts Hume, how do we know that we have minds? Only
through having ideas of our minds. But an idea of a mind is an
idea, not a mind. If an idea of a mind is merely an idea, and nothing
more, then what need is there to suppose that minds exist apart from,
or in addition to, ideas? If we infer that a mind is not just an idea,
but is that which has ideas or causes ideas to exist, then this inference, too, is based upon the assumption that the principle of causality is a necessary one. However, if this principle is derived from

sensory experiences, it is not necessary. If it is not necessary, then we are not warranted in inferring that minds must exist since ideas exist. Hume concludes, therefore, that we can be certain about the existence of neither minds, nor God, nor real things, if by these we mean something external to our present ideas.

If one cannot be certain, then, he must remain in doubt, or sceptical. A "sceptic" is one who doubts or is unsure. One may be sceptical about anything—about the weather, about his own ability to succeed, about his memory, about the testimony of others. Hume was an epistemological sceptic, doubting our ability to know the existence or nature of anything that is not either given as a sensory impression or as an idea derived from sensations. He called himself a sceptic, but many later interpreters of his views prefer to name him an "agnostic," a term coined later by T. H. Huxley. Agnosticism, Huxley says, "may be stated in various ways, but they all amount to this: that it is wrong for a man to say that he is certain of the objective truth of any proposition unless he can produce evidence which logically justified that certainty." [11]

Again, one may be agnostic about the truth of any particular judgment—about whether it will rain, about whether his memory is accurate, about the existence of God (thus agnostics cannot be atheists, for an atheist believes he knows that no God exists, whereas an agnostic believes that he cannot know whether a God does or does not exist). Hume was an epistemological agnostic, believing that we cannot have certainty concerning the existence of anything outside immediate experience. Although there have been many kinds of agnostics before Hume's time, Hume's agnosticism has been particularly influential in determining the course of modern thinking about the nature of knowledge.

?	PERCEPTIONS	?	
	1. Impressions		
	2. Ideas		

Hume brought into sharp focus the empiricist theory of truth. Truth does not consist in those ideas which copy real things, nor does falsity consist in those ideas which do not. Truth does not

[11] Thomas H. Huxley, *Essays upon Some Controverted Questions*, p. 350. D. Appleton and Co., New York, 1892. Used by permission of Appleton-Century-Crofts, Inc.

consist in those ideas caused in us by God. Rather, true ideas are those which are faithful copies of impressions. Our original perceptions, i.e., sensory impressions, are neither true nor false. They are simply "given." When we recall these impressions or when we abstract general ideas from many such impressions, it is these ideas which appear in recollection or in abstract thinking that are true or false, and true or false in proportion to their faithfulness in copying the original impressions. Truth, for Hume, has its reference entirely within experience and needs no extraexperiential conditions or causes. Thus, Hume is even more subjective than Berkeley, and, as a consequence, gave added support to the idealistic philosophies which followed. Hume's denial of certainty about anything outside experience gave impetus to a more thorough examination of experience itself. Such studies have often magnified the importance of experience as a key to existence.

Does Hume's critique of certainty leave us resourceless? If we cannot know that things exist as they seem to, or if we cannot know that things never happen without being caused to happen, shall we stop all inquiry? Shall we merely sit motionless and spend our time doubting? No, says Hume. Half a loaf is better than none. Just because we cannot be certain, does it follow that we can have no knowledge at all? No. We still have all the knowledge that we had before, all the same interests and desires that we had before, and the same possibilities for learning new things that we had before. What Hume has done is to help us become aware that we do not have the certainty we assumed. But we did not have it before, even though we thought we did. Thus, Hume has led us really to wider knowledge by creating in us an awareness of the limitations of certainty. Hume has no objection to our having faith in God, in science, in other people, in one's own mind, or in the future, but his point is that we will be safer if we recognize that these faiths are not certainties. Hume has taught us to be more cautious, more considerate, and more wary about our assertions. His influence has led us to examine in detail what we now call "theory of probability," and to be concerned about the precise degrees of evidence for and against our views. Hume's agnosticism is responsible for much of the insistence upon the tentativity that has come to be a fundamental part of the scientific attitude, as we conceive it today.

Hume did not succumb to hopelessness because of his agnostic conclusions, nor did he advise others to do so. His life continued quite normally. "I dine, I play a game of back-gammon, I converse, and I am merry with my friends. . . . Here then I find myself absolutely and necessarily determined to live, and talk, and act like other people in the common affairs of life." [12] However, "in all the incidents of life we ought still to preserve our scepticism. If we believe that fire warms or water refreshes, it is only because it costs us too much to think otherwise. . . . Where reason is lively, and mixes itself with some propensity, it ought to be assented to." [13] Furthermore, we should not jump too quickly from the conclusion that we can know nothing with certainty to the conclusion that therefore we are certain that we can know nothing with certainty. This would be to make the very mistake we are seeking to avoid. "A true sceptic will be diffident of his philosophical doubts, as well as of his philosophical conviction; and will never refuse any innocent satisfaction which offers itself on account of either of them." [14]

Our agnosticism should not prevent us from enjoying life. We should enjoy life, even if we cannot understand it or be certain about it. Nor should it prevent us from seeking to be scientists. If experience does, in fact, present us with uniformities that we have come to call the laws of nature, we can hardly shut our eyes to these empirical facts. Since, however, we have no empirical certainty that the future must be like the past, we must take upon ourselves the risk of believing that regularities which have held in the past will hold likewise in the future. Some implications of Hume's agnosticism have been drawn out by positivists and pragmatists, whom we shall meet in later chapters.

How does Hume's agnosticism compare with the six statements describing naive realism? According to Hume:

1. Objects known do depend upon being known. Whether anything exists apart from knowledge, we have no way of ascertaining. Therefore, of course, we must proceed as if such objects did not exist.

2. The qualities of objects exist just as they are known; but the only existence they have, that we know of, is as objects in our present experience.

3. So far as we can be sure, objects have their entire existence within experience; although we cannot assert what causes them (we

12 Hendel, *op. cit.*, pp. 97–98.
13 *Ibid.*, p. 99.
14 *Ibid.*, p. 102.

cannot even say that our experience itself causes them), nevertheless, we have no reason to conclude that they have any other nature than that which is presented in them as they appear.

4. Objects seem as they are and are as they seem. However, if our ideas do not faithfully copy the impressions from which they are abstracted, then we may have some false ideas, but their falsity is strictly a failure to copy impressions and not a failure to copy real things.

5. Objects are known directly. They exist in our experience and, thus, there is nothing between them and our experience of them.

6. Objects are private. In fact, we cannot even be sure that there are other people, for if they are independent of our ideas of them, we cannot know them as they are, and if they consist merely in our ideas of them, they are ideas in our minds rather than being other minds. Even if other people do exist and if they do have ideas similar to ours, there is no test we can use with perfect assurance.

Criticisms

No matter how reasonable Hume's arguments may seem, his conclusion flies in the face of our inborn tendency to believe. We naturally rebel against such persistent and utter doubt. Our faith in naive realism, no matter how untenable we may have found it, remains sufficiently strong in us to demand that we doubt so much doubting. Our faith in reason, too, remains strong even in the presence of Hume's "reasonable" arguments against it. But note, here, that Hume, in presenting reasonable arguments against rationalism, was both reasoning and appealing to our reason. He was presupposing and using in practice the very tool which he sought to deny. Of course, he did not deny that we should reason. What he denied was that we have any innate faculty equipped at birth to reason. Yet, a rather obvious part of his purpose was to refute the reliability of reason in seeking certainty, regardless of whether it was innate or acquired. His own use of reason, however, leaves us unconvinced that we can dispense with it entirely or, even, that we cannot have such certainty as reason may involve. To demonstrate that certainty cannot rest on sense experience does not prove, thereby, that certainty cannot be found by other means. Rationalists, mystics, gestaltists, phenomenalists, neo-realists, pragmatists, etc., become significant partly in proportion to their providing a partial answer to Hume.

A problem still remains for Hume, as it did for Berkeley and Locke; namely, why do objects, colored, solid tables, for example, appear as if they were real? Hume must admit that he cannot explain this phenomenon and he does not attempt to do so. Why human nature is what it is, or why our experiences are what they are, he cannot say, for to do so would be to presuppose a knowledge of their causes which, as he has taken great pains to show, is a kind of knowledge of which he cannot be certain. But, again, our natural realistic tendencies will persist among our faiths unless Hume can present more cogent arguments to compete with the obvious reality of apparently real things. Although the pendulum, swinging between belief and doubt, has swung a full span from naive realism (the obvious) to agnosticism (the obviously not obvious), we have not completely escaped thereby from a degree of faith in the obvious; for even our belief in the impossibility of certainty is a belief. Mere doubts cannot stand by themselves, for we must at least believe that what we doubt is doubtable, and therefore we remain believing something.

As later critics have pointed out, even though we cannot have certainty, we may still have probability. Of course, Hume admitted this, but he did not spend much time and effort developing constructively what probabilities there are and how far we may rely upon them. Furthermore, as the verifications of many of our beliefs increase, at first independently of each other, and then through mutual corroboration, we come to hold, as probable, conclusions which imply doubts about a thorough agnosticism. The apparent impossibility of certainty seems to become less impossible. Scientific experiments based upon the faith that knowledge of real things is possible have brought satisfactory results. So, on the basis of satisfaction alone, we find that our faith in realistic inferences is preferable to our faith in the arguments which Hume presents for agnosticism. To this fact Hume makes no reply. If a person prefers to be a realist, with or without justification, Hume cares to do nothing about it. He merely seeks to show that there are some arguments for agnosticism which are fairly obvious and should be considered before one publicly proclaims that his views should be accepted unquestioningly by others.

We may add a final, if somewhat trivial, criticism. How did Hume arrive at his own doctrine of agnosticism? Did he derive it simply from his own sensory impressions? If so, then did they not "cause" his ideas constituting this doctrine? Then, does he not presuppose the doctrine of causality which he refutes? If not, he must have arrived at his theory by some other reliable means; otherwise the doctrine itself is unreliable, and we are not obligated to accept it. Hume could reply, however, that he does not know how he came by his doctrine, and we could not blame him for claiming what he does not claim.

The Egocentric Predicament

Before leaving the subjectivistic viewpoint of Hume, it may be well to introduce a convenient term, "the egocentric predicament," which was coined by Ralph B. Perry almost two centuries later. We may not be able to accept Hume's agnosticism in total, but we had better not take leave of him until we realize fully the significance of his conclusions for all subsequent philosophy. Perry evaluates the subjectivistic contributions, due partly to Locke and Berkeley as well as to Hume, as "one of the most important original discoveries that philosophy has made. No thinker to whom one may appeal is able to mention a thing that is not an idea, for the obvious and simple reason that in mentioning it he makes it an idea. No one can report on the nature of things without being on hand himself. It follows that whatever thing he reports does as a matter of fact stand in relation to him, as his idea, object of knowledge, or experience. In order to avoid making inferences unawares, it is necessary to have a name for this situation just as it stands. It will be convenient to call it 'the ego-centric predicament.'" [15]

No matter how strong our prejudices may be for belief in the existence of real things, they can hardly be stronger than our rational demand for believing this argument regarding the egocentric predicament: an object known is an object known; [16] unknown objects are unknown; we cannot know objects without coming into the relationship of knowing, and thereby they are related, not unrelated, to our knowledge; if we are thinking of objects, they cannot be independent of our thinking of them, so we know them only when they are dependent upon our knowledge of them as objects; if things ever exist without being known, we thereby do not know them and cannot say what they are like.

[15] Ralph Barton Perry, *Present Philosophical Tendencies*, p. 129. Longmans, Green and Co., New York, 1912, 1921.

[16] See George T. W. Patrick, *Introduction to Philosophy*, revised edition, p. 347. Houghton Mifflin Co., Boston, 1935.

Regardless of our other faiths, can we remain reasonable while rejecting this argument? If we cannot reject it, then it follows that, whatever else we may hold about the nature of knowledge, it must somehow be accounted for in a way which will concede that knowledge is inherently subjective. Knowledge may not be exclusively subjective, but it is essentially subjective. All epistemologists after Hume's time have had to reckon with this basic argument. If it can be established that knowledge is at least subjective, then even though we cannot fly off on the wings of our dream of penetrating reality, we have, nevertheless, pinned down one corner of the problem of knowledge. Even if the pin is placed rather uncomfortably, and in a place quite different from where we had hoped, nevertheless, if it is attached to a solid foundation, and one to which we will have to come eventually, perhaps we should be very thankful to Hume that he has forced us so early in our modern investigations to recognize the necessity for at least some subjectivity. When fumbling in the dark, we can feel our way better and with more assurance if we have first found a stable landmark, even if it is quite different in nature and location than we had expected.

· 6 ·

Phenomenalism

The methodical, punctual professor, Immanuel Kant (1724–1804), who during all his life traveled but a few miles from his native city, Koenigsberg, Germany, produced theories that have pervaded the entire body of Western science, and have profoundly influenced the trend of philosophical thinking. Trained as a rationalist, he remained a disciple of G. W. Leibniz and Christian Wolff [1] until Hume, as he says, aroused him from his "dogmatic slumber." [2] Whereas Hume did convince him that dogmatic assertions about the existence of things outside experience is unwarranted, Kant, in turn, detected that Hume was dogmatic about his agnosticism. "To Kant both empiricism and rationalism were dogmatic; the one because it assumed the validity of sensations, the other because it assumed the existence of innate ideas." [3] Kant is important because, among other things, he was the first thinker to give a decisive reply to Hume. Kant answered Hume, not just for himself, but, in a sense, for all mankind. Hume was considered a thoroughgoing agnostic. Kant refuted such agnosticism, but only partly. Kant sought and found a compromise between the extremes of agnostic empiricism and dogmatic rationalism. In doing so, he kept some elements of both empiricism and rationalism. He concluded that there are certain facts accepted by both, which cannot be ignored, and he did so by recognizing certain rationalistic factors inherent in the nature of mind, which Hume had overlooked.

Kant agreed with Hume's conclusion about the impossibility of having knowledge of real things or, as he called them, "things-in-

[1] Alfred Weber, *History of Philosophy*, p. 352. Charles Scribner's Sons, New York, 1896, 1925.

[2] Herbert Ernest Cushman, *A Beginner's History of Philosophy*, Vol. II, p. 242. Houghton Mifflin Co., Boston, 1911, 1920.

[3] *Ibid.*, p. 243.

themselves." We are stuck with the egocentric predicament. We must be agnostic about the nature of real things. On the other hand, this doubting does not make science impossible. If we can have no knowledge of what lies outside experience but only of what occurs within experience, then science does not deal with what lies outside experience, but only with phenomena, with what lies within. This has always been its function. Science seeks universal and necessary laws of phenomena.

We can roughly equate what Kant means by phenomena with what we have been calling experience, consciousness, awareness, and its objects, or with what, in interpreting Locke and Berkeley, we have called ideas. Kant agrees with Berkeley and Hume that the only world we know is the phenomenal world, hence the term "phenomenalism." The aim of science is to discover the laws of nature, of natural phenomena, or, simply, phenomena. If we cannot know what is outside experience, then all the phenomena which science can investigate are within experience. It behooves us, therefore, to direct our epistemological investigations upon the nature of experience itself, if we would see how science is possible.

This Kant did. In fact he spent most of his life in a tremendous, ponderous, tedious study. He invented, for his purposes, a highly technical language to express a multiplicity of fine distinctions that he found necessary to make. In what follows, we shall seek to re-state his views in a language similar to that of Locke, Berkeley, and Hume, introducing as few Kantian terms as possible.

Kant's solution began by distinguishing, much as Locke, Berkeley, and Hume had done, between two fundamental aspects of our experience, namely, the perceptual and the conceptual, or the empirical and the rational. However, his analyses were somewhat more intricate. He accepted the empiricist dictum that there can be no experience (except, perhaps, experiences of pure thoughts) without sensations, and thus there can be no knowledge of objects without involving sensations. But (a) mere sensations are not knowledge, and certainly they are not science, and (b) we do not, except on very rare occasions, have experiences consisting merely of bare sensations. Ordinarily, our experience involves also meanings, significance, relations, ideas, concepts, or whatever one may wish to call them. We do not usually have mere sensations, but sensations of something. We do not just perceive sensations; we perceive objects. We experience something as existing in a particular place at a particular time. Mere sensations are meaningless until we have located them as objects which we call things. Both sensation and conception are required to produce knowledge. "Conception without perception is empty; perception without conception is blind." [4]

If conceptions are not presented to the mind by sensations, then they must be contributed to experience (i.e., to phenomena) by the mind itself. Hume held an inadequate theory, even an inconsistent theory, concerning the function of the mind in producing experience. For, on the one hand, he held that the mind is passive, like a blank tablet, in receiving sensory impressions; but, on the other hand, he spoke of the mind as active in abstracting ideas from impressions. He overlooked the full significance of the activity of the mind in producing experience, partly, perhaps, because he sought to prove that we can have no certainty of the mind's existence. It is to this activity of the mind that we must look in order to discover more fully the factors essential to the production of our experiences or of our phenomenal world.

We cannot look directly into our minds. In fact we cannot be sure what our minds are like or that we have minds which are anything like we conceive them. Kant agrees with Hume in being agnostic about the real nature of the mind itself as well as about the real nature of things-in-themselves. But he disagrees with Hume's ignoring them altogether. If concepts do exist in experience and if they are not contributed by sensations then they must come from some other source. Although Kant was very cautious about his statements concerning this other source, he very definitely accepted it as necessary to explain the nature of experience. We shall introduce some of his language and arguments later, but it seems better to continue to speak, even if somewhat inaccurately, of this other source as being the mind, just as Locke, Berkeley, and Hume did. We cannot examine our minds directly; but we may infer that they must perform certain functions, if we can discover that these functions are actually performed and that they are not performed by our sensations.

First, Kant observed what seemed to him to be the universal and necessary characteristics of objects as experienced. Then he sought to figure out from these observed features what kinds of functions or faculties are required to produce these features. This was a delicate task and, even if we do not accept the results exactly as he left them, we should be able to see that he offered some profound insights,

---

[4] *Ibid.*, p. 253

which we must continue to take account of in arriving at our own theories of knowledge and science. To make his long story short, we may summarize his conclusion, following Burtt's convenient interpretation for beginners,[5] under three headings. Kant distinguishes three "faculties," as he called them, the faculty of sensibility, the faculty of understanding, and the faculty of reason.

1. The first of these, sensibility, is needed to account for the fact that whenever we experience things, such as chairs, landscapes, and stars, we always perceive them as if in space and time. Never do we find an exception to this principle. Each thing is experienced as spatial, and as temporal. If bare sensations themselves do not give us space and time, such characteristics must be provided by the mind. These two "forms," as he called them, of space and time, are present in all perception, whether or not we understand or reason about them. Therefore, some capacity of the mind must be assigned the task of contributing these forms to all perceptual experiences. Thus, he thought, we must recognize this faculty of sensibility, which is merely that ability of the mind which causes us to perceive things as spatial and temporal.

Notice that here Kant is admitting Hume's contention that we do not directly apprehend any time or space external to experience and that if we are to account for how we experience things as spatial and temporal we must do so in terms of what is inside experience. Whether there is anything like space or time beyond experience we cannot know. We have no sensation of space or time as we have of color and solidity, yet all our sensations of color and solidity take spatial and temporal forms. Therefore, such forms must be contributed by some faculty of the mind. When we examine the spatial characteristics of objects, as a mathematician or carpenter does, what are we investigating? We are examining something contributed to these phenomenal objects by our minds. The geometer can reason about the geometrical nature of space, then apply his conclusions to the objects he experiences, and his conclusions will fit. Why? Because the spatial features of the objects are rational, not empirical, and are contributed by the mind, not through the senses. A science of mathematics is possible, not because there is a real world, as Locke thought, with real extension that is really measurable. Rather, it is possible because it deals with characteristics of objects contributed to them by the mind. Kant, the rationalist, rescues mathematics from

[5] Edwin A. Burtt, *Types of Religious Philosophy*, pp. 252–262. Harper & Bros., New York, 1939.

Hume, the empiricist, who found no possibility of certainty in mathematics because he believed it to be derived wholly from sensory experience.

2. The faculty of understanding, Kant believes, is needed to account for the discovery that the mind seems compelled constantly to hold certain beliefs about the nature of things. The mind cannot think about the objects it perceives without being obliged to think of them as having been caused. The principle of causality, that nothing happens without being caused to happen, is inherent in the way the mind thinks about objects. Granted that Hume is correct in holding that the principle of causality cannot be derived with certainty from sensory impressions, it merely follows that his empiricism is inadequate and needs to be supplemented by a recognition of those rational aspects of experience that are uniformly present. These universal and necessary characteristics of experience Kant called "categories," a term widely used in metaphysics. Kant included among his categories, and groups of categories, quantity, quality, relation, existence, possibility, and causality. We cannot think of a chair, for example, without thinking of it as one chair, as having some quality, as being related or not related to other things, without existing, without it being possible. Not many thinkers today accept his list precisely as he formulated it, but many do continue to accept some of them and have added others also. Following Burtt, we shall consider only two of Kant's twelve categories, namely, causality and existence.

The principle of causality, which has proved so important in the history of thought, comes in here for another overhauling. Kant recognizes this principle, so basic to both science and theology, as necessary. The mind itself is constituted in such a way that it demands that all things be interpretable as having been caused. Although the principle of causality is rescued from Hume's attack, it is rescued only so far as the knowledge of phenomena is concerned, but does not apply to things outside experience. Previous and later arguments, relative to the nature of atoms or of God as unknown causes of experience, which claim to extend the principle of causality to things outside experience, Kant finds unwarranted. He still insists that Hume is right in asserting that we cannot know whether the principle applies outside experience. All he claims is that it does necessarily apply within experience, because the mind, one of the two contributors to experience, is such that it supplies this category of causality to the experience which it helps to produce.

The category of existence likewise is furnished by the mind. One cannot think of a chair without thinking of it as existing. Whether a chair exists when we are not thinking of it is uncertain, as Hume has pointed out. Whether a particular chair has any existence apart from our experience of it, we do not know. But we can have no experience of a chair except as something that exists. Existence, then, is a universal and necessary characteristic of perceived objects which, since not contributed by sensations, must be contributed by mind. Thus, in a sense, another category has been rescued from Hume. We can be sure that the objects which we experience exist. But we cannot be sure whether they have any existence apart from experience. Here we have the important contribution of Kant: agnosticism regarding what is unexperienced, combined with rationalism regarding part of what is experienced. Both in theology or physics, we can with certainty assert that God or atoms, if they are objects in our experience, exist. But whether atoms or God exist beyond experience, we have no way of knowing. Therefore, although we can have certainty regarding phenomenal objects, we can have no certainty at all regarding the "noumenal," or objects beyond experience.

3. The faculty of reason appears necessary to account for the three "ideas of reason": our idea of soul (mind), our idea of the world, and our idea of God.

If our senses present to experience a multiplicity of different sensations, and if our understanding presents experience with a multiplicity of concepts, what combines them in, or as, experience? How does it happen that all these different parts of our experience cohere in the way they do? If they do not hang together accidentally, then must we not conclude that there is some principle involved in their remaining together and functioning together uniformly? If some such principle exists, what is it? Kant, in examining this need, concluded that such a principle must be inclusive of, and thus must transcend, all the particular perceptions ("apperceptions," he called them). It must unify them or synthesize them into one experiential whole. Thus, without concluding that there is a complex mind attached to a complicated brain that exists as a real thing outside of, and causing, the unity of our experience, he simply concluded that, as a minimum, there must be some transcendent unifying principle which he called, therefore, "the transcendental synthetic unity of apperception." Thus, whereas he remained largely agnostic about the nature of mind as a real cause of experience, he felt not only justified in inferring, but he was also required to infer, that if our experiences are unified there must be something which unites them. Thus, there must exist some principle of wholeness, some soul, which performs this function. The term "soul" was a part of the accepted terminology of Kant's day, and those who reject it must find another term to represent that principle which performs this experience-unifying function. For convenience, we shall continue to use the term "mind," even though it may signify much more than Kant was willing to grant.

Not only does experience demand subjective unity, a mind, soul, or whatever one may wish to call it, but also an objective unity. That is, not only do all my experiences seem to cling together as mine, but also the objects, the chairs in this room, for example, seem to have a stability and a continuing togetherness which appears not to depend merely upon the unity of my experience. This objective unity, which our experience seems to have, we call "the world." The world of objects is different from and opposed to me, as a subject. These objects seem to remain together even though I seem to move as I walk. They appear to have a coherence of their own, different from my subjective unity. If these many objects do not hold themselves together, there must be some principle which binds them. What the real nature of this principle is, if it has any real nature, we cannot know. Kant adopted the term "noumenon" to name whatever exists beyond phenomenon. Phenomenon is experienced. Noumenon is beyond experience. Yet, if our sensations do not cause themselves, and if the unity of our phenomenal objects does not cause itself, then some principle of causation for sensations and for objective unity seems required. Again, irrespective of whether we turn out to be spiritualists, materialists, or agnostics, regarding the nature of what exists outside experience, we still must, somehow, answer the question of how it is that our objective world appears to be held together.

If we have two unities, a subjective unity and an objective unity, are these separate or are they united in some still larger whole? Experiences are such only because they are experiences of objects. Objects are objects precisely because they are experienced. The two are inseparably related and involve each other. But, if these two unities, as different unities, cannot unite with each other by their differences, is there not needed some further principle which unites them? Kant concludes yes. That which unites everything, that principle of allness or wholeness, of holiness, traditionally we have called "God." Kant infers, however, only that there is some principle which unites all experience He is not inferring that there exists some "real" God, some noumenal God, some unexperiencable, all-powerful, all-knowing, all-good personality called God. Like Hume, he remains agnostic at this point about both the existence and nature of any external God. At least there is nothing in our "pure reason" [6] which yields us any certainty that such a God exists. Yet he concludes that reason demands that we recognize an actual need for some principle of totality. If our entire experience cannot be held together without a unifying principle, then we must assume that there is such a principle. Whether we call this God or not, can we be satisfied with our theory of knowledge until it somehow accounts for this principle of total unity of experience?

Before answering finally the question, what is science and how is it possible, Kant finds it necessary to make still further distinctions. So far, we have presented his conclusion that science deals with phenomenal objects, with the world as we experience it, not with noumena or the unexperienced things-in-themselves. Furthermore, exact science is possible to the extent that it deals with those aspects of phenomena that are contributed to phenomena by the mind through the forms of space and time and the categories which "make experience possible." [7] In Kant's language, "although all our knowledge begins with experience, it does not follow that it arises from experience. For it is quite possible that even our empirical experience is a compound of that which we receive through impressions and of that which our faculty of knowledge (incited only by sensuous impressions) supplies from itself, a supplement which we do not distinguish from that raw material, until long practice has roused our attention and rendered us capable of separating one from the other." [8] ". . . there exists a knowledge independent of experience and even of all impressions of the senses. Such knowledge is called *a priori,* and is distinguished from empirical knowledge, which has its sources *a posteriori,* that is, in experience." [9]

A priori knowledge is possessed before, or prior to, experience, whereas *a posteriori* knowledge is achieved after, or posterior to, experience. "Since the mind prescribes its laws to nature, it follows

[6] Norman Kemp Smith, *Immanuel Kant's Critique of Pure Reason.* Macmillan and Co., London, 1929.

[7] Frank Thilly, *A History of Philosophy,* p. 404. Henry Holt and Co., New York, 1914.

[8] Theodore M. Greene, *Kant, Selections,* pp. 26–27. Charles Scribner's Sons, New York, 1929.

[9] *Ibid.,* p. 27.

that we can know *a priori* the universal forms of nature. We can know that the perceived world will always be connected" [10] in a certain order because the mind supplies that order. Kant subscribes to the doctrine of innate ideas, not in the sense that we have ideas of tables, chairs, and men already in our mind at birth, but only in the sense that the mind cannot think, reason, judge, or experience without employing certain necessary forms and categories. The categories are inherent in the mind. Categories are not objects, but only aspects, or characteristics, without which objects cannot be experienced. The mind has no innate objects, but only innate categories, no innate experiences, but only innate potentialities. The mind does not know until it judges. In judging about sensible objects, since we cannot have knowledge of them before the sensations occur in experience, we can construct such objects only as such sensations occur in experience.

Still another distinction is needed before Kant's final conclusions on science can be reached. "Judgments are divided by Kant into two large classes—analytic and synthetic. . . . An analytic judgment merely expresses in the predicate something that is contained in the . . . subject." [11] That is, the predicate merely states a part of what is already meant by the subject. If by "sky" we mean something that is "blue," then if we say, "The sky is blue," we are merely asserting what we already know to be meant by "sky." The judgment is analytical because it analyzes, or takes apart, or takes a part out of, the subject. "A synthetic judgment is one in which the predicate is not contained in . . . the subject. It is a statement of something new about the subject in hand." [12] It is synthetic because something new is added to, or synthesized with, what is known about the subject. For example, if one says, "My shirt is ripped," where by "shirt" he does not mean that it must be "ripped," then he adds something new to what he means by "shirt" in this circumstance.

If we merely analyze what we already know (or assert an *analytic a priori* judgment), we get no new knowledge. If we merely synthesize what we get from our sensory impressions, we get something new, but not something necessary. A *synthetic a posteriori* judgment gives us new knowledge of a particular thing, or of particular things, but does not give us knowledge upon which we can rely universally. The kind of knowledge that science seeks is of general laws which

---

[10] Thilly, *loc. cit.*
[11] Cushman, *op. cit.*, p. 256.
[12] *Ibid.*

hold universally and without exception. It wants universal and necessary knowledge of the objective world, not just of the workings of the mind. Science seeks to know what it does not already know. It looks for new knowledge. But it also wants certain knowledge. Therefore, since the universal and necessary characteristics of phenomena are contributed by the mind, the certainty which science seeks can be found only in *a priori* judgments. Since new knowledge can be found only in *synthetic* judgments, science seeks only *synthetic a priori* knowledge. For example, the conclusion that "all equilateral triangles are equiangular" is *a priori*, since it can be deduced with certainty from the universal and unchanging nature of the way in which the mind is able to conceive triangles, but it is *synthetic* because people do not know this until they have had some experience with particular triangles which they have observed and measured. Thus, such knowledge as we acquire in studying mathematics is new (*synthetic*) and yet certain (*a priori*). Kant concludes that certainty is possible in science, but we cannot achieve such certainty merely from empirical (*synthetic a posteriori*) experiences alone. Science deals with the world of natural phenomena, and it can achieve certainty in its conclusions about such natural phenomena because the mind itself contributes the *a priori* elements needed when it contributes its part to the production of the phenomena we experience.

(MIND)	PHENOMENA	NOUMENA
?	Objects as experienced	?
Faculties	→ 1. Concepts	
a. Sensibility	→ *a.* Space and time[13]	
b. Understanding	→ *b.* Categories	
c. Reason	→ *c.* Ideas of reason	
	2. Sensations ←	Things-in-themselves

    Truth, for Kant, as for Hume, is found entirely within experience. It does not involve some relation of correspondence between what is within and what is without experience or between phenomena and noumena. Also, like empiricists Locke, Berkeley, and Hume, Kant agrees that mere sensations are neither true nor false but are simply present in experience. The faculties of the mind that provide experience with the forms of space and time, the categories, and the ideas

[13] Kant called space and time, not "concepts," but *a priori* "forms" of perception—a distinction too technical to enter into here.

of reason, cannot be in error, for they are merely potentialities, or necessary conditions, of knowing. Instead, error arises only when we judge. In perceptual judgment we unite the sensory and the mental, the objective and the subjective, and here we may make mistakes. We are in error whenever we "confuse the subjective with the objective," [14] mistaking the rules of thought as if they were rules of things, or attributing uniform and necessary regularity to the sensuous when it does not belong to it. To assert that the principle of causality inheres in sensations is almost as bad as attributing causality to the noumenal world for, although we can have no true ideas about the noumenal world, we can be in error in attributing to either sensations or noumena what the mind contributes to phenomena.

A conceptual judgment, in contrast to a perceptual judgment, is true so long as it conforms to the *a priori* principles existing in the mind. But, since judgment is an activity of the mind, and may or may not be given in accordance with these *a priori* principles, judgments may be in error. Kant accepted a distinction, commonly made by traditional logicians, between "formal" and "material" error. Formal error occurs in analytical judgments when something in the predicate, which was not contained in the subject, is attributed to the subject. Formal error involves a violation of the mind's *a priori* principles. Material error occurs in synthetic judgments when some *a priori* characteristic is predicated of a subject as if it were something new due to *a posteriori* sources. But, at any rate, all truth and error occur in judgments that have no existence apart from experience. Kant confirmed Hume's agnosticism regarding external truth, and greatly influenced later idealistic and other semiempiricistic philosophies.

How does phenomenalism compare with naive realism? 1. Objects, i.e., phenomenal objects (for all objects of knowledge are phenomenal), depend for existence upon their being known. They have no existence apart from this experience, and, being composites of both sensory and conceptual ingredients, they have no existence apart from the cooperation of both elements.

2. Qualities of objects likewise depend for their existence upon the objects being experienced. Some qualities, like color and solidity, are produced in objects by sensory impressions, whereas others, such as space and time (Kant calls them "forms"), are contributed by the mind. But, although the potentialities for the production of these

[14] Leo W. Keeler, *The Problem of Error from Plato to Kant,* p. 238. Pontifica Universitatas Gregoriana, Rome, 1934.

qualities have some we-know-not-what noumenal cause, the qualities of objects themselves have no such external existence.

3. Since phenomenal objects exist only when known, knowing them affects them, not by changing their nature, but by creating their nature.

4. Objects seem as they are, if we take them merely as they are given. But, since, in judgment, our assent or dissent is likely to be influenced more by the vividness of impressions than by the rigorousness of *a priori* principles, we may mistake something objective for something subjective, or vice versa, and may thus err. If, then, we do not accept the objective and subjective factors just as they are given, we do not see them as they are. Objects seem as they are, except when we are in error.

5. Objects are known directly. They occur in experience; consequently, there is nothing between them and our experience of them. They are not distorted by any intervening medium, although in hasty judgment we may produce a distorted object, in which the subjective and objective factors are confused.

6. Are objects private or public? Unfortunately, Kant was so preoccupied with his analysis of experience itself that he never got around to dealing effectively with this problem. His writings leave unsettled the problem of how the various experiences of different people are related. Some idealists have concluded that Kant thought of the whole universe as consisting of one great intricate experience, but the present writer thinks it more probable that he should have held that the objects experienced by a particular person are private, and that we might expect different people to have knowledge of the same kinds of objects only if their minds were equipped with the same *a priori* faculties and happen to have the same kinds of sensory impressions occurring in the same way. Kant's agnosticism, like Hume's, should have extended to the existence of other minds and their experiences. But, in the absence of specific statements, different schools of thought have been free to make their own interpretations.

Criticisms

Even though Kant's theory is complicated, it has proved so important in the development of modern thought, and has stimulated so many questions and answers which might otherwise have been overlooked, that we do well to learn of Kant's importance.

Although Kant's rescue of exact science from Hume's extreme empiricism may leave us somewhat less dissatisfied than before, nevertheless Kant retains so much agnosticism about what is beyond experience that our realistic instincts call upon us to doubt his extreme phenomenalism. Of course, Kant himself, in the moral part of his philosophy, which we have not discussed, accepted faiths in the existence of God, freedom, and immortality, but he was careful to point out that these practical faiths are not rational certainties. As pragmatists point out, if we have practical faiths almost as demanding as rational faiths, then perhaps some reconstruction of our interpretation of reason to include the practical may provide a more satisfactory solution.

The problem perplexing all empiricists, namely, why does it happen that, if phenomenal objects are not real, they still seem to be real, remains in Kant's picture. Although he answered this objection much better than Hume, by admitting the existence of a noumenal world which is needed to account for the way our impressions are caused, and, thus, in effect, admitting the existence of real causes (things-in-themselves), nevertheless, if phenomenal objects are not like noumenal things-in-themselves, why do they appear as if they were real things-in-themselves?

The regularities, universal and necessary, which scientists seek, also appear to be real, i.e., the laws of nature do not appear to be *a priori* contributions of the mind. Although a careful reading of Kant mitigates the force of this criticism somewhat, nevertheless most scientists think they are discovering objective, not subjective, laws. The so-called neutrality, or objectivity, claimed for the ideal scientific attitude is praised as significant because objective, not subjective, factors in experience are believed to be the ultimate source of reliable knowledge. Shall we say that such scientists have naively ignored Kant or that Kant has overstated his case?

His conception of science, as requiring only certainty, has been given up, at least somewhat, since his time. Nowadays, scientists seek probability—high degrees of probability, of course, but still only probability. Empiricism, apparently, has had more influence in determining some contemporary notions concerning the nature of science than have rationalistic ideals, which held sway among scientists in the seventeenth, eighteenth, and nineteenth centuries. Perhaps, of course, we may have been too easily misled by empiricism, and, possibly, by placing our philosophical ears closer to the message of Kant, we may save ourselves from some of the evils of extreme empiricism.

Critics often object to Kant's specific list of categories, rejecting some and adding others. Perhaps he reserved too many functions for the faculties of the mind and gave too little credit to objective factors in creating objects in experience. Especially common is the rejection of his faculty psychology, which has been replaced in favor of functional psychology, gestalt psychology, and other theories based on more dynamic conceptions of the mind. However, if Kant were writing today, he could change his language from "faculty" to "function" without changing his meaning very much, for Kant discovered the faculties because, in analyzing experience, he found need for a term describing certain functions. Yet, even so, Kant's failure, from the contemporary point of view, to take into fuller consideration genetic factors, individual differences, and environmental influences that modify the structure of minds, leaves his philosophy inadequate today. But, if we reject Kant merely on account of his flaws, we may be at a disadvantage for having ignored his strengths. The stress today on previously ignored individual differences induces us to ignore individual similarities, and the essential contributions of minds to their experiences, or of subjects to their objects.

Some think that Kant's distinction between *a priori* and *a posteriori,* like Locke's distinction between primary and secondary qualities, is improperly drawn. Locke considered space a primary quality of real things. Kant considers space as a form of perception contributed by the mind. The dispute about classifying qualities and forms has continued, and the idealists who followed Kant have rejected his classifications much as the idealist, Berkeley, who followed Locke, rejected Locke's distinction between primary and secondary qualities.

Finally, as we shall see in the next chapter, an important criticism made by objective idealists is that, if the noumenal world performs no intraexperiential function, and if the ideas of mind, world, and God find their significance as implications of experience itself, our continuing to talk of an unknowable noumenal world is a bit of nonsense which had better be forgotten. Idealists, who find that experience is self-explanatory, think it unnecessary to appeal to an unknowable cause.

· 7 ·

Objective
Idealism

Another German professor of philosophy, Georg Wilhelm Friedrich Hegel (1770–1831), of Jena, Heidelberg, and Berlin, whose thought reflects the viewpoints of other German philosophers such as Fichte and Schelling, as well as of Kant, constructed one of the most grandiose and influential systems in Western thought. Like Kant, Hegel wrote in a language not translatable into terms easily understood by the common man, because his thinking soared to heights which can be expressed only through unusual concepts. Yet we owe ourselves at least an attempt to interpret his contribution to more recent viewpoints.

Hegel agrees with much of the agnosticism of Hume and Kant. Of course, there can be no knowledge of what we cannot know. Or, whatever is totally outside experience cannot be known, and may well be ignored. It is, indeed, a waste of time to assume the existence of an unknowable noumenon or an unknowable mind when, after all, the only reason for inferring their existence is that they appear to be implied by what exists within experience. But, if we investigate logical implications, we discover that they have an inner nature, an internal structure, a necessary unity, which cannot be cut apart, as Hume, Kant, and even Berkeley seem to have done, into what is inside and what is outside experience. If one idea implies another, the two are internally, not externally, related. So, to assume that something exists completely outside experience is to overlook the fact that "inside" and "outside" get their meanings only by being defined in terms of each other. What is "outside" experience is outside only relative to what is "inside." Therefore, since implications of meanings exist only in or for experience, the term "outside experience" has meaning only for experience. Any "outside experience" which had no meaning for some experience would be nothing. When we talk about the unknown, we talk only about the unknown which we know as being unknown, not about what we do not know as unknown. Therefore, we do not escape experience, but merely expand experience, in making such inferences.

It was Kant, rather than Hume, who had the greater insight into the nature of knowledge, for, although he did not avoid agnosticism, he was on the right track in noting that experience itself has an inner structure, and in seeking to discover this structure. Every knowing situation involves a judgment, as Kant pointed out, and every judgment involves relationships, at least the relationship between subject and object, or knower and known. Most previous thinkers, though critical of naive realism, retained and reasoned with the somewhat naive logic developed in the Aristotelian tradition. This logic had its basis in a false emphasis upon the doctrine of external relations. According to this doctrine, if two things are different they are not the same, and their relations to each other are not parts of them but are between them, and, thus, are external to them. For example, this chair which is here on this floor can be picked up and moved elsewhere. This chair does not depend for its nature upon the nature of the floor, and the nature of this floor does not depend upon the nature of this chair. They are independent entities. Their temporary relations to each other do not in any way constitute their own nature.

But, from Hegel's point of view, this is indeed a naive view, which overlooks something more fundamental. Let us examine more carefully what we mean by "this chair" and "this floor." If by "this chair" we mean this chair as it is now, and if it is now on this floor, then we do not mean some other chair, or this chair at some other time in some other place. Thus, "being on this floor" is part of what we mean by "this chair." We cannot define fully what we mean by "this chair" without involving in our definition what we mean by "this floor." Therefore, when we realize more fully what we mean, we discover that what we mean by "this chair" and "this floor" do depend upon each other, and that they are not merely externally related, but are also internally related. We find that the meaning of the one cannot be fully stated without stating the meaning of the other. It is only when we do not understand fully what we mean that we say they are externally related. It is true that "this chair" is not "this floor" and, thus, each is not the other, and, to this extent, each is external to the other. But this truth is not the whole truth about "this chair" and "this floor." Those who accept the doctrine of external relations accept what is true, but only partly true, and so fall short of the whole truth. If science and philosophy seek the whole truth, they cannot succeed with a logic based solely on a doctrine of external relations.

In examining the implications of judgment, Hegel found that part of what is meant by each thing is that it is not some other thing. I.e., not only is each thing something in itself, or what it is "for itself," but also it is something in relation to other things, or "for other things," because, at least, it is not these other things. Our understanding of anything cannot be exhausted either by discovering what it is "for itself" or what it is "for other things." The whole truth about it involves both what it is for itself and what it is relative to all else.

Science, seeking universal and necessary laws, must examine these relations between things. But even external relations are not merely external, for all relations unite objects instead of separating them. For, it is the individuality of each thing which makes it separate, whereas relations unite it with other things. Even the relation of negation, e.g., "this chair is not this floor," unites "this chair" and "this floor" in such a way that the exclusion of the other is an essential part of the meaning of each. The more we discover what a thing is not, the more we discover what it is, in the sense that it is that which is not what it is not. When I discover that a chair is not a floor, I have thereby discovered something about the nature of the chair. That a chair is not a floor is just as true about that chair as that it has four legs. Science, then, in seeking the whole truth, seeks to know what a thing is not as well as what it is, because "that it is not what it is not" is necessarily implied in the nature of whatever it is.

Hegel discovered, further, that the implications of our judgments are dynamic (not just static, as traditional logicians seemed to hold) and that the relationship of negation involves a change, growth, and development. As our experience emerges into existence, it seems to do so in accordance with a certain natural movement which he called "dialectic." Dialectic, says Hegel, in his *Encyclopaedie*, "is no novelty in philosophy. Among the ancients Plato is termed the inventor of dialectic. . . . In modern times it was, more than any other, Kant who resuscitated the name of dialectic, and restored it to its position of honor." [1] The dialectical process, inherent in thinking, develops in such a way that every view we hold, "taken precisely as it is given,

---

[1] J. Loewenberg, *Hegel, Selections*, p. xvi. Charles Scribner's Sons, New York, 1929.

naturally veers round to its opposite," [2] if we will but follow its lead and not rest satisfied with half-truths. "The truth is that every particular point of view ineluctably suffers from a warped perspective. . . . The dialectical method . . . simply consists in laying siege to every typical attitude or belief by rendering its partisan claims logically ridiculous." [3]

If, for example, I say that "I exist," and thereby identify myself with existence, and thus existence with me, then I assert what is both true and false. For, whereas "I exist" is true, that "You exist" is also true. Then we are both identified with existence and we are both the same as existing. But also, you are not I and I am not you, or we are not the same. Thus, I do exist as myself, yet I do not exist as you; so, in this sense, I do not exist. There is a sense in which I do not exist (as you) as well as a sense in which I do exist (as I), but it takes both of these senses to make up the whole truth about me. For each judgment (thesis) which we take as true, we can find an opposite judgment (antithesis) which is also true. And when we have two opposite statements both true, we have the truth (synthesis) which is the truth that both are true. If we say, "This is a chair" (thesis), and then examine what we mean by "this chair," which is actually on this floor, we find that although "this chair" means "not this floor," nevertheless, and therefore, "not this floor" is part of what this chair means or is (antithesis). Even if we said that "this chair is in no way related to this floor," we would thereby be saying that "we mean by 'this chair' something which 'is in no way related to this floor.'" Thus, we would need to state what we mean about the relation of "this chair" and "this floor," in order to assert that they are "in no way related." To say that "two things are in no way related" (thesis) is a way of relating them (antithesis). We can know the "whole truth" (synthesis) about this statement (thesis) only if we know that its opposite statement (antithesis) is true and, thus, that it is true that both are true (synthesis).

Hegel's great insight is that "all concepts are dialectically related," [4] and that these dialectical relationships are the key to the structure of experience. It follows from this that the scientist who seeks to know the structure of the world he investigates need not look, with Locke, outside experience to discover some independently real, or primary, qualities, but should examine, as Kant did, the structure of experience itself. Hegel obviously was rationalistic in his outlook.

[2] *Ibid.*, p. xvii.
[3] *Ibid.*, p. xix.
[4] *Ibid.*, p. xviii.

For him, however, reason operates dialectically, not merely in accordance with the traditional logic of static classes externally related. When we are fully aware of reason's dialectical operations, "each concept may be seen to imply its own opposite as a necessary and inseparable part of itself." [5]

What, then, is Hegel's estimate of empiricism, which played such an important part in the philosophies of Locke, Berkeley, and Hume, and which has seemed so central to more recent philosophies of science? First, if we would be typically Hegelian, we must inquire concerning what we mean by empiricism. If, by it, we mean that knowledge originates in sensory impressions, then our view is inherently ridiculous. Each sensory impression is a particular, unique, temporary experience, whereas scientific knowledge consists in universal, necessary, unchanging laws. If we had a single sensory impression, entirely unrelated to our concepts, we could not know it, for all knowledge is conceptual. "We never succeed in specifying the particular save in terms that define the type or the class of things to which it belongs." [6]

If we call it a "sense impression," we already are interpreting it conceptually, however, for the term "sense impression" is itself a concept, not a sense impression. Therefore, the empiricist's knowledge could not possibly originate in sense impressions, for he must already know, conceptually, what a sense impression is before he can judge that he has one. "Empiricism, though intending to safeguard the reality of the particular, is doomed to silence, since it cannot without abandoning the particularity of its objects name or specify them. Empiricism, in a word, cannot say what it *means* (i.e., particulars) and it cannot mean what it *says* (i.e., universals). Either speechlessness or self-contradiction—this is the dilemma to which philosophical empiricism is reduced. As long as it chooses to be articulate, empiricism ceases to be true to itself; in equating the immediately perceived object with the conceptually described object, it becomes, in fact, indistinguishable from its rival. Not content with silence, empiricism turns into rationalism. It becomes, as Hegel says, its own other." [7] Hegel does not urge that we should not be empirical. He merely says that empiricism cannot stand by itself, and the more we insist that it stand by itself the more ridiculous does our thesis become. Our proofs (and Locke's, Berkeley's, and Hume's proofs)

[5] *Ibid.*, p. xvii.
[6] *Ibid.*, p. xxiv.
[7] *Ibid.*, p. xxv.

of empiricism must appeal to reason, and in appealing to reason we establish rationalism at least as much as we support empiricism.

What about scepticism? Hegel gives it the same treatment. If anyone, for whatever reason, concludes that he has the right to think as he pleases and to doubt whatever he wishes to doubt, Hegel will point out that such a thesis, like all theses, is partial and incomplete and, to an extent, false. One cannot doubt everything, for, first, he must believe that he is doubting, and such a belief is a belief, not a doubt; and, secondly, he must believe that he, as a doubter, exists, for if he does not exist as a doubter, then there is no doubting, and thus his supposed doubt is not a doubt. Furthermore, "doubt implies a standard for testing the adequacy of our human beliefs," [8] and, since the very reason for doubting is the belief that there is something to be doubted, doubt implies the existence of belief in the value of doubting, in terms of some such standard of value. "Doubt and belief are inseparable." [9] Scepticism cannot stand by itself. It cannot be the whole truth. It demands its opposite, its other, i.e., faith or belief. We cannot follow Hume and believe scepticism without thereby also being believers and not doubters.

What happens to the principle of causality in Hegel's hands? Hume had explained our beliefs about causality as arising from a habitual association of objects, from which was inferred a necessary causal connection. He maintained that we sense no transference of power from cause to effect, and have no sensory impressions of necessary connection between them. Hegel agrees with Hume in holding that necessary connection cannot be sensed, but he discovers its source in implication. The meanings of any two terms that are related, as is especially clear with terms forming pairs of opposites (theses and antitheses), necessarily depend upon each other because they derive their meanings partly from each other. The terms "cause" and "effect" are no exception to this rule. "Cause" and "effect" do indeed have a necessary connection, which cannot be sensed, but which lies inherent in their meanings. If by "cause" we mean "cause of an effect," and if by "effect" we mean "effect of a cause," then "cause" and "effect" imply each other.

Such necessity as is involved in causality, then, is to be discovered in the implications of meanings involved in a cause-effect relation.

[8] *Ibid.*, p. xxvii.
[9] *Ibid.*, p. xxv.

If critics object, "But by 'causality' we do not refer to the 'meaning' of cause but to the cause itself," Hegel would reply, "You can say this only if you *mean* 'cause itself.' You cannot say that you refer to a cause you do not mean, for you can only refer to such a cause by *meaning* to refer to it. Thus, to think that you can separate (relate merely externally) the cause you mean from your meaning that cause, when they are inseparable (also internally related), is to conclude falsely." All science which remains content to state its conclusions in terms of causality defined merely in terms of external relations seeks only half-truths, and when it mistakes these half-truths for the whole truth, it thereby defeats itself and misunderstands itself as well as its objects.

Dialectic does not stop merely with the discovery that each concept implies its "opposite as a necessary and inseparable part of itself," [10] or that each thesis generates its own antithesis. If antitheses were merely antagonistic, they could not get along together. But since antitheses are internally related, they merge in a higher unity, a synthesis of thesis and antithesis. "Synthesis or federation of antithetical categories is what the dialectical logic is designed to accomplish." [11] But the synthesis itself then stands as a new thesis and, like all theses, generates its opposite. If cause (thesis) generates effect (antithesis), then together cause and effect constitute causation (synthesis); but causation generates its opposite, i.e., that which is not causation. "Thus a stone in motion is a cause," but it also involves "shape, color, and so on, which do not enter into its causal nature." [12] There is more to that which causes than its causality, and this more is not (i.e., is antithetical to) its causality. But when there is that which is both a cause and also not (because more than) a cause, this "that which" exists as a synthesis of both such causality and such non-causality, a synthesis to which Hegel gives the name "substance." Substance, too, as thesis, generates its antithesis and synthesis.

Without going further into the details of Hegel's system, we may summarize by saying that "this repetitive pattern—mutual antagonism and consequent reconciliation—is the fate to which all concepts must submit." [13] Moreover, even concepts themselves must submit

[10] *Ibid.*, p. xvii.

[11] *Ibid.*

[12] W. H. Johnston and L. G. Struthers, *Hegel's Science of Logic*, Vol. II, p. 197. The Macmillan Co., New York, 1929.

[13] Loewenberg, *op. cit.*, p. xviii.

to dialectical fate. For concepts require the non-conceptual, and the logical requires the non-logical. Although Hegel's *Science of Logic* is devoted primarily to abstract concepts, his *Phenomenology* deals not with "abstract terms or categories, but with the perennial types of human experience. Here Hegel sets in opposition passionate conceptions rather than bloodless concepts. Different and recurrent views of life—sensuous and intellectual, emotional and reflective, practical and theoretical . . . —are here induced to voice the will to believe in their own exclusive reasonableness. And reasonable each does appear from the point of view of its own perspective. But, alas, each human attitude in the process of contending for mastery always finds its claim to power rebuked and impugned. For there is no human view or belief without its rival. And the rival is no less emphatic in asseveration of its rights. Life, as Hegel conceives it, is an incessant strife of partisan views. They are partisan because they are particular. Indeed, partisanship and particularity are synonymous. Whatever is particular—a particular art, a particular religion, a particular philosophy—is self-absorbed and self-centered and hence never free from bias. The truth is that every particular point of view ineluctably suffers from a warped perspective." [14]

A viewpoint can lose its warpedness only by escaping from its particularity, by transcending itself, by changing into its opposite to the extent that it can regard itself as others see it, and then by grasping, somehow, the truth that it and its opposite viewpoint are actually parts of a larger one that is truer than either of the two alone.

For this process Hegel uses the term *aufgehoben*. *Aufgehoben* conveys "at once three distinct meanings . . . to annul, to preserve, to elevate." [15]   "Everything . . . be it a scientific concept, a literary movement, a national policy, a religious creed . . . vanishes into its opposite, and nothing ever passes away." [16]   Each thesis and its antithesis remain gathered up into their synthesis, for the synthesis could not be a synthesis without retaining both thesis and antithesis. The minutest bit of falsity (e.g., the truth that falsity is false) must remain as part of the truth, without which the whole truth cannot be the whole truth. If one part is omitted, it is not the whole. So, despite the dynamic, growing, developing, evolving character of the dialectic, it is a growth in which nothing is ever lost. One who seeks more knowledge does not seek to forget what he already knows. He

[14] *Ibid.*
[15] *Ibid.*, p. xiii.
[16] *Ibid.*

merely wishes to add more to his knowledge. Even if he learns that his former views were false, e.g., that his naive realism was in error, he must retain his knowledge of that naive realism in order to know that it is false, otherwise he would not know what it is that he knows is false.

Not only each particular judgment, not only each particular person's knowledge, but even each particular science suffers from its particularity. Physics, economics, biology, each aims to tell a whole story, and each fails because its story is not complete until it includes all the different sciences. Whoever is acquainted with the specialities of physics, economics, or biology, for example, is already acquainted with the fact that these fields suffer "from an exaggerated sense of their importance, each seeking to draw all others within its particular orbit, each regarding itself as the essential and favored representative of the whole."[17] But since each fails to tell the whole story, the more each pretends that it does so, the more will the other sciences see it otherwise.

Only as we rise above all the particular sciences and their perspectives of each other to "science" can we escape the falsity of their particular viewpoints. Moreover, "science" itself is partial, and passes over into its non-scientific opposite, and these two become *aufgehoben* in something higher. The process continues until, at last, it reaches The Whole—that whole which includes everything. But does not it have its opposite also? Yes, but since the opposite of "whole" is "parts," the opposite of The Whole is all its parts. If so, then must we not have that which transcends and synthesizes both The Whole and all its parts? Yes, and this is The Absolute. Beyond it the dialectic cannot go, since The Absolute contains its own opposition within itself. For, first of all, there can be nothing outside of that which contains everything, and, thus, it can have no external opposite. Secondly, as the ultimate synthesis, it must somehow be that which is the opposite of all opposition. As the opposite of all opposition it is without opposition, not in the sense that it is not opposed to all opposition, but in the sense that nothing opposes it in its functioning as that which opposes all opposition. So, in The Absolute, dialectic comes to its end in that which includes both all dialectic (which involves negation and generation) and the opposite of all dialectic (which involves no negation and no generation) in an ultimate synthesis.

[17] *Ibid.*, p. xxxv.

What is the ultimate goal of science, then? To know the whole truth, i.e., to know The Absolute. But can The Absolute be known? No, at least not completely. A person's perspective of The Absolute is not The Absolute's perspective of itself, and the perspective which any science has of its subject matter is not The Absolute's perspective of itself (if, indeed, we should speak of that which transcends all perspectives as having "a perspective"). "Only an absolute subject can grasp and personify the whole truth. Conversely, the whole truth . . . must be the object of a mind universal in extent . . . a spirit with prodigious tentacles, so to speak, to clutch it. . . . The absolutely known . . . coalesces in the end with the reality of an absolute knower. The known *is* the knower; thought and being are one." [18] The Absolute, then, as the goal of human knowledge, is unreachable by man, even by the scientist, because of his finite perspective. Yet, men, including scientists, cannot be other than they are, searching for a truth which they can never fully reach. On the other hand, men can succeed in progressing to knowledge of greater portions of The Absolute. Men cannot help but know The Absolute, in part, for there is nothing beyond The Absolute for men to know.

Why is Hegel's view called "objective idealism"? It might better have been termed "subjective idealism" (since no knowledge exists apart from a subject, or, ultimately, from the Absolute Subject), had not history already allotted this term to Berkeley's system. For Berkeley, "to be is to be perceived," by either the infinite or finite subjects; but each subject is different from, or external to, every other subject and, thus, each is real or independent of the others. For Hegel, all finite subjects are internally related to the infinite subject and have their existence and nature dialectically bound up with it in such a way that not they, but only The Absolute, is the ultimate subject. If Hegel's epistemological view were named after the "point of view of The Absolute," it would have to be named "subjective idealism" for all that is known depends for its existence upon its being known by, or in, or through, The Absolute. On the other hand, from the point of view of a human knower, other knowers, other knowledge, even the objects of each knower, are other than, or different from, and to this extent external to, him. Furthermore, not only are objects other than subjects, but also every judgment, including those which dialectically relate antitheses, involves two different things which it relates. These differences, despite their in-

[18] *Ibid.,* p. xxxiii.

ability to escape their union in a single Absolute, nevertheless are differences. In so far as two things are different, each is, to this extent,
"independent" of the other. To the extent that they are independent,
each is "real" with respect to its other. Thus, in this sense, the objects of knowledge are real relative to their subjects or knowers. They
are, then, independent as well as dependent. Hegel, therefore, is a
realist as well as an idealist, "if realism is a name for the belief that
. . . reality possesses an independent nature not conforming to mind
but rather exacting submission from it. This is indeed a fundamental tenet of Hegel's philosophy, in behalf of which the dialectic
is so generously employed, so long as mind is understood to be
merely human."[19] Although objects are not completely real (not
wholly independent of subjects), they are at least real (have at least
some independence of subjects), and thus, perhaps, the term "objective idealism" best names this kind of independence. Objects appear
real to us because they are, to a degree, real, and because their nature is such that, through dialectic necessity, they transcend their
own natures and are, even if only to a degree, genuinely real with
respect to us.

How does objective idealism fare in comparison with naive realism?

1. Objects depend for their existence upon being known. They
have no existence apart from knowledge. However, the knower does
not create his objects at will, but is as much a creature of his objects
as his objects are of him. Subjects and objects depend upon each
other, and so, in a sense, create each other.

2. Qualities of objects depend upon objects for existence. A thing
and its qualities depend on each other, for a thing's nature consists
in its having qualities, and qualities are nothing if not qualities of
things. But a thing and its qualities, which together constitute an
object, both depend upon some subject for their existence as object.

3. Since objects of knowledge have no existence apart from such
knowledge, their nature, as objects, is determined completely by
their functioning in such knowledge. However, in so far as that
which serves as an object of knowledge (thesis) has other functions
(antitheses), it is, also, not determined merely by its being known.

4. Objects seem as they are and are as they seem. Yet, also, in so
far as the term "seem" means "not real," "seeming" implies that there
is more to objects than their seeming. Appearances, as such, are not

[19] *Ibid.*

realities. Yet, since there is an internal relation between antitheses, the apparent and the real also involve each other. What seems obviously so is so; yet it is not all that is so. Since "so" and "not so" have no meaning apart from each other, "what seems obviously so" and "what seems obviously not so" together form parts of a higher "so" which neither alone is adequate to represent.

5. Objects are known directly. There is nothing between them and our knowledge of them, except their difference from the knowledge which knows them. They occur in experience, but they remain different from, or differentiated in, experience; for without difference there could be no judgment and no experience. Between knowledge and its objects exists no intervening medium, for the difference between knowledge and object is all that intervenes.

6. Objects are private to the extent that my objects are mine and not yours and yours are yours and not mine. Yet we cannot know the same Absolute without having the same object. There is only one Absolute, and although we cannot know it exactly as it is, as Absolute, nevertheless, there is nothing outside it for us to know. In knowing, we must know The Absolute—some of it, not all of it—and to the extent that we know it, we have the same (i.e., public) object of knowledge.

Before turning to criticisms, perhaps it is worth noting that historians attribute to Hegel considerable influence (1) upon Nietzsche, and, consequently, upon the development of Nazism, (2) on Karl Marx and, thus, upon the development of dialectical materialism, which is basic to orthodox Communism, (3) on academic philosophy, first in Germany, then in England (T. H. Green, B. Bosanquet, F. H. Bradley), and in the United States (Josiah Royce), both through appreciative followers and through revolts (John Dewey began his philosophical career as something of an objective idealist), and (4) on the thought of many orthodox Christians who have felt forced to abandon Thomism, Neoplatonism, and other philosophies traditionally used to interpret Christianity.

Criticisms

Hegel is even more abstruse, incomprehensible, and ponderous than Kant. The full grandeur of his system can be appreciated only by experts. His thought is too cumbersome to be popular, and, thus, so far as the populace is concerned, his thought, like other imponderables, had better be forgotten. Hegel has had his great influence chiefly through his effects upon other thinkers who have, in turn, incorporated some of his ideas into their apparently less incomprehensible systems. Of course, Hegel might reply that he is merely stating the common-sense view of any person who stops to reflect. Anyone who has attained even a small insight into his ideas must realize that he "has something." Nevertheless, the fact that parts of the Hegelian theory may be acceptable does not entail acceptance of his entire doctrine.

Hegel was critical of himself, or found inherent in his system its own antithesis, its own negation, its own defeat. "His logic . . . suffers no philosophy to escape from the fate of its dialectical decrees. Hegel's own method decrees his own system to be ultimately jettisoned." [20] His entire system was his own knowledge, not The Absolute's, and even if we understood Hegel's system as completely as he did, we would still be far short of knowing the whole truth.

A most common criticism of Hegelianism is that it is impractical. The Absolute is unknowable to man, and it seems preposterous to make the goal of knowledge something unknowable. It is just as impractical to try to reach that which transcends experience as that which realists say exists outside experience. As William James later remarked, "It is not necessary to drink the whole ocean in order to know that it is salty." But Hegelians can reply that man in his most practical moments, in his life crises, knows that he depends upon some higher destiny. The age-long demand for faith in God, which is universally present among the religions of mankind, testifies to a practical, vital, inner, persistent demand for assurance of protection by some higher power. The ethical insights of the ages proclaim that man cannot "gain his life unless he lose it" in something higher than himself. Even so, critics contend, this is hardly what we call practical.

Again, it is condemned as "unscientific," though this term has to be defined. Hegel thought of himself as being objective, i.e., of following the necessary demands of the dialectic wherever they might lead. How could anyone be more scientific than this? But the term "science" has come to mean more than willingness to be objective. Scientists have come to take sides on the issue of whether scientific knowledge is exact or inexact. Hegel held that the dialectic is exacting, even though not mathematically exact. But science has come to mean the mathematically exact, or, if we fall short of exactness, then

[20] *Ibid.*, p. xiv.

the mathematically probable. In comparison with this ideal, the followers of dialectic are considered mystical, intuitive, idealistic, visionary, vague, and romantic. Science, it is claimed, can rely only on the dependable, upon the definite, on the fixed and unchanging uniformities of nature. Pursuit of the transcendental should be reserved for religion, poetry, and dreams.

Furthermore, despite continuing uncertainties about the nature of causality, scientists usually prefer to distinguish between causation and implication. Abstract ideas imply each other; things cause each other. When Hegel identifies things and thoughts, he contradicts a basic premise without which realistic scientists feel they cannot operate.

Finally, critics condemn Hegelianism as totalitarian and conservative. Man, by his very nature, is subordinate to that which is higher or that which transcends him. Since a group transcends its members and is a higher synthesis of their individual differences, each individual is naturally subordinate to his group. This philosophy of the nature of man has contributed to both Nazi and Communist types of political philosophy. Those who believe that individuality should receive the larger respect reject the implications of Hegelianism which subordinate persons to groups. Also, it contributes to certain types of conservatism; for if each part of the whole has its proper place in the whole, then each part, whether good or bad, is as good or bad as every other part in making an essential contribution; and, thus, there is provided no motive for improvement. "Ruler" implies "someone ruled." Each is necessary to the other, so there can be no point in trying to get rid of rulers. These attacks [21] against Hegelianism are not aimed directly at its theory of knowledge, but they do express some of the reasons why it has become unpopular; and its epistemology, internally related to the rest of it, has remained unpopular also.

[21] The writer does not wish to imply that such attackers always understand what they are attacking.

· 8 ·

Positivism

Frenchman Auguste Comte (1798–1857), would-be reformer, would-be professor, and would-be suicide, is credited by historians as being the founder of a widespread philosophy of knowledge. "Having from his earliest years a strong humanitarian and reforming impulse, and being an intimate associate of Saint-Simon, he sought to find in positivism a basis for a social reconstruction which would serve as a safeguard against the disintegrating tendencies of revolution."[1] His own life showed considerable personal disorganization, yet, for a while, he taught mathematics, gave a few lectures on his philosophy, published several books, and gathered a cult of followers of his new religion of science or "religion of humanity."

His significance, for our purposes, is to be found in the sharp contrast which positivism bears to Hegel's objective idealism, against which Comte reacted violently. His reaction was not merely to Hegel, but against "metaphysical speculation" of all kinds, including that of Catholic Thomists, under whose philosophy he was reared. He had studied natural science and was familiar with its increasing number of striking successes. These achievements were understandable by ordinary people who could see the results. They were within the grasp of the intellect of the average man. They were closer to the more immediate results which men want than Hegel's Absolute which, as Hegel himself acknowledged, is forever beyond the reach of men. To Comte, the goal of science should be one that can be reached. The purpose of science, in the first place, is to seek knowledge that will help men live healthily and happily. Science "organizes knowledge. It gives us the power of prediction and

[1] Alfred Weber, *History of Philosophy*, p. 492. Charles Scribner's Sons, New York, 1896, 1925.

enables us to control nature in many ways and to harness her to the service of human progress and happiness." [2]

Not only should we devote ourselves to mathematics and the physical sciences. "The scientific method must be extended, the scientific point of view must be developed, and life must be reorganized on a scientific basis. Thus only can the world be saved. If this can be done, if we can become as scientific in our estimation of moral and social phenomena as we are in our dealings with physical events, then we may succeed in formulating a new positivistic philosophy of life by which human beliefs and attitudes will be inspired and moral stability will be regained. What we need, therefore, is a science of social behavior to which men may pin their faith." [3] These were high ideals. They inspired men, then and now, and the science of sociology, in the minds of some historians, has its beginnings in Comte's vigorous efforts to spread these ideals of a scientific study of society as a means of promoting human welfare.

If the Hegelian Absolute is too high up in the clouds of metaphysical speculation to make it worth while for ordinary mortals to play hide-and-seek with tricky dialectic (while their stomachs cry for food), what, then, shall science seek? Positivism first goes back to Hume, rejecting "all hypothetical construction of entities regarded as existing apart from and beneath the sensible universe." [4] Locke's primary qualities, Berkeley's God, Kant's noumenon, and Hegel's Absolute, are all "metaphysical," or beyond that in experience of which we can be sure or "positive." But Hume's conclusion, his scepticism or agnosticism, were, as Kant had pointed out, too negative. Comte's enthusiasm for promoting the benefits of science could not let him remain agnostic about the results of science. Science has succeeded. It has produced positive, not negative, results. Here we find a double meaning of the term "positive." The positive means both affirmative and certain. Positivism rejects as metaphysical [5] that knowledge of

[2] B. A. G. Fuller, *A History of Philosophy*, Vol. II, p. 506. Henry Holt and Co., New York, 1938.

[3] *Ibid.*, p. 503.

[4] *Ibid.*, p. 504.

[5] Unfortunately the term "metaphysics" has a variety of meanings. In its most general sense, metaphysics is an area of investigation of being, or existence. Such a conception does not prejudge whether the existence referred to is inside or outside experience. This is the more usual meaning in both Eastern and Western philosophy both before and after Comte's time. However, misunderstanding this, and identifying the metaphysical with only that which is outside of, or transcends, experience, Comte greatly influenced the establishment of this

things outside experience of which we are unsure, uncertain, and not positive. Recognizing the success of science, positivism has faith that it can and will bring good (positive) rather than bad (negative) results.

In rejecting the negativism of Hume, positivism then has the job of showing what there is, in experience, besides sense impressions, of which we can be certain. This job was attempted, but not too successfully dealt with, by earlier positivists. "Science does not consist in merely amassing facts, nor is its advance simply an enlargement of the field of vision. Science also infers from the behavior of phenomena certain laws which their behavior exemplified and follows. . . . These laws, however, are not regarded . . . as governing and determining the behavior of the sensible world. They are not the causes of things. As long as science considers them such it has not yet risen above the metaphysical level. Natural laws are no more than descriptions of how phenomena do behave. They are not explanations of why they behave as they do. Why things behave as they do, we cannot know. The causes of things are unascertainable." [6] Thus, the positivistic treatment of the principle of causality follows Hume in denying that we can be certain about it. Scientific laws, as descriptive rather than explanatory, can be used for purposes of prediction, so long as we presuppose that future experiences will be like those which have passed. "Comte, however, realizes that at this point he . . . is assuming the uniformity of nature and the prevalence of certain habits of action throughout all space and time. He is himself indulging in one of those metaphysical hypotheses that he condemns. He hastens to modify the dogmatism of his assertion. Laws are not necessarily absolute in the sense of being of necessity universally true. The establishment of absolute laws, which we could be sure held for everything in all times and places, would require a complete scientific observation of all phenomena whatsoever, past, present, and future, throughout the entire universe. Obviously such completeness is impossible, since scientific observation is limited to a small portion of space and time, and scientific inferences cannot be made with certainty beyond the range of scientific observation.

narrower meaning as one of the now-common meanings of the term. Since, for Comte, science is limited to the "positive" which is inside experience, "the scientific" and "the metaphysical" are entirely opposed to each other. This is contrary to the view taken in this text which considers metaphysics a philosophical science.

[6] Fuller, *op. cit.*, pp. 504–505.

Furthermore, scientific thinking is relative to the nature of the human organism. . . . All in all, then, Comte admits, scientific laws are at best approximations." [7] Nevertheless, they are better than unobtainable absolutes and ultimates. For, even with mere approximations, science has helped mankind and can continue to do so.

Fundamental to Comte's thinking was his "Law of the Three Stages." In his book, *The Positivist Philosophy*, "Comte approaches a statement of the meaning of positivist philosophy through a great fundamental law of cultural development. This law is that each and every branch of human knowledge passes through three stages—the Theological, the Metaphysical, and the Positive. In the first stage, men seek for final causes, in the second for abstract forces, and in the third for exact laws. Each stage reaches a highest culmination. In the first one it is God, in the second one Nature, and in the third one universal law. Two sets of facts prove this law, one is that every science shows that it has passed through each stage and the other is that every individual's development recapitulates that of the race." [8] The Theological Stage represents the childhood of mankind, when there is a tendency to anthropomorphize things, passing from animism through polytheism to monotheism. Knowledge in this stage is obtained from oracles, mystic revelations, reading the stars, and from the authority of those who claimed to have revelations. The Metaphysical Stage represents the youth of mankind, when men reason for themselves instead of accepting authoritative revelations—a trick we learned from the Greeks. But for the gods we substitute metaphysical principles, such as Plato's Idea of the Good, Aristotle's Prime Mover, Hegel's Absolute, etc. When mankind reaches its manhood, or the Positive Stage, men give up their search for prime movers, absolutes, essences, and all speculation about what we do not experience, and then limit their investigations to such experiences as can yield positive scientific knowledge.

Comte is significant because of the part he played in founding positivism, and positivism is important partly because it has served as a rallying point for many who have become enthusiastic about their faith in science and who have also rejected theologies and metaphysics as suitable explanations of the nature of science. Positivism capitalized upon Hume's agnosticism by uniting it with an enthusiasm for scientific and social progress which Hume lacked. Its influence

---

[7] *Ibid.*, pp. 505–506.

[8] Daniel S. Robinson, *An Anthology of Modern Philosophy*, p. 697. Thomas Y. Crowell Co., New York, 1931.

has spread as time has increased the need for some acceptable philosophy to use in support of revolts against the traditional philosophies. In South America, especially, it has reigned almost without competition as the dominant anti-catholic philosophy, and, as such, it has gathered together under its banners many varieties of naturalistic, agnostic, positivistic, materialistic, and revolutionary temperaments. In the United States, it has been much less significant, for, until recently, it has found successful competitors in an indigenous naturalism, i.e., pragmatism; in many other epistemologies, such as neo-realism and critical realism; in certain metaphysical views, especially materialism; and in various forms of protestantism which, in satisfying many different kinds of rebellious temperaments, have effectively opposed catholic influence. But, about the time of World War II, immigrants from Europe, especially from Vienna, brought and planted the seeds of a particular variety of positivism sometimes called "logical positivism," and sometimes "logical empiricism." This movement has found favorable soil in America, and we shall now focus our attention upon it as the heir and contemporary form of the Comtean outlook.

Logical Empiricism

Although "logical empiricism" derives its name from its emphasis on both the logical and the empirical aspects of experience, as in Kant, also, like Kant, logical empiricists are actually more concerned with the logical than the empirical—the latter being a concern of the specific sciences. However, like Hume, they reject "both the thesis of the reality of the external world and the thesis of its irreality" [9] as something not only unworthy of investigation but beyond the range of sensible inquiry. Thus, although retaining Kant's concern for logical and empirical ingredients in experience, they repudiate, as being foolish, Kant's concern for noumenal causes. But, like Comte, they continue to misuse the term "metaphysics," and consequently find that "one of the most gratifying trends in the history of science is the gradual liberation of theory from metaphysical bondage." [10] However, critics have forced some modification of earlier thorough-

[9] Rudolf Carnap, "Empiricism, Semantics, and Ontology," *Revue Internationale de Philosophie*, Jan. 15, 1950, pp. 32–33. Reproduced in *Semantics and the Philosophy of Language*, edited by Leonard Linsky, University of Illinois Press, 1952.

[10] Herbert Feigl, "Logical Empiricism," in D. D. Runes, *Twentieth Century Philosophy*, p. 386. Philosophical Library, New York, 1943.

going antimetaphysical views. According to a later version, "the positivistic critique of metaphysics is primarily an attack upon confusion of meanings and not intended as a wholesale repudiation of what has been presented under that label."[11] "There is no sharp line between inductive generalizations of common sense and science on the one side and those of cosmology on the other."[12] "Inductive metaphysics is merely the risky, sanguine, and disreputable extreme of science."[13]

What is new in logical empiricism is its emphasis upon analysis of meanings and the logical structure of language. "The systematic pursuit of the problem of meaning by means of a logical analysis of language distinguishes logical empiricism from earlier, more psychologically oriented, types of empiricism. . . ."[14] "Not the origin and psychological development but its logical structure and empirical validation are the subject of a thus reformed epistemology."[15] "If all psychological considerations are excluded and only logical ones admitted, this results in an analysis of derived terms and sentences as logical constructions erected on primitive terms and sentences which have direct experiential reference."[16] "The unique characteristic," then, of logical empiricism, "is the exclusive use of logical analysis to demonstrate positivistic theses."[17] This involves a presupposition that all, or almost all, meanings are analyzable, without residue, into logical parts. In contrast with Hegel, who accepted a doctrine of relations as both internal and external, logical empiricists are exclusively concerned with the external relatedness of meanings. Even the ordinary conceptions of implication are replaced by specifically restricted definitions such as "material implication." Since everyday language is pervaded with ambiguity, and since the ideal of science is exactness, some separation of the ambiguous from the exact "should be undertaken for the sake of greater clarity and avoidance of confusion."[18] "The main contribution [according to some logical empiricists] lies in . . . thinking which possesses the virtues characteristic of science: clarity and consistency, testability and adequacy, precision and objectivity."[19]

---

[11] *Ibid.*, p. 384.
[12] *Ibid.*
[13] *Ibid.*, p. 385.
[14] *Ibid.*, p. 377.
[15] *Ibid.*, p. 387.
[16] *Ibid.*, p. 392.
[17] J. R. Weinberg, *An Examination of Logical Positivism*, p. 1. Routlege and Kegan Paul, London, 1936.
[18] Feigl, *op. cit.*, p. 378.
[19] *Ibid.*, p. 376.

In pursuit of such clarity, a basic distinction has to be made between "analytical propositions" and "empirical propositions," or between "logical sentences" and "factual sentences." Thus, we have knowledge of two sorts, the former pertaining to the "rules of language," the latter to "matters of fact" about "states of affairs." "A pair of Kant's distinctions, though not his philosophy as it elaborates them, are most helpful here. He distinguishes between analytic (i.e., true by definition) and synthetic (i.e., factual) sentences, and between a priori (i.e., logically independent of experience) and a posteriori (i.e., empirical) validity." [20] ". . . we distinguish today: (1) Logically true sentences, also called analytic sentences. (2) Logically false sentences, also called contradictions . . . [which] are true or false . . . by virtue of their form. (3) Factually true and (4) factually false sentences whose validity depends upon their correspondence with observed fact." [21] Except for "(5) emotive expressions," which are not knowledge, these two types, the logical or analytical and the empirical or factual, are the only kinds we have to deal with.

1. Logical propositions are both necessary and arbitrary. "The locus of 'necessity' . . . lies . . . exclusively in the relation of logical implication between premises and conclusions." [22] But which primitive propositions we use, what rules of language we adopt, or how our logic is constructed, is arbitrary. "From a purely formal point of view a system of logic is just one calculus among an indefinite number of others." [23] "The rules of deduction belong to the internal regulative mechanism of a consistent language. They merely enable us to express in one form precisely what we have already said in another." [24] "The meaning of words, then, or of signs quite generally, consists in the way in which they are used, the way they are connected with other words or related objects of experience. The definition of a term, the declaration of its meaning, amounts to a statement of the rule according to which we employ or intend to employ the term." [25] "Inasmuch as it is the cognitive meanings that we are interested in, idealized models, or in the extreme limit, an ideal language . . . may be used. The tools developed in modern symbolic logic prove of utmost value for this purpose." [26] "On the technical side logic has been developed not only by further extensions and applications of symbolic logic proper, but also by the introduction of

[20] *Ibid.*, p. 387.
[21] *Ibid.*, p. 383.
[22] *Ibid.*, p. 397.
[23] *Ibid.*, p. 394.

[24] *Ibid.*
[25] *Ibid.*, pp. 379–380.
[26] *Ibid.*, p. 380.

meta-languages, i.e., languages about languages, for the purpose of syntax and semantics."[27] But "we must connect language with something outside of language, with experience."[28]

2. "Empirical propositions are one and all hypotheses, which may be confirmed or discredited in actual sense-experience."[29] They have "factual meaning" if and only if their assertion or denial implies "a difference capable of observational (experiential, operational, or experimental) test."[30] "If a sentence is considered true when it corresponds to an existing state of affairs, a sentence is factually meaningful only if we are in principle capable of recognizing such a state of affairs as would either validate or invalidate the sentence."[31] "But this is not to be interpreted as if it meant acceptance of a *belief* in the reality of the thing world; there is no such belief or assertion or assumption. . . ."[32] "To recognize something as a real thing or event means to succeed in incorporating it into the framework of things at a particular space-time position so that it fits together with other things recognized as real, according to the rules of the framework."[33] Therefore, even in discussing the nature of empirical propositions, logical empiricists restrict what an empirical proposition can mean to what is admitted as meaningful within a particular framework of arbitrarily accepted logical premises. "Concepts and assertions are meaningless if no operations can be specified that define the former and test the latter."[34]

The scientific ideal of logical empiricism is, by means of analysis, to reduce the number of premises and rules of operation to the fewest possible. "By stepwise procedures all terms are reduced to a comparatively small number of basic or primitive terms."[35] Even the principle of induction itself, if we must have one, "had better be formulated not as a piece of knowledge but as a rule of procedure."[36] Strictness in defining such primitive terms and rules of procedure, and rigor in operating only within definitely set limits, will insure exact and reliable conclusions. Since the logical limits laid down in the original definitions determine what may properly be treated by a scientist, all undefined terms must be considered irrelevant for any

[27] *Ibid.,* p. 395.
[28] *Ibid.,* p. 380.
[29] Alfred J. Ayer, *Language, Truth and Logic,* p. 132. Oxford University Press, New York, 1936.
[30] Feigl, *op. cit.,* p. 382.
[31] *Ibid.*
[32] Carnap, *op. cit.,* p. 23.
[33] *Ibid.,* p. 22.

[34] Feigl, *op. cit.,* p. 382.
[35] *Ibid.,* p. 380.
[36] *Ibid.,* p. 389.

investigation. If one is to speak, as scientists often do, of causality, the precise meaning of causality must be defined in relation to other terms and rules of the adopted system.

Although, strictly speaking, a logical empiricist might adopt any definition of causality he chooses, one of them asserts that "causality is neither 'mere regular sequence' nor an 'intrinsic bond' but a functional relation between events and magnitudes. . . ."[37] The term "functional relation" here refers, not to what realists might call real physical functions, but to logical or systemic functions, i.e., operations permitted by the rules of procedure adopted in establishing the particular logical system. However, since logical empiricists insist that part of the purpose of science is to deal with experience, the scientific task is unfinished until various alternative logics, each with its different rules and definitions of terms, have been tried out and have either succeeded or have failed in predicting future events.

Does all this mean that the logical empiricist is merely a subjectivist? Most realists would say yes. However, since, like any other term, the term "real" may be submitted to rigorous logical definition, it may then be readmitted into a logical empiricist's language. "We take the position that the introduction of new ways of speaking does not need any theoretical justification because it does not imply any assertion of reality."[38] Once the "meaningless and absurd" use of the term reality is eliminated, then a logical empiricist is free to use the term "real" "in a clear sense."[39] "The reality, in this sense, of rocks and trees, of stars and atoms, of radiations and forces, of human minds and social groups, of historical events and economic processes, is capable of empirical test."[40] "In asserting that the scope of the natural universe is wider than human experience on the basis of which it is known, no illegitimate transcendence is introduced. As long as we do not forget that existential assumptions must be in principle capable of test, though most of these tests are indirect, we remain within the range of the factually-meaningful. . . . So in the outlook of empirical realism we assume certain broad features of the physical world simultaneously with certain hypotheses concerning the process of perception. Each enforces the presumptive validity of the other."[41] It also assumes that "the objectivity—or, more precisely, the intersubjectivity—of knowledge is warranted right from the start."[42]

[37] *Ibid.*, p. 398.
[38] Carnap, *op. cit.*, p. 31.
[39] Feigl, *op. cit.*, p. 390.
[40] *Ibid.*
[41] *Ibid.*, p. 391.
[42] *Ibid.*, p. 392.

How does logical empiricism compare with naive realism?

1, 2, 3. Do the objects of our knowledge exist independently of our knowing them? If the object is a logical concept, a defined term, a rule of linguistic procedure, it is dependent upon our use of it, and its existence is relative to us. But, as to whether sensory objects have independent status, the logical empiricist wishes to remain agnostic. However, if our adopted system admits as "meaningful" any "indirect testing," then we may find ourselves in agreement with others concerning our logical concepts, definitions, and rules of logic. Then we may credit objects with having such testable independence as is needed for our cooperation with other people. If we wish to consider whether the table in this room is "real," i.e., independent of an observer, then we might devise a test, such as having one person stay in the room to observe it, while another person leaves. If the person who stays testifies that the table continues to be an object, whereas the other testifies that when he was absent from the room he no longer saw it, they may agree to define as "real" the table remaining in one experience though not in the other. However, those beliefs in the existence of allegedly real things, regarding which no rule for testing can be formulated, are "metaphysical," and persons who concern themselves with such beliefs are dealing with "pseudo problems."

4. Are appearances realities? If we have not already defined these terms in our language in such a way that either they are identical or definitely different, then we must discover some empirical test for distinguishing them. For example, if one chooses to test whether his money is "real" or "apparent," by trying to exchange it for goods, then he has a clear proof of the difference between the million dollars he dreamed he found last night and the dollar he just now put in his pocket. He can prove that the million dollars is not real and the dollar real by trying to spend them.

5. Are objects known directly? Is there any intervening medium? The logical empiricist replies by examining what is meant by "known directly." If you mean that you are aware of an object without being aware of anything between it and your knowledge of it which you can test, which you can locate by any means at your disposal, you accept it as immediate. To say that there is an intervening medium which you cannot locate by any possible test is to express a meaningless statement. But, on the other hand, if you can discover some intervening medium by means of some test, then such an object may be appropriately judged to be known indirectly. If you can wave your hand in the space between your eye and object, you can say that

some "distance" intervenes. Or, if you can perform some optical test, you may conclude that light rays intervene.

6. Are objects public? Again we must ask what we mean and devise an appropriate test. If I ask, "Do you see this chair?" and you answer "Yes," and if I have already sufficiently verified your existence as another person, then I can take this as a test that you see what I do and that this chair is thus public. But if I ask, "Did you feel bad when you fell off the roof in my dream last night," and if you say, "I was not in your dream last night," I can take this as a test of privacy. These may be incomplete tests. In fact, no empirical observation can ever be tested completely. Nevertheless, until further evidence comes along, we may accept our objects as either private or public, depending upon what evidence we have.

Criticisms

As a group, logical empiricists, although having training in the mathematical sciences that has given them special facility in the field of mathematical logic, have largely neglected to study the history of philosophy. As a consequence, they easily fell prey to hasty adoption of Comte's mistaken use of the term "metaphysics"—a term serving as a keystone of their outlook. As their language has spread, it has led others to misinterpret both historical and contemporary philosophies where the term is used. Although a logical empiricist might reply that anyone has a right to use a term in any way he pleases, critics will acquiesce only when logical empiricists cease deliberate condemnation of other philosophies by means of obviously implied moral connotations in their allegedly innocent language.

In rejecting metaphysics, logical empiricists have been forced to invent meta-languages, meta-logics, and meta-mathematics, which are as incomprehensible to the layman as Hegel's Absolute. Anyone who seeks to understand *Principia Mathematica*, for example, will find it almost as difficult as Hegel's *Science of Logic*. Logical empiricism devotes itself more completely to a logic of external relations than Hegel does to a logic of internal relations. But, worse still, from the point of view of those who take philosophy with moral seriousness, logic, with all of its supposedly necessary meta-languages, is looked upon as merely a game—one which we do not have to play, and one for which we can invent our own rules as we please or exchange for other rules, provided only that we do not switch rules during a particular game. Logical truth and falsity have no duties to empirical reality but only to such rules as have been arbitrarily adopted at the outset of any logical game. Why this proviso applies to all logics is something never explained.

Critics point out that logical empiricists presuppose, in many different ways, the kinds of metaphysics they reject. First of all, they presuppose the existence of a mind in which all this logic-play and factual-meaningfulness-testing takes place, even though they may often ignore the mind as "metaphysical" because its existence cannot be "tested." Yet, on the other hand, they have accepted as testable the existence of other minds and the existence of intersubjective knowledge and the existence of "real things," so long as testable. Different logical empiricists sometimes accuse each other of being "metaphysical" when they disagree upon what is considered testable. Any shift in what are deemed to be the appropriate upper or lower limits of testability will produce a shift from the "metaphysical" to the "empirical" or vice versa. Any redefining of "meaningful" may change what is meaningless into what is meaningful. The brief history of logical empiricism has shown rapid growth in granting what was earlier condemned as metaphysical as now testable and, even, "warranted right from the start." If this trend continues, we may find that eventually all that has been rejected as metaphysical will gradually come to be considered testable.

Critics discover in the logical empiricist demand that "we describe the world in a way that does not impoverish it by artificial reductions [and we reject] . . . the multiplication of entities beyond necessity" [43] a fault in which logical empiricists are themselves most perverse. In their search for clarity, through mathematical logic, they condemn common-sense language as being weighted with confusion, which science and philosophy seek to dispel. They thereby falsely presuppose that clarity is to be found only by analysis, or by taking meanings apart and separating them into some presupposed ultimate constitutents. If, at times, we are clearly unclear, such unclarity is as genuine a part of experience as any formal clarity. To presuppose that formal clarity must somehow underlie our unclear experiences is to be unempirical and to demand that the empirical be subordinated to the logical. Although it is easy to see how one troubled with vagueness would idealize perfect clarity, if we but listen to the Hindu condemnations of all distinction as illusion, we may well question whether the logical empiricist's profusion of logics and meta-logics

[43] *Ibid.*, p. 375.

is not a multiplication of entities beyond necessity. If there is something about experience which is clearly unanalyzable, to presuppose the possibility of complete empirical analysis is to presuppose falsely.

This extreme devotion to external relations creates many difficulties concerning the relations between many factors in experience which logical empiricists cannot account for, but must either overlook or assume not to be difficulties: 1. First of all, logic and experience are held to be not identical, not similar, and not interpretable in terms of each other. Yet, logical empiricism cannot be both logical and empirical without assuming some working relation between these two unlikenesses. The assumption that these two unlike constituents of knowledge cooperate in all sorts of intimate ways is something accepted without explanation. In fact, to "explain" would be to involve "metaphysics," so the logical empiricist thereby thinks himself excused from all need for "explaining" why his theory that experience operates in accordance with his doctrine of external relations must be so. But what is logical empiricism if not an explanation? Furthermore, if all propositions are either empirical or logical, then this proposition (i.e., "All propositions are either empirical or logical") is either an empirical or a logical proposition. If it is an empirical proposition, then it is, like all empirical propositions, uncertain; and thus logical empiricism itself is uncertain. If it is a logical proposition, then it is, like all logical propositions, based upon some arbitrary assumptions concerning the basic rules of logic and language; and thus logical empiricism itself is infected with the arbitrariness which can make no demands upon our belief unless we happen to like it.[44] If there is a third alternative, that this proposition involves a confusion of both the logical and the empirical, then it entails a kind of confusion which logical empiricists seek to avoid, and can claim no superiority over either common-sense or "metaphysical" propositions on grounds of clarity.

2. It has been objected that it is absurd to say that "we must connect language with something outside of language,"[45] for obviously language occurs within experience. 3. "Logical reconstruction is independent of the grammatical."[46] 4. The logical is also separated from the psychological. "Most logical empiricists fight shy of psy-

---

[44] For further criticisms of this type see Carlton W. Berenda, "A Five-Fold Skepticism in Logical Empiricism," *Philosophy of Science*, April, 1950, pp. 123–132.

[45] Feigl, *op. cit.*, p. 380.

[46] *Ibid.*

chology, and therefore have little to say about meaning or significance. This makes them, in my opinion, somewhat narrow, and not capable of producing an all-round philosophy." [47] 5. The cognitive has nothing to do with the emotive (nor facts with values) unless they are mistakenly confused with each other. 6. Even the truth of a meaningful proposition depends upon something external to it. It may be capable of being confirmed, but its confirmation is an operation external to it which in no way modifies or determines its nature, even though, nevertheless, its truth depends upon such external confirmability. 7. All the varieties of alternative logics which may be chosen at will are external to each other as well as to all empirical propositions.

[47] Bertrand Russell, "Logical Positivism," *Revue Internationale de Philosophie,* Jan. 15, 1950, p. 18.

·9·

Neo-Realism

Platonic Realism

Although neo-realism, or the new realism, originated after 1900 in England and America, it has roots in a metaphysics which goes back historically to Plato (427–347 B.C.) and which is sometimes called "Platonic realism." Plato was both an "idealist" and a "realist" —an idealist in metaphysics ("Ideas" are the ultimate realities) and a realist in epistemology ("Ideas" exist prior to and independently of minds which know them). By "Ideas" Plato meant not ideas in our minds, as Locke, Berkeley, and Hume held, but forms, patterns, types, or universals, which must first be, if any particular thing which has such form or pattern or type can exist.

If a thing can exist, its kind must first be; it could not be a thing of this kind if there were no such kind. Thus, thought Plato, kinds or types or Ideas of things must be prior to the existence of these things themselves, and our personal ideas of the kind, or nature, of any thing depend upon our knowing, or having already in our minds, some knowledge of such natures or kinds. Plato lived long before the full force of empirical criticisms of innate ideas was felt in epistemology, and Plato accepted the doctrine of innate ideas. In fact, he believed that minds had a pre-existence in which they had firsthand acquaintance with all such Ideas and, although through the shock of birth all such pure knowledge was forgotten, perceptions help us to recall, at first vaguely and later more clearly, the precise nature of these kinds, or Ideas. "The world of sense is the copy of the world of Ideas." [1] The apparent world of our sensations is a faint image of, and is less real than, the world of Ideas. The Ideas are the most real; what we commonly call "real things" are less real, and our personal

[1] Alfred Weber, *History of Philosophy*, p. 62. Charles Scribner's Sons, New York, 1896, 1925.

118

notions of these real things are still less real than these things. Of these two worlds, this world of sensations and images that are temporary, transitory, impermanent, and the other world of eternal, fixed, unchanging Ideas, the other world is more real.

We may understand more fully how Plato arrived at his view if we consider an example. We perceive many particular things all of which are circular, such as a circular coin, a circular wheel, a circular plate, etc. We may note that they are all alike in being circular or in having circularity in common. This circularity has its being, not just in one of the round things, but in all of them. It transcends them. It exists outside them as well as in them, and it is the same circularity outside as in. If we make another round wheel, it is possible for us to do so only if we incorporate into that wheel the same circularity which already exists in other round things. Thus, the same circularity that exists in other round things before the new wheel is made has its being prior to its embodiment in this new wheel. Plato believed that such circularity existed even prior to the existence of any round things. Its pre-existence was held to be necessary for the very first round thing to come into existence as round. A further point to notice in understanding this view is the fact that each of our particular perceptions of round things involves perception of imperfect circularity, for, if we examine each round thing closely enough, through microscopes of higher and higher power, we find that no particular round thing is perfectly circular. But we have an idea of perfect circularity. If we have it, and if we did not derive it from particular circles, because all of them are, in fact, imperfect, then we must have had, in some previous experience, prior acquaintance with perfect circularity. So it is with all other forms, shapes, patterns, ideals, laws. In the world of eternal Ideas, there exists an original type, or archetype, for all existing things, including justice, beauty, virtue, government, man, truth, goodness, as well as for squares, triangles, and circles. Particular tables and chairs and men and governments, and our notions of these, come into existence and cease to exist, but ultimate reality—the eternal Ideas—remain unchanged. They alone truly are.

What is knowledge? All knowledge, ultimately, is knowledge of the Ideas. We know that this particular thing is circular because we are apprehending the Idea of circularity embodied in it, and thus in knowing that this is circular we are really knowing circularity. We first know the Idea circularity through perceiving particular round things, but then, when we have abstracted from many round things the concept roundness, we begin to approach the true Idea of circularity. Complete certainty we cannot have, in this life, or so long as our minds are imprisoned in our sensuous bodies. But the more we deal with purely abstract forms, the closer do we approach the Ideas themselves, to reality itself, to those Ideas to which our ideas must conform if they would be true. The Ideas themselves are neither true nor false, but our ideas are true to the extent that they represent the Ideas themselves, and false to the extent that we mistake them to be independent of the Ideas. We perceive truly to the extent that we perceive the universal (i.e., Idea) through the particular, but we are in error if we mistake the particular itself to be the universal when it is not.

Platonism was taken over by early Christian fathers and used as a metaphysical groundwork for Christian theology (Jesus, although a theist, was not a theologian, and since he provided no metaphysics or epistemology, it was left to Christian theologians to find a supporting metaphysics where they could). Plato's distinction between this world of sensation, or appearance, and the other, real, eternal realm of fixed and unchanging Ideas provided such support. Later, Aristotle, a pupil of Plato, who partly accepted and partly rejected Plato's views, and added a Prime Mover to Plato's philosophy, replaced him as the most respected supporting philosopher. It is not our purpose to examine these philosophies in any detail, but we cannot overlook their contribution to both metaphysics and epistemology and the influence they still exert. So important is the problem of the existence and nature of universals that Whitehead has remarked that the whole history of Western philosophy is largely a series of footnotes to Plato. During the medieval period, Platonic realism (which did not include all of Plato's views, for there is much more to Plato's thought than the doctrine of real universals) was represented by William of Champeaux who held that universals (Ideas) alone are real, or substantial. Erigena, Anselm, and Abelard, among others, continued, in modified form, the view that such universals are at least more real than particular things or our particular ideas of them. This view provided the backbone of all philosophies which appealed to reason, as against revelation, and provided modern philosophy with its rationalistic background, and with much of its support. This long history is interesting in itself and in informing us on the background of our modern philosophical problems. But space allows only brief mention of the importance of a representative type of epistemology contributed by the past.

Neo-Realism

"The new realism is a revival of what has been referred to as 'the antiquated metaphysics, which talks about existence *per se* out of all relations to minds.'" [2] But neo-realism is significant, for our purposes, because it was formulated after the rise of empiricism and after three or four centuries of modern epistemological criticism. In England, Bertrand Russell and G. E. Moore, and in the United States, E. B. Holt, W. T. Marvin, W. P. Montague, R. B. Perry, W. B. Pitkin, and E. G. Spaulding, are outstanding representatives of this viewpoint—all being twentieth-century thinkers. New realism is new, not only in contrast with naive realism, representative realism, and many other varieties of realism, but also in the sense that it is a new presentation, with some modifications, of the older Platonic realism. "This new realism, while it insists, as all realism must, that things are *independent*, asserts that when things are known, they *are* ideas of the mind. They enter *directly into* the mind; and when they do, they become what are called 'ideas.'" [3] "Things may be, and are, directly experienced without owing either their being or their nature to that circumstance." [4] This sounds very much like naive realism, yet, as we shall see, the real entities of the neo-realist turn out to be eternal in nature like Plato's Ideas.

Neo-realists reject representative realism as dualistic—i.e., as separating our ideas of objects known from the objects themselves. Once this separation has been made, then arises the difficult, if not impossible, task of trying to get ideas and objects back together again. When we make this attempt, we naturally either accept our ideas themselves as objects (as Berkeley, Hume, and Kant did) or we reject the possibility of knowing real things (as Hume, Kant, and Comte did). That is, we end up either with mere subjectivism or with agnosticism, or both. If we are to have a theory of knowledge of reality, we shall have to accept as a basic premise that reality is itself knowable rather than that only ideas which represent it are knowable. We must reject "the representative theory of knowledge according to which we can have direct knowledge only of our ideas

[2] Ralph Barton Perry, *Present Philosophical Tendencies*, p. 306. Longmans, Green and Co., New York, 1912, 1921.
[3] *Ibid.*, p. 308.
[4] *Ibid.*, p. 315.

which, as phenomena, are numerically distinct from the real objects which can merely be inferred to exist behind them." [5]

In contrast with this dualistic type of realism, neo-realism holds that the object known and the idea of the object are one and the same. Real things are perceived directly, not indirectly, and enter into consciousness with nothing between them and our consciousness of them. Yet nothing that becomes an object thereby "forfeits its objective or self-subsistent character by chancing to stand in the consciousness relation. All the contents of consciousness or experienced qualities are objects of the same order of reality, each one being a constituent member of the same spatio-temporal system of nature. Consciousness itself is a relation between these objects." [6] "Being known is something that *happens* to a preexisting thing. The characters of that preexisting thing determine what happens when it *is* known. When the knowing takes place, the preexisting characters remain undisturbed. . . . The content of knowledge (that which lies directly before the mind when knowledge takes place) is numerically identical with the thing known. In the end all things are known through being themselves brought directly into that relation in which they are said to be witnessed. In other words, things when consciousness is had of them become themselves contents of consciousness." [7] Instead of treating objects as ideas in a mind, wherein there is involved a substantial mind which has or holds or receives these ideas, objects happen to be held together externally, not by a mind, but by an external relation called "consciousness." Consciousness is not a substance, not an attribute of a mind, but a relation. "If consciousness is a relation, objects of consciousness must be real independently of their standing in that relation, while conversely, if objects are real independently of a consciousness or knowledge of them, then that consciousness or knowledge can not be anything other than a relation between them." [8] "If it be admitted that consciousness is a relation and not a substance, then there arises once more the question of the nature and significance of the so-called secondary qualities." [9] The question is settled "by ascribing them to the objectively real things." [10] Primary and secondary qualities are equally real, and both the color and shape of the real table enter directly into consciousness together.

---

[5] W. H. Werkmeister, *A History of Philosophical Ideas in America*, p. 377. The Ronald Press, New York, 1949.

[6] *Ibid.*, pp. 378–379.   [9] *Ibid.*, p. 375.

[7] *Ibid.*, p. 409.   [10] *Ibid.*

[8] *Ibid.*, p. 374.

If the dualistic division of experience into real things and ideas of things is abandoned for a monistic view that things and their qualities enter directly into consciousness, we find that "the elements of the physical and the psychical . . . are the same. . . . Color itself is neither physical nor psychical." [11] "When mind and body are so conceived, there is no longer any peculiar difficulty involved in the perception of bodily objects. For the relationship which invests a term with a bodily character does not preempt it; so that at the same time it is bodily by virtue of one relation, it may also be content of perception by virtue of another relation." [12] "The difference between knowledge and things, like that between mind and body, is a relational and functional difference, and not a difference in content. . . . The thing transcends the thought . . . [or] the immanent may at the same time be independent. . . . The cardinal principle of neo-realism is the independence of the immanent." [13] The analogy of the searchlight is sometimes used to describe the function of consciousness. As the light falls upon objects it reveals them as being all together, even though each differs from and is separate from the others. Likewise, consciousness is merely an awareness of pre-existing things, and in this awareness they appear all together, but their connection is due merely to their being related by this external relation, consciousness, thrown upon them like a light.

Bertrand Russell has summarized this view by saying, "I believe that the stuff of our mental life, as opposed to its relations and structure, consists wholly of sensations and images." [14] And "I contend that the ultimate constituents of matter are not atoms or electrons, but sensations, and other things similar to sensations as regards extent and duration." [15] "When several people simultaneously see the same table, they all see something different; therefore 'the' table, which they are all supposed to see, must be either an hypothesis or a construction. 'The' table is to be neutral as between different observers; it does not favor the aspect seen by one man at the expense of another. It was natural, though to my mind mistaken, to regard the 'real' table as the common cause of all the appearances which the table represents (as we say) to different observers. . . . Instead of

[11] Perry, *op. cit.*, p. 310.
[12] *Ibid.*, p. 311.
[13] *Ibid.*, pp. 312–313.
[14] Bertrand Russell, *The Analysis of Mind*, p. 109. G. Allen and Unwin, Ltd., London, 1921.
[15] *Ibid.*, p. 121.

supposing that there is some unknown cause, the 'real' table, behind the different sensations of those who are said to be looking at the table, we may take the whole set of these sensations (together possibly with certain other particulars) as actually *being* the table. That is to say, the table which is neutral as between different observers (actual and possible) is the set of all those particulars which would naturally be called 'aspects' of the table from different points of view. . . . I suggest . . . that these particulars, together with such correlated others as are unperceived, jointly *are* the table; and that a similar definition applies to all physical objects." [16] "A piece of matter . . . is . . . the collection of all those correlated particulars which would normally be regarded as its appearances or effects in different places. . . . On the other hand, all the happenings in a given place represent what common sense would regard as the appearances of a number of different objects as viewed from that place. All the happenings in one place may be regarded as the view of the world from that place. I shall call the view of the world from a given place a 'perspective.'" [17]

Now, all the various aspects, which function sometimes as aspects of *things* and sometimes as *aspects* of things, are in themselves neutral and may be called "neutral entities." An aspect is, in itself, neither mental nor material, neither an idea nor a real thing (i.e., the whole of a real thing as common sense sees it). If we consider an aspect as one aspect of a real thing, which real thing consists entirely of all of the aspects of it—from all possible points of view of it—taken together, then this aspect is part of a real thing, and as such it is physical or material. But this same aspect, when participating in a point of view of the whole world, is known together (con-scious) with other things from this point of view. When aspects of several different things thus function together in one "perspective," consciousness exists, and such an aspect is then mental.

But aspects, or neutral entities, are independent of all other aspects, whether related together as a material thing or related together as objects in some consciousness. All the views that we might have of a table, from all possible points of view, constitute "the" table, whereas all the objects which appear together in my present perspective constitute my present consciousness. But, my present view of the table from my present point of view is both a part of the table and a part of my consciousness. Thus, while I do not now experience the

16 *Ibid.*, pp. 97–99.
17 *Ibid.*, p. 101.

whole of the real table, i.e., all its aspects from all points of view, the one aspect of the table which I do experience is the table itself from this point of view. In this way, for Russell, real entities enter directly into our knowledge.

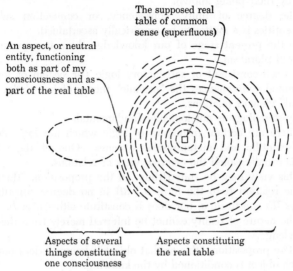

The supposed real table of common sense (superfluous)

An aspect, or neutral entity, functioning both as part of my consciousness and as part of the real table

Aspects of several things constituting one consciousness

Aspects constituting the real table

Causality, according to Russell, "in the only sense in which it can be practically applied, means 'nearly invariable antecedent.'"[18] When the various aspects of the table seem invariably related to each other, we consider them causally related and seek to name some one cause, "the" table, to account for their invariable association. But, likewise, it is because our perceptions of numerous objects together in one moment of consciousness appear to be invariably connected with something called "I" that we infer that there must exist an "I" which causes the invariable association of my ideas as experience of mine. But, if we recognize that all we are assured of is invariable connection, we can get rid of the common-sense notion that there are mysterious causes hiding behind what we see and that causality itself, as invariable connection, enters directly into our consciousness or knowledge.

Perhaps the best summary of the American neo-realist position is contained in the "Platform of Six Realists," which appeared first in the *Journal of Philosophy* in 1910.[19]

[18] *Ibid.*, p. 96.
[19] Reproduced in Werkmeister, *op. cit.*, pp. 388–389.

1. The entities (objects, facts, etc.) under study in logic, mathematics, and the physical sciences are not mental in any usual or proper meaning of the word "mental."

2. The being and nature of these entities are in no sense conditioned by their being known.

3. The degree of unity, consistency, or connection subsisting among entities is a matter to be empirically ascertained.

4. In the present stage of our knowledge there is a presumption in favor of pluralism.

5. No self-consistent or satisfactory logic (or system of logic) so far invented countenances the "organic" theory of knowledge or the "internal" view of relations.

6. Epistemology is not logically fundamental.

7. There are certain principles of logic which are logically prior to all scientific and metaphysical systems. One of these is that which is usually called the external view of relations.

8. This view may be stated thus: In the proposition, "the term a is in the relation R to the term b," aR in no degree constitutes b, nor does Rb constitute a, nor does R constitute either a or b.

9. The nature of reality cannot be inferred merely from the nature of knowledge.

10. The proposition, "this or that object is known," does not imply that such object is conditioned by the knowing.

11. Realism holds that things known may continue to exist unaltered when they are not known, or that things may pass in and out of the cognitive relation without prejudice to their reality, or that the existence of a thing is not correlated with or dependent upon the fact that anybody experiences it, perceives it, conceives it, or is in any way aware of it.

12. Cognition belongs to the same world as that of its objects. It has its place in the order of nature.

13. The objective content of consciousness is any entity in so far as it is responded to by another entity in a specific matter exhibited by the reflex nervous system. Thus physical nature, for example, is, under certain circumstances, directly present in consciousness.

14. The specific response which determines an entity to be content of consciousness does not directly modify such entities otherwise than to endow them with this content status. In other words, consciousness selects from a field of entities which it does not create.

15. The same entity possesses both immanence, by virtue of its membership in one class, and also transcendence, by virtue of the fact that it may belong also to indefinitely many other classes. In other words, immanence and transcendence are compatible and not contradictory predicates.

16. The realist holds that things known are not products of the

knowing relation nor essentially dependent for their existence or behavior upon that relation. He holds that this doctrine has three
claims upon our acceptance: first, it is the natural, instinctive belief
of all men, and for this, if for no other reason, puts the burden of
proof upon those who would discredit it; secondly, all refutations of
it presuppose or even actually employ some of its exclusive implications; and, thirdly, it is logically demanded by all the observations
and hypotheses of the natural sciences, including psychology.

17. Realism, while admitting the tautology that every entity which
is known is in relation to knowing or experience or consciousness,
holds that this knowing, etc., is eliminable, so that the entity is known
as it would be if the knowing were not taking place. That is to say,
the entity, in its being, behavior, and character, is independent of
the knowing. This position agrees with common sense and with
science in holding (1) that not all entities are mental, conscious, or
spiritual, and (2) that entities are knowable without being known.

18. The fact that terms are in the cognitive relation does not imply
that the terms are mutually dependent on, or capable of modifying,
either each other or the relation, any more than this dependence,
etc., is implied for any two terms in any other relation.

If we realize that Russell's aspects or neutral entities are what they
are independent not only of knowledge but also of each other, that
they are constituents of things and of minds and thus exist prior to
things and minds, then they should resemble Plato's ideas in that
they precede in reality the reality of all things and minds into which
they enter. They do not exist in space and time, but they constitute
space and time. They "subsist," and "it is this doctrine of subsistence
which constitutes the crux of the neo-realist position." [20] If there are
two realms of being for the neo-realist, they are the realm of existence—of spatio-temporal events—and the realm of subsistence—of
entities which do not depend upon space or time for their being.
"The entities of this [subsistent] universe have no substance. They
are related by external relations." [21] But external relations themselves subsist, as do propositions, and other logical forms. For example, the proposition, "2 plus 2 equals 4," depends for its being
neither upon this time nor this place but is true regardless of times
and places. The fact which this proposition asserts is a real fact, i.e.,
does not depend upon anyone's knowledge of it in order for it to be.
Yet, when it is known, it is known directly. It enters directly into
conscious experience and does not have to be represented by ideas

[20] Werkmeister, *op. cit.*, p. 412.
[21] *Ibid.*, p. 416.

of it. But its being known by one person directly does not in any way prevent it from being also the same fact which others know and the same fact which is unknown to still others and sometimes unknown to anyone. Logicians, when analyzing logical structures, analyze real structures. Neo-realists are logical realists because they believe that logical structures which subsist independently of all knowledge can be known directly and analyzed directly when they appear in our conscious experience. Like Plato's ideas, they subsist prior to our knowing them, yet enter directly, even if not clearly, into our ideas of them.

If we understand neo-realism by now, we should already be quite clear concerning its relations with naive realism.

1. Both agree that objects which are known exist independent of their being known, can endure without being experienced by anyone, and are not created by our knowing them. However, neo-realism distrusts the existence of wholes, or objects as wholes, but accepts some ultimate "aspects," or "neutral entities," or "logical atoms," as the real objects.

2. Both agree that qualities are parts of the objects known and that these, too, do not derive their nature from their being known. Both agree in making no distinction between primary and secondary qualities and in having all known qualities enter directly into experience.

3. Both agree that our knowledge of objects in no way changes the nature of these objects.

4. Both agree that objects seem as they are and are as they seem and that all appearances are also realities, though not all realities need appear. However, what seems obviously so may not be so. That is, error is possible. Neo-realists recognize the possibility of error and endeavor to deal with it, but, as will be pointed out in the criticisms, this problem "was truly the Achilles' heel of the neo-realists" [22] as it was of the naive realists. "Error and truth arise from the practical discrepancy or harmony between subjective manifolds and the manifolds of some independent order." [23] But, despite much effort and verbal fumbling, how this discrepancy could possibly occur has never been stated satisfactorily in terms merely of neo-realistic assumptions.

5. Both agree that objects are known directly, that they occur in experience when known, that there is nothing between them and our

[22] *Ibid.*, p. 398.
[23] Perry, *op. cit.*, p. 325.

knowledge of them, and that we know them exactly as they are without any distortion by an intervening medium. However, for neo-realists, we may not know the whole of each real thing which enters experience, for each thing has several aspects, and enters into several other relationships, which do not participate in the particular relationship which constitutes one particular present conscious experience.

6. Both agree that objects are public, but only logical entities can be fully shared, for a "physical object" is such that only one, or at most a few, of its aspects can enter into a particular consciousness at a particular time. If we see a table from two different perspectives we see two different aspects of the table, and thus, in so far as we see aspects of the same table, we have a public object, but in so far as we see different aspects of the table, we have private objects.

That neo-realism is influential goes without saying, for those who know of Bertrand Russell's enormous popularity. It has gained support among British, American, and other European philosophers and scientists who have found the assumption that logical and mathematical propositions have an existence independent of particular minds supports the view that scientists discover formulas and do not merely invent them. This doctrine provides a basis for the view that scientists are dealing with reality in their formulas, equations, and deductive analyses. Bertrand Russell, collaborating with A. N. Whitehead, wrote *Principia Mathematica,* probably the most thorough analysis of the logical foundations of mathematics. The development of symbolic logic probably owes much more to logical realists than to logical empiricists, who, apparently, have taken it over from the logical realists. Logical realists and logical empiricists are alike in their emphasis upon analysis, upon accepting a logic of external relations as prior in importance and reliability to a logic of internal relations, upon ignoring the need for some principle of activity which functions (as a mind) to make experience possible, and in taking inadequately into account what we have called the intraorganic and extraorganic conditions of perception. The neo-realist view that mathematical relationships subsist independently of things or of knowledge is one which mathematicians and logicians hold almost instinctively unless they have been made sceptical through epistemological questioning. While neo-realism appears to be declining somewhat, in the eyes of professional philosophers, as a respectable epistemology, it will continue to compete with logical empiricism, critical realism, pragmatism, and various other epistemologies for favor among scientists seeking philosophical foundations. Neo-realism has given the age-long Platonic realism a new form and, although we may expect further modification, Platonic realism will not die out easily.

Criticisms

Despite its appeal to mathematical instincts and its surface similarity to naive realism, neo-realism also rubs some of our common prejudices the wrong way. Distinctions between mind and body, between ideas and real things, between truth and falsity, are so deeply embedded in our normal outlook that it will take a lot more explaining to rid us of our old habits of thinking.

The problems of error, illusion, of memory, of things which do not now exist, and of creative imagination—all these remain to plague the neo-realist. If real things enter directly into our experience and if consciousness is nothing but an external relation between real things which happen to wander in, all that enters consciousness must be treated as if it were real. "Neo-realism has been forced to hold that memory is the actual presence of the past event itself." [24] No mind is assumed which is active in remembering, in modifying, changing, abstracting, or creating the ideas occurring in consciousness. Thus, ultimately, there can be no subjective factor to modify real things as they enter the relation of consciousness. If errors, illusions, new ideas occur, must they not also be real? The neo-realist must answer yes. But, at the same time, he cannot admit that there are "real" errors, "real" illusions, "real" creative imagination, apart from experience. If he resorts to the view that the mind does not merely take objects just as they are given, but modifies them somewhat, in order to allow for some disharmony between ideas and objects as required in falsity, then the view that consciousness is merely an external relation without active power has to be given up. If false propositions are entertained, or have entered our mind directly, what would prevent us from accepting the false as true? Bertrand Russell has to admit that his own account "does not throw any light upon our own preference for true beliefs rather than false ones." [25] "Basic disagreement among neo-realists with respect to the problem of error" [26] leaves many unwilling to go along very far with them until this problem has received better treatment.

[24] R. W. Sellars in *Essays in Critical Realism*, p. 216. Macmillan and Co., Ltd., London, 1920.

[25] Russell, *op. cit.*, p. 278.   [26] Werkmeister, *op. cit.*, p. 421.

Among the most objectionable features of neo-realism are its relational view of consciousness and its denial of mental causes participating in the construction of objects. Little consideration is given to the intraorganic and extraorganic conditions of knowing. Although these matters are taken up from time to time under the prodding of critics, they are never treated with full seriousness. Russell's view, for example, that each consciousness is simply a perspective of the world which includes all the aspects of different things from that particular point of view, gives no reason why there should not be consciousness from every such possible point of view, or why the world is not filled completely full of such consciousnesses; whereas, at the same time, he seems content to accept the view that consciousness exists only in persons, animals, and the like, which, although numerous, are widely scattered. Also, if consciousness depends upon perspective, and if two people could exchange places and perspectives, then they should, in effect, exchange consciousnesses. Of course, we do, somewhat, but why not completely? Why there should be any consciousness at all remains unexplained.

Furthermore, if consciousness is merely an external relation, it is merely between the objects which are experienced, and thus the objects are not in consciousness. If, on the other hand, consciousness is anything more than an external relation, what this more is, or in how far it is an internal relation, is something which has remained undeveloped. In fact, this doctrine of external relations "is 'somewhat of a boomerang'; for if it is impossible to infer the dependence of things upon experience, then it is equally impossible to infer their independence." [27] For, after all, if two things are independent of each other, they depend upon each other for that independence.

Neo-realism, although appealing to mathematical temperaments, is essentially nonempirical, and, as a consequence, gives no support to empirical science. For, if there is no mind and no memory, there can be no learning by experience. "If the realistic doctrine means that contents do not undergo change in knowing taken as an active process of inquiry, then, Dewey maintains, it is obviously false; for the meaning of a term—e.g., mammal, species, metal, orchid, circle, etc.—is quite different at the end and at the beginning of scientific reflection." [28]

[27] *Ibid.*, p. 386.
[28] *Ibid.*, p. 390.

The distinction between existence and subsistence, and both the assumption that there is a realm of subsistence and that it is more real than existence, are made without proof. "There is only one way by which 'neutral entities' existing beyond experience may be secured, namely, by begging them from the start." [29]

The idea of causality disappears completely from neo-realistic doctrine when it is consistent, and the doctrine becomes inconsistent when it is brought in unwittingly from time to time. A real table consists of real neutral entities or aspects but these are not caused by any real table other than these aspects themselves which, apparently, are self-caused. Objects occur together in consciousness, but consciousness in no way causes their togetherness. If one should happen to entertain the appearance that one thing causes another, this apparent causality is itself merely a subsistent aspect in a really noncausal reality.

[29] *Ibid.*, p. 386.

· 10 ·

Critical
Realism

Critical realism began, as an organized movement, with the publication in 1920 of *Essays in Critical Realism; A Co-operative Study of the Problem of Knowledge* by seven American philosophy professors: Durant Drake, Arthur O. Lovejoy, James Bissett Pratt, Arthur Kenyon Rogers, George Santayana, Roy Wood Sellars, and Charles A. Strong. This beginning as a concerted movement was preceded by individual efforts represented in numerous articles and some books such as Sellars' *Critical Realism; A Study of the Nature and Conditions of Knowledge.*

"The doctrine here defended, while definitely realistic, is distinctly different from the 'new' realism of the American group, whose volume, published in 1912, was a signal example of the value of co-operative effort in crystallizing and advertising a point of view in philosophy. Our realism is not a physically monistic realism, or a merely logical realism, and escapes the many difficulties which have prevented the general acceptance of the 'new' realism. It is also free, we believe, from the errors and ambiguities of the older realism of Locke and his successors." [1] "Critical realism differs from naive realism in its denial that the physical thing is intuited. Knowledge for it involves the distinction between the content and the object of knowledge. Yet it agrees with naive realism in its belief that the physical thing is the direct object of knowledge." [2] "Let us contrast it with the epistemological monism of the neo-realists. For them, the datum presented *is* the ultimate reality. The idea is the object. [And it is] an independent reality which only temporarily enters into an external and non-modifying relation to the individual percipient. If this is epistemological monism, then critical realism is a form of

---

[1] Durant Drake, and others, *Essays in Critical Realism*, p. vi. Macmillan and Co., Ltd., London, 1920.

[2] Roy Wood Sellars, in *Essays in Critical Realism*, p. 199.

epistemological dualism; it holds that knowledge of objects is mediated by ideas which are *in some sense* distinct from the objects of knowledge. Mere identification, at least, does not meet the essential difficulties." [3] "The more one reflects upon the situation, the more one realizes that the mind is not a searchlight, and that the self does not possess an 'eye' which has the power of bringing it into contact with the surfaces of things in a ghostly fashion. By its very origin and locus, human knowledge cannot contain the material object." [4]

Critical realists have chosen the difficult (some critics think impossible) task of steering a course between neo-realism, which, like naive realism, claims that the real object itself is directly given or present in experience, and representative realism, which holds that real objects are never themselves present in experience but only represented by ideas, primary and secondary, which indirectly reveal its nature, especially through primary ideas which supposedly copy primary qualities. But "the copy theory of truth is simply absurd." [5] Therefore critical realists must somehow account for the fact that "I do seem to see and know the real object directly. . . . But the object itself remains forever transcendent to experience." [6] "How then . . . can we compare a thing which we meet in experience with one which we never meet?" [7]

The way out of this difficulty involves a recognition of all the various kinds of intra- and extraorganic conditions of perceptions [8] and the activity of the mind in constructing ideas of things. Real things stimulate our sensory end organs, our nervous systems, our brains, but our ideas are produced only after our brains have reacted to these stimuli. Thus our ideas are different from, and have to be different from, the real things which stimulate them. "We use not only our sense organs and nervous system, but also our perceptual images, and . . . if any one of these means or implements were lacking, perception would be impossible. . . . To have a perceptual image *is* to perceive an object and to perceive it directly. In having

[3] *Ibid.*, p. 190.
[4] *Ibid.*, p. 201.
[5] W. H. Werkmeister, *A History of Philosophical Ideas in America*, p. 444. The Ronald Press, New York, 1949.
[6] *Ibid.*
[7] *Ibid.*
[8] See Roy Wood Sellars, *The Principles and Problems of Philosophy*, pp. 46ff. The Macmillan Co., New York, 1926.

a perceptual image I do not perceive a perceptual image; I perceive the object, and I do so by means of the image. In like manner, in thinking of my friend, I do not think of my thought of my friend; but I have a thought of him, a thought which means him and which . . . corresponds to him. Nevertheless the perceptual image is in itself no more the object perceived than my thought of my friend is 'my friend himself.'"[9] Furthermore, "innumerable different images may be derived from one physical object, either by different observers at the same time or by the same observer at different times; for if there are many different images of the same object, it is hard to see how they can all be *identically it.*"[10]

"Now if the subject plays a part in 'conditioning' perception, what part does it actually contribute to the nature of the percept? At this point the traditional distinction between 'primary' and 'secondary' qualities again takes on special significance [and] . . . must therefore be restated. Now the objective colors, tones, etc., i.e., the so-called secondary qualities, as attributed to the things, are measurable only in terms of primary qualities. The objective color we specify by wave-length, refractive index, etc.; the objective pitch, by frequency of vibration; the objective temperature, by the volume of fluid, etc. To this extent the objective conditions of the perceived colors, tones, and temperatures merge with those of perceived figures and forces; and the old primary qualities remain in a special sense primary after all."[11]

Real things have real qualities sometimes called "essences." Some of these may be unknowable. But some of them become "contents" of experience, despite the fact that what is experienced is partly a product of mental activity. That is, some of the qualities of real things which are independent of experience are the same as or identical with some of what is experienced. "The content given is the essence of the object. It is a way of saying that the content is relevant to the object, that it has a sort of revelatory identity with the object, that it contains its structure, position, and changes. . . . The content of knowledge offers us the fundamental categories, such as time, space, structure, relations, and behavior, in terms of which we think the world. . . . We can conclude that the physical world reveals itself in the data of observation. This revelation is causally

9 Werkmeister, *op. cit.*, p. 453.   11 *Ibid.*, pp. 456–457.
10 *Ibid.*, p. 454.

mediated and is furthered by mental operations. . . . in knowledge we claim to grasp reality in some measure, and yet we cannot intuit it. . . . Knowledge rests upon the use of data as revelations of objects because of what may, I think, be rightly called a logical identity between them." [12] "Knowledge is a claim to know an object in terms of this content. The object is known but not intuited; the content is intuited but not known. . . . there is no need for the assumption of a cognitive relation connecting the object and the knower. The physical existent is not an object in its own right. It is *made* an object by the selective activity of the percipient organism. . . . The relation of the existent to the organism is causal; it is the source of stimuli. But the selection of one existent rather than another *as object* is due to the *interest* of the organism. . . . The existent sends out stimuli of a causal character, and, in return, organisms respond to them in accordance with the capacity of their nervous systems. *Being an object* is an honor done to a thing by an organism, an honor of which the thing is quite unaware. . . . In perception, therefore, the causal relation is from the thing to the organism, and not the reverse, but this internal veering of attention upon the thing is so important and so intimately experienced that it seems to leap across space to the thing and terminate on it. . . . a thing's *being an object* is an expression of the subject." [13]

But how can we be sure of all this? Even though we cannot have absolute assurance, still we can have practical assurance, and our practical assurance is "pragmatically justifiable. . . . Everything is *as if* realism were true; and the *as if* is so strong that we may consider our instinctive and actually inescapable belief justified." [14] But is it merely a matter of luck [15] that a mental content and the essence of an object happen to be the same? No, at least it is not wholly a matter of luck. For "my behavior is successfully guided by this claimed knowledge through contents; and it is hard to understand why there should be this successful guidance if the contents did not give knowledge." [16] "And what more could we have in the way of proof? . . . there is no such thing as guaranteed proof, of the Q.E.D. sort, except in the purely hypothetical realms of logic and mathematics. An independently existing world is proved to exist in the

[12] Sellars, in *Essays in Critical Realism,* pp. 200–203.
[13] *Ibid.,* pp. 212–214.
[14] Drake, in *Essays in Critical Realism,* pp. 5–6.
[15] Werkmeister, *op. cit.,* p. 471.
[16] *Ibid.,* p. 475.

same sense, and with as great certainty, as *anything* can be proved to exist."[17]

If we can be so sure, what about error? "The definition which critical realism gives of error is briefly this: When we 'know' an object, we are assigning a certain 'essence'—a character or group of characters—to some reality existing independently of the knowledge-process. And as truth is the identity of this essence with the actual character of the reality referred to, so error stands for the lack of such agreement, and the ascribing of an ideal character to what we are mistaken in supposing to be real, or the ascribing to reality a wrong character instead of a right one."[18] "What, then, is the precise meaning of truth? It is the affirmation of a knowledge-claim after doubt. It is the assertion that the object is revealed in the idea-content. And error is the denial of a knowledge-claim. To say that an idea is false is to say that the content does not reveal the object, does not give the actual characteristics of the object."[19] But if ideas are different from real things, how can we ever have truth? "It is a contradiction, of course, to suppose that something can be in experience which is not experienced, but . . . it is not a contradiction that something can be *known* which is not experienced; for it may be known in the sense of 'being referred to.' Of course the referring is experienced, and also the 'nature' of that which is referred to."[20] "The function of the percept is to stand for and point to the object."[21] It is this "pointing to" that is "direct." An idea is produced by a complicated and indirect causal process supposedly beginning with a real thing and stimulating sensory end organs, the nervous system, and the brain to create ideas. Thus perception is a causally indirect process. Nevertheless, the real thing itself becomes an object known directly in the sense that it is pointed to or referred to by the idea. Thus an idea involves both "content" and "reference." We are in error if we refer a wrong content to an object, as when we mistake an orange flower for a yellow flower, or if we refer to a wrong object, as when one mistakes his mirror image for another person. In any case, error arises from wrong reference.

[17] Durant Drake, *Invitation to Philosophy*, pp. 159–160. Houghton Mifflin Co., Boston, 1933.
[18] Arthur K. Rogers, in *Essays in Critical Realism*, p. 117.
[19] Sellars, *The Principles and Problems of Philosophy*, p. 167.
[20] Werkmeister, *op. cit.*, p. 460.
[21] *Ibid.*

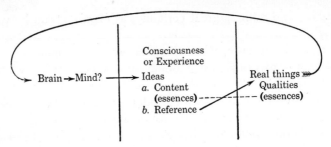

Naive realism and critical realism are similar in being direct real-isms, except that critical realism is highly critical about the kind and degree of directness that is possible.

1. Both agree that objects which are known are or may be inde-pendent of being known. They can endure or continue to exist with-out being experienced by anyone. However, critical realists insist that although knowing things as objects does not create them as things it does create them as objects. That is, being an object of knowledge is something that happens to a thing only when some knower selects it as its object.

2. Both hold that things which are objects have qualities which are parts of them and which do not derive their existence or nature from the knower.

3. Critical realism claims that real things become objects only by a mental act of reference, but it concurs with naive realism in think-ing that knowledge in no way influences the qualities of real things in making objects of them. No real thing is an object unless known, but becoming an object does not change the nature of the thing known.

4. Critical realism rejects the naive realistic view that what seems obviously so is so. Since error is possible, what appears may be so or may not be so. In fact, since the mind, conditioned by compli-cated causal processes, enters creatively into the production of the contents of ideas, we should expect these contents to be at least partly different from the qualities of real things. But this does not prevent some essences from being the same in both the contents of ideas and the qualities of real things. When this is the case, then, so far as sameness prevails, what appears is identical with what is real.

5. Whereas both agree that objects are known directly, critical realism holds that knowledge of objects is both indirect and direct—

causally indirect and referentially direct. Whereas naive realism holds that we know objects exactly as they are without distortion by any intervening medium, critical realism holds that ideas which are produced by complicated intervening causal media may, nevertheless, refer directly to objects without media intervening in such reference. When we refer to objects, we refer directly to them, and when the essences of objects and contents are the same, we refer to objects by means of the same essences which the objects themselves have.

6. Both agree that objects are, or may be, public. Two or more people may see the same object and see it exactly as it is. However, although critical realists insist that this is a possibility, they recognize that, also, much of what we see, when we claim to see the same object, may be quite different. For our end-organ-nervous-system-brain-mind-idea-producing causal systems differ. They may be as different from each other as our facial features, for example, are from each other; yet they are also probably quite similar, even as our facial features are more similar than different. Therefore, we should be able to infer that the contents of our ideas will be somewhat different and, thus, that the essences that we refer to a real thing may be quite different. Yet, on the other hand, in so far as sameness is possible, as it appears to be, especially regarding mathematical and logical essences, it is also possible for two persons to have exactly the same essences as contents of their ideas.

Criticisms

Although critical realism promised to be highly significant, its effectiveness was greatly diminished by the fact that, a few years after the publication of the *Essays*, "the critical realists [were] sharply and hopelessly divided into two major camps,"[22] one, represented by Santayana, Strong, and Drake, defending an "essence theory" in metaphysics, and the other, represented by Sellars, Lovejoy, and Pratt, supporting a "nominalistic theory," with Strong adhering first to the essence and later to the nominalistic view. The essence theory holds that essences are eternal unchangeable natures subsisting quite independently of either things or ideas in which they come to be embodied (a view perhaps best presented in Santayana's *Realm of Essence*), whereas the nominalistic theory holds that what is meant

[22] *Ibid.*, p. 462.

by essences is merely whatever nature a real thing or idea has when and while it exists and that, apart from such existing things or ideas, no such essences need exist. This split, which was accompanied by a shift in emphasis in interests from epistemology to metaphysics, was followed by a growing antagonism. "Realist stands thus pitted against realist, and the controversy deteriorates into a repetitious statement of old arguments—of arguments which, because of their repetitious restatements, have lost all power to convince." [23] However, the discussions appearing in philosophical journals did stimulate various critical debates which still reverberate in the philosophical atmosphere.

Some critics claim that, since critical realists admit a dualism of idea and real thing, they are merely restating an old-fashioned representative realism which history has already discarded. The same old difficulties in differentiating an unexperienceable from an experienced world and primary from secondary qualities recur all over again, even if in subtler and more complicated statements.

Although it takes account of the possibility error, it admits that it gives us no sure way to detect error. Critical realists themselves are forced to use coherence and pragmatic tests in seeking assurance of the truth of their ideas, and these tests are never certain.

Critical realists try to eat their cake and have it too, by claiming that an idea can be both the same as and different from its object. Traditional logic, which critical realists have not found necessary to reject, holds that if two things are different, they are not the same, or if they are the same, then they are not different. To hold that ideas (or their contents or essences) and real things (or their qualities or essences) are identical, even though different, stretches this traditional logic too much. If we cannot intuit an object, but do intuit contents, and if the essences of the object and of the content are sometimes the same, then are we not intuiting the object through intuiting its essence?

Furthermore, to call the reference of an idea to an object "direct," when it is admitted that it may miss its mark, is to play upon the meaning of the word "direct." It may be true that an idea is directed toward an object, but it may be so directed without reaching it at all, let alone reaching it directly.

Different criticisms apply to each of the two different camps concerning their treatment of essences. If essences are, with Santayana, eternal unchanging subsistents, how does it happen that they get

[23] *Ibid.*, p. 486.

entangled in existing things? If essences are, with Sellars, merely the natures of particular things or ideas as they are produced by somewhat unique causal factors, how can we expect that existents as different as ideas and real things will be exactly alike? Although we cannot pursue these types of criticism here, they do become troublesome as we go more deeply into them.

· II ·

Intuitionism

Another Frenchman, Henri Bergson (1859–1941), "is deemed by acknowledged philosophers worthy of comparison with the greatest" because he produced a revolution in our ways of thinking "equal in importance to that effected by Kant, or even by Socrates."[1] His revolution consisted primarily in his criticisms pointed against both realists and rationalists, against realists because they insist on seeing things from the outside, and against rationalists because they believe that dynamic, vital, changing reality can be captured in fixed and unchanging concepts. The existing world as we know it first hand, in our own life, is experienced as a growth, development, and passage through varieties of different occasions. In fact, "there are no two identical moments in the life of the same conscious being."[2] When we experience existence thus from the inside, so to speak, we find it a unity of variety. "The inner life is all this at once: variety of qualities, continuity of progress, and unity of direction."[3]

But what happens when we seek to know other things, to know things from the outside rather than from the inside? We interpret them through images and concepts. Then, in seeking more knowledge, we seek more images and more concepts. We analyze our object, but since "analysis is the operation which reduces objects to elements already known, that is, to elements common both to it and other objects,"[4] we do not thereby discover what it is in itself but only "as a function of something other than itself. All analysis is thus a translation, a development into symbols, a representation

---

[1] Edouard LeRoy, The Philosophy of Henri Bergson, pp. 1–2. Henry Holt and Co., New York, 1913.

[2] Henri Bergson, An Introduction to Metaphysics, p. 12. G. P. Putnam's Sons, New York, 1912.

[3] Ibid., p. 15.

[4] Ibid., p. 7.

taken from successive points of view from which we note as many resemblances as possible between the new object which we are studying and others which we believe we know already. In its eternally unsatisfied desire to embrace the object round which it is compelled to turn, analysis multiplies without end the number of its points of view in order to complete its always incomplete representation, and ceaselessly varies its symbols that it may perfect the always imperfect translation." [5] ". . . we easily persuade ourselves that by setting concept beside concept we are reconstructing the whole of the object with its parts, thus obtaining, so to speak, its intellectual equivalent. . . . [But] these concepts, laid side by side, never give us more than an artificial reconstruction of the object, of which they can only symbolize certain general, and, in a way, impersonal aspects; it is therefore useless to believe that with them we can seize a reality of which they present to us the shadow alone. . . . [Also] the concept generalizes at the same time as it abstracts. The concept can only symbolize a particular property by making it common to an infinity of things. It therefore always more or less deforms the property by the extension it gives to it." [6]

Such analyzing, such conceptualizing, such intellectualizing, such rationalizing, which all give external knowing, and especially scientific and philosophical knowing, extracts from concrete realities static "pictures" which, when put end-to-end, may be likened to a movie film. But no matter how many pictures we take of a real thing, we cannot capture either its inner or its entire nature. "Were all the photographs of a town, taken from all possible points of view, to go on indefinitely completing one another, they would never be equivalent to the solid town in which we walk about." [7] In science, where we seek not pictures or images but first abstract concepts and then symbols of those concepts, we get farther away from, rather than closer to, reality. "The very idea of reconstituting a thing by operations practiced on symbolic elements alone implies such an absurdity that it would never occur to any one if they recollected that they were not dealing with fragments of the thing, but only, as it were, with fragments of its symbol." [8]

If science cannot reveal reality, because science is too rationalistic and because reason can work only with static concepts or symbols of such concepts, what about empiricism and empirical science? "Both

[5] *Ibid.*, pp. 7–8.
[6] *Ibid.*, pp. 18–19.
[7] *Ibid.*, p. 5.
[8] *Ibid.*, p. 29.

empiricists and rationalists are victims of the same fallacy. Both of them mistake *partial notations* for *real parts*. . . . The empiricists say quite rightly that psychological analysis discovers nothing more in personality than psychical states. Such is, in fact, the function, and the very definition of analysis. The psychologist has nothing else to do but analyze personality, that is, to note certain states. . . . But rationalism is dupe to the same illusions. It starts out from the same confusion as empiricism, and remains equally powerless to reach the inner self. Like empiricism, it considers psychical states as so many fragments detached from an ego that binds them together. Like empiricism, it tries to join these fragments together in order to recreate the unity of the self. Like empiricism, finally, it sees this unity of the self, in the continually renewed effort it makes to clasp it, steal away indefinitely like a phantom. But whilst empiricism, weary of the struggle, ends by declaring that there is nothing else but the multiplicity of psychical states, rationalism persists in affirming the unity of the person. . . . I see in this matter only one difference between empiricism and rationalism. The former, seeking the unity of the ego in the gaps, as it were, between the psychical states, is led to fill the gaps with other states, and so on indefinitely, so that the ego, compressed in a constantly narrowing interval, tends towards zero, as analysis is pushed farther and farther; whilst rationalism, making the ego the place where the mental states are lodged, is confronted with an empty space which we can have no reason to limit here rather than there, which goes beyond each of the successive boundaries that we try to assign to it, which constantly grows larger, and which tends to lose itself no longer in zero, but in the infinite." [9]

What, then, is the way out of this predicament? If we try to reason our way out of a kind of difficulty which reason itself has gotten us into, will we not only get deeper and deeper into the same trouble? "Our mind, when it follows its natural bent, proceeds on the one hand by solid perceptions, and on the other by stable conceptions. It starts from the immobile, and only conceives and expresses movement as a function of immobility. It takes up its position in ready-made concepts, and endeavors to catch in them, as in a net, something of reality which passes. . . . we place ourselves in the immobile in order to lie in wait for the moving thing as it passes. . . . With stoppages, however numerous they may be, we shall never

[9] *Ibid.,* pp. 30–36.

make mobility. . . . Fixed concepts may be extracted by our thoughts from mobile reality; but there are no means of reconstructing the mobility of the real with fixed concepts. . . . But because we fail to reconstruct the living reality with stiff and ready-made concepts, it does not follow that we cannot grasp it in some other way. . . . The truth is that our intelligence can follow the opposite method. It can place itself within the mobile reality, and adopt its ceaselessly changing direction; in short, it can grasp it by means of that *intellectual sympathy* which we call intuition. This is extremely difficult. The mind has to do violence to itself, has to reverse the direction of operation by which it habitually thinks, has perpetually to revise, or rather recast, all its categories." [10]

If intuition is the only method by which we can penetrate reality, how does it function? It is knowing from the inside, not from the outside. Intuition is knowing something as it is in itself, not as it is in relation to something else. But how can we know other things from the inside when they are other than or outside us? "There is one reality, at least, which we all seize from within, by intuition and not by simple analysis. It is our own personality in its flowing through time—our self which endures. We may sympathize intellectually with nothing else, but we certainly sympathize with our own selves." [11] "It is true that no image can reproduce exactly the original feeling I have of the flow of my own conscious life. But it is not even necessary that I should attempt to render it. If a man is incapable of getting for himself the intuition of the constitutive duration of his own being, nothing will ever give it to him." [12] If we grant that we know ourselves from the inside and in knowing ourselves know reality, we still have not shown how we can know other things from the inside. Of course, if they are completely other, we cannot know them at all. We must, with Hume, remain agnostic about such otherness.

But, on the other hand, the objects which we experience are not completely outside; they are already in our experience as our own objects. Still, they are objects. If we are to know our objects from the inside we must, so to speak, project ourselves inside them. Even though we cannot do this completely, for we would then be these things themselves, we can make the attempt. That we can partially succeed is evident from our appreciation of dramas and novels. "Con-

[10] *Ibid.,* pp. 66–69.   [12] *Ibid.,* pp. 15–16.
[11] *Ibid.,* p. 9.

sider a character whose adventures are related to me in a novel. The author may multiply the traits of his hero's character, may make him speak and act as much as he pleases, but all this can never be the equivalent to the simple and indivisible feeling which I should experience if I were able for an instant to identify myself with the person of the hero himself. Out of that indivisible feeling, as from a spring, all the words, gestures, and actions of the man would appear to me to flow naturally. . . . The character would be given to me all at once, in its entirety. . . ." [13]

American football fans easily recall their sympathetic attempt to help their team put the ball over the goal line. This is our clue to insight into reality. In order to know any particular dynamic reality as it really is, I must attribute to it "an interior and, so to speak, states of mind; I also imply that I am in sympathy with those states, and that I insert myself in them by an effort of imagination. Then, according as the object is moving or stationary, according as it adopts one movement or another, what I experience will vary. And what I experience will depend neither on the point of view I may take up in regard to the object, since I am inside the object itself, nor on the symbols by which I may translate the motion, since I have rejected all translations in order to possess the original. In short, I shall no longer grasp the movement from without, remaining where I am, but from within, as it is in itself." [14]

Does Bergson advise us to reject all attempts to know things from the outside, all reasoning, all science? No. We should not reject science. But we ought to recognize its limitations. It cannot give us insight into reality as it is in itself. It is merely, at best, an outside look. It mechanizes, and thus falsifies, life. "The human intellect feels at home among inanimate objects, more especially among solids, where our action finds it fulcrum and our industry its tools; . . . our concepts have been formed on the model of solids; . . . our logic is, pre-eminently, the logic of solids; . . . consequently, our intellect triumphs in geometry, wherein is revealed the kinship of logical thought with unorganized matter. . . ." [15]

Nevertheless, we cannot abandon intellect, any more than a Christian soul can abandon its material body. "It is, therefore, natural and legitimate in daily life to proceed by the juxtaposition

[13] *Ibid.*, p. 3.
[14] *Ibid.*, pp. 2–3.
[15] Henri Bergson, *Creative Evolution* (translated into English by Arthur Mitchell), p. xix. The Modern Library, New York, 1944.

and portioning out of concepts." [16] We should not reject reason altogether, but need to recognize "in the faculty of understanding an appendage of the faculty of action." [17] Once we realize its true function, we find that science itself has been dependent upon intuition and that "a profoundly considered history of human thought would show that we owe to it all that is greatest in the sciences. . . . The most powerful of the methods of investigation at the disposal of the human mind, the infinitesimal calculus, originated from this very inversion. Modern mathematics is precisely an effort to substitute the *being made* for the *ready made*, to follow the generation of magnitudes, to grasp motion no longer from without and in its displayed results, but from within and in its tendency to change; in short, to adopt the mobile continuity of the outlines of things." [18]

It is the same with other scientific developments. Scientific activity is itself growth, development, and a groping for form. Science does not consist in the cut-and-dried conclusions in the answer section at the end of a laboratory manual. These are merely tracks left in the mud which has now dried. We may retrace the steps of other scientists and thus, in a measure, try to capture from the inside, as nearly as we can, what the scientist was doing when he first worked out (in an active living process) the problems now left for us to do over again repetitiously. But ink marks stored in books are not science itself, which is inseparable from the living activity of scientists at work on their problems. In fact, "modern science dates from the day when mobility was taken as . . . a reality. Galileo, setting a ball rolling down an inclined plane . . ." [19] started rolling also a movement which has helped us, finally, to realize that it is not Platonic Ideas, unchanging universals, or eternal essences, which are most real, but changing, flowing, growing, living beings. Biology, not physics, is the primary modern science. In his *Creative Evolution*, Bergson applies in some detail to the life sciences his philosophy, here summarized briefly.

What about causality? Those who abstract cause from effect and effect from cause, and seek to measure the cause and then relate it to measurements of the effect, lose all contact with real causality. The felt force of one's own self experiencing effort in enduring and in

[16] Bergson, *An Introduction to Metaphysics*, p. 42.
[17] Bergson, *Creative Evolution*, p. xix.
[18] Bergson, *An Introduction to Metaphysics*, p. 70.
[19] *Ibid.*, pp. 75–76.

dealing with problems is what causation is from the inside. The feeling of effort in helping the ball across the goal vividly illustrates internally experienced causation. If we abstract causes from the flux of life we lose real causation. Intuition of causation is achieved neither through conceptualizing it in terms of external relations between cause and effect nor through conceiving it in terms of necessary or internal relatedness, but by grasping it from the inside. Inside, we are spiritual, not material; irrational, not merely rational; both one and many, not just many or even merely one. The feeling of causal efficacy within our own experience cannot be reduced truly to any symbolic formula. Each intuition is in some sense unique, just as each different moment of existence is in some sense different from every other. So, if we would retain sensitiveness in knowing, we must expect and seek uniqueness in our intuitions, not try to reduce all knowledge to static pictures or fixed concepts.

What is Bergson's attitude toward naive realism?

1. He states as the first of his nine basic principles that "there is a reality that is external and yet given immediately to the mind. Common sense is right on this point." [20] Real things can endure without being experienced by anyone else, but no living thing can endure without experiencing its own duration. It is only from the outside that things appear dead or static or without experience. The hardest and most durable granite has been discovered to be composed of energetic atoms, lively electrons, pulls and tensions between electrons and protons. All this we have discovered from our external examinations of atoms. If we could experience the processes, tensions, and changes taking place in the atoms themselves, we would find them, not exactly like, but nevertheless analogous to, our own inner experiences. In so far as they are unlike, of course, we cannot know them even by intuition.

2. Qualities of an object are known either intuitively or conceptually. If intuitively, they blend harmoniously with the rest of the experienced object because they are inherent parts of the concrete flux of its inner nature. If conceptually, they appear as external essences incomprehensively concatenated, at war with each other and with the object to which they attach. Naive realists are naturally intuitive. In so far as we naively intuit, we grasp reality immediately. Nevertheless, it is also natural for human minds to reflect, to reason, to analyze, and through this reflective process we are led farther and

[20] *Ibid.*, p. 65.

farther away from our more naive, but often more true, insight into reality.

3. Does our knowledge of objects change the nature of the objects? When we intuit them, we do not change them; intuition is a dynamic grasping of dynamic reality. But when we conceptualize and mathematize and systematize, we change the dynamic into the static, the fluid into the stable, the changing into the permanent. Of course, we are not really changing the nature of reality, but we reconstruct a substitute for reality, and, in so far as we take the substitute to be a real object of knowledge, we deceive ourselves.

4. Objects are as they seem from the inside, and seem, through intuition, as they are. Dynamic reality appears as it is in dynamic intuition. But, actually, objects are not what they appear to be from the outside.

5. Objects are known directly through intuition, indirectly through conception. In intuition there is no distorting medium intervening. But conceptualizing distorts by interjecting, between living reality and our living experience, conceptions which falsify. The more we conceptualize, the more distortion we place between us and the reality we seek to apprehend. Our intellectual folly reaches its final deception through our conceiving some eternally perfect system of externally related essences incarcerating all life in the prison of some supreme intellect.

6. Objects are public, and some, at least, can be known both intellectually and intuitively. Some objects, such as a table between us, can be known by both of us from the outside. We can each form concepts of it, and, in comparing concepts, may find ourselves in considerable agreement about them. But, it is also possible for two people, both watching the hero of the drama strive to fulfill his deepest desire, to lose themselves fully in their empathetic intuition of his feelings. To the extent that they succeed, both, even at the same time, live inside their hero's struggles. This inside is not a spatial inside, for space, as usually understood, may be occupied by only one thing at a time. But lived space, the space of our own inner experience, permits our percepts, concepts, desires, hopes, doubts, errors, fears, etc., to intermingle harmoniously without contradiction, for it is the intellect which first creates barriers and then condemns, as inconsistent, whatever crosses them. Where intellect has not yet done its work, there can be no inconsistency in having multitudes share the same object through intuition.

Criticisms

Few can read Bergson sympathetically without feeling that he expresses a fundamental point. Yet, at the same time, he overdoes it. Intuition is a sympathetic projection of oneself into an object. But this is impossible, except imaginatively, and surely this is merely our imagination, not real projection and identification. Furthermore, even if we try, and seem to ourselves to succeed, in a measure, then, if we are still on the outside, we have fooled ourselves; and the more we seem to be on the inside of something else, when we are not, the more we deceive ourselves.

Furthermore, feelings are not enough. To feel as another person does, when, for example, he is conceptualizing, we, too, must conceptualize as he does. Even though there may be a sense in which all the different objects in our experience appear to be intuited at once, nevertheless, the differences between our objects are genuine differences and the similarities are genuine similarities; so, when our intellect abstracts these differences and similarities, it may tend to generalize too hastily, but it is not dealing with no actuality. Conceptualizing itself is a part of the flux of experience and, as such, even on Bergson's own terms, is actual, vital, dynamic. Granting that we have succumbed too easily to the call of reason and that we have overdone our rationalizing of the irrational, nevertheless (a) some good results have come from science, and (b) the remedy for overrationalizing is hardly overirrationalism.

If each individual's experience involves uniqueness, then no intuition of one unique experience by another unique experience can be had without destroying some uniqueness. The most successful intuition of any other thing must, at best, be a matter of degree.

If our understanding of what Bergson means by his philosophy must be by intuition, then we are doomed to considerable failure because his experiences are being conveyed to us, as we read, through highly abstract concepts cast into the molds of an artificial language and conveyed through printed symbols. If he knew this, he should have remained silent; for, by his own claim, we cannot reconstruct an intuition from static concepts set side by side. "It has often been said that his entire philosophical enterprise constitutes an inconsistency: the use of intellect to discredit intellect." [21]

[21] Harold A. Larrabee, *Selections from Bergson*, p. xvi. Appleton-Century-Crofts, Inc., New York, 1949.

Although Bergson applied his philosophy to biological sciences with some success, it has not been generally acceptable to physical scientists. He never succeeded in working out systematically a whole philosophy. Of course, if he had done so, he would have contradicted his own tenets. Nevertheless, his chief contribution to philosophy is negative, rather than positive. He attacked the enduring ramparts of Platonism and its various rationalistic successors, but only partly succeeded, and, although he tried, he failed to give us a substitute which can be used with as much confidence and widespread success. Yet Bergson has stimulated the philosophical imaginations of many rebels in many lands. "His works stirred William James to the point of ecstasy. . . ." [22]

[22] *Ibid.*, p. viii.

· 12 ·

Pragmatism

If there is any one predominantly American philosophy, it is pragmatism. The two most outstanding representatives are William James (1842–1910) and John Dewey (1859–1952). However, William James credits Charles Sanders Peirce with originating the term. George Herbert Mead (1863–1931), Max Otto (1876–   ), C. I. Lewis (1883–   ), Stephen C. Pepper (1891–   ), Charles W. Morris (1901–   ), Sidney Hook (1902–   ), and many other American philosophers claim adherence to the movement. In England, F. C. S. Schiller (1864–1937) preferred to call his variety of pragmatism "humanism."

William James

Harvard Professor William James, better known to some as a psychologist, developed his practical, down-to-earth, "cash-value" philosophy partly out of the American cultural milieu and partly out of his own psychological studies of varieties of religious experiences. Although he was able to find no great uniformity of doctrine among peoples practicing different religious beliefs, he did discover that these beliefs have effects, beneficial or otherwise, but often beneficial, upon the lives of the practitioners. In examining these beliefs more carefully, and comparing them with other beliefs which we hold about various ideals, James noted that "often enough our faith beforehand in an uncertified result is the only thing that makes the result come true." [1] If one desires to know whether or not he has the ability to attend a college and to graduate from it, then if he does not have enough faith that he has such ability actually to enroll, he will never know; or, rather, he proves to himself, by not enrolling,

[1] William James, *The Will to Believe*, p. 59. Longmans, Green and Co., New York, 1897.

that he does not have this ability. On the other hand, if he does have enough faith in this belief to enroll and work hard and succeed, then, finally, he knows that he has that ability. In such a situation, his own faith itself was a factor in making a difference in the outcome. Without faith, or without a will-to-believe, one cannot know whether his desires can be satisfied or his ideals realized. If your life is in danger and you fear that you may drown before reaching shore, then you should "believe what is in the line of your needs, for only by such belief is the need fulfilled. . . . Refuse to believe, and you shall indeed be right, for you shall irretrievably perish. But believe, and again you shall be right, for you shall save yourself. You make one or the other of two possible universes true by your trust or mistrust,— both universes having been only maybes, in this particular, before you contributed your act." [2]

Although not all our knowledge situations are crisis situations, nevertheless in them we may find a clue to what we seek in wanting to know. "The pragmatic method . . . is to try to interpret each notion by tracing its practical consequences. What difference would it practically make to anyone if this notion rather than that notion were true? If no practical difference whatever can be traced, then the alternatives mean practically the same thing." [3] "Mr. Peirce, after pointing out that our beliefs are really rules for action, said that, to develop a thought's meaning, we need only determine what conduct it is fitted to produce: that conduct is for us its sole significance. And the tangible fact at the root of all our thought-distinctions, however subtle, is that there is no one of them so fine as to consist in anything but a possible difference of practice. To attain perfect clearness in our thoughts of an object, then, we need only consider what conceivable effects of a practical kind the object may involve—what sensations we are to expect from it, and what reactions we must prepare. Our conception of these effects, whether immediate or remote, is then for us the whole of our conception of that object, so far as that conception has any positive significance at all." [4]

What is truth? "True ideas are those that we can assimilate, validate, corroborate, and verify. False ideas are those that we cannot. . . . Truth happens to an idea. It becomes true, is made true by events. Its verity is in fact an event, a process: the process namely

[2] *Ibid.*
[3] William James, *Pragmatism*, p. 45. Longmans, Green and Co., New York, 1907.
[4] *Ibid.*, pp. 46–47.

of its verifying itself, its veri-fication." [5]   "The possession of true
thoughts means everywhere the possession of invaluable instruments
of action. . . . The importance to human life of having true beliefs
about matters of fact is a thing too notorious. We live in a world of
realities that can be infinitely useful or harmful. Ideas that tell us
which of them to expect count as true ideas . . . and the pursuit
of such ideas is a primary human duty. The possession of truth, so
far from being here an end in itself, is only a preliminary means towards other vital satisfactions. . . . The practical value of true ideas
is thus primarily derived from the practical importance of their objects to us. Their objects are, indeed, not important at all times. . . .
Yet since most any object may some day become temporarily important, the advantage of having a general stock of extra truths, of
ideas that shall be true of merely possible situations, is obvious. We
store such extra truths away in our memories and with the overflow
we fill our books of reference. Whenever such an extra truth becomes practically relevant to one of our emergencies, it passes from
cold-storage to do work in the world and our belief in it grows active.
You can say of it either that 'it is useful because it is true' or that 'it is
true because it is useful.' Both of these phrases mean exactly the
same thing, namely, that here is an idea that gets fulfilled and can be
verified. . . . From this simple cue pragmatism gets her general notion of truth as something essentially bound up with the way in which
one moment in our experiences may lead us towards other moments
which it will be worth while to have been led to. Primarily, and on
the common-sense level, the truth of a state of mind means this function of a leading that is worth while." [6]   "For one truth-process completed there are a million in our lives that function in a state of
nascency. . . . Truth lives, in fact, for the most part on a credit-
system. Our thoughts and beliefs 'pass' so long as nothing challenges
them, just as bank-notes pass so long as nobody refuses them. But
all this points to direct face-to-face verifications somewhere, without
which the fabric of truth collapses like a financial system with no cash-
basis whatsoever." [7]   " 'The true,' to put it very briefly, is only the
expedient in the way of our thinking, just as 'the right' is only the
expedient in the way of our behaving." [8]   Ideas "become true just
in so far as they help us to get into satisfactory relation with other
parts of our experience. . . . Any idea that will carry us prosperously
from one part of our experience to another, linking things satisfacto-

[5] *Ibid.*, p. 201.   [7] *Ibid.*, pp. 207–208.
[6] *Ibid.*, pp. 202–205.   [8] *Ibid.*, p. 222.

rily, working securely, simplifying, saving labor; is true for just so much, true in so far forth, true instrumentally." [9]

All this sounds as if James were merely a subjectivist. But, he retorts, "my account of truth is realistic, and follows the epistemological dualism of common sense. Suppose I say to you 'The thing exists'—is that true or not? How can you tell? Not until my statement has developed its meaning farther is it determined as being true, false, or irrelevant to reality altogether. But if now you ask 'what thing?' and I reply 'a desk'; if you ask 'where?' and I point to a place; if you ask 'does it exist materially, or only in imagination?' and I say 'materially'; if moreover I say 'I mean that desk,' and then grasp and shake a desk which you see just as I have described it, you are willing to call my statement true. . . . This notion of a reality independent of either of us, taken from ordinary social experience, lies at the basis of the pragmatist definition of truth." [10] The belief that there are real things is one that works so well that we could hardly get along without it.

What, then, is the pragmatist's conclusion concerning knowledge of objects? Apart from the general view that ideas are instruments useful in achieving satisfactory results, he cares to offer few specific details. As a pragmatist, he makes no demands that a particular metaphysical viewpoint be presupposed in order to make knowledge as he sees it possible—except, of course, that somehow the possibility of experience and its ideas and their workability be provided for. Pragmatism "does not stand for any special results. It is a method only. . . . If you follow the pragmatic method, you cannot look on any . . . word as closing your quest. You must bring out of each word its practical cash-value, set it at work within the stream of your experience. It appears less as a solution, then, than as a program for more work, and more particularly as an indication of the ways in which existing realities may be changed. Theories thus become instruments, not answers to enigmas. . . . At the outset, at least, it stands for no particular results. It has no dogmas, and no doctrines save its method. As the young Italian pragmatist Papini has well said, it lies in the midst of our theories, like a corridor in a hotel. Innumerable chambers open out of it. In one you may find a man writing an atheistic volume; in the next some one on his knees in

[9] *Ibid.*, p. 58.

[10] William James, *The Meaning of Truth*, pp. 217–218. Longmans, Green and Co., New York, 1909.

prayer for faith and strength; in the third a chemist investigating a body's properties. In a fourth a system of idealistic metaphysics is being excogitated; in a fifth the impossibility of metaphysics is being shown. But they all own the corridor, and all must pass through it if they want a practical way of getting into or out of their respective rooms. No particular results then, so far, but only an attitude of orientation, is what the pragmatic method means." [11]

If pragmatism's conclusions are merely methodological, shall we rest the matter there? If it allows us to be either theistic or atheistic, idealistic or materialistic, metaphysical or anti-metaphysical, is it broad enough to tolerate all possible workable alternatives? But perhaps it is too tolerant. What works for one fails for another. Beliefs which one pursues satisfactorily now may frustrate him in the long run. A belief is true while it is working successfully, false when it fails, true while it satisfies, false when it frustrates. Is truth then fickle, flip-floppish, wishy-washy, unreliable? James would reply that if no fool-proof assurance of absolute and unchanging certainty is available, as a practical workable idea, then the best we can do is to seek the most reliable beliefs we are able to find. But how shall we test their reliability? By experimental trial-and-error methods. In this process, some are bound to fail. Some will survive longer than others, but still fail. If we have no alternative, then we must make the best of this method. By learning from experience, by retaining those beliefs that work and rejecting those that fail, we gradually build up a greater fund of working capital. Of course, it remains a possibility that the whole banking system may fail, and we shall have to start all over again. Philosophical, religious, political, scientific, and moral systems that have worked for centuries as "the truth" have come, in later centuries, to be discarded and replaced by other philosophies, other religions, other governmental systems, other scientific hypotheses, and different moral standards. Pragmatism has the virtue of accounting for our varieties of disagreements and yet allowing us to retain our own individualistic and private local funds of truth.

In treating "The Relation Between Knower and Known," [12] James remarks that "throughout the history of philosophy the subject and its object have been treated as absolutely discontinuous entities; and thereupon the presence of the latter to the former . . . has assumed

[11] James, *Pragmatism*, pp. 51–54.
[12] James, *The Meaning of Truth*, Ch. IV.

a paradoxical character. . . ." [13] But the paradox disappears when we realize that what is meant by an object is merely whatever practical difference it makes in our experience. If someone tells us of a new restaurant just opened up in town, we take his idea as true if, by following it, we can come eventually to the restaurant. That is, we can achieve certain experiences which we call "being in the restaurant" and which terminate the desire we had for arriving there. "Knowledge of sensible realities thus comes to life inside the tissue of experience. It is made; and made by relations that unroll themselves in time. Whenever certain intermediaries are given, such that, as they develop towards their terminus, there is experience from point to point of one direction followed, and finally of one process fulfilled, the result is that their starting-point thereby becomes a knower and their terminus an object meant or known. That is all that knowing (in the simple case considered) can be known-as, that is the whole of its nature, put into experiential terms. . . . That is what we mean here by the object's being 'in mind.' Of any deeper, more real way of its being in mind we have no positive conception, and we have no right to discredit our actual experience by talking of such a way at all." [14]

Involved here is a distinction between "knowledge by acquaintance" and "knowledge about." "Where direct acquaintance is lacking, 'knowledge about' is the next best thing, and acquaintance with what actually lies about the object, and is most closely related to it, puts such knowledge within our grasp." [15] "But the whole system of experiences as they are immediately given presents itself as a quasi-chaos through which one can pass out of an initial term in many directions and yet end in the same terminus, moving from next to next by a great many possible paths. Either one of these paths might function as a substitute for another, and to follow one rather than another might on occasion be an advantageous thing to do. As a matter of fact . . . the paths that run through conceptual experiences . . . are highly advantageous to follow. Not only do they yield inconceivably rapid transitions; but, owing to the 'universal' character . . . , they outstrip the tardy consecutions of the things themselves, and sweep us on towards our ultimate termini in a far more labor-saving way than the following of trains of sensible perception ever could.

[13] *Ibid.*, p. 102.
[14] *Ibid.*, pp. 106–107.
[15] *Ibid.*, p. 119.

Wonderful are the new cuts and short circuits the thought-paths make. Most thought-paths, it is true, are substitutes for nothing actual; they end outside the real world altogether, in wayward fancies, utopias, fictions or mistakes. But where they do re-enter reality and terminate therein, we substitute them always; and with these substitutes we pass the greater number of our hours." [16]

Although James claimed that pragmatism is merely a method and a theory of truth, he himself reached, by the use of this method, some conclusions which he called "Radical Empiricism" [17] and "A Pluralistic Universe." [18]   We shall not go into these here.   Differences among pragmatists are to be expected regarding which epistemological, metaphysical, and other theories work best. But, also, we find that pragmatists differ somewhat concerning which is the most workable conception of what constitutes the "practical" or the "pragmatic." James was primarily concerned with what is workable for individuals, whereas Dewey, as we shall see, placed more emphasis upon the importance of social practice.

Criticisms

Many critics point out that the view that "ideas work because they are true" is more widespread than the view that "ideas are true because they work." Does this not mean that the former is therefore more successful, more workable, even more practical, and that, as a pragmatist, James should admit the inferiority of his own hypothesis? Many object to the saying that "the truth of an idea lies in its future," because we commonly think of ideas as being true or false now, even though we may admit that proof of truth or falsity may come only in the future. Furthermore, many feel very uneasy when James claims that the same idea may be true for a while (i.e., at first, when it works) and then false for a while (i.e., later, when it fails to work). Few are willing to accept a view of truth so wishy-washy that the same idea may be true for one and false for another or false at one time and true at another. The problem of error, which started our search for an improvement on naive realism, gives evidence that

[16] *Ibid.*, pp. 112–113.

[17] William James, *Essays in Radical Empiricism*. Longmans, Green and Co., New York, 1912.

[18] William James, *A Pluralistic Universe*. Longmans, Green and Co., New York, 1909.

errors also "work" for a while, and thus, for James, all errors which work must also be truths.

John Dewey

Conceiving man as a biological being evolved by a process of adaptation to environment, Dewey finds his clue to the nature of knowledge in the fact that what adapts itself survives, whereas what fails to adapt itself perishes. Animals possessing grasping hands could find food when others with hoofs could not; those with more complex nervous systems, more sensitive sensory end organs, longer memories, and more generalized responses could adjust where others could not. Ideas, for Dewey, are biological instruments which an animal uses in making adjustments. An idea is a tool useful in helping its possessor survive. If men have ideas which fail them, then both these men and their ideas perish. If men have ideas which help them survive, then both these men and their ideas are likely to survive. But, even though ideas do not save us or kill us, nevertheless, as James pointed out, those ideas which bring us satisfactory results we keep and use again, whereas those ideas which bring us dissatisfaction we discard. So, there is competition among ideas for survival as our most suitable instruments. Intelligence consists in ability to adapt to relatively new situations. Those of us who acquire ideas which help our adaptation thereby acquire intelligence, or more intelligence, and the most intelligent beings are those who have the greatest ability to acquire new intelligence.

"Thinking is adaptation *to* an end *through* the adjustment of particular objective contents." [19] "There is no miracle in the fact that the tool and material are adapted to each other in the process of reaching a valid conclusion." [20] The kinds of ideas we have about the goals we wish to reach have resulted partly from the varying needs arising in the situations we get into. If a person faces the danger of freezing to death, he conceives the problem of protecting himself from the cold. In this situation, he develops ideals of shelter, and a cave becomes perceived as a shelter. Then he calls it not a cave (mere hole) but a shelter. This is what the cave means to him now, because he intends it to perform the function of sheltering him. But this person's first attempts, such as, when blowing on his hands to

[19] Joseph Ratner, *Intelligence in the Modern World: John Dewey's Philosophy*, p. 929. Random House, New York, 1939.
[20] *Ibid.*

keep them warm, he idealizes some big warm blow, may prove useless in his predicament. Then he tries other ideas: first some clothes, then a tent, then a constructed house, then fires in fireplaces, furnaces, etc. "All knowledge, as issuing from reflection, is experimental in the literal physical sense of experimental." [21]   Unless we try out our ideas, they do not become knowledge. In fact, knowledge "does not come into existence till thinking has terminated in the experimental act which fulfils the specifications set forth in thinking. But . . . the object thus determined is an object of *knowledge* only because of the thinking which has preceded it and to which it sets a happy term. . . . In short, the object of knowledge is its objective; and this objective is not constituted till it is reached." [22]

What is science? Does it deal with real objects? Science, for Dewey, is a further extension of reflective thinking which the biological animal does when problematic situations arise. The problems of pure science are merely personal problems generalized and dealt with in a more general way and on a wider scale. The purpose of science is not to discover and to contemplate eternal verities, but to serve human needs. Science is incomplete, has not reached its objective, until human needs have been served. "What is sometimes termed 'applied science' may then be more truly scientific than is what is conventionally called 'pure science.' For it is directly concerned with not just instrumentalities, but instrumentalities at work in effecting a modification of existence in behalf of conclusions that are reflectively preferred. . . . Thus conceived, knowledge exists in engineering, medicine, and the social arts more adequately than it does in mathematics and physics." [23]

Science, then, is a process, a function, an activity. It is not a body of knowledge or set of conclusions stored away. Science, as an activity of problem-solving, is better represented by the verb "sciencing" than by a noun which connotes completeness. Scientific activity does not begin until there is a problem, and does not cease until the problem has been solved or forgotten. Problems naturally beget suggested solutions, for one can hardly be clear as to just what his problem is unless he thereby conceives some notion as to how to solve it. Our first impulsive guesses usually fail us, and then we need to examine our problem more carefully to determine more clearly its

21 *Ibid.*, p. 931.   23 *Ibid.*, p. 945.
22 *Ibid.*, pp. 932–933.

conditions, and what we may do about changing them. The more our suggestions fail us and the more we are frustrated in solving our problem, the more reflective we become. We try out all sorts of imaginary solutions before exerting too much effort in actual labor. Each imaginary solution, or hypothesis, is used as a guide in solving the problem. Its purpose is to guide us to where we want to go. First we test it by reasoning about it, deducing conclusions to see whether these fit other facts of our experience relative to the problem. If these all seem to work unchallenged, then we try out the hypothesis in actual practice. If it works, the hypothesis was true and we have reached our goal. If it does not, we discard it, and begin again.

Since man is a social animal, Dewey, who is more concerned than James with social experimentation and political instruments, believes that man must try out various forms of social adjustment before he finds one that is most suitable. Our ideas about what kinds of social conduct are best, or right, likewise evolve from social experimentation. Those ideas which bring good social results we keep, and, if they come to be deemed necessary for group welfare, they are then enforced as mores and laws. But, if times and conditions change, then our social needs change. When they do, we discover the need for new laws, and thus we must experiment again. Sometimes mores become obsolete because they are solutions to social problems which no longer exist. Social intelligence requires abandonment of useless customs and their replacement by more useful methods. If societies survive better through anticipating future problems and planning ahead to meet them, then social planning seems as necessary to social survival as individual planning is to individual survival. Social knowledge has social goals as its object or objective. With Dewey, the social sciences come to equal or surpass the physical and biological sciences as instruments useful in human adaptation.

Criticisms

Dewey's instrumentalism seems to rest upon the assumption that man is a biological animal evolved through a struggle for existence and a survival of the fit. Irrespective of the weak links in proof of such evolution, do we not first have to set up our epistemology and its principles of proof before we can prove biological evolution, instead of first assuming biological evolution as a basis for our theory of knowledge? Although persons reared in a culture saturated with biological assumptions find that pragmatism fits nicely into their pattern of preconceptions, critics who do not hold the same preconceptions claim that such pragmatists assume, in effect, the very point to be proved.

The hypothesis that all ideas are merely biological instruments which are more or less useful, but never certain, rules out all possibility of achieving certainty. Those who have faith that our desires for perfection in knowledge and certainty are satisfiable, feel, not without some reason, that pragmatists rudely frustrate this faith. The conviction that there is a realm of eternal Ideas, universals, or essences, has been instrumentally useful for centuries and continues to be so. Even on instrumentalist grounds, non-instrumentalist views are true, for it is only in the twentieth century that instrumentalism as a philosophy has emerged, whereas men have been getting instrumentally useful philosophical results for centuries. In other words, the instrumentalist himself must admit that other philosophies have worked longer and possibly better than instrumentalism itself.

Considering James and Dewey together, what is the pragmatic attitude toward naive realism?

1. Pragmatists recognize that many of our naive and unreflective ideas are true because they work successfully. The selective processes of biological struggle have favored the survival of those who are able to adapt themselves somewhat automatically and unreflectively. Naive realism is a very useful tool. Nevertheless, some problems cannot be dealt with unreflectively, and, when these problems arise, naive realism proves inadequate. Then we must experimentally seek some other epistemology which will be more adequate. Pragmatists accept realism as a useful doctrine. "That realities exist independently of their use as intellectual data, and that meanings exist apart from their utilization as hypotheses," [24] are permanent truths which we will continue to find useful, although the view that there are eternal unchangeable essences or Platonic Ideas is a fallacy. Since the truth of ideas depends upon their usefulness, the truth of realism continues to depend upon its remaining useful.

2, 3. Although objects have qualities which may have existed independent of our knowing them, objects and their qualities do not become objectives until they enter actively into a problematic situation —a situation wherein we are confronted with a problem, in which these objects, being useful in getting us out of a predicament, become

[24] *Ibid.*, p. 937.

significant. Since "no knowledge is ever merely immediate," [25] we can know no objects which are not also in some sense objectives, and all objectives are conditioned by their being goals relative to our aims. Thus, although objects do not acquire all their qualities by being known, they do acquire their character as objectives from our interest in them.

4. Whether or not "what seems obviously so is so," depends upon whether it works out in the way predicted. If something seems obviously so, and if nothing arises to challenge its seeming so, then it continues to work satisfactorily as so. But, whenever something arises to challenge such seeming, then, at that moment and on that account, it is no longer merely obviously so. Naive realism itself is accepted as true until the problem of error arises to challenge it. This challenge itself is what makes naive realism no longer tenable.

5. Objects are known directly at some times, and indirectly at others. "Knowledge by acquaintance" is direct, but sometimes we seem to have "knowledge about" objects not immediately present, to which we have to be led through other experiences with their other ideas.

6. Whether objects are public will depend upon whether they stand up under what we demand as a test of public knowledge. If, for example, I ask you to hand me a chair, and you do so, and I sit on it, I have satisfied myself that you knew what I was talking about, and since my assumption of such publicness creates in me no disturbing problems, I am satisfied. But if I ask you to look for the thousand dollars I dreamed of hiding in my dresser drawer last night, and you cannot find them, a problem is created. My faith that these dollars are public is shattered if I continue to have more faith in your apparent veracity than in the vividness of my recollected dream. Whether two people can see a public object exactly as it is will depend upon how much agreement they reach, and upon how much agreement is demanded by what they choose to mean by "exactly."

Other Pragmatists

The fact that there are many varieties of pragmatism may be taken either as a virtue—it is broad, tolerant, and adaptable—or as implying a vicious criticism—i.e., if pragmatism were a good theory, why should there be so much disagreement among pragmatists? Prag-

[25] *Ibid.*, p. 927.

matism's basic doctrine, that any view which works successfully is true while it works, has resulted in a welter of conflicting views among pragmatists, because they are able to find opposing views workable. Even during the first decade of the twentieth century, when pragmatism was still struggling to get started, an article appeared on "The Thirteen Pragmatisms." [26]   In the subsequent decades, the varieties of pragmatism proliferated into multitudes. Thus, pragmatism, in coming to serve as a support for everything, because every view which is held must be working while it is held, ends in meaning nothing very distinctive. Nowadays, almost every one is a pragmatist, regardless of what else he believes. Thus, when a person says he is a pragmatist, one cannot, from that alone, infer much about what he does believe.

However, since there are some fundamental differences between pragmatists, criticisms which apply to some may not apply to others. Dewey's social concerns made good a shortcoming in James. Schiller's version added a social criterion of truth which James' more individual emphases lacked. "Truth, then," says Schiller, "to be really safe, has to be more than individual evaluation; it has to win social recognition, to transform itself into common property." [27]   This feature of pragmatism is partly responsible for the common requirement of experimental scientists that an experiment is not considered reliable until it has been repeated by other persons. Truth continues to depend upon workability, but demands public workability. Charles Sanders Peirce carries this idea farther in holding that true ideas are those which are fated to be agreed upon by all who investigate. That is, not merely current and local agreement is required, but an agreement which will be reached after all who have investigated have turned in their evidence, so to speak. C. I. Lewis [28] rejects James' "verification theory" in favor of a "verifiability theory"; i.e., instead of saying that only those ideas which have been verified are true, Lewis holds that all ideas which either have been or could be verified are true. This view both admits unverified truths and yet defines truth in terms of verifiability. The foregoing illustrates some

[26] Arthur O. Lovejoy, "The Thirteen Pragmatisms," *The Journal of Philosophy,* Jan. 2, 1908, pp. 5–12, and Jan. 16, 1908, pp. 29–39.

[27] F. C. S. Schiller, *Humanism: Philosophical Essays,* p. 58.   The Macmillan Co., London, 1903.

[28] See his *Mind and the World Order.*   Charles Scribner's Sons, New York, 1929.

trends among pragmatists which, doubtless, will continue, until more specific names come to be found more significant.

Conclusion to Part I

The foregoing selection of typical epistemologies is intended as a sampling, not as a complete survey either of all of the kinds or of their varieties. Although much of the material presented may have been too difficult for full or easy comprehension, none of it could have been fairly omitted, once the aim of representing major types had been adopted. Perhaps a reminder, at this point, may be useful to readers who have felt increasing dismay at the complicated problems and perspectives involved in the attempt to answer the simple question: What is knowledge? The primary aim of an introductory text is not so much to provide a detailed acquaintance with the views treated (although this may be of considerable value in itself, inasmuch as all of the views treated are quite commonly referred to in current literature), as to have raised some questions, to have offered some suggestions, and to have helped the reader to begin his quest toward a satisfactory solution or, at least, to a less dogmatic attitude toward beliefs. Since, usually, a person's first step is to discover that "he knows not, and knows he knows not," if one's having grown to feel appallingly lost implies that he has become less dogmatic, a major achievement has been reached.

Perhaps, since the reader has a right to know where his author stands, some confession of position is in order. The writer has resisted the temptation, at this point, to include another chapter expressing his own viewpoint. Since it is not sufficiently different from some of the varieties of pragmatism to warrant presenting it as a special type for introductory purposes, only a few words seem advisable. His view is based upon a doctrine of organic relations, which becomes fully clear only after presentation of the writer's metaphysical views in Chapter 20. Nevertheless, it may be observed here that the writer accepts the implications of the egocentric predicament and faith in the existence and partial knowability of external realities. Hume, Kant, and Comte are correct in claiming that we cannot be certain of whatever may exist beyond experience. Yet, as James and Dewey have indicated, we are justified in holding beliefs about real things so long as they work. Therefore we may trust our "animal faiths" [29] in real things when they persistently appear "as if" [30] real. Subjects and objects depend upon each other, and yet may function independently. Appearances of real things remain both appearances and also apparently real. However, the Platonic and neo-realistic beliefs regarding independently subsisting Ideas or essences seem to have relatively little utility. Positivism, in most of its forms, subscribes to a rather useless, and even harmful, agnosticism based upon a too narrow conception of experience. Hegel's dialectic may be very useful when not handled by careless or biased minds. Throughout all, sensitive combinations of doubt and faith, tentativity and trust, wariness and willingness to risk oneself in experimental belief, persist as ideals.

The philosophical quest may be compared to shopping for a suit of clothes. Each of the different views which men have fashioned and offered for acceptance may be likened to intellectual suits which must be tried on, one after another, to see how well they fit before one makes a final selection from among those ready-made, or before one sets about making a pattern of one's own, combining the more suitable parts of each suit tried on. The writer prefers the experimental attitude because, even if one should find a suit that fits him perfectly at an early age, he may require several refittings as he grows taller or more portly in his intellectual dimensions, to say nothing of what concern he may have for his social fitness relative to changing fashions in intellectual styles.

Finally, a reminder may be helpful regarding the structure of this book. Although some philosophies have been selected here as representative primarily of either epistemological or metaphysical types, such selection is not intended to neglect the fact that all fully developed philosophies involve theories of both knowledge and reality and values. It should be obvious from Part I that epistemological problems and solutions hinge upon those in metaphysics. Parts II and III should reveal more clearly how metaphysical and axiological solutions depend upon those in epistemology. Some epistemological types may accompany many different metaphysical types. Pragmatism, for example, might lead a thinker to any one of the following metaphysical views. However, if a thinker holds one of the following views as primary, he might not be able to be a pragmatist. When-

[29] See George Santayana, *Scepticism and Animal Faith*. Charles Scribner's Sons, New York, 1923.

[30] See Hans Vaihinger, *The Philosophy of "As If*," Harcourt, Brace and Co., New York, 1924.

ever any outlook is taken as primary, either epistemological, metaphysical, or axiological, one's other views tend to adhere to it. Not only do epistemologies, such as agnosticism and positivism, place limits upon what is considered possible in metaphysics, but, in turn, as we shall see, metaphysical views, such as dualism, materialism, or spiritualism, imply limitations upon what kinds of knowledge are considered possible.

· 13 ·
Dualism

Metaphysics

Metaphysics is that science which has as its job the investigation of the nature of reality, or being, or existence. Although no completely satisfactory definition of metaphysics can be given—so the reader should reserve judgment about its meaning until he has at least been able to develop his own conception by studying the metaphysical views presented in this part of the text—nevertheless some additional [1] general remarks seem needed. Inasmuch as the terms being, existence, reality, etc., have somewhat different meanings in the contexts of various systems, no one of these terms can be taken as basic to all meanings of the term metaphysics.

Metaphysics is concerned with being, but also with nonbeing, with existence, but also with subsistence, with reality, but also with appearance. It is common to say that the metaphysician seeks to know ultimate reality, or the most real. The term real, although one of the most ambiguous of all philosophical terms,[2] continues to be commonly used. Especially important for introductory students is a recognition that this term has somewhat different uses in epistemology and metaphysics, for although in epistemology the real is usually considered independent of being known, in metaphysics the real is that which "most is" whether known or not. In some systems, these two meanings of the term merge, because that which is most real is also independent of knowledge, whereas in some other systems the most real being is the knowing experience itself and, thus, what is metaphysically real may be epistemologically subjective.

[1] See pp. 5, 105.
[2] Cf. William Gerber, *The Domain of Reality*, for a study of its meanings. King's Crown Press, New York, 1946.

Perhaps the simplest way to describe metaphysics is to say that it is concerned with the " 'stuff' out of which the world is made." [3] What ultimate substances, or kinds of substance, if any, exist, and what are their most ultimate characteristics? When investigation is focused upon the kinds of being, it may be called ontological, and when attention is paid primarily to the ultimate characteristics of being, it is often called cosmological.

René Descartes

According to Frenchman René Descartes (1596–1650), who, possibly more than any other man, set the course of modern metaphysics, the universe is composed of two distinct kinds of substance, namely, mental or spiritual substance, and material substance, or, more simply, spirit and matter. Meaning by "substance" anything which can stand by itself without depending upon anything else, or any "existent thing which requires nothing but itself in order to exist," [4] he held "that each substance has a principal attribute, and that the attribute of mind is thought, while that of body is extension." [5] That is, a mental being is essentially a thinking being, whereas a material being is essentially a spatial thing. "There is always one principal property of substance which constitutes its nature and essence, and on which all others depend. Thus extension in length, breadth and depth constitute the nature of corporeal substance; and thought constitutes the nature of thinking substance. For all else that may be attributed to body presupposes extension, and is but a mode of this extended thing; as everything that we find in mind is but so many diverse forms of thinking. Thus, for example, we cannot conceive figure but as an extended thing, nor movement but as in an extended space; so imagination, feeling, and will, only exist in a thinking thing." [6] Matter, then, can exist without depending upon mind or spirit, while spirits can exist also without depending upon bodies or matter. "The mind or soul of man is entirely different from the body," [7] i.e., ". . . is entirely and absolutely distinct

[3] G. T. W. Patrick, *Introduction to Philosophy*, revised edition, p. 181. Houghton Mifflin Co., Boston, 1935.
[4] Ralph M. Eaton, *Descartes, Selections*, p. 275. Charles Scribner's Sons, New York, 1927.
[5] *Ibid.*, p. 276.
[6] *Ibid.*
[7] *Ibid.*, p. 161.

from any body."[8]   Not only is there "a great difference between
mind and body, inasmuch as body is by nature divisible, and the
mind is entirely indivisible,"[9] but also "body is everything that mind
is not; mind is the absolute negation of everything that body is.   The
two substances entirely exclude each other, they are entirely opposed
to each other: body is absolutely soulless; the soul, absolutely im-
material."[10]

In expressing such an extreme view, Descartes was trying to give
a rational account of a view commonly held by Christians.   Descartes was himself raised as a Roman Catholic, was trained by Jesuits
until he was seventeen, and "won his place in the history of philosophy by attempting to harmonize the old scholasticism with the
new science. . . ."[11]   He "shows, on the one hand, all of the conservatism of a churchman of mediaeval times in his respect for institutional authority; on the other hand, his intellectual activity places
him among the leading scientists of the Renaissance."[12]   "All my
opinions," he says in one place, "are submitted to the authority of the
Church."[13]   "Although . . . his works were placed upon the *Index*
by Catholics, they created a profound impression on the theology,
science, and literature of the second half of the seventeenth century,"[14] and on modern thought since his time, not only in theology,
science, and literature, but on the popular religious views influenced
by them.   Probably many of the readers of these pages find themselves somewhat at home in Descartes' thought, somewhat familiar
with his reasoning, but also, as we shall try to show, somewhat perplexed as a consequence of sharing his predicaments.

Descartes' dualistic metaphysics grows naturally out of a distinction between mind and body which we all find necessary to make.
It "is favored by the grammatical structure of our language."[15]   The
terms mind and body occur in our language, in fact in all languages,
because they represent something different.   Certainly, a dualistic

[8] *Ibid.*, p. 152.
[9] *Ibid.*, p. 160.
[10] Alfred Weber, *History of Philosophy*, p. 251.   Charles Scribner's Sons, New
York, 1896, 1925.
[11] Herbert E. Cushman, *A Beginner's History of Philosophy*, Vol. II, p. 77.
Houghton Mifflin Co., Boston, 1911.
[12] *Ibid.*, p. 76.
[13] Eaton, *op. cit.*, p. 311.
[14] Cushman, *op. cit.*, p. 90.
[15] Durant Drake, *Invitation to Philosophy*, p. 349.   Houghton Mifflin Co.,
Boston, 1933.

metaphysics supports the distinction in ways in which other metaphysical views cannot. Many concepts have significance with reference to only one of these terms. For example, we do not speak of square yards of love, pounds of hope, or inches of thought. Nor do we say that stars love, atoms hope, or rocks think. Furthermore, errors, illusions, mirages, and imagination can be accounted for only if there is something non-material in which they occur. Memory of material things which have perished presupposes their existing in some nonmaterial kind of being. Dreams seem to involve experiencing things which do not exist materially. And death has long been accounted for by a spirit leaving the body, since a dead body seems different from a live person even when no material alteration is observable. Also, certain traditional religious beliefs, such as the hope and promise of life after death, seem warranted only if some non-physical or non-material substance remains when the body disintegrates. Men believe that God is just, and since it appears obvious that people differ in their rewards and punishments in this life, there must be another life in which justice is done. One will have to be conscious in order to recognize his rewards in another life, otherwise they would not be genuine. Therefore, there must be some conscious, thinking, knowing part of a person that lives on separately from his body, if not permanently, at least until his old body is resurrected or a new body somehow provided. Finally, attempts to reduce all spirit to matter, as materialists do, or all matter to spirit, as spiritualists do, fail to be satisfactory, as we shall see. Dualism, by accepting the equally ultimate existence of both matter and spirit, escapes many of the difficulties inherent in these views.

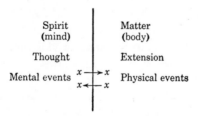

Criticisms

Advantageous as dualism may seem at first sight, it is shot through with perplexing inconsistencies. Despite Descartes' holding that spirit and matter are absolutely unlike, he holds also that they interact in a mind-body relationship. Physical events may cause mental events, as when a stubbed toe, or decaying tooth, or empty stomach produces in the mind a feeling of pain. On the other hand, mental events influence physical events, as when a desire to raise one's arm causes his arm to rise. In fact, "the soul is really joined to the whole body, and we cannot, properly speaking, say that it exists in any one of its parts to the exclusion of others, because it is one and in some manner indivisible. . . ."[16] But where does interaction take place? Not throughout the body, but only in some specialized place, namely, in the pineal gland. "Let us then conceive here that the soul has its principal seat in the little gland which exists in the middle of the brain, from whence it radiates forth through all the remainder of the body. . . ."[17] Although Descartes' guess was perhaps a shrewd one, and his attempt represents the kind of effort all dualists need make in order to account for interaction of mind and body, nevertheless, few are satisfied with his answer. Although mind and body are entirely unlike, the mind being non-spatial and body spatial, yet the mind has a location in space in the pineal gland and "is really joined to the whole body." How does the mind know when to be ready to respond to physical stimulus and why does it not respond to all of them? Why may not one body have two minds? How does the mind get caught in its body cavity in the first place and what happens when it is freed? How does it happen that one mind does not stimulate some other bodies? What about animals? Do they have souls? Descartes says No; we are not warranted in holding "that brutes can think."[18] But they have pineal glands. What is to prevent a soul from getting caught in the pineal gland of an animal since it is so much like that of persons? The foregoing perplexities, puzzling as they are, fade into insignificance, for metaphysicians, in the face of four other difficulties.

1. Descartes' interactionism involves a violation of the principle of the conservation of matter, which Descartes accepted. Matter, says Descartes, can be neither created nor destroyed, nor even increased or decreased in the slightest, for to increase is to create. In any cause-effect situation, there must be just as much in the cause as in the effect, and as much in the effect as in the cause. If there is more or less in effect than in cause, then matter has been either created or destroyed in some measure. But, when mind and matter interact,

---

[16] Eaton, *op. cit.*, p. 371.   [18] *Ibid.*, 355.
[17] *Ibid.*, p. 374.

if mental causes produce material effects, then the material effect is a product, not merely of material causes, but also partly of spiritual causes. Since, in interaction, spiritual causes affect the outcome, a material effect is produced partly by a spiritual, or non-material, cause. In this case, there is more matter in existence after than before. Or, when the reverse is true, i.e., when a bodily injury produces mental pain, part of the effect of a material cause is non-material, and, thus, some matter is destroyed. The law of the conservation of matter is violated by some matter escaping into mind or spirit whenever action of matter upon mind takes place.

Now, if it should occur to the reader, as it does to many, that what happens is not an increase or decrease of matter, but merely a transformation of material energy into spiritual energy, or vice versa, then he is substituting a monism of energy for a dualism of mind and matter; for if the same energy can take first a material form and then a spiritual form, it is one thing having two forms, not two different kinds of substance which are absolutely unlike in their nature, as Descartes held. If we are to hold to both an extreme dualism and at the same time to interactionism, then we have to conceive the mind as a causal agent of material events such as to make matter obey the laws of mind in following its orders as well as the laws of matter. Interactionism thus seems to involve a set of miracles, one each time the mind influences the body. If Descartes is to adhere strictly to his doctrine that there must be as much in an effect as in a cause, spiritual causes can have only spiritual effects and material causes only material effects. Or, if a material cause produces an effect in a mind, must there not be a material effect in that mind? No matter how the question is answered, there are difficulties.

2. An epistemological paradox is involved also. True ideas, according to Descartes, copy real things. Ideas about rectangular material table tops are true if they copy the rectangular spatial forms of those material tops. To copy is to be like. But Descartes asserted that mind and matter are entirely unlike. If mind and matter are entirely unlike, then no idea, which is mental, can be like a table top, which is material. If ideas cannot be like material things, then there can be no true ideas of such things. But since Descartes believes there are true ideas of material things, he is inconsistent again, and here again his theory breaks down.

3. There is a logical difficulty in his view if he draws out all the implications of his extreme dualism. If mind and matter are so unlike each other as to be completely independent, they are unrelated

to each other. For, if two things are joined by the same relation, they are like each other at least in sharing this same relation. It is precisely because they seem to be related in persons that the theory that they are two, and different, arises. Thus, they must be related. Furthermore, if it is claimed that they are related, they must be related by a relation which itself is either a material relation, or a mental relation, or neither. If it is a mental relation, how can it attach to the physical? If it is physical, how can it connect with the mental? If neither, then a third kind of being is needed to relate them, and again dualism breaks down logically.

4. What caused the two worlds of material and spiritual substance to exist in the first place? If there were two kinds of being, were they self-caused or caused by something else? If by something else, then by one, or by two? If by two, were there two first causes, two Gods? If by one, is this cause itself a material cause, or a spiritual cause, or neither, or both? If one answers both or neither, then ultimate dualism is given up. This is what Descartes did. He said there is one God, the creator, or creating substance, who is distinct from matter and spirit as created substances. Thus, ultimately, there are three substances (triplism), i.e., spirit, matter, and God, or only one (monism), i.e., God. This latter is what most dualists have been inclined to accept. A further consequence of Descartes' view was that, since there must be at least as much in the cause as in the effect, God, as cause of both spirit and matter, must be at least both spiritual and material. If the material and the mental exist together in God, then they are, ultimately, one, and not two. In any case, Descartes ended with God as the one and only substance and so, in effect, refuted his own dualism.

Parallelism

Dualistic followers of Descartes, who sought to rescue dualism from the maze of inconsistencies involved in his interactionism, were much more successful, logically and theologically, in substituting "parallelism" for "interactionism" as an explanation of mind-body relationships. Arnold Guelincx (1625–1699) and many others [19] found a solution much more consistent with traditional theology. If, as Descartes held, God is the cause of everything, then he is the cause

[19] Cf. Frank Thilly, *A History of Philosophy*, pp. 288–289. Henry Holt and Co., New York, 1914.

of both mind and matter. But if God is all-powerful, i.e., if whatever God wills will be done, then God could destroy or change or stop anything. Since he is all-knowing, he knows before an event happens that it is going to happen. Therefore, if he wanted it not to happen, he could prevent its happening. In effect, then, whatever happens, God wills it to happen. If this is so, God is not only the original creator of mind and matter, but is also the continuing creator of each mental event and each material event. If God is the actual cause of all events, why is there any need for mental events to cause material events or of material events to cause mental events? What need is there for interaction between mind and body when God is the constant cause of both? The hypothesis of interaction is superfluous and, since it results in a multitude of contradictions, why not give it up?

Parallelists claim that when a mental event, such as a desire to raise an arm, occurs (and God wills it to occur since he knows about it and can, but does not, stop it), it is sometimes accompanied by the rising of my arm (which God also wills to occur). The desire and the rising accompany each other, but they do not cause each other, for God is the cause of everything. Instead, the desire is the occasion (this kind of parallelism is sometimes called "occasionalism") for God to cause my arm to rise. "God knows what I am going to will, although my will is free; and the entire universe has been arranged in accordance with that knowledge. God in his infinite wisdom has instituted laws of motion, so that a movement which is entirely independent of my will and power coincided with my free volition."[20]

Criticisms

Parallelism, too, gives up dualism, in effect, for although mind and matter are still kept independent of each other, even completely uninfluenced by each other, both are not only originally but constantly and continuously dependent on the will of the One God who is the only ultimate reality.

Furthermore, it allows the mind no true causal power. For, although it insists that the mind has free will, is free to cause, it denies that it has any power not already bestowed upon it by something upon which it is dependent. A mind can do nothing of itself, can make no real difference in the world, is fatalistically determined in all

[20] *Ibid.*

it does. The material world, likewise, has no influence upon mental events. Mind is "useless in biological evolution." [21] If matter is but a functionless accompaniment of God's causing ideas in minds, it seems more reasonable to discard matter altogether, as Berkeley did.[22]

No matter how flawlessly this view fits into perfectionistic theologies, it does not really satisfy the ordinary man. The reason dualism arose in the first place was that our everyday experiences give rise to the distinction between a mind and a body which act upon each other. Thus, parallelism is not a satisfactory solution to the original problem, in the light of common sense. It adds what many will consider an absurdity: God's intervening knowingly and specifically on each petty occasion.

Finally, the supposed parallelism between mind and body, or between mental and physical events, is incomplete. Not all mental events have their physical correlates (such as dreams, imaginings, errors), and not all physical events have mental companions (not everything that happens in our body or even in our brains appears in consciousness). Why sometimes and sometimes not? These rationalistic occasionalists were embarrassed by having no rational explanation, and they hardly wished to leave the matter to whimsicalness of God. Although parallelism once had considerable vogue, it has largely passed from favor as a satisfactory metaphysical outlook.

[21] G. Watts Cunningham, *Problems of Philosopy*, p. 296. Henry Holt and Co., New York, 1924.
[22] See Ch. 4.

·14·
Neutral
Monism

Benedict Spinoza (1632–1677), a Dutch Jew who was excommunicated from his synagogue on charges of atheism, shared Descartes' faith that men can, through reason, discover the truth about existence. But, like the occasionalists, he rejected Descartes' interactionism and drew, more logically, the conclusions implied in assuming that God is the only ultimate substance. Upon examining more precisely what we mean by substance, Spinoza concluded that if a substance is really something that stands by itself, is independent of all else, then there can be only one such substance. For if there were two, they would depend upon each other for their relations to each other. Thus, if there were two or more things which were dependent upon each other, they would not be true substances.

Therefore, if there is any substance at all, there can be but one. "If substance is that which needs nothing other than itself to exist . . . , if God is *the* substance and everything else dependent on him, then, obviously, there can be no substance outside of God. Then thought and extension cannot be attributes of separate subsubstances, but are merged . . . in God; they are attributes of one single independent cause and bearer of all qualities and events, the one principle in which all things find their being. He is the one thinking and extended substance—the dualism of substance disappears, but the dualism of attributes remains. There can be no interaction between the two attributes, between mental and physical processes; the two series are parallel to each other and never intersect. And wherever there are mental processes, there must be physical processes and vice versa."[1]

[1] Frank Thilly, *A History of Philosophy*, p. 293. Henry Holt and Co., New York, 1914.

Spinoza explains the mind-body relationship somewhat as the occasionalists did, by holding that "these attributes are absolutely independent of one another and cannot influence each other; mind cannot produce changes in body nor body changes in mind. When two things have nothing in common with one another, the one cannot be the cause of the other; for since the effect would contain nothing that belonged to the cause, everything in effect would be a creation out of nothing." [2] But these two attributes or aspects are, nevertheless, attributes or aspects of the same underlying substance. Both express it. Or, it expresses itself through them.

The way in which substance manifests itself through its attributes may be likened to the way in which a pencil which is both yellow and shiny manifests these qualities. The yellowness does not cause the shininess and the shininess does not cause the yellowness, but, rather, both are caused by the substance of the pencil which, in itself, is neither yellow nor shiny, and yet, since it is manifest as both yellow and shiny, is both. Again, substance and its attributes may be compared with a meaning which is expressed in two or more languages. Two words, in different languages, may be entirely different in their structure, spelling, pronunciation, and linguistic context, and yet may express exactly the same meaning.

So God, the one and only substance, expresses itself through its attributes and modes (like languages and their words). Since God is completely independent, he is infinite, for if he were finite or limited there would have to be some other substance which limited him. But since there is only one substance and no other, this one must be infinite. Being infinite, it expresses itself in an infinite number of ways. That is, it has an infinite number of attributes, of which the mental attribute and the material attribute are but two. God expresses himself not in just two languages, but in an infinite number of them. He himself is not a language, but is what these languages express. That is, God, or substance, is neither merely material in nature, nor merely mental in nature, but is neutral, as between these two attributes or aspects. The one substance is a neutral substance (hence the view is called "neutral monism"), which manifests itself equally as matter and as mind and also in an infinite number of other ways. God is not caused by, or influenced by, what happens in any particular mind or particular material thing. Rather, God is the cause of all. God is self-determined or self-caused or is a *causa*

[2] *Ibid.*, p. 297.

sui. In this sense God alone is completely free. Freedom consists in being self-caused, not in being uncaused. If one is caused from the outside, by something else, especially if he is dependent upon this something else, then he is unfree. For man, there is no genuine free will. In both mind and matter, all is determined, mind by reason, matter by mechanical law. Since mind and matter are entirely different kinds of attributes, will cannot cause bodily movement nor can hunger influence desire for food. For, if both are independent expressions of an underlying substance, each is simultaneously determined by this underlying cause.

How is Nature related to God? For Spinoza, the two are one. There can be only one substance, so whatever we call Nature and whatever we call God are the same substance. Undoubtedly Spinoza's beliefs, that there is nothing in God which is not also in Nature and that God's, or Nature's, products were necessary and impersonal, rather than by God's personal choice, were responsible for his expulsion from his synagogue. The fight that has prevailed in the history of both Jewish and Christian thought, regarding whether God is a person with undetermined choices or a magnificent automaton which does merely what it has to do according to its own nature, has been long and bitter. Spinoza's faith in reason, as against revelation, led him to seek a completely rational explanation. Reason itself is deterministic, logical, demanding, necessary. No personal whim is permitted in strict deduction. Spinoza, using "the geometrical method," beginning with self-evident axioms, some definitions, then using deductive procedures, and not stopping until he reached Q.E.D., sought to establish a more completely reasonable faith. This he did, perhaps more successfully than any other thinker. But, alas, there is more to life than logic, more to experience than reason, more to happiness than an "intellectual love of God." [3]

Nevertheless, Spinoza's pantheistic conception is one of the grandest, most magnificent, of all time. The same man who was rejected as atheistic by his local synagogue has been eulogized time and again by historians as "the God-intoxicated man." [4] God, for Spinoza, is an eternally perfect, rationally complete, mathematically exact, system. "The ultimate structure of the world, from which all events flow by geometrical necessity, is God. God is absolutely in-

[3] John Wild, *Spinoza, Selections,* p. 390. Charles Scribner's Sons, New York, 1930.

[4] Arthur K. Rogers, *A Student's History of Philosophy,* third edition, p. 255. The Macmillan Co., New York, 1932.

finite and absolutely perfect, but his perfection is, of course, not that
of an ideal personality. It refers rather to the completeness of his
power and the unqualified rigor with which all that happens is determined by his nature; it is mathematical, not moral, perfection." [5]
Human beings, too, are eternal, not as separate and independent substances who will some day dwell near God, but as parts of his rational
nature which is inherently eternal. "When knowing truly, the human
mind transcends its otherwise hampering finitude; it apprehends its
objects under the form of eternity." [6] In knowing truth, which is
eternal, we participate directly in the eternal. In this sense, we are
eternal now, if we know the truth. Since all things, including ourselves, are parts of God, our "knowledge is a part of God's knowledge
of himself, which is not subject to change or destruction. And the
love of God, since it arises from true knowledge and depends solely
upon it, cannot be transitory emotion but is likewise eternal." [7] "He
who clearly and distinctly understands himself . . . loves God, and
loves him better the better he understands himself . . ." [8] and "the
more we understand individual objects the more we understand
God." [9] The more we realize our dependence upon God, the more
we love God without wanting that "God should love us in return," [10]
for our welfare depends upon his nature because our nature is part
of his nature. We depend upon him, as attributes on a substance,
not he upon us, for a substance does not depend on anything.

Spinoza succeeded in drawing out the logical conclusions of a theology presupposing a completely rational universe. He solved the
mind-body problem without the maze of contradictions left by Descartes. In conceiving God as supremely rational, he freed God from
the whimsical imperfections of more anthropomorphic conceptions,
and his many insights have stimulated the imaginations of multitudes
of subsequent thinkers.

Criticisms

But Spinoza did too good a job. He overdid the logical and rational aspects of both theology and everyday life. In identifying

[5] Edwin A. Burtt, *Types of Religious Philosophy*, pp. 190–191. Harper &
Bros., New York, 1939.
[6] *Ibid.*, p. 191.
[7] *Ibid.*
[8] Wild, *op. cit.*, p. 379.
[9] *Ibid.*, p. 385.
[10] *Ibid.*, p. 380.

God with Nature, he involved himself in the "pantheistic heresy" which both Jewish and Christian orthodoxy fought persistently. If God is everything, he is both cause and effect, both premise and con- clusion, both determiner of everything (within himself) and com- pletely self-determined. But this leaves man merely a determined part with no genuine individuality, no true freedom of will, no possi- bility of sinning. Religion traditionally has sought to save man from sin; Spinoza, on the contrary, sees man not as sinful, but as merely ignorant as a consequence of his finite nature.

Traditionally, religion has revealed that God saves men by grace, by his living personal interest in them, but for Spinoza, God, the neu- tral substance, cannot love except through the attribute, mind, which expresses emotions. When he does this, he loves through men, rather than loves men. Spinoza's doctrine that "God loves himself with an infinite intellectual love" [11] does not set well with those who prefer to picture God as completely unselfish. Spinoza does not mean to interpret God as selfish, but he is merely drawing out the logical con- sequences of the view that if there is only one substance, only one thing that is completely independent, and if this is God, then there is nothing besides God for God to love. God cannot love himself directly but only through the love which men, who are parts of him, have for him. Of course, each man, in loving God, is, in a sense, lov- ing himself, for each man is nothing apart from God. While all this is reasonable, most people, including most theologians, prefer to be less reasonable.

In rejecting dualism, Spinoza irritated our natural preferences for believing that our minds and our bodies are not only different sub- stantially but that they interact with each other. We dislike his con- clusion that matter is insubstantial and that mind is ineffective. We do not like to be considered merely bits of the universal logic come to consciousness. We feel that we have some genuine freedom of choice and that we can be effective in the world. His interpretation of all causation as consisting merely in logical implication leaves us uncomfortable. His view that "thought and being are identical" [12] gives us no satisfactory account of errors, illusions, dreams. He de- nies that there can be any genuine novelty in the world, for it is in- herently rationally perfect, and thus allows no possibility for evolu- tion. Finally, although he claimed that substance is neutral, as be- tween mind and matter, he interpreted substance as being inherently

[11] *Ibid.*, p. 391.
[12] Thilly, *op. cit.*, p. 294.

rational, and thus thoroughly mental. Spiritualists have done a more satisfactory job of accounting for existence, for there is more to the spiritual than the rational, more to the life of spirit than deductive necessity.

Spinoza leaves us wondering why men can span two independent attributes, mind and matter, but no more of the infinite number of them. It stretches our credulity to believe that, if we can participate in two absolutely different attributes which parallel each other but do not interact, we are unable to have the least inkling of the other attributes which are also inherent in our underlying nature. Finally, it is difficult for us to understand how we can be eternal now through knowing truth.

· 15 ·

Spiritualism

The view that existence is mind or spirit, or like mind or spirit, goes under many names: mentalism, idealism, psychical monism, panpsychism, spiritualism, and others. Probably the most commonly used term is spiritualism. The terms "mental," "spiritual," "psychical," and "ideal" are often used interchangeably, although in some specific contexts sharp distinctions may be made. Also, different spiritualists disagree about details in interpreting the nature of mind or spirit. Some emphasize it as primarily rational, others as mainly emotional or voluntaristic; some as deterministic, others as free; some as an ultimate unity, others as a multiplicity of "Ideas"; some as eternal, fixed, unchanging, others as purposive, growing, developing; some as inherently valuable or as intrinsic value, others as beyond value. There are so many outstanding idealists that it is difficult to pick one or two to represent them. However, they fall into two general groups, those holding that there are many different minds, and those believing that there can be but a single mind or mental system.

1. The former, who may be called "pluralistic spiritualists," we have already met [1] in the philosophy of George Berkeley, who held, as a good idealist, that "to be is to be perceived" or "to be is to be a perceiver." Minds and their ideas are all that exist. Matter is nothing but an idea, for ideas of material things are ideas, and, since ideas are caused in minds by minds, there is no need for the useless hypothesis of material substances to cause them. Berkeley refuted both Locke and Descartes and the occasionalists by pointing out that if God causes everything which our minds do not cause, and if he does so directly, the supposition of an extra intermediary, matter, is superfluous. No matter really exists.

[1] See Ch. 4.

One of the earliest of modern idealists, G. W. Leibniz (1647–1716), is usually interpreted as a pluralistic idealist because he held that existence consists of monads, or simple substances. "These monads are the real atoms of nature and, in a word, the elements of things." [2] "Each monad must be different from every other. For in nature there are never two beings which are perfectly alike. . . ." [3] "If we give the name soul to everything which has perceptions and desires . . . then all simple substances or created monads might be called souls; but . . . the name of souls should be given only to those in which perception is more distinct, and is accompanied by memory." [4] "Nothing but this (namely, perceptions and their changes) can be found in a simple substance." [5] However, "God alone is the primary unity or original simple substance, of which all created or derivative monads are products and have their birth, so to speak, through continual fulgurations of the divinity from moment to moment, limited by the receptivity of the created being, of whose essence it is to have limits." [6] "Although each created monad represents the whole universe," [7] from its particular point of view which is different from every other point of view and which, thus, is definitely individualistic, it can cause nothing outside itself. Seen from the inside, it is spiritual. Seen from the outside, it is material. When one person sees another, he sees him as a material body. But he experiences himself as spiritual, unless he also looks at himself from the outside, so to speak, as when he looks at his hand. So it is with all monads, each being spiritual in itself, but appearing as material from external points of view. Thus matter does not really exist but is merely the external appearance of what is actually spiritual.

Leibniz held that monads in no way influence each other, but each develops its own internal history in such a way that what happens within it corresponds exactly with the way it is seen from without, because this monad, and the views of it which other monads have of it, develop in accordance with a "pre-established harmony" which God, the Monad of monads, introduced of rational necessity in the beginning. "The soul follows its own laws, and the body likewise

[2] G. W. Leibniz, *The Monadology*, paragraph 3. Quoted in Robert Latta, *Leibniz, The Monadology and Other Philosophical Writings*, p. 218. Oxford University Press, London, 1898.

[3] *Ibid.*, par. 9 (Latta, p. 222).   [6] *Ibid.*, par. 48 (Latta, pp. 243–244).
[4] *Ibid.*, par. 19 (Latta, p. 230).   [7] *Ibid.*, par. 63 (Latta, p. 253).
[5] *Ibid.*, par. 17 (Latta, p. 228).

follows its own laws; and they agree with each other in virtue of the pre-established harmony between all substances, since they are all representations of one and the same universe." [8] Although we cannot elaborate on Leibniz' outlook here, he is recognized as having some acute insights and as important in influencing the course of idealistic speculation. He was not, strictly speaking, a pluralist, for all created monads cooperate of necessity in one harmonious system determined by the Monad of monads. But pluralistic spiritualists seem to have taken considerable comfort from his views.

In America, a widespread movement called "personalism" has been represented by Bordon P. Bowne (1847–1910), George H. Howison (1834–1916), Alfred C. Knudson (1873–   ), Ralph Tyler Flewelling (1871–   ), Edgar S. Brightman (1884–   ), and many others. In Philadelphia in 1940 a group of personalists organized themselves together as a movement and adopted a platform with twenty-two principles.[9] They hold that "a person is (or many persons are) the supreme reality; i.e., the highest in value and dominant in power. . . . The realm of nature (including the human body) is the phenomenal product of the energizing of God's will, thus having no independent existence. The metaphysical basis of all the laws of nature is the orderliness of God's volition. . . . The interaction of created selves does not consist in direct causal effects on each other, but only on God through whom they work. . . . The only causality experienced is the act of willing." [10] Flewelling says "that reality is in some sense personal; that there are only persons and what they create; that personality is self-conscious and self-directive both in finite individuals and in a supreme creative Intelligence which is the world-ground and source of all reality." [11] Since many chairs of philosophy in Methodist colleges, universities (e.g., Boston University, University of Southern California), and theological schools have been, and are, occupied by personalists, some have come to think of it as the official philosophy of the Methodist Church. However, the Methodist Church has no officially adopted metaphysics, as such, and personalists compete with humanists and neo-orthodoxists at present for followers among theological students.

[8] *Ibid.*, par. 78 (Latta, p. 262).

[9] Cf. W. H. Werkmeister, A *History of Philosophical Ideas in America*, pp. 326–329. The Ronald Press, New York, 1949. Werkmeister devotes Chs. 7, 8, and 15 to personalism.

[10] *Ibid.*

[11] In D. D. Runes, *Twentieth Century Philosophy*, p. 324. Philosophical Library, Inc., New York, 1943.

2. The latter, those who hold that all existence is comprehended in a single mind or mental system, often are called Absolute Idealists. In addition to Hegel,[12] Johann Gottlieb Fichte (1762–1814), Friedrich Wilhelm Schelling (1775–1854), Arthur Schopenhauer (1788–1860), and E. Von Hartmann (1842–1906) represent German idealists; Thomas Hill Green (1836–1882), F. H. Bradley (1846–1924), and Bernard Bosanquet (1848–1923), British idealists; and Josiah Royce (1855–1916), G. W. Cunningham (1881–   ), and Brand Blanshard (1892–   ), American idealists. Many other American idealists of varying shades of conviction regarding whether one or many minds predominate include: Ralph Waldo Emerson, James Ward, Mary Whiton Calkins, C. A. Strong, R. M. Wenley, J. W. Creighton, Hartley Burr Alexander, Herbert Wildon Carr, Wm. E. Hocking, Durant Drake, DeWitt H. Parker, and Gustav Mueller.

An example of spiritualistic doctrine expressed in the writings of a popular religion, "The Church of Christ, Scientist," or simply "Christian Scientists," is found in Mary Baker Eddy's *Science and Health with a Key to the Scriptures.* "In the material world, thought has brought to light with great rapidity many useful wonders. With like activity have thought's swift pinions been rising towards the realm of the real, to the spiritual cause of those lower things which give impulse to inquiry. Belief in a material basis, from which may be deduced all rationality, is slowly yielding to the idea of a metaphysical basis, looking away from matter to Mind as the cause of every effect. Materialistic hypotheses challenge metaphysics to meet in final combat. In this revolutionary period, like the shepherd-boy with his sling, woman [Mrs. Eddy?] goes forth to battle with Goliath. In this final struggle for supremacy, semi-metaphysical systems [i.e., dualisms] afford no substantial aid to scientific metaphysics, for their arguments are based on the false testimony of the material senses as well as on the facts of Mind. . . . From first to last the supposed coexistence of Mind and matter and the mingling of good and evil have resulted from the philosophy of the serpent. Jesus' demonstrations sift the chaff from the wheat, and unfold the unity and the reality of good, the unreality, the nothingness, of evil. . . . The categories of metaphysics rest on only one basis, the divine Mind. Metaphysics resolves things into thoughts, and exchanges the objects of sense for the ideas of Soul. These ideas are perfectly real and tangible to spiritual consciousness, and they have this advantage over the

[12] See Ch. 7.

objects and thoughts of material sense,—they are good and eternal. . . . The theories I combat are these: (1) that all is matter; (2) that matter originates in Mind, and is as real as Mind, possessing intelligence and life. The first theory, that matter is everything, is quite as reasonable as the second, that Mind and matter coexist and cooperate. Only one of the following can be true: (1) that everything is matter; (2) that everything is Mind. . . . If one is real, the other must be unreal. Only by understanding that there is but one power, not two powers, matter and Mind, are scientific and logical conclusions reached." [13]

Although the advantages and difficulties of each variety of spiritualism vary somewhat, we shall try to summarize them in a general way for all spiritualistic systems. Spiritualists have an initial and basic advantage over materialists because they begin with something certain, indubitable, immediate. Each person, no matter what else he believes, must believe that his own experience or consciousness exists. The existence of the thinking mind seems necessarily presupposed in each thought, including the thought of anyone who thinks there is no mind. Even though everything else be dubitable, one cannot doubt that he doubts. Although recognition of this fact does not thereby prove that the whole universe is mental or spiritual, and nothing besides mental or spiritual, it does prove conclusively that mind or consciousness does exist. It does not prove that it is the ultimate existence, but it does prove its existence. "Since physics can tell us nothing about the inner nature of what exists, we may be thankful if our awareness of our own inner life gives us a clue, however vague, to the inner nature of the world stuff out of which we were born, and of whose very substance we are." [14]

Proof that reality is at least partly mental leads to the next step, the attempt to prove that all reality is mental. If we distinguish between what we experience and what is beyond our experience, and if what we experience is mental or spiritual, then which is the more probable hypothesis: to suppose that the world which we do not experience is unlike what we experience, or like what we experience? Is it not more reasonable to suppose that the world which we do not know is like that which we know? What basis could we have for

[13] Mary Baker Eddy, *Science and Health with a Key to the Scriptures,* Ch. X. Trustees under the Will of Mary Baker G. Eddy, Boston, 1875, 1925.

[14] Durant Drake, *Invitation to Philosophy,* p. 383. Houghton Mifflin Co., Boston, 1933.

supposing that it is unlike, when all of our guesses must themselves be mental? "Our mental life is the nearest bit of reality to us, the only portion of reality that we know at close range. Is it not plausible to suppose that the rest of reality, which we know only at arm's length, as it were, is homogeneous with this bit we know so intimately?" [15] If anyone assumes the principle of the uniformity of nature, and if the part we are acquainted with is mental, then should not the rest of it, uniformly, be mental also?

Spiritualism escapes all of the logical difficulties involved in dualism in its interactionistic form and succeeds better in providing some ultimate unity than does either occasionalism or neutral monism. Since matter is accounted for as consisting simply of those ideas or parts of mind which are ideas-of-matter, the origin of matter is explained quite simply: ideas-of-matter originate in mind just as other ideas do. Whereas dualism sets for itself the task of reconciling irreconcilables, spiritualism begins and ends without this handicap.

Spiritualism also escapes the shortcomings of materialism. Materialists, as we shall see, have difficulty in explaining how mind can arise in a purely mechanical world; but spiritualists, in taking mind as basic, not only can account for the conservation of matter in terms of the eternality of mind and its ideas, but also provides more reasonable explanations of our ideals. Beauty, for example, is as real as matter or numbers, for both have their origin, their existence, and their end, within mind or spirit. Our romantic nature, including the values of love, faith, desire, purpose, goals, etc., is accounted for. We can believe that justice, rightness, duties, etc., are not merely illusions in a world of mechanical atoms but are spiritual realities. Spiritualism justifies man's belief that he is worth something because his kind of being is the center of reality, whereas the materialist must hold that man is nothing but an insignificant speck of cosmic dust that glimmers for, at most, part of a century and then puffs out into nothingness. God, as spiritual, is natural to spiritualism; doubts about God's existence trouble us less, therefore, if we begin with spiritualism. Spiritualism permits man to feel at home in nature. The whole universe is something like ourselves. Since its nature is akin to ours, we can feel justified in our pursuit of values. Spiritualism provides a healthier, more hopeful outlook, by supplying motivations concerning the worth-whileness of living.

[15] *Ibid.,* p. 385.

Criticisms

However, spiritualism overtaxes our common sense. "It strains our credulity to think of sticks and stones and dirt and the ocean as 'psychic' in nature."[16] When we are ill, we doctor our bodies, not our minds. When we have a broken leg, diphtheria, or a toothache, we go to a physician, not to a psychiatrist.

Spiritualism is unscientific, at least as most scientists see things today. Scientists seem to be dealing with real things, not with mere ideas. They investigate atoms, chemicals, diseases, planets, etc. These certainly do not seem to them to be merely mental. It is not customary, in physics laboratories, either to look for spirits or to call upon some greater spirit to provide some spiritual solution. The objective scientist seeks to know the laws of nature, not the laws of his mind. He wants to discover regularities, uniformities, structural relationships, and his success, so far, satisfies him that he is on the right track.

The evidence for dualism still stands. Our common-sense beliefs in the difference between our minds and bodies do not easily respond to the proposal that our bodies are illusions. "The brain acts mechanically by pushes from behind, as it were. The mind acts teleologically, by foresight of future consequences."[17] Spiritualism is impractical, for the theory that material bodies exist, both our own and those of real tables, works better in actual practice.

The idealistic argument, that it is more plausible to believe that the unexperienced world is like, rather than unlike, experience, is, at best, a matter of plausibility, not of absolute proof. Once this mere plausibility is accepted, then spiritualists proceed as if there were no further doubt. But, after all, is it not more plausible to argue that what we do not experience is not like what we experience, or that what is unexperienced is unlike experience? It is only on the assumption of the uniformity of nature that this argument is plausible, and this argument is usually associated with materialistic contentions.

Finally, spiritualists disagree among themselves almost hopelessly concerning what, precisely, constitutes spirit. Not only are they

---

[16] *Ibid.*, p. 388.
[17] *Ibid.*, pp. 388–389.

divided into pluralists and absolutists, but they disagree as to whether spirit is essentially rational or irrational, free or predestined, fixed or growing, temporal or eternal, causative by will or by logical implication, merely good, both good and evil, or beyond good and evil. They differ, too, in the ways in which they accept the conclusions of contemporary sciences as influencing both their basic presuppositions and their explanations of particular phenomena.

· 16 ·

Materialism

Materialism may be stated simply: All is matter. In direct contrast to spiritualism, which holds that all is spirit, materialism denies any substantial existence to spirit or mind. Whatever exists is material in nature and is composed, ultimately, of material particles which alone can stand by themselves. All else is composed of these particles and depends upon them for continuing to exist. If matter is all, what, then, is matter, and what is a particle? The history of materialism [1] is long and complicated. We can do little more than summarize two examples of materialism.

1. Democritus (c. 460–370 B.C.) and his teacher, Leucippus, are given credit by historians as being the earliest Greek thinkers to formulate clearly the view that existence consists of an infinite multiplicity of indivisible or uncutable particles, or atoms (the Greek term "atomos" means indivisible). Democritus "affirms the homogeneity of all bodies; . . . he conceives this indeterminate matter as divided into an infinite number of infinitely small molecules, which come together and separate. In that way bodies are formed and destroyed. These molecules are infinite in number and indivisible, without, however, being mathematical points, for an unextended thing would be nothing. They are identical in chemical quality, but differ in size and form. They are endowed with perpetual motion, which they do not receive from a transcendent principle, but which belongs to their essence. The force which moves them acts according to necessity, and not according to design and purpose. Democritus rejects all teleology, but denies chance also. . . . Nothing in nature happens without a cause; all things have their reason and necessity. . . . The perpetual motion produces a whirling movement among the atoms, in consequence of which they

[1] Cf. Frederick A. Lange, *The History of Materialism.* Houghton Mifflin Co., Boston, 1879–1882.

are combined according to their external affinities,—that is, according
to size and form; for since they are all chemically the same, they
neither attract nor repel each other. The heaviest atoms naturally
move downward in infinite space, while the lightest form the atmosphere. Some atoms have uneven, rough, sharp, or hooked surfaces.
These catch hold of each other and form acid or bitter substances;
while atoms with smooth surfaces form substances which impress
the senses agreeably. The soul consists of the finest, smoothest, and
therefore most nimble atoms. When such atoms exist in isolation,
or are mixed together in small quantities, the soul-atoms are in-
sensible; when they are joined together in larger masses, they acquire the faculty of sensation. They are scattered over the entire
body, but gathered together more numerously in the sense-organs,
where sensation is produced; in the brain, the seat of thought; in
the heart, the seat of the affections; and in the liver, the seat of
desire. Sensation and perception are explained as follows: Efflu-
ences go forth from all bodies and enter our organs of sense, where
they excite sensation, and the brain, where they produce ideas or
images of things. Sensation is the only source of knowledge, and
there is nothing in thought that has not passed through the channel
of the senses. Our ideas represent our impressions, that is, the relations existing between ourselves and the external world; they are
not direct reproductions of the objects themselves, the inner essence
of which is concealed from us. We are conscious so long as the
soul-atoms remain intact in the body; sleep ensues, and with it loss
of consciousness, when a certain number of atoms escape; when
nearly all of them escape, and but a few remain, we fall into a state
of seeming death; and, finally, when all the psychical atoms are
separated from the body at once, we die. Death cannot destroy
these atoms, because the atom is indivisible and therefore inde-
structible; it destroys their temporary union in a body, and, consequently, the individuality formed by such a union. Since feeling
does not belong to isolated atoms, but is produced only by a combination of atoms in the brain and other organs, death puts an end
to feeling and destroys the personality. The gods are more powerful beings than man, but their immortality is not absolute. Since
they are composed of atoms, like mortals, they eventually succumb
to the common fate of all, though they may live longer than human
beings." [2]

[2] Alfred Weber, *History of Philosophy*, pp. 36–38. Charles Scribner's Sons,
New York, 1896, 1925.

This view, that matter consists of hard, supposedly inert particles which are indivisible, uncuttable, irreducible, unpurposive, obedient to mechanical laws, and moving about in space, continued largely unchanged down to the modern period. After Socrates, Plato, and Aristotle had done their antimaterialistic thinking, Epicurus (341–270 B.C.) revived materialism. Lucretius, the Roman poet, adopted it. In England, Thomas Hobbes (1588–1697), in France, J. O. La-Mettrie (1709–1751), Denis Diderot (1713–1784), Baron P. d'Hol-bach (1723–1789), and Cabanis (1757–1808), and in Germany, Karl Vogt (1817–1895), J. Moleschott (1822–1893), L. Buchner (1824–1899), and Ernst Haeckel (1834–1919), expounded it. However, to Isaac Newton (1642–1727) goes the credit for giving to material-ism its classical formulation. "The Newtonian system, stated with schematic simplicity, . . . is as follows. There is an absolute space, composed of points, and an absolute time, composed of instants; there are particles of matter, each of which persists through all time and occupies a point at each instant. Each particle exerts forces on other particles, the effect of which is to produce accelerations. Each particle is associated with a certain quantity, its 'mass,' which is in-versely proportional to the acceleration produced in the particle by a given force. The laws of physics are conceived, on the analogy of the law of gravitation, as formulae giving the force exerted by one particle on another in a given relative situation. This system is logically faultless." [3]

However, logical flawlessness and empirical adequacy are two different things. Increasingly the Newtonian system has been found wanting. "It was criticized on the ground that absolute space and time are meaningless, and on the ground that action at a distance was inconceivable. This latter objection was sanctioned by New-ton, who was not a strict Newtonian." [4] As scientific investigations gradually revised our conceptions of matter, materialists have had to change their views of the nature of the ultimate particles. Al-though modern chemists adopted the old Greek term "atom" because they believed that they had, at last, found the ultimate indivisible particles, atoms have since been broken down into electrons, protons, and neutrons; with positrons, nutrinos, positrinos, mesons, and other elements, entering into the picture. The result is a quite different

[3] Bertrand Russell, *The Analysis of Matter,* pp. 13–14. Harcourt, Brace and Co., New York, 1927.
[4] *Ibid.*, p. 14.

conception of matter and, consequently, of what materialism stands for.

2. Gradually, especially since the middle of the nineteenth century, Newtonian ideals of absolute space, with its three static dimensions, and absolute time, with its single direction or dimension, have given way to a more complicated dynamic concept of a four-dimensional space-time continuum. The supposed mass of inert particles has been discovered to be dynamic. "Mass is found to be energy, and energy is found to have mass. Hence the old laws of the conservation of mass and the conservation of energy are transformed into one law of the conservation of mass-energy." [5] Matter becomes "mattergy." Energy is not something to be located merely at or within a body, but is conceived, like gravitational forces, as constituting a field surrounding a body or as between it and other bodies. It is "not the behavior of bodies but the behavior of something between them, that is, the field," [6] which also forms an ultimate part of the metaphysical picture.

With the acceptance of field concepts involved in relativity theory and the replacement of inert particles by quanta of energy as ultimately indivisible units, one may raise the question as to whether materialism itself has not been transformed into something else. Since materialism aims to reduce all else to ultimately indivisible units, any recognition of fields which are not so reducible involves a partial surrender of such aims. To the extent that one recognizes something ultimate or irreducible over and above the supposed smallest independent units, he ceases to be wholly materialistic. Just as spiritualism seeks some ultimately indivisible whole, or spirit, to which such reality as other things have may be reduced, so materialism searches for some finally indivisible parts or particles to which all wholes may be reduced.

Even as the spiritualist who admits some plurality into his system falls short of spiritualistic perfection, so the materialist who allows unity or wholeness some place in his system fails to be fully materialistic. "If a 'new materialism' is to arise it must certainly be vastly different from its philosophic forerunner." [7] Many former materialists who have accepted the newer concepts in physics still consider

[5] Eugene Garrett Bewkes and others, *Experience, Reason and Faith: A Survey in Philosophy and Religion*, p. 582. Harper & Bros., New York, 1940.

[6] A. Einstein and L. Infeld, *The Evolution of Physics*, p. 312. Simon and Schuster, New York, 1938.

[7] Bewkes, *op. cit.*, p. 383.

themselves materialists. But it seems better to reserve the name "materialism" for those who idealize pluralities of indivisible, externally related parts and to adopt some new terminology for those who accept some measure of unity, or organization, or field of force as having an ultimate place in their outlook. In Chapters 18, 19, 20, and 21, we shall examine typical views which do this.

Materialists have, for a long time at least, proceeded quite satisfactorily in explaining the nature of tables, planets, atoms, but have had some trouble in accounting for life, mind, society, goodness, rightness, and God. Nevertheless, they are not without answers.

Life is not a special creation by a divine will. It is a product of biochemical processes. The more scientists search for the "building blocks" of the animal body, the more they discover. Many complicated vitamins and hormones have been synthesized artificially. Although biochemists have not yet been able to initiate life from sterile inanimate materials, their constant progress in reproducing part after part of the physiological constitutents maintains their hope that they may some day do so. Biological evolution, as interpreted by materialists, is a product merely of material forces acting and reacting upon each other in our complex terrestrial system.

Mind is not a substance. A body has no soul. The unity of personality is temporary and is a product of the cooperation of the body's electrons, atoms, molecules, cells, organs. Each animal body has a brain, and the way a body behaves depends upon the way its brain behaves. Materialists have developed a school of psychology known as "Behaviorism." [8] "Modern psychology regards mind not as a thing but as a function. Mind is what the brain does. This is no more a metaphysical problem than is the relation of locomotion to a locomotive. The locomotion is not inside the locomotive, nor outside it, nor beneath it, nor part of it, nor is it a 'mysterious essence which permeates it.' It is simply what the locomotive does." [9] There is no mind apart from brain. When a brain dies or ceases to function, mind automatically disappears. When an animal behaves in a certain way, we say he is conscious. When a man reflects about a mathematical problem, we note that his behavior is somewhat more complicated. He has delayed responses. But we can infer what is happening in his internal behavior only by observing external behavioral results. Materialists solve the mind-body problem rather simply: there is no such thing as mind, except as a functioning of

[8] Cf. John B. Watson, *Behaviorism.* W. W. Norton and Co., New York, 1925.
[9] Joseph K. Folsom, *Social Psychology*, p. 18. Harper & Bros., New York, 1931.

the body. The old idea of freedom of will disappears. Although it is possible for a person to do what he wants to do, his wants are determined by his bodily nature, his environment, and the stimuli which influence him. Every choice is completely determined. Purpose, for materialists, is a product of evolution; evolution is not a product of purpose.

Society, likewise, is merely a more complicated arrangement of matter, of the ultimate constituent parts, but it is still material in nature. People associate with each other through sound and light waves, i.e., through physical contacts. Government can be carried on only through physical instruments, such as ballots, legislative halls, police courts, etc. War is a complicated "dance of atoms," all of which could have been predicted by anyone who might have known the positions, mass, motion, and relations between all of the various particles involved.

Goodness and badness are not ultimate characteristics of existence. Atoms, electrons, and quanta are neither good nor bad. The ultimate constituents of existence are neutral. When physiological organisms evolve sensitivity, and feelings of pleasantness or unpleasantness in connection with it, they respond accordingly. Physiological psychologists have sought to find the physiological basis of our feelings and desires and emotions. The parts played by glandular secretions in producing emotions is quite well known. The effects of these secretions upon neurones and synapses is not so widely known. One psychologist has pointed out that pleasant feelings accompany decreasing synaptic resistance while unpleasant feelings accompany increasing synaptic resistance.[10] Values, then, arise as a consequence of physical processes and remain in existence only so long as those particular processes continue. When all living beings cease to exist, all values will disappear from the universe.

Rightness is explained by one materialist as follows: "If our existence is based on the play of blind forces and only a matter of chance; if we ourselves are only chemical mechanisms—how can there be an ethics for us? The answer is that our instincts are the root of our ethics and that the instincts are just as hereditary as is the form of our body. We eat, drink, and reproduce, not because mankind has reached an agreement that this is desirable, but because, machine-like, we are compelled to do so. We are active,

[10] Cf. Leonard Troland, *The Mystery of Mind.* D. Van Nostrand Co., New York, 1926.

because we are compelled to be so by processes in our central nervous system; and as long as human beings are not economic slaves the instinct of successful workmanship determines the direction of their action. The mother loves and cares for her children, not because metaphysicians had the idea that this was desirable, but because the instinct of taking care of the young is inherited just as distinctly as the morphological characters of the female body. We seek and enjoy the fellowship of human beings because hereditary conditions compel us to do so. We struggle for justice and truth since we are instinctively compelled to see our fellow beings happy. Economic, social, and political conditions or ignorance and superstition may warp and inhibit the inherited instincts and thus create a civilization with a faulty or low development of ethics. Individual mutants may arise in which one or the other desirable trait is lost, just as individual mutants without pigment may arise in animals; and the offspring may, if numerous enough, lower the ethical status of a community. Not only is the mechanistic conception of life compatible with ethics; it seems the only conception of life which can lead us to an understanding of the source of ethics." [11]

God does not exist, for materialists, except as ideas in the minds of men. Physics, not theology, is the basic science. If all is matter, then God, or whatever the term "God" can mean metaphysically, is matter. In fact, if we examine carefully some of the qualities traditionally attributed to God in comparison with characteristics predicated of matter, we find that they turn out to be very much the same.

God	Matter
1. Eternal, everlasting.	1. Can be neither created nor destroyed.
2. Omnipresent, everywhere.	2. Everywhere.
3. Creator, cause of all.	3. Everything originates in matter.
4. Nothing caused God.	4. Nothing caused matter.
5. Omnipotent, all-powerful.	5. No non-material power exists.
6. What God wills must be.	6. What mechanical laws determine must be.
7. Unseen except through manifestations.	7. Unseen except through manifestations.
8. Transcendent.	8. There is more to matter than exists in any of its parts.
9. Immanent.	9. Matter exists also in each part.

[11] Jacques Loeb, *The Mechanistic Conception of Life*, p. 31. University of Chicago Press, Chicago, 1912.

God	Matter
10. Omniscient, all-knowing.	10. All knowledge exists in material brains. No knowledge apart from matter, thus matter is all knowledge or has all the knowledge that exists.
11. Omnibenevolent, all-good.	11. If there is nothing beside matter, only matter can be good; since matter contains all goodness, it is all-good.
12. Personal. Although God has many superhuman or impersonal traits, God is often spoken of as a person or as appearing in personal forms.	12. If all life and mind is material, then all personality is material. But if so, then matter manifests itself in or as persons, and since there are no nonmaterial persons, matter itself is personal.

Materialism has become a widely popular metaphysics, especially among some physical scientists and their followers who find in the physical sciences their most hopeful clues to interpreting the ultimate nature of existence. Since it accepts a faith in the sciences as its foundation, it is considered by many of its supporters as the most scientific metaphysics. It frees us from superstition and sentimentality. It gets us out of the difficulties involved in spiritualism and its usual theistic explanations. To claim that all is created out of nothing by an unknowable God stretches and strains our belief too much. Materialism is freed from such strain because it considers matter itself as the eternal, uncaused source of all that is. Materialism likewise relieves us from the contradictions of dualism. The principle of the conservation of matter, energy, or mattergy, can never be violated because matter, or mattergy, is the only substance. The pragmatic argument, that materialism works well, also is accepted as in its favor by some.

Criticisms

Others say that materialism is unscientific. For, although it is true that early modern scientists tended increasingly to be materialistic, later scientists reversed this trend. "It is noteworthy that physicists as a class are the least materialistic of scientists. This apparent anomaly seems explainable on the basis of the relative development of the sciences; physics had built its cities before the life-

sciences cleared their forests. The psychologist or biologist has before him a maze of unresolved and highly complex secondary phenomena; consequently he is not pressed on the question of fundamentals, and it is easy for him to anticipate an inclusive solution
of his problems in purely mechanistic terms. The physicist, however, has exhausted the possibilities of mechanism. He has seen one
rigid conceptual entity after another resolved into components of
greater complexity and subtlety, until the whole world is unstable
and fluid, space, matter, and energy intermingling chameleon-like
in an elusive, impenetrable complex." [12]

Materialism is considered unscientific in another way. By basing
its conclusions upon the physical sciences only, it neglects the conclusions of the psychological and social sciences, of aesthetics, ethics,
and economics, for example. If these are sciences also, then is not
materialism unscientific in ignoring these sciences just as much as
other metaphysical views may be in minimizing the physical sciences?
A metaphysics based upon all of the sciences, this argument states,
is more scientific than those based on only one or a few.

Materialism is nonevolutionary, strictly speaking. For, although
evolution is accounted for in materialistic terms, matter itself does
not evolve. Materialism assumes matter as its eternal absolute. The
non-evolutionary particles are metaphysically prior to evolutionary
changes in the relations between these particles. The evolutionary,
then, is less real than the non-evolutionary. Emergentists, whom we
shall meet in Chapter 18, condemn materialists as too unevolution-
ary. Materialists are in the same fix as those theists who say that
all evolution has taken place in accordance with an unchanging plan
of an unchanging God. The materialist today "faces a peculiar dilemma. He is convinced that the original principles of [materialism],
physical matter and motion, are sufficient to express completely whatever is real. But he is convinced equally that evolution has occurred
and that novel levels of being over and above the original levels of
physical matter and motion now exist. If he recognizes this greater
richness of being as a fact, however, he is committed to the view
that the world of fact is wider than the principles of [materialism].
If he is serious about his evolutionism, there is no possible reduction
without remainder of emergents to pre-existents." [13]

[12] From an unpublished paper by physicist J. H. Rush.
[13] D. W. Gotshalk, *Metaphysics in Modern Times*, pp. 27–28. University of
Chicago Press, Chicago, 1940.

Materialists disagree among themselves concerning the nature of matter. Some posit three primary principles: material particles, space, and motion. They disagree not only concerning whether the ultimate particles are static or dynamic, but also as to whether motion is inherent in the particles or contributed to them from the outside, and as to whether the particles exist in space or whether space is merely a product of their external relatedness. A sharp cleavage exists between those who believe that every particular motion is completely determined and those who feel that all that is needed to account for the world is pure chance. The latter hold that, given an infinite number of particles and an infinite length of time, all possible combinations of arrangements will take place; therefore, the present run of arrangements, including our galaxy, biological evolution, human history, mind with its love of beauty and God, all are sufficiently explained by pure chance. If all possibilities must happen in infinite time, then this present one must also, so it needs nothing else, certainly neither God nor materialistic determinism, to account for it. However, many materialists prefer a middle course between complete determinism and pure chancism. They subscribe to tychism, the view that holds that in a largely deterministic world chance factors do operate to influence the course of events. Until the part that chance plays has been clearly demonstrated, materialists will remain divided among themselves.

Materialism is caught in another difficulty. In assuming that existence is ultimately a multiplicity of particles, it asserts that plurality is more ultimate than unity. In fact, there is no real unity of things. Each thing, such as the earth, an animal, a cell, an atom, has no genuine unity about it, for ultimately it is merely an association of those particles which alone are real. However, materialism does not entirely escape the notion of unity, since it assumes that the ultimate particles are indivisible units.

However, materialism is also involved in an opposite difficulty. It is too rationalistic. Although it denies that human reason is anything more than a temporary function of temporary brains, nevertheless it assumes that matter, in operating mechanically, conforms to mathematically predictable patterns of behavior. It is often said that if a mind knew enough about the location, size, motion, and aggregation of the ultimate particles, it could predict with certainty what would happen at any time in the future. Although granting that no mind that knew this much could actually exist, materialists nevertheless assume that matter follows mathematical laws exactly. If reason (including mathematical reasoning) is a function of mind, rather than of matter, in making matter obey rational laws, do not materialists thereby imply a rationalistic spiritualism hidden behind their pronouncements?

In fact, if matter and God have practically the same attributes, as pointed out above,[14] then materialism is simply a kind of theism in verbal disguise. If believing in God as traditionally described is a kind of superstition, then materialism is also a superstition which thinks itself free from such criticism simply because it has adopted a different name. The criticisms raised against deterministic theism apply equally well to materialism, except in so far as its emphasis upon plurality of particles negates the utter unity of monotheism. However, either this pluralism is not as complete as assumed, or the problem of the interrelation of the particles begets difficulties. Either some God-like unity, or wholeness of matter, with rationalistic determination, is involved, or the chance associations of independent, externally related particles leave mechanical processes unpredictable. Determinateness and predictability presuppose something more than externally related particles. Again, if, as pointed out previously,[15] materialistic rationalism presupposes the principle of the uniformity of nature, then this unity, or uniformity, is something external to the particles themselves, and, thus, materialism itself presupposes the existence of more than material particles.

In accepting, at least partially, the changing conceptions of matter, materialism tends to evolve beyond itself. Some think that in exchanging inert for dynamic units materialists have become spiritualists, for what is a spirit but a center of activity. Leibniz' monads were conceived as indivisible energy units which, nevertheless, were determined in nature and action by a larger rationalistic determiner, the Monad of monads. How does materialism differ from pluralistic spiritualism, if matter is interpreted in terms of energy?

Finally, materialism fails to satisfy our natural demands for faith in the reality of values. If materialism is true, life is not worth living, or at least not worth living for more than the temporary pleasures which one happens to enjoy. "Life is much more real, and so are love and desire and longing and poetry and friends and society and work and play and beauty. Just what do we mean by

[14] See pp. 197–198.
[15] See p. 189.

the word *reality,* when we say that matter and atoms are more real than these other things?   Browning's line

> Sun-treader, I believe in God and truth
> And love;

meets with more response than the legend of the materialist who says: "I believe in mass particles in motion." Why not say that the *interesting* things in life are the *real* things?" [16]

Epiphenomenalism

Some materialists, recognizing the difficulties in denying the existence of mind altogether, yet wishing to escape the difficulties inherent in interactionistic dualism, have sought a way out through epiphenomenalism.   These thinkers accept the ultimacy of matter but not the complete nonexistence of mind or consciousness.   Consciousness, however, is not given the status of a full substance, something that can stand independently by itself.   Consciousness is dependent upon the brain, but the brain is not dependent upon consciousness.   Originally, all was matter, but matter at times, i.e., when it forms itself into brains, gives rise to mind which is not matter.   But mind disappears as soon as it fails to be supported by matter.   Thus, we have a semidualism in which there is no interaction, but only a one-way action.   Matter causes mind, but mind does not cause matter.   Mental events accompany the function of the brain, but in no way influence its operation.   The analogy is sometimes used, comparing brain and mind to a train and its shadow.   As a moving train casts a shadow which reflects some of the activities on the train, so some of the brain's activities emerge into consciousness.   But, even as what happens in the shadow of the train in no way causes the train or its events to be different, so what happens in consciousness or mind leaves the course of material events in the brain entirely unaltered.   Epiphenomenalism, thus, recognizes the existence of mind, but preserves intact the principle of the conservation of matter, since no substantial interchange between mind and matter takes place.

mind
↑
MATTER

16 G. T. W. Patrick, *Introduction to Philosophy,* p. 225.   Houghton Mifflin Co., Boston, 1924.

However, critics point out that most of the main criticisms of materialism still stand. The mind is left ineffective. Our common-sense experiences demand more than mere existence of mind as an evanescent shadow. "Now, although there are many cases in which consciousness seems helpless, there are also many cases in which consciousness seems to be the controlling factor. Whenever we plan, will, exert effort, our mental life feels active, efficacious, rather than a passive accompaniment of our bodily life." [17] "Consciousness may be, from the physical, dynamic point of view, a by-product. But it is this by-product alone which gives *worth* to the activities of organisms and the universe that gives them birth." [18] Epiphenomenalism leaves us both without explanation of "a very difficult problem, viz., How *can* physical bodies generate consciousness?" [19] and of why there should be any need of consciousness occurring at all in a purely materialistic world. Epiphenomenalism hardly satisfies the needs of those who feel that mind has some reality. In fact, it stands as an admission of weakness in materialism, which leads to further abandonment of strict materialism in the thinking of emergentists.

[17] Durant Drake, *Invitation to Philosophy*, p. 366. Houghton Mifflin Co., Boston, 1933.

[18] *Ibid.*, pp. 374–375.

[19] *Ibid.*, p. 375.

· 17 ·

Emanationism

Plotinus (205–270), who lived first in Alexandria and later in Rome, represents a metaphysical view which has been highly influential in Western thought, especially in its effects upon Christian theology. Although Plotinus was not a Christian, he influenced Christian thinkers, from St. Augustine to contemporary churchmen such as Dean Ralph W. Inge.[1] In the battle between the thought of Plato and Aristotle for recognition and acceptance by later Christian thinkers, it was a Neoplatonism, something like that of Plotinus, which won out; for despite the fact that Aristotle was finally acclaimed as "The Philosopher," the spirit of Platonic thought, modified by various Neoplatonic thinkers, suffused Christian theology, even though the words and ideas were more often attributed to Aristotle. Plotinus is important for our purposes because his view represents a crystallization of Neoplatonism as a type. Despite the absence of historical documentation, his view may be looked upon as a remarkable synthesis of three major philosophical trends: Platonism, Brahmanism, and Hebrew-Christian thought.

Plato conceived reality as a scale of being, ranging from completely perfect being to completely imperfect non-being. Being consists primarily in Ideas,[2] or Archetypes, after which created things were patterned by the Demiurge, or Creator. These Ideas which constitute the realm of being also form a hierarchy in which the highest Idea is the Idea of the Good. This Idea is the most real of all beings. The world created by the Demiurge includes a world soul, rational souls, irrational souls, inanimate bodies, in a descending order, and, finally, "indeterminate matter" as a lower limit of being in the scale ranging from being to non-being. The upper

[1] W. R. Inge, *The Philosophy of Plotinus.* Longmans, Green and Co., New York, 1918.
[2] See p. 118.

part of the scale represents greater reality, the lower parts lesser realities. These lesser realities have their source in the higher realities and, ultimately, in the Idea of the Good.

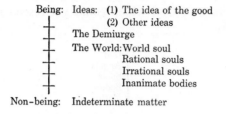

```
Being:  Ideas:  (1) The idea of the good
  ┬              (2) Other ideas
  ┼        The Demiurge
  ┼        The World:World soul
  ┼                  Rational souls
  ┼                  Irrational souls
  ┼                  Inanimate bodies
  ┴
Non-being:  Indeterminate matter
```

Brahmanism, likewise, pictures existence as ultimately a perfect, eternal, indivisible, attributeless unity called Brahman.[3] This perfect being manifests itself as Atman, which is the ultimate unity of Brahman plurified implicitly and suffusing the world as the ultimate reality underlying the souls of men. Souls acquire the illusion that their plurality is real and then suffer a round of rebirths, rising and falling on the scale of being according as their deeds are good or bad. The law of Karma automatically determines whether they shall be reborn higher or lower in a caste system or animal system. A favorable balance of good deeds permits one eventually to practice yoga and to lose his illusory and unreal individuality in a beatifically blissful union with Brahman in a state called "nirvana." Herein he is freed from his lesser reality, his illusory individuality, and he achieves perfect reality through loss of all illusion of individual separateness.

```
Brahman    (Perfect unity)
Atman      (Unity that pervades all plurality)
  │ Souls   Plurality that is really unity
  │ Bodies  Plurality that is mistaken for reality
  │ Castes  Levels of social classes
  │ Animals Levels of animal life
  │ Plants  Levels of plant life
  ▼ Matter  Levels of decomposition
```
(Illusion)

Hebrew-Christian thought also developed a hierarchy including God, the angels (Lucifer among them), souls, bodies, matter. Creation of all was from God alone. Next to God in perfection were angels who were bodiless and uncontaminated by fleshly concerns. Souls also were created perfect, but were endowed with freedom of choice and power to sin. This freedom was unwisely used by Adam and Eve, who discovered their nakedness, i.e., that they had bodies,

---

[3] See p. 236.

and mistakenly believed that their bodies were real and good and that their selfish and fleshly desires were the true values. Humanity was thus condemned to live a carnal life through the fall of man, and could be saved only through seeking to crucify the flesh and through the Grace of God which could yet rescue men from their mortal unreality.

> God
> Angels
> Souls
> Bodies
> ↓ Matter

Plotinus grasped, perhaps better than any other Western thinker, the nature of perfection and how it can pervade imperfection, or how imperfection is a sort of watered-down perfection which has no reality at all apart from such perfection. Perfect being he called the "One." The One has no parts, and, thus, cannot be taken apart or destroyed. It was, of course, never put together. It must be eternal, for time involves a succession of moments, but the One has no parts to succeed each other and, thus, cannot be temporal. It involves no conflicts, because it has no parts which can conflict. It really can have no name, for to pronounce a name is to utilize syllables or vocal motion, i.e., parts, whereas the One has no parts and, therefore, cannot be represented truly by anything with parts. All names which imperfect beings give it are imperfect names; and any imperfect name given to a perfect being must misrepresent it. However, for the sake of exposition, Plotinus called it the One. We cannot even truly say of the One that: It exists, It is eternal, It is perfect, for all these, as imperfect terms, cannot represent perfection adequately. Perfection is beyond adequate representation. It cannot even be known, for knowledge involves distinction, whereas the One is beyond all distinctions, is without distinctions, is indistinct, for it is superior to all distinctions. Only through intuition, knowledge that is not knowledge, can we get a temporary glimpse of its indistinctness. Then, of course, we intuit our own indistinctness from (or union with) it.

Such perfection has no relations, for relations entail separation, and, therefore, plurality. Perfect unity is without any plurality whatsoever. Yet plurality exists in the imperfect world in which men live. How is it to be accounted for? Perfection is in no way related to imperfection, for if it were, perfection would have an imperfect relation and thus be imperfect. However, imperfection (that which is by its very nature not perfect) is derived from that which it is not. Just as perfection is unity, imperfection is plurality. Just as unity is without opposition, plurality is filled with opposition. Just as perfection is good, so plurality is evil.

How is the imperfect world created by such a perfect being? Not by an act of will, for willing involves a willer, what is willed, and the activity of willing. But these are many, whereas the One is but one. Creation follows by a sort of logical necessity. Imperfection, that which is not perfect, is logically implied by perfection. What is logically implied must be. Imperfection gets its meaning, thus its being, from perfection. But, of course, since perfection is prior to imperfection, perfection does not get its meaning from imperfection. Plotinus expresses these ideas through an analogy. Like the sun, which (he believed) gives off light eternally without diminishing its energy one bit, the One emanates the world continuously with "no lessening of its perfection." [4] Or, logically, a premise implies its conclusion eternally without the premise being diminished in the strength of its power to imply its conclusion. The imperfect world is created, then, by a process of emanation (hence "emanationism") in which it comes into being of logical necessity from the One, which is perfect reality and which is in no way influenced, diminished, or increased by, or even related to, creation. The One is pure substance, in the sense that it depends upon nothing. In fact, it is the only substance, for all else depends upon it. Thus, ultimately, emanationism seems very much like spiritualism. But the emanations are not nothing. This world is a real world, even if imperfect. Imperfect being is not no being. Only completely imperfect being is no being. This Plotinus called the "Void."

Between the One and the Void are three stages of created being: Nous, Soul, and Body. 1. Nous is the first level of emanation. It is the unity, or oneness, of created being. But it is differentiated into two aspects, or levels. (a) First of all, it is undivided in itself, even though it is divided from the One which is unrelated to anything. It constitutes the unitary being of the created world which, as such, most nearly reflects the unity of the One. As such it involves no differentiation, no plurality of relations. However, it also (b) entails implicitly all possibilities for further creation. This second level of Nous is something like Plato's realm of Ideas, or like the mind of an all-knowing God in which all possibilities of created things exist implicitly before (and after) any particular possible thing is actually created. Not all these possibilities need be actual-

[4] Joseph Katz, *The Philosophy of Plotinus*, p. xvi. Appleton-Century-Crofts, New York, 1950.

ized. In this level of Nous, all is thought at once (i.e., eternally). Both universals (types, kinds; e.g., manness) and particulars (individual persons; e.g., John Smith) subsist eternally. Each universal (e.g., man) is more unified than each particular (John) and, thus, is more real, because more fully reflecting the unity of the One. Unactualized possibilities are more real than actualized possibilities because they are less infected with plurality, which is unreality. Nous, as the first level of emanation, exists eternally in all the fullness of its perfection as compared with the lower levels of creation, yet it is imperfect because it falls short of the complete undifferentiated perfection of the One.

2. The second level of emanation, Soul, constitutes the everlasting unity of all actual existence. Whereas Nous is eternal (timeless or prior to temporal distinctness), Soul is everlasting (pervades and yet transcends all times). Soul also involves two aspects, or levels, the unitary and the pluralistic, or (a) the undivided world soul, and (b) the many individual souls. "There are both many souls and one; and from the one soul proceed the multiplicity of different souls." [5] Each individual soul has its own indivisible nature. Each is undivided in itself, even though it is divided both from other souls and from the world soul. As simple, each soul reflects the unity of the world soul, the unity of the Nous, and, ultimately, the unity of the One itself. But each soul degenerates, emanates, or evolves distinctions within itself in various ways: Consciousness occurs, and since consciousness involves distinction between subject and object, between different objects, and between ideas as they become distinct from one another, plurification sets in. Desires arise, and desires involve separation of the desirer from the desired object, and the more desires one has the more separation (evil) occurs. A mind begins to think, to reason, to clarify, and, in so doing, involves itself in chains of reasoning with their multiplicities of separate links. The more distinctions a mind makes, the more it knows matter, or that which is relatively unreal. The more it devotes itself to the making of distinctions, the more materialistic it becomes and the farther away does it get from the One.

3. Body, the third level, subdivides itself into two sublevels. (a) The body of the world as a whole is emanated from the world soul. The everlasting and space-transcending world soul degenerates itself throughout all passing times and particular spaces. However, the body of the world as a whole has more unity, and thus more reality, than any of the many particular bodies into which it degener-

[5] *Ibid.*, p. 105.

ates. (b) Each particular body emanates from an individual soul, just as the world body emanates from the world soul. Each body again is subdivided into its own bodily whole and its many separable parts. A body is needed by each soul to account for the many distinctions it makes. A soul cannot make spatial distinctions without body, since a soul as a whole is indivisible, whereas space involves infinite divisibility. Body is the principle of endless differentiation. But each body is first a body as a whole. It is a single body, not merely an aggregation of chunks of matter. It is, however, distinct from its soul, its principle of wholeness. Thus arises the distinction between the spirit and the flesh. A body "looks to" its soul to unify it, to give it life, to animate it. But each body exists also as parts, or as matter. When a body decays, loses all relation to its soul, it disintegrates into particles of dust and becomes even less real. Materialism, from the emanationist viewpoint, is the worst of all possible philosophies, with the exception of complete nihilism.

Finally we must consider, 4, the Void, which is really not being at all, but nonbeing. As complete absence of being, it is pure negativity, not something positive. It is like completely empty space, or it is as with light that shines so far into distance that it finally loses itself in complete darkness, where darkness is merely the absence of light. The dust particles of degenerate bodies are much more real than the Void, for the Void consists not even of infinite particles, for a particle has its own unity as a particle. The Void is complete diversity without the being of anything that is diverse. It is such complete plurality that there are not even any units of plurality. The Void is as completely nothing as the One is completely perfect being.

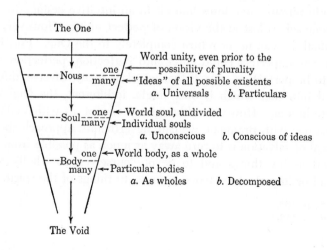

This scale of levels of being is also a range of good and evil. For the One is perfect goodness, whereas the Void is complete evil. Nous, Soul, and Body represent decreasing degrees of goodness as well as increasing unreality. Emanationism is pessimistic, since it holds that all creation is evil, and the more creation that occurs, the more evil (i.e., less goodness) that exists. Of course, the One, being all-good, does not create evil by an act of will, for the One has no will. The evil of imperfection flows by a logical necessity from the nature of the goodness of the perfect One. The One has no personality, no consciousness, no desires, no intentions. Thus it cannot be blamed for evil consequences. Evil must simply be accepted as a necessity of imperfect existence. Then, all existence, apart from the One, is evil. But, on the other hand, it is also good; all save the Void partake of being and, thus, of goodness. There is still some hope. For we can turn ourselves away from matter, away from our fleshly bodies, away from our selfish desires and multiplicities of distracting ideas. Our souls can "turn again towards the existence from which they proceeded." [6] Since "no soul, not even ours, enters into the body completely" [and] "by her higher part the soul always remains united" [7] with higher unity, each soul is already partly pure and can purify itself further simply by refraining from further descent into impurity. Like Christians and Hindus, we should crucify the flesh and seek release from the bonds of our illusory material bodies. Then, by devoting ourselves to the unity within our selves, to the higher unity which is the world soul, to the eternal unities contemplatable as a system of Platonic Ideas, and, finally, to the world unity itself, we may increasingly approach complete identification with the One. As in Hindu nirvana, one loses himself in an intuitive ecstacy in which his whole self is lost in the vision of perfect unity. However, as an individual, he can never return completely to the One. For, if that which was imperfect could enter into perfection, perfection would cease to be perfection. Or, if that which is many, diverse, different, entered into that which is one, single, indifferent, the One would cease to be one. However, although we cannot, as with Vedantists, become one with Brahman, we can, nevertheless, approach the One. The goal of salvation is to turn away as much as possible from material and fleshly things and to devote ourselves, as wholly as our material or imperfect existence permits, to things of the spirit.

[6] *Ibid.*, p. 106.
[7] *Ibid.*, p. 112.

For Plotinus, there is no genuine freedom of will. That is, the One, or perfect being, has no such freedom, because will involves desire, and desire implies separation of the desirer from the desired. But in the One there is no separation whatsoever. It is true that in the imperfect world there are desires and, in a sense, there is freedom of choice, but this freedom follows from imperfection. In the Void there is complete freedom, but nothing which is free. In the One there is complete being, but no freedom. If the individual seeks salvation, then he must seek to get rid of his separate individuality with all its desires, or all its freedom of will. Plotinus' views suggest both Hindu abhorrence of individuality and Christian rejection of selfishness. The goal of life becomes rejection of self and this world. But a soul cannot, of itself, will to reject this world. For in so willing, it exerts desires, and desire is the very evil one seeks to avoid. So one's success comes not from desiring, but from not desiring, i.e., from accepting one's fate. In Christian terminology, this becomes a willingness to accept the will of God as one's own will.

Plotinus and Neoplatonism have this advantage. They show us that the world, even though evil, is ultimately good. The evil we experience is unreal, or partly unreal, and good, ultimately, triumphs, even if not completely. Evil is merely negative good. Plotinus' insights, at least many of them, have lived on through Christian theology, and have survived doubtless because they have worked well in the practical experience of Christian thinkers and practitioners. Man is a humble creature who stands a better chance of achieving goodness by realizing his humility. God is good and in no way responsible for evil. Being perfect, the One is without whim or caprice, and so we can rely upon the necessity of its goodness.

Criticisms

In making spiritual unity most real, and material plurality comparatively unreal, Plotinus seems to support the reality of mind as against that of body. Our bodies are less real than our minds, he holds, but this seems contrary to much of the evidence supplied by the sciences of medicine and genetics. It seems as if our bodies grow first and then our minds. Our bodies seem more stable than our minds, which at first appear undeveloped, then at times insane or unconscious, and finally seem to disappear at death. He fails to give matter as much causal power, as much substantiality, as much reality, as we expect. Matter, for him, is mere negativity, mere absence of substance, mere causation of a thing by what it is not, or by its own unreality. Thus matter has no real causative powers. Although this view may have seemed reasonable in the ancient world, modern science has revealed so much that is positive about matter and energy that emanationism can hardly remain satisfactory. Furthermore, if plurification produces unreality, evil, and error, then the analytical quest for knowledge brings us only more error instead of knowledge of the truth.

Plotinus is too deterministic. There is no genuine freedom of will. Not even the supreme reality, the One, has any freedom of choice, because it has no choice at all. Freedom of choice itself is an evil, for Plotinus. All this is contrary to our common-sense experience. Even though Plotinus' views have influenced Augustinian, Calvinistic, and later Christian theology, predestinarianism has always entailed a host of problems which leave believers uneasy. If salvation presupposes the possibility of freely chosen faith, then such extreme determinism is both unchristian and contrary to the evidences of our own immediate experiences in making choices.

Emanationism is too antisocial. For it holds that the way to perfection is private and personal, not social. He who would seek spiritual elevation should flee this world and shut himself away from its multiplicities of attractions, including his interest in other people. In fact, the more people one is interested in, the more he diversifies, materializes, or worsens himself. The good is to be sought in solitude and contemplation, in destroying, discarding and forgetting the flesh.

For many Christians, Plotinus' One is too impersonal, cold, indifferent, dead, and too loveless. If God is love, then, since Plotinus' One is indifferent to love, without love, beyond love, he cannot care about human troubles. From the point of view of spiritualists, the One is, indeed, spirit, but it is a spirit without life. Most spiritualists want a living spirit, even if it must contain some opposition, conflict, plurality, within it. Hegel, for example, accepted the Absolute as an identity-in-difference, not as a mere identity. Spiritualists, then, even in denying to matter as much reality as Plotinus gave it, do not always destroy the activity of spirit so completely as to make it lifeless and powerless to produce real changes. For materialists, Plotinus underestimates the importance of matter by granting it only a dependent reality, and by making it the most unreal of all partly real beings, whereas, for materialists, matter is the only true reality. Evolutionists reject Neoplatonism because it allows only devolution, degeneration, descendence, with no genuine novelty of being, but only greater and more complicated non-being.

· 18 ·

Emergentism

In contrast to emanationism, which holds that both mind and body have some reality although mind has more reality than body, emergentists hold that though both have some reality, body is more real than mind. C. Lloyd Morgan (1852–1936),[1] Samuel Alexander (1859–1938),[2] and Roy Wood Sellars (1880–   )[3] will be taken as examples of those who hold emergentist views.[4] All agree that reality is organized into levels of being, higher levels being substantially different from lower levels, yet dependent upon them. Lower levels depend less upon higher levels than higher levels depend upon lower levels. Thus, lower levels are more substantial and more ultimate than higher levels. All agree that there is some lowest level which is most permanent, substantial, and ultimate, and, in this sense, most real.

Morgan and Sellars agree with materialists that matter has always existed, can be neither created nor destroyed, depends upon nothing else for existence, and is the most substantial kind of being. So, generally, emergentists agree with materialists so far as matter itself is concerned. But they reject the materialist contention that only matter exists. "The whole doctrine of emergence is a continued protest against mechanical interpretation, and the very antithesis to one that is mechanistic."[5] Whereas materialists contend that the universe is complete, emergentists feel that it is unfinished. Whereas materialists say there can be no genuinely new substance in the world,

[1] C. Lloyd Morgan, *Emergent Evolution.* Williams and Norgate, London, 1923.

[2] Samuel Alexander, *Time and Deity.* The Macmillan Co., London, 1920.

[3] Roy Wood Sellars, *Evolutionary Naturalism.* The Open Court Publishing Co., Chicago, 1922.

[4] Others include Jan Christian Smuts (cf. his *Holism and Evolution.* The Macmillan Co., New York, 1926).

[5] C. Lloyd Morgan, *Emergent Evolution*, p. 7.

emergentists believe that new substances emerge from time to time. Since all is completely determined for materialists, there can be nothing really new, nothing that is unpredictable in principle, nothing substantial that did not exist before. Emergentists insist on the actuality of novelty, the evolution of new substances, the arising of new kinds of being. "The orderly sequence of natural events, historically viewed, appears to present, from time to time, something genuinely new. Under what I call emergent evolution, stress is laid on this incoming of the new. . . . But if nothing new emerge—if there be only regrouping of pre-existing elements *and nothing more*—then there is no emergent evolution." [6]

A major clue to the difference between emergentism and materialism is to be found in Morgan's distinction between "emergents" and "resultants." Since materialists say there can be nothing new in the world, unless it be simply a new arrangement, a new collection, a new association of material elements, they therefore consider such happenings as are said to be new as merely new sums—as in mathematics when 5 and 7 are added together for a first time, the number 12 is said to be new, but there is nothing in twelve that was not already implied in 5 and 7. Or, when one billiard ball is hit by two others, the motion imparted to it is new for the balls, but the motion, the kind of behavior, is not a new kind of behavior. The amount and direction of the motion could have been predicted precisely if the direction and motion of the other two balls had been known. And there is nothing in the moving ball which could not be explained directly as a result of the motion and direction (and other similar factors such as slope of surface, air resistance) of the other two. The motion of the billiard ball is explainable as the resultant of the motion of the other two balls. Emergentists say that each emergent involves resultants, but it involves something more. "When carbon having certain properties combines with sulphur having other properties, there is formed, not a mere mixture but a new compound, some of the properties of which are quite different from those of either component. Now the weight of the compound is the additive resultant, the sum of the weights of the components; and this could have been predicted before any molecule of carbon-bisulfide had been formed. One could say in advance that if carbon and sulphur shall be found to combine in any ascertainable proportions there will be such and such weight as resultant. But sundry other properties are constitutive of emer-

[6] *Ibid.*, p. 1.

gents which could not be foretold in advance of any instance of such combination." [7]

When an emergent first appears in the world, what is it that is new? There are new units of stability, new organized structures, new properties, capacities and functions, new laws of behavior, and new centers of control or causation.

1. Each emergent depends for its existence and stability upon the existence and stability of its constituent units. For example, a molecule depends upon its atoms, a cell upon its molecules, a body upon its cells, a social group upon the bodies of its members. Instability in any necessary constituent affects the stability of the emergent unit. But, also, each emergent has a stability in addition to the stabilities of its constituents. For example, some molecules may retain their molecular structure despite an exchange of atomic parts; cells retain their living structure even though there be an increase or decrease or exchange of molecular contents; bodies continue to function through loss or addition (birth or death) of cells; [8] and social institutions constituting the structure of lasting human relationships may endure for centuries even though the various persons upon which they depend live for less than a hundred years. Emergents have a stability of their own, over and above the stabilities of their participants, a stability which often outlasts the participants. Each emergent as a stable unit functions as a substance. In so far as an emergent outlasts its constituents, it is more substantial than they are. So, although emergents are dependent, in the sense that they cannot exist without constituents, they are independent of some of them and therefore not completely or entirely dependent upon them. To the extent that emergents remain while constituents come and go, such emergents are more substantial than their constituents. To this extent, emergents are genuine substances, not merely functions of matter.

2. Each emergent has a structure which is different from, external to, and in addition to, the structures of its constituents. The structure of a molecule consists in the external relations of its atoms. That is, in addition to the internal structure of each atom—relations between electrons, protons, etc.—there are external relations between atoms in molecules, and these relations, external to the atoms but internal to the molecule, are different and additional relations constituting the

---

[7] *Ibid.*, p. 3.

[8] Some biochemists say that the molecular content of the human body is completely replaced once every seven years.

structure of the molecule. The structure of a living cell with its functions of growth, reproduction, etc., is external to its molecules and is something added to the structure of the molecules and atoms involved. The structure of a human body is more complex, perhaps, than that inside a single cell. The structure of a family, a city, a nation, etc., is different in nature from that of a body, cell, molecule, or atom. No structure of a higher-level unit can be reduced to the structures of lower units. When a group or body or cell disintegrates, its structure disappears, but it cannot be explained merely in terms of the structures of lower units.

3. Each emergent has certain properties which permit it to function differently than can its constituents. It has some capacities for acting and reacting which its constituents do not have. It can perform functions not possible for its units. For example, molecules have properties which their atoms do not have; cells can function in ways which molecules cannot; bodies have abilities that cells do not; societies can do things which single individuals cannot. Since these capacities are peculiar to the emergent unit, they did not exist in the world before it did.

4. The behavior of each new kind of emergent forms patterns, or laws, which are peculiar to the units of this kind, or level. Each new kind of functioning generates new laws. "The law connecting the properties of [the emergent] with those of [its constituents] and with the structure of the [emergent] is, so far as we know, an *unique* and *ultimate* law." [9] The laws of molecular behavior differ from those of merely atomic behavior. Those of cell behavior involve more than those of molecular behavior. The laws of bodily functioning cannot be limited to those of cell behavior. The laws of behavior of social groups cannot be reduced to laws of bodily stimulus and response. The attempt of materialists to reduce all sciences to physics is rejected as false, for if what is new at each level of emergence cannot be reduced to lower levels, and if each level has its own kinds of behavior and laws of such behavior, then each constitutes a genuinely different subject matter for scientific investigation. The distinctness of sociological, psychological, and biological sciences from physical sciences is no accident of human whim but depends upon really different kinds of behavior of different kinds of substance. This does not mean that each science is completely autonomous, but only that

---

[9] Charles D. Broad, *Mind and Its Place in Nature*, p. 65. Harcourt, Brace and Co., Inc., New York, 1925.

there is some real basis for their difference. Since higher-level units continue to depend upon lower-level units, the functioning of the laws of behavior of the higher units continues to depend upon that of the lower. A biologist has much to gain from physics. He cannot be a good biologist without knowing something of physics. But no physicist could possibly formulate the laws of biological behavior merely from his knowledge of physical laws.

5. Each emergent is not only a substance but also a causal agency. An emergent is itself causal, not merely a transmitter of effects. Although each is dependent upon its constituents, and so is to this extent insubstantial, its constituents are, in turn, dependent upon it, in a certain sense, and, to this extent, it is more substantial than they are. Once lower-level units participate in an emergent organization, their behavior is conditioned by that fact. Their behavior is modified, controlled, directed, to a certain degree, by the limits set upon them by their participating in the emergent system. The action of an atom, for example, depends partly upon the kinds of limitations which the molecular structure puts upon it. The behavior of a molecule in a cell depends upon the use it serves in the life of the cell. The behavior of a cell in a human body depends upon the function it is called upon to perform within the body (e.g., certain blood corpuscles are called into existence to heal wounds as demanded by bodily needs). The behavior of a person is affected by the kinds of groups and culture patterns in which he participates and by the kinds of roles he plays in his society. The causal efficacy of emergent units cannot be reduced to the causal activity of the lowest particles of matter. These lowest units are not the only substances, even though they may have been the first, and may be the last, if there are to be some last, substances. But the emerging processes evolve new substances which function causally to produce effects which could not have been caused by any other kinds of substance. Each level has a kind of causal ultimacy about it. There are many levels of being. Each is a kind of reality. Emergent levels may be destroyed, but they cannot be reduced completely. Each emergent has a kind of organization, a kind of unity, a kind of wholeness which cannot be analyzed into parts. Each emergent whole is more than a mere sum of separate parts. That is, each emergent involves more than resultants. Existence cannot be reduced merely to matter in motion.

In contrast with emanationism, which holds that unity or oneness is prior to plurality, emergentism claims that the plurality of units of matter is prior to emergent unity. Unity is an evolutionary achieve-

ment. New units or new unities emerge. Organization is a consequence of progressive integration. Creation is an integrative process,
not disintegrative; is a generative process, not degenerative; is growth
in organization, not disorganization. Whereas both emanationists
and emergentists agree that unity or wholeness involves more than a
sum of parts, emanationists consider the whole (the One) as prior
to the parts, and emergentists believe that the parts, or the lower-level
constituents, are prior to higher-level wholes. If integrity is better
than disintegration, then emergentism is much more optimistic about
the future than emanationism, for new entities are yet to emerge
from continuing progressive integration; whereas for emanationists
the One was originally perfect, and, therefore, creative processes can
produce only degeneration. The only hope for emanationists is to
return backwards as far as they can to that from which they have
come. Emanationism is thus backward-looking, emergentism for-
ward-looking.

How many levels of emergence are there? "It is beyond the wit of
man to number the instances of emergence." [10] "Salient examples
are afforded in the advent of life, in the advent of mind, and in the
advent of reflective thought. But in the physical world emergence is
no less exemplified in the advent of each new kind of atom, and of
each new kind of molecule." [11] "Within each, of course, there are
many emergent sub-orders of relatedness. It is for science to work
out the details—for psychology, for biology, for chemistry and
physics." [12] Selecting a few major levels for purposes of comparison,
we may diagram them in a pyramid. Sellars, who adds a social level
to those which Morgan selects for consideration, says "The base of
the pyramid stands for inorganic nature in its full scope; the next
level for living things of all grades and kinds; the next, mind and intelligence; and finally we come to social processes, to human beings
and their social relationships, to civilization." [13] Alexander, influenced by Einstein's theory of relativity, prefers to consider "Space-
Time" as a level lower than "Matter," from which matter emerged.
Electrons or quanta of energy may derive their existence from "kinks"
in the dynamic curvature of space-time. He considers especially important a level emerging out of the human mind, namely, "God."

[10] Morgan, *op. cit.*, p. 1.
[11] *Ibid.*
[12] *Ibid.*, p. 22.
[13] Roy Wood Sellars, *The Principles and Problems of Philosophy*, p. 345. The
Macmillan Co., New York, 1926.

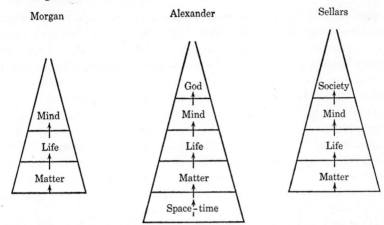

Morgan   Alexander   Sellars

What causes emergents to emerge? There must somehow be inherent in the lowest levels of matter or space-time a tendency toward increasing organization. Existence has basic to it an urge to emerge. Morgan and Alexander give it a name, "Nisus." Morgan speaks of it as "Activity" (capital "A"), or as "God as directive Activity within the scheme." [14] Morgan and Alexander are theists, so find it convenient to identify "the Creator" with the principle of creativity of new emergents immanent in existence even at its lowest levels. This principle of emergence itself emerges from level to level and so exists as the yearning of each level for one that is higher. Alexander speaks of each higher level as "deity" to lower levels. That is, matter is deity to space-time, life is deity to matter, mind is deity to life, and God is deity to mind. God consists in that ideal which has emerged in human minds as that toward which minds strive. But just as mind aspires to become Godlike, life strives to become conscious, matter to become alive, space-time to become matter. However, although Alexander's view is shot through with theistic conceptions—Nisus, deity, God— Sellars is an atheist who sees no need of accounting for emergence in other than naturalistic terms. The tendency of dynamic matter toward increasingly higher levels of organization is present in matter, but there is no point in deifying it. Emergentism, then, requires no theistic commitments, nor atheistic ones either. In any case, Alexander's God is itself an emergent which is dependent upon men's minds. If men's minds ever disappear, the God to which men aspire will disappear also. However, this does not mean that God is merely

[14] Morgan, *op. cit.*, p. 33.

a figment of the human imagination, for once the ideal has emerged, it, in turn, controls the behavior of those who hold it as an ideal. Those who believe in God, who aspire to become Godlike, who organize their energies and activities about a pattern of behavior directed toward becoming Godlike, behave differently. Thus this ideal, this emergent God, does, in fact, control their lives so long as they believe in or aspire to him. Sometimes such ideals are passed on from generation to generation, and then such an ideal God endures substantially and causally longer than some of its supporters. In this way, Alexander accounts for the obvious power which God has over the lives of people. But such a God, while real and substantial in some obvious degree, is less real, less substantial, less enduring, than the ultimate constituents of matter or space-time.

How are mind and body related, according to emergentists? Body with its brain is more real than mind, as epiphenomenalists had previously maintained.[15] But mind, once it emerges upon or within a brain, achieves a kind of substantiality of functioning and causing such that it, in turn, influences brain activity. A mind continues to depend upon its brain and dies with it, but once a mind emerges it functions as a director of much of the brain's activity. Ideas, whether of simple geometrical figures or of complicated scientific systems, are not parts of the brain. They arise only in minds, and in accordance with mental laws. But our ideas of unsolved scientific problems cause our bodies endless research labor. Our bodies normally respond to control by our minds so long as our bodies sustain consciousness. However, some activity within the body, which is connected with the brain through the nervous system, influences conscious experiences. Thus, there is interaction between these two kinds of being. Emergentism involves interactionism, just as the dualism of Descartes and much of common sense does. But the interaction is between two substances which are partially dependent upon each other, not between two completely independent and unlike substances.

All substances, for emergentists, are partially dependent substances, or partial substances, except the lowest level of matter. A mind is a less real substance than a brain, but their difference in reality is a matter of degree. So long as a mind functions substantially it is, to this extent, a substance. Some minds which become intensely mental, completely domineering over their bodies, demanding of bodily submission, become nervous, unhealthy, insane. Minds which

15 See p. 202.

demand more from their brains than can be given, die with the death of their brains. A mind tends to survive in proportion to its service to its brain. The existence of partial substances at different levels depends upon their mutual cooperation, for the integration of mind and brain, or of any of many different levels into a newer and higher level, depends upon such cooperation between different kinds of partial substances. The more successfully they cooperate, the more permanently do they survive as a consequence of such cooperation.

What about freedom? Emergentists are primarily determinists. Lower levels determine higher levels, but are, in turn, determined by them to a certain extent. If survival of higher levels depends upon a particular kind of organized cooperation, then this demand conditions the urge to survive and determines what it must do. However, "there are degrees of freedom in nature, and the higher up we go in the scale of evolution the more freedom there is because the greater is the internal organization and plasticity of realities." [16] "We rightly feel that in most of our actions we are not pushed around from the outside. There is choice, adjustment, response to these external demands upon us. It is because of this that relative autonomy is a feature of the world." [17] "Organisms have designed themselves because design is natural to the physical world. But such design is a growth-design and not a planned design. It is only machines which are planned designs." [18]

Freedom is a relative matter and nothing is completely free. But the ultimate particles of the lowest level, if they be complete, perfect, without parts, and thus without an internal direction, must be controlled entirely from the outside. Thus, the ultimate units are completely unfree. It is only the emergents which exercise control over their constituents as well as having some influence over other similar emergents which are free. The higher the level, the more internal control or self-control, and thus, in this sense, the more freedom. Whereas Plotinus found freedom of choice an evil because it represented degenerate being which could be remedied only by one's giving up such freedom, Sellars finds freedom a good which emerges from an essentially unfree origin and which promises more and more freedom as the emerging process proceeds to higher and higher levels. This does not mean that freedom is freedom from determination. It

[16] Sellars, *The Principles and Problems of Philosophy*, p. 372.
[17] *Ibid.*, p. 375.
[18] *Ibid.*, p. 377.

means merely that higher emergents become more fully self-determining.

What is goodness and how does it come into being? Matter is neutral, neither good nor bad. Yet, somehow, values emerge. Life and mind arise from lower tendencies to emerge and express this tendency inherent in them as desires. "Anything which we desire, need, want, enjoy either for its own sake or as a means is a value." [19] "Organisms desire objects, tend toward them, are filled with emotion at the sight of them, select them, give them value-meaning." [20] Thus values arise as a consequence of the emergence of desires, both historically and in each desiring occasion. But, if each desiring situation involves both an aim and a goal, which is primary? For emanationists, the One, the ultimate goal of all our deepest desires, exists prior to the desires. We desire the One because it is desirable.

Emergentists, on the other hand, find desires arising out of needs. As we strugggle to conceive what we lack, we formulate ideas, or ideals, of what will meet our need. Such ideals, then, are taken as our goals. Our inner urges, molded by environmental conditions, are the source of our aims. Aims, then, are primary, goals are derivative. Alexander, for example, sees God as that ideal to which we aspire, an ideal which grows out of our awareness of incompleteness. When we feel ignorant, we idealize all-knowingness. When we feel powerless, we idealize omnipotence. When we fear our temporariness, we idealize everlastingness. When we feel restrained, we idealize perfect freedom. All of our ideals, then, become ideally harmonized as God, that goal in which all our aims will be perfected. Once such an ideal emerges, it guides, and thus controls, our conduct in pursuit of such aims. But God, as such a supreme goal, originates in human needs. For Sellars, further, "It is society that creates values. They express social aspirations or ideals." [21] Such social values also "mingle and interact with one another" [22] and give rise to newer and more complex desires serving as a basis for the evolution of still higher values. "Human personality reaches its highest point where values are developed and overlap." [23]

Emergentism has the tremendous advantage of combining many insights of previous views, while avoiding some of their difficulties. It

[19] *Ibid.*, p. 434.

[20] Roy Wood Sellars, *Bougle's Evolution of Values*, p. xxi. Henry Holt and Co., New York, 1926.

[21] *Ibid.*, p. xxxv.   [23] *Ibid.*

[22] *Ibid.*, p. xxxvi.

retains an interactionistic view of mind-body relationships without being subject to the difficulties of extreme dualism. It retains matter as its ultimate basis and, thus, has most of the advantages of materialism. But, since it recognizes genuine novelty and the emergence of higher levels of behavior, it also justifies the existence of the nonphysical sciences. In doing so, it is more scientific than materialism since it takes into account the substantial results of all of the major sciences. "And the advantage of it is that it explains the coexistence in nature today of things so different as minerals and government, the stormy ocean and the human mind which contemplates it and sees in it beauty and destruction." [24] It gives mind efficacy, power of control, substantiality, without making it either the sole substance or superior to matter or even equal to matter. It allows for an immanent deity and can account for the controlling power which religious ideals have over the lives of men. It is optimistic, even though deterministic. It allows for increasing freedom, without abandoning determinism. Also, it is, as compared with materialism, genuinely evolutionary. For, it holds that the stuff and substance of the universe has evolved from matter and continues to do so.

Criticisms

Criticisms of emergentism are offered by every other philosophy. Dualists find that, since emergentists accept interaction, either emergentism is involved in the same difficulties as dualism, or mind and matter are not both substances. That is, the difficulties of dualism can hardly be avoided unless dualism of substances is given up. The emergentist agrees that mind and matter are not complete, perfect, or mere substances, but only partial substances. Those who cannot accept the notion of partial substances reject emergentism as founded upon an inconsistent conception. To the extent that they interact, mind and matter are not substances, and to the extent that they are substances they do not interact. This is hardly interaction of substances.

Emergentists are involved in an epistemological difficulty, similar to, if not quite the same as, that of dualists. How can one emergent, i.e., mind, know other emergents which are different from it? Of course, mind and other emergents are alike, in being emergents, but different in kind. If each level has its own kind of laws, how can

[24] Sellars, *The Principles and Problems of Philosophy,* p. 364.

mind, operating in accordance with its own unique laws, know (be like) other levels subject to different laws? Although the emergentist doctrine does not imply that knowledge of matter is as completely impossible as Descartes' extreme dualism necessitates, it leaves such knowledge partly impossible, to the degree that other emergents are different from mind.

Materialists feel that emergentists add nothing, except difficulties, to the materialism that is their basis, or starting point. Materialists grant that levels of organization of matter exist, but these so-called higher levels are merely levels of greater complexity of association of pre-existing units. Such association creates no new substance. The substantiality of the so-called higher levels is illusory. A whole is merely the sum of its parts. Higher wholes are merely more complicated sums. If a whole were more than the sum of its parts, then where did this more come from? Either the new substance was spontaneously created, or involves some energy mysteriously brought in from elsewhere, or entails some sort of mystical transformation of energy which we are unable to account for.

Emergentists reply that some energy from one level may be lost to that level when a new level of organization emerges from it, but the universe as a whole neither gains nor loses energy. There is no unbridgeable gap between levels of oganization of energy. Cosmic energy involves not merely transformation, as materialists hold, but also a new formation of energy which materialists cannot account for merely in terms of their basic assumptions. The natural tendency of amateur dualists to find no difficulty in the transformation of material into spiritual energy, and vice versa, in interaction, has been accepted by emergentists and explained in terms of levels of partial substances involving levels of transformation and new forms of energy.

However, materialists may put their criticisms in another way. If there is more in an emergent than in a resultant, then the law of cause and effect, that the cause must contain as much as the effect, is violated. Emergentists reply that, in a sense, the effect contains no more, i.e., transforming energy into new forms gives us something new and different and, in this sense, more, but there is no more energy in the universe as a whole, just because a particular whole involves more than its parts. Such "more" comes not from nowhere, but from other forms of energy, not all of which can be captured in the equations of materialists, whose calculations are limited largely to one level only.

Then the materialist replies that emergentism overthrows the principle of the uniformity of nature, not only in holding that there can be more in emergents than in resultants, but also in claiming that each level generates its own and different set of laws. There is no one set of laws for the whole universe, no legal uniformity, but an increasing number of different varieties of laws which have no predictable relation to those previously in operation. Emergentism involves a chaotic growth of laws to whose growth there is no apparent end. Emergentists reply that laws follow functioning and do not pre-exist to force functions to conform. Whenever there are new forms of behavior, there must be, naturally, new laws. Materialists falsify the facts of experience when they insist that new laws of behavior must conform strictly to old and pre-existing laws. If matter must conform to eternal laws, materialists, then, have succumbed to a sort of Platonic idealism, in which laws are prior to matter. However, materialists, so long as they remain materialists, obstinately reject emergentism as unnecessarily mystical.

Spiritualists and emanationists join in condemning emergentism for subordinating spirit to matter, unity to plurality, the higher to the lower, and lesser reality to greater reality. Emergentists make God an evanescent emergent, a temporary development which may become extinct like other already extinct species. God is a product of matter, rather than matter a product of God. Also, creationists and organicists, as we shall see, join dualists in condemning emergentists for their overemphasis upon matter.

Numerous other questions remain to plague emergentists. Why did emergence begin in the first place? Why did not the material level remain merely material? If emergent processes have been going on forever, why have we not emerged even farther than we have? If one level can emerge from another, why stop (or start) with the material level? Perhaps there are lower levels than matter (as one emergentist, Alexander, already recognizes in space-time). What causes emergents to decline, disintegrate, become extinct? Why has not the whole emergent process returned to its material origin? If it will eventually do so, is not emergentism just as pessimistic, ultimately, as materialism, about the conservation of values in the universe?

· 19 ·

Creationism

Swedish-born American philosopher John Elof Boodin (1869–1950), Professor of Philosophy at the University of California at Los Angeles, is significant for having synthesized emergentistic and emanationistic types of metaphysics into a single system. Whereas emergentists find only matter and emanationists find only spirit (the One) as the ultimate substance, Boodin accepts two kinds of ultimate substance, i.e., both spirit and matter. But, unlike Descartes, who considered his two substances, spirit and matter, as independent, Boodin holds that the two kinds of ultimate substance are never completely independent of each other nor, even, of other emergent substances, which depend upon both of them. For Boodin, a lowest level of matter and a highest level of spirit, i.e., God, have always existed, and together they have created and continue to create (hence "creationism") all other substances through their joint cooperation.

Boodin is an evolutionist who develops his system by comparing "three views of evolution: (1) merely temporal emergence, which means a passage from the lower to the higher without formal guidance [e.g., the type of emergentism dealt with in the preceding Chapter], (2) preformation, according to which all forms and levels are present in the process from the beginning [e.g., as exemplified in the emanationism of Plotinus], and, finally, (3) creation, by which is meant emergence with guidance. Both emergence and preformation deal with evolution as a one-way process." [1] "Neither . . . can be true by itself." [2] "The theory of creation which I propose recognizes . . . the emergence of real novelties in the local history—new events, forms, and levels, which are probably not matched in detail

[1] John Elof Boodin, *Three Interpretations of the Universe*, p. 487. The Macmillan Co., New York, 1934. This volume and a companion volume, *God*, together constitute a set also entitled *God and Creation*.
[2] *Ibid.*, p. 488.

226

anywhere else. But, in contrast to materialism, it holds that events run their course within wholes; and these exist within a universal whole which is compresent with the events and guides the events. With the preformation theory, it recognizes the reality of structure as guiding the individual history. But in contrast to the preformation theory, it holds that structure in particular histories emerges under the guidance of the whole, and is not latent from the beginning in the particular history. . . . Nature, as we now conceive it, consists of pulses of energy—quanta of radiation, positive and negative electric charges—within an electromagnetic field and gravitational field. These pulses of energy are integrated into a series of patterns and levels. . . ." [3] "There must be a plurality of fields of energy, and these must take account of one another . . . and they must take account of one another in terms of their unique history and inertia. But above all there must be some cosmic control within which the re-arrangements are guided, so far as the history and inertia of the various centers and milieux of centers permit. Such a process of synthesis by interaction of parts within a whole, I call creation." [4]

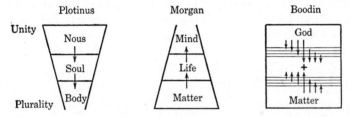

"The material out of which the cosmic structure is built is the same everywhere," but also "everywhere in nature we have evidence of control." [5] "Emergence can be no accident. . . . To say that the new manifestations—laws, events, qualities, levels, individuals—emerge from the organizations of the stuff of nature, is true enough. . . . To say that they happen when the adequate conditions are present is a truism. The question is what conditions must we postulate as adequate to account for the progressive series of organization, the outcome of which is the mind of man?" [6] "The ultimate impetus to advance must come from the cosmic whole. The evolution of nature— from atom to human art—is a process of trial and error response on the part of the individual, at a particular stage of its evolution, to ex-

[3] *Ibid.*, p. 489.
[4] *Ibid.*, p. 490.

[5] *Ibid.*, p. 492.
[6] *Ibid.*, p. 495.

press the structure of the whole in terms of its own individuality and limitations." [7] "The whole process of evolution is a process of spiritualization." [8] "In the last analysis all organization is spiritual." [9] However, "this cosmic control does not evolve, but everything evolves within it." [10] "Matter [i.e., those organized levels we are acquainted with] has no privileged position. Matter and the laws of matter emerge in the evolutionary process. Matter is not conceived as the mere downward trend of life—the débris of organization, as Bergson [and Plotinus] conceives it. But matter [in this sense] is part of the evolutionary ascent from the comparatively formless situation in the primitive nebulae to higher and higher degrees of organization. Matter itself as we find it is already spiritualized through organization." [11] "The part at any rate is not a mere passive instrument of the whole. There is no merely passive matter." [12] "There is nothing really static in nature. Everything is in transition." [13] "The cosmic environment acts upon matter, or better, the cosmic whole stimulates the part, for the earth and the parts of the earth develop in the womb of the cosmos and under its control." [14]

Each emergent is a product of the interaction of matter and spirit, or of parts and wholes. Each is a new whole of parts, both as a new whole of its parts and a new part of the larger whole within which it developed. Every new thing is a result of both the higher and the lower (like the Chinese Yang and Yin, positive and negative, or male and female) principles which create between them new progeny, new substances which function as new wholes of parts and as new parts of larger wholes in furthering the ongoing emergent processes. "Spirit and matter have complementary properties. Matter is characterized by inertia, spirit by spontaneity; matter by entropy, spirit by creativeness. Matter is ever losing potential. Life and mind increase potential. The law of spiritual activity is the reverse of material activity. For matter, activity means loss of energy; for spirit, activity means a gain." [15] Whereas, for Plotinus, spirit is positive being, matter negative being, for Boodin, both spirit and matter have positive being, though spirit is positive in activity, matter negative in

[7] *Ibid.*, p. 498.   [10] *Ibid.*, p. 493.
[8] *Ibid.*, p. 499.   [11] *Ibid.*, p. 496.
[9] *Ibid.*, p. 491.   [12] *Ibid.*, p. 502.
[13] *Ibid.*, p. 491.
[14] John Elof Boodin, *Cosmic Evolution*, p. 73. The Macmillan Co., New York, 1925.
[15] John Elof Boodin, *God*, p. 115. The Macmillan Co., New York, 1934.

activity (i.e., has inertia). Boodin reverses Plotinus' view that spirit (especially perfect spirit or the One) is inactive in opposition to matter which is evil activity. For Boodin, it is spirit which is active and activity is good. However, since spirit penetrates or organizes the lowest units, there is no merely passive matter. Although pure matter, if there were any, would be formless, and pure spirit, if there were any, would be without content, every existing being involves both. There is no God apart from the material world, no world apart from God.

Like Aristotle (384–322 B.C.) who long ago claimed that there can be no substance without both form and matter, Boodin denies their separate existence. However, whereas Aristotle was inconsistent with his general doctrine on three counts, Boodin is more consistent. For Aristotle, "God, the intelligences believed to control the celestial spheres, and the creative reason which is the highest faculty of the human soul" are "capable of existing as pure form without any admixture of matter." [16] This inconsistency, a failure to reject fully Plato's doctrine of an independently subsisting realm of Ideas, made him more acceptable to Christian theologians who sought to retain Neoplatonic conceptions of God, and yet also have more common-sense conceptions of man. Boodin is more consistent, if less orthodox, at this point.

The mind-body problem, explained unsatisfactorily by Descartes in terms of two independent substances, by Spinoza as aspects of one underlying substance, by spiritualists and materialists by each denying the existence of the other's body or mind, by emanationists and emergentists through subordination of body to mind or mind to body, finds in creationism both equality and mutual subordination, both substantiality and interfunctionality, both independence and dependence, treated with greater justice. "We can neither express the lower levels as functions of the higher levels, nor can we express the higher levels as functions of the lower levels." [17] Mind and body as higher and lower, or as more spiritual and more material, each has its own kind of substantiality and its own kind of contribution to make to the interactive situation. Whereas, for emergentists, mind controls body only after it has emerged from body, Boodin holds that the emergence of the body itself was determined by larger wholes.

[16] Edwin A. Burtt, *Types of Religious Philosophy*, pp. 53–54. Harper Bros., New York, 1939.
[17] Boodin, *Cosmic Evolution*, p. 173.

In his book, *The Social Mind,* he develops an example of higher control. A group is a unity, a spirit, relative to which its members are matter. Such group-spirituality does not deprive the individual of any of his own spirituality, but adds and enriches it by providing a larger spirit within which it is molded, protected, evolved. Each personality is a product both of its biological and its sociological heritage. Each personality is molded by its group as truly as by its cells and, as it emerges into maturity, it, in turn, modifies its cell structure by its acquired habits of eating and exercise and by medical prescriptions. The minds of other persons, and what may be spoken of as the "social mind," pre-exists to guide the mind of the particular individual as it develops. "In fact, the nurture of the younger generation by the older with its milieu of habits is the condition of the existence of all higher animal life." [18]

All the combined influences from higher and lower levels dynamically determine the unique character of the emerging personality. But, once it emerges, it functions, in turn, as a substantial determiner of other things. Each personality both influences its own bodily and cellular behavior and also the constitution of its group and its group's behavioral patterns. Mind, then, becomes substantial and causative. It is not just an emergent which originates wholly from lower levels, for in this event, as materialists point out, matter seems to be acting, even indirectly, back upon itself. But it is like a substance which has its own contribution to make, and which is derived partly from still higher sources, instead of originating in matter only.

What about freedom and determinism in the creationistic picture? "It is a fundamental law, including all reality, that the degrees of freedom increase with the degrees of complexity." [19] "At the lowest stage the organization is precisely determined." [20] But higher up the scale there is greater freedom because the higher-level units, being more complex, contain within themselves as unities greater and more various possibilities for growth. In part-whole situations, a whole, being a higher-level guide to the behavior of its parts, is freer than its parts. Yet "in this inter-relation the parts have their say. They are not mere functions of the whole. We know of varying degrees of freedom as between the parts and wholes open to our observation. The degrees of freedom in atoms are different from those in molecules, different in molecules from those in molar masses, different in

[18] *Ibid.,* p. 99.
[19] Boodin, *Three Interpretations of the Universe,* p. 500.
[20] *Ibid.*

organic masses from living beings, different in the unicellular organism from that of the multicellular organism, different in an organism endowed with mind from one in which there is no such endowment, and different within the isolated person from persons in society. The degrees of freedom in the cosmic whole must present still greater ranges. As the human organism is not just one history, but a vast number of histories, atomic histories, molar histories (such as that of the heart), all running their course within the organic whole, so in the cosmos there are an indefinite number of histories running their course within the whole. But the degrees of freedom must be vastly greater in the cosmic whole than in the economy of the human organism." [21]

Creationism has most of the advantages of emergentism. It keeps the interactionistic view, not only without the disadvantages of extreme dualism, but also without the emergentistic difficulties of deriving greater from lesser unity. Emergentists must posit original unity somehow and do so as activity inherent in the lowest levels of matter, but this appears to many as getting more unity in higher emergents than the original dispersement of matter warrants. Boodin not only presumes sufficient unity of the cosmic whole to satisfy our needs, but he retains a basis for whatever demands we may feel for the eternal ultimacy of God. Whereas Alexander's God may become extinct, Boodin's never can. Boodin is equally evolutionary regarding the world's novelty, he thinks, and yet retains all the advantages of materialism that even a materialist could want, unless he is unduly squeamish about those unitary or spiritual factors which he has failed, even in his own eyes, to account for. Creationism is even more scientific than emergentism in that higher levels of organization have a greater genuineness about them than emergentists can give. Sociology is as ultimate a science as physics, because the social mind is as much a real determiner of personality as are molecules. Creationism, too, is both deterministic and optimistic. It accounts for the evolution of new substances even more convincingly than emergentism. It has the advantage also of subordinating neither mind to body nor body to mind, thereby supporting the long philosophical, religious, and common-sense faith that persons have a genuinely dual character.

On the other hand, Boodin not only escapes the difficulties of Descartes' ultrasubstantialistic dualism, but also some of the difficulties in Aristotle, and in St. Thomas Aquinas, who based his philosophy upon Aristotle. Although Aristotle, too, held that form and matter

[21] Boodin, *God,* pp. 83–84.

cooperate in the production of each substance, thus obviating Descartes' difficulties centuries before Descartes discovered his dualism, he accepted Plato's fixity of forms. Aristotle's essential forms were eternally unchangeable, so he could not account for evolution or emergence of novelty. Boodin, having the advantage of modern science at his disposal, surpasses both Aristotle and Descartes in synthesizing dualistic interactionism with the development of genuine novelties through the creative interaction of substantially different principles. Each new person is both unique and novel. Each mind is a realm of emerging ideas which resemble the ideas in similarly emerging minds, and yet each person's ideas are also uniquely his own.

Criticisms

Again, every different viewpoint will have objections to creationism similar to those raised against emergentism,[22] for creationism incorporates much of the emergentistic doctrine. In addition, emergentists will reject the eternality of spiritual control. Creationism contends that the lower emerges from the higher as much as the higher emerges from the lower. In fact, although Boodin claims that spirit and matter have complementary properties, he attributes life and creativeness to spirit, inertia and deadness to matter. Thus, even though the two are supposedly equal, spirit is superior in activity and power of control. Contemporary conceptions of matter as dynamic are hardly consistent with the claim that such activity as belongs to matter is due to the influence of higher spirit. Even though field theories are gaining credence in physics, physicists hardly accept the field as the sole source of activity.

Boodin's identification of action with spirit and passivity with matter ignores also those traditional attributes of God as peaceful. This, of course, brings to the fore the paradoxes involved in having a God who is both an all-powerful creator, or principle of activity, and a God who is eternally unchanged, peaceful, placid, perfect. Although Boodin is not, of course, responsible for this theological predicament, his forgetting God's inertness, as inherent in his eternal unchangeableness, leaves a gap in his system. If God, too, is inert in that he cannot be changed, and if inertness is a property of matter, then is not God, too, properly considered, the biggest particle of matter?

[22] See pp. 223–225.

If all other levels of substantiality have emerged except some lowest level of material inertness or the highest level of cosmic organizing activity, why stop with these? Why must there be a lowest level? May not the divisibility and plurality of matter be infinite? Need there be a first level? Why must there be a highest level? May not the emergence of each new highest level of organization thereby generate a new plurality demanding a still higher level of unity? Need this process of increasingly complex unity ever stop? Organicists, at least, reject top and bottom levels, without rejecting the universal operation of the higher and the lower, or the spiritual and the material, principles in each causal situation. These criticisms will be developed further in the following chapter.

· 20 ·

Organicism

Organicism, the writer's (1907–   ) own view, is presented here as a tentative explanatory hypothesis to be tried out in competition with other views. Consistent with his pragmatic spirit, previously confessed,[1] the writer intends that his view, like all others presented in this book, shall be considered as a tentative proposal to be examined for its relative merits as a general interpretive hypothesis. One may say of it what William James said of pragmatism: It is "a new name for some old ways of thinking." [2] Of course, every new view must claim either that it has been held before or that, somehow, mankind has been mistaken up to now. Organicism is not, as will be shown, an entirely new way of thinking, but an old way which men naturally follow when they are not enticed into extremes. However, it does claim to be a sufficiently new kind of emphasis upon "the middle way" in metaphysics to warrant presenting it here as a distinguishable type. There have been middle ways of many kinds proclaimed before, especially in moral matters, but never, so far as the writer knows, has middle-of-the-road-ism been pursued so persistently as a means of discovering the nature of the metaphysically ultimate.

But also, the new name, "organicism," is not entirely new. The term "organic" is an old one which has already acquired a variety of meanings. Some of these are relevant only to certain specialized fields, such as biology or organic chemistry. Others are intended to be more general, yet are defined in specifically limited ways, as in Whitehead's "Philosophy of Organism." [3] One may find the word "organicism" used with reference to any of these meanings of "or-

[1] See pp. 165–166.
[2] William James, *Pragmatism, A New Name for Some Old Ways of Thinking.* Longmans, Green and Co., New York, 1907.
[3] See Ch. 21.

234

ganic." However, despite such variety, there appears to be something of a common core of meaning running through most uses of this term which seems closer to the writer's key idea than that expressed by any other term. What this general meaning is, it is hoped, will become clear as the chapter develops. When the meaning of a common term is sufficiently expanded to represent vast metaphysical contexts, it undergoes a kind of change which makes it partly new. However, the novelty of organicism as a metaphysics, or the novelty of the expanded meaning of the term "organic," is a matter of degree. Any difference in degree, nevertheless, if considered sufficiently significant, may be taken as a difference in kind. Not only is it true, as William James has said, that there is no difference but difference in degree between difference in degree and no difference,[4] but also there is no kind of difference but difference in degree between difference in degree and difference in kind. Whether organicism is different in kind or in degree is something which the reader will, doubtless, decide for himself.

The relationship of organicism to the theories previously discussed may be represented by the following diagram.

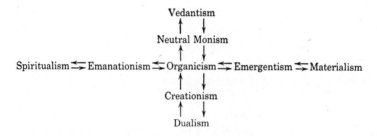

Spiritualism holds that only spirit exists. Materialism claims that only matter exists. Emanationism pictures matter as dependent upon spirit for its existence, whereas spirit does not depend upon matter. Emergentism claims that spirit depends upon matter for its existence, but that matter does not depend upon spirit. For organicism, spirit and matter both exist, but interdependently. That is, they are partly independent of and partly dependent upon each other. Conceiving spirit as unity or wholeness and matter as plurality or partiality, it sees the relationship between spirit and matter as almost the same as

[4] Paraphrased from William James, *The Will to Believe*, p. 297. Longmans, Green and Co., New York, 1896.

that between a whole and its parts. Just as a whole is not its parts and the parts are not their whole, so spirit and matter are not each other and are, in this sense, independent of each other. And yet, just as no whole can exist separated from its parts, and just as nothing can be a part of a whole independently of that whole, so neither spirit nor matter can exist apart from each other.

Dualism holds that spirit and matter both exist, but in complete independence of each other, and, also, that there is nothing upon which both depend.[5] Creationism, although claiming independence for spirit (God) and matter, frankly recognizes the dependence of each upon the other in all creative processes. Yet, here too, there is nothing upon which spirit and matter depend. Neutral monism, on the other hand, considers spirit and matter as two dependent attributes or aspects of an underlying neutral substance. This substance is that upon which spirit and matter depend for existence, but it does not depend on them. Vedantism, or at least Samkara's conception of Nirguna Brahman, similarly sees Brahman as that upon which all else depends for existence but which depends upon nothing else. However, in Brahman even the distinction between spirit and matter disappears. Neither spirit nor matter, ultimately, exist, but only that which has the spiritual and the material as illusory aspects exists.[6]

Organicism finds itself between creationism and neutral monism in holding (1) that there is a sense in which spirit and matter genuinely exist and (2) that each functions also as an aspect of something which underlies both. Not only do wholes and parts exist interdependently, but also that which is both whole and parts exists. In sum, spirit and matter both exist and that which is both spiritual and material exists; spirit and matter are partly independent of each other and yet also partly dependent upon each other, and that which is both

---

[5] These dualistic ideals, clearly expressed in Descartes' dualistic statements, are contradicted both by Descartes' interactionistic statements (spirit and matter do depend upon each other for their interaction with each other) and his theistic statements (spirit and matter are created, i.e., dependent, substances whereas God is the only uncreated substance). See Ch. 13.

[6] Except for brief and incidental mention of Brahmanism (see p. 205), no exposition of Vedantism is included in this text. Its significance as a type relative to organicism should be sufficiently clear from the foregoing statement. For details, the reader is referred to S. Radhakrishnan, *Indian Philosophy, Vol. II,* Ch. VIII; M. Hiriyanna, *The Essentials of Indian Philosophy,* Ch. VII; Swami Nikhilananda, *The Upanishads, Vol. I,* pp. 25–49.

spiritual and material is partly independent of, and partly dependent upon, spirit and matter. Whatever is both spiritual and material can be reduced neither to the spiritual nor to the material; spirit cannot be reduced to matter, matter cannot be reduced to spirit, and neither spirit nor matter can be reduced to that which is both spiritual and material.

For organicism, then, each of the other eight theories expresses a fundamental truth in its positive assertions, but each is inadequate to the extent that its negative assertions deny fundamental truths embodied in the positive assertions of the others. That is, spiritualism is correct in claiming that spirit exists, but mistaken in denying that matter exists. Materialism is correct in believing that matter exists, but incorrect in claiming that spirit does not exist. Emanationism is right in saying that matter depends upon spirit, but wrong when it says that spirit does not depend upon matter. Emergentism is true when it says that spirit depends upon matter, but false in its presupposing that matter may be completely independent of spirit. Vedantists and neutral monists truthfully claim that spirit and matter are aspects of something underlying both, but falsely deny that spirit and matter have no independence whatsoever. Dualists and creationists rightfully hold that spirit and matter both exist, somewhat independently, but they are mistaken to the extent that they claim complete independence of matter and spirit from each other and from something which underlies or includes both. Organicism, then, opposes each of the other theories by rejecting their negative statements, but embodies the positive claims of each within itself.

How does organicism deal with the problem of levels of existence, discussed in the three preceding chapters? In contrast with emanationism and creationism, both of which require a highest level—the universe as a whole (called the One or God)—which is not included within anything higher, organicism claims that any whole which, for any reason, is taken as the highest, in any sense, functions also, in other ways, as part of some still higher whole—and this without exception. In opposition to emergentism and creationism, both of which posit, at least in principle, some lowest level of many indivisible parts or particles, organicism believes that any unit which is taken as the lowest can be seen, in some other sense, to involve its own infinite variety of parts. Only by admitting no completely highest or lowest levels can organicism maintain its faith in the constant interdependence of unity and plurality, wholeness and partiality, spirit and matter. Since the view that there must be either a highest or lowest level, or both, is so widespread and persistent, it is clearly demanded of organicism that it give its reasons for differing at this point.

First, regarding a supposed highest level which is inclusive of everything, organicism, accepting change as an ultimate characteristic of existence, sees every existing whole, including "the universe as a whole," as changing somewhat whenever there is change in its parts. When a whole is involved in a change in any of its parts, it thereby changes as a whole—not completely, into a wholly different whole, but partly, into a whole with a different part. In so far as it is a whole with the same parts, it is the same whole; but in so far as it is a whole with different parts, it is a different whole. Being both the same and different, it does not escape either its sameness or its difference.

Now, any supposed highest level of unity, or "the universe as a whole," also not only remains the same, in whatever sense there is no change in it, but also becomes different, in whatever sense there is change. To the extent that there is change, existence must include both "the universe as a whole" before such change and "the universe as a whole" after such change. Thus, although "the universe as a whole" is the highest level of unity, in one sense, "the universe as a whole," after such change, is a still higher level of wholeness for it includes a previously nonexistent and not-included event. Since change continues, increasingly higher levels of inclusiveness continue to emerge. Thus, although in one sense there is a highest level, or universe as a whole, in another sense no level is the absolutely highest level. However, to the extent that any level is unique in some respect, it is the highest level in that respect. In this sense, every level is in some sense the highest level. "The ultimate is not something far removed from us, rather it is *here* and *now*." [7]

Turning, secondly, to the opposite end of the whole-part polarity, we may note that each part is related to its whole and to the other parts in this whole. Now, each thing which is related to other things has such relations as parts of itself. Thus, though part of a larger whole, each thing must, by that very fact, have many parts of its own. Having such parts, no thing which is a part can be an absolutely smallest part or a lowest level of particles (wholes without parts).

[7] A. R. Wadia, "The Place of the Philosopher in Modern Society," *Silver Jubilee Commemoration Volume,* p. 72. Indian Philosophical Congress, Bangalore, 1950.

However, in so far as anything is unique as a part, it is the lowest part of its kind. In this sense, every part may be a lowest part without detracting in any way from other parts being lowest in their own ways.

The foregoing reasoning involves a doctrine of organic relations which may be contrasted with the doctrines of external relations and of internal relations. To the extent that materialists and emergentists are motivated by pluralistic ideals, they tend to conceive existence as consisting ultimately of many separate particles which are independent of, or external to, each other. Relations between such particles are believed to be external to the particles and to have no influence whatsoever upon their nature. Spiritualists and emanationists, on the other hand, in considering plurality subordinate to unity, presuppose that all relations, ultimately, are internal to, or inside of, the things related, because things have no existence apart from their identity with the more ultimate one. No external relations exist ultimately.

Dualists and creationists contend that each of these two kinds of relations exists, but without overlapping, except when interacting. Internal relations and external relations are entirely unlike in nature, for dualists, but interact creatively, for creationists. For vedantists and neutral monists, neither internal nor external relations exist since, ultimately, no relations exist, except either as illusory (for vedantists) or dependent (for neutral monists) aspects of something that is nonrelational.

For organicism, every relation has both external and internal aspects, for each relation both separates its terms from each other and unites them to each other. Consequently, a relation between one thing and another is, on the one hand, neither of those things, but, on the other, serves also as parts of both of them, since neither could exist, as related to the other, apart from both that other thing and this relation between them. To the extent that things are related, they are interdependent; i.e., they are both independent of each other, in being different things, and depend upon each other for being what they are as related to each other. Even the relation of negation, the most external of all relations, is partly internal, for two things cannot be not each other without being dependent upon each other for such notness. If there were no such other thing, the one thing could not be what it is as a different thing. Two supposedly completely different things must be alike at least in being different from each other.

Also, the relation of identity, the most internal of all relations, is partly external, for each relation has two ends which, as different ends, are somewhat external to each other.

The two preceding examples, pertaining to spirit-matter and to external-internal relations, illustrate some organicistic theses, namely, that existence, as experienced, presents its apparently essential conditions as polar opposites and that, whenever such polarities appear, nine types of explanatory theories develop. Other examples of polar categories of existence are:

1. One, unity	Many, plurality
2. Identity, sameness	Difference, otherness
3. Continuity	Discontinuity
4. Particular, unique	Universal
5. Being	Nonbeing
6. Things	Space
7. Quality	Quantity
8. Immanence	Transcendence
9. Permanence	Change
10. Substance	Function
11. Duration	Events
12. Old	New, novelty
13. Actual	Potential
14. End	Means
15. Goal	Aim, tendency
16. Intrinsic value	Instrumental value
17. Finite, finished	Infinite, unfinished
18. Perfect	Imperfect
19. Cause	Effect
20. Good	Evil
21. Free	Determined
22. Intelligence	Unadaptability
23. Essence, definiteness	Indeterminateness, indefiniteness
24. Absolute	Relative
25. Hierarchy, inequality	Reciprocity, equality
26. Active, agent	Passive, patient [8]

The nine types of theories may be arranged on a generalized Diagram of Types similar to the diagram on p. 235. This diagram is convenient both for revealing organicism's relation to other types and for deriving organicism's conceptions with respect to each polarity.

[8] See Archie J. Bahm, "Existence and Its Polarities," *The Journal of Philosophy*, Sept. 29, 1949, p. 630.

Coining some convenient, if atrocious, terms for this purpose, we may picture the relations between the nine types as follows:

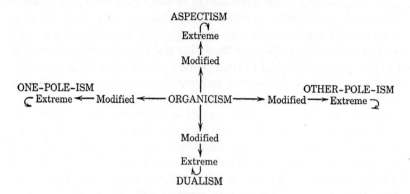

The meaning of each of these types may be stated generally as follows: 1. Extreme one-pole-ism: One pole of the polarity exists; the other does not exist. 2. Modified one-pole-ism: One pole exists prior to the other pole. The other pole depends upon the one pole for existence, but the one pole does not depend upon the other. 3. Extreme other-pole-ism: The other pole exists; the one pole does not exist. 4. Modified other-pole-ism: The other pole exists as prior to the one pole. The one depends upon the other for its existence, but the other does not depend upon the one. 5. Extreme dualism: Both poles exist independently of each other. Neither depends upon the other for its existence. 6. Modified dualism: Both poles exist, independent of each other for what they are in themselves, but dependent upon each other for what they are in relation to each other. 7. Extreme aspectism: That which is polar exists, but its poles do not exist. Both poles are merely apparent aspects of that which is polar. 8. Modified aspectism: That which is polar exists, and its poles depend upon it for their existence. That which is polar does not depend for its existence upon its poles. 9. Organicism: Both poles exist and that which is polar exists—interdependently, i.e., partly dependently and partly independently. Each pole is partly independent of and partly dependent upon its opposite pole, and that which is polar is partly independent of and partly dependent upon its poles. That which is polar can be reduced neither to one nor to both of its poles, neither wholly nor partly; a pole can be reduced neither to its opposite pole nor to that which is polar, neither wholly nor partly.

Organicism, thus, is defined in terms of its relations to the other eight types. It is both dependent upon them (identical with their positive assertions) and independent of them (different from them in denying their negative assertions). It claims to be a new synthesis: a synthesis because of its way of relating itself to these other types and of gathering up their truths within itself, and new because of its unique pattern of denial of their denials and because of the resulting kind of spirit and operational technique involved in its solutions to metaphysical and to other philosophical problems.

Perhaps another example is needed to clarify the way in which this organicist technique works. Selecting the substance-function polarity for examination, we may note that extreme substantialism (extreme one-pole-ism) would hold that only substance exists, without any existing functions. This view may be illustrated by the Taoist ideal that "the way to do is to be," in contrast with the ideals of extreme functionalists (extreme other-pole-ism) who would have us believe that "the way to be is to do" or, in more familiar language, "a thing is what a thing does." Modified substantialism considers substance as primary, functions as secondary; i.e., functions depend upon substances whereas substances do not depend upon functions. Modified functionalists, who are becoming increasingly popular these days, consider action as primary, the actor as secondary. If a thing is what a thing does, then there must be that thing, even though it acquires such dependent being as it has as a result of its functioning in such activity. Extreme dualism would hold that both substances and functions exist, but independently of each other. If this seems absurd, surely it is not much more so than the spirit-matter dualism of Descartes. Modified dualism would accept substances and functions as equally real and as essentially independent of each other, though dependent upon each other in so far as they are interrelated. For extreme aspectism, neither substance nor function really exist, but only that which appears to manifest itself as both substance and function. Modified aspectism admits existence for both substance and function, but only as aspects dependent upon an underlying neutral something which is not dependent upon them.

Organicism, drawing out and summing up the positive truths in the foregoing types, claims that substance exists, that function depends on substance, that function exists, that substance depends on function (for substance must function as substance), that substance and function are independent of each other (neither can be reduced to the other), that they are dependent upon each other ("A substance is that which functions and a function is whatever a substance does." [9]), and that substance and function are aspects of something upon which they depend and which depends upon them. Both substantialism and functionalism are partly true; acceptance of the interdependence of both parts (there can be no being without doing and no doing without being) is organicism. But organicism accepts dualism and aspectism also as partly true, for (1) being and doing must both be (neither can be reduced to the other) and (2) that which both is and does depends for its existence upon both its being and its doing, and its being and doing depend for their existence upon it.

Not only may the Diagram of Types be used to define the organicist view relative to each particular polarity, but all such particular organicist views (the list of polarities given above is incomplete) together constitute a beginning definition of organicism as a metaphysical type. That organicism is also an epistemological and axiological type needs to be mentioned, but cannot be developed here. In addition to the polar categories of existence, there are many polar categories of experience (e.g., subject-object, apparent-real, concrete-abstract, reason-emotion, belief-doubt, explicit-implicit, real-ideal) which appear in organicism as an epistemology definable through the Diagram of Types. The spirit of organicistic epistemology is captured in the following statement by Alexander: "Even Realism and Idealism as philosophical schemes are excellent examples. . . . Why not accept both sources of knowledge? . . . Therefore, let us regard each as experimental, to be probed to the extreme and then retracted, to some mid-point, . . . the point of maximum significance." [10] Although distinction is made between experience (the epistemological) and existence (the metaphysical), since organic relations hold between them, neither can be treated adequately in isolation.

If organicism, in aiming at the middle way, consistently avoids extremes, does it not itself thereby become another kind of extreme, i.e., extreme middle-of-the-road-ism? No, for it claims that we are no more able to reach and stop at an extreme middle than we are to reach and remain at either extreme pole. Existence is dynamic, tending always to proceed more in one than in the other of two polar

[9] Archie J. Bahm, "Organic Unity and Emergence," *The Journal of Philosophy,* April 24, 1947, p. 244.

[10] Hubert G. Alexander, *Time As Dimension and History,* p. 119. University of New Mexico Press, Albuquerque, 1945.

directions. Each pole, being an essential aspect of an existent, vies with its opposite for dominance and occasionally succeeds.

But each success for one pole becomes a failure for its existent to the extent that the other pole, also essential to the existent, is defeated. Since, if one pole succeeds completely in doing away with its opposite, it destroys not only an essential aspect of its existent, but also the existent itself, and thus the pole itself. Therefore, existence involves a dynamic tension between polar tendencies and limits beyond which these tendencies cannot go without destroying themselves. Each surge of dominance by one polar aspect thus tends to be followed by a reverse tendency toward dominance by its opposite aspect. Consequently, rhythmical patterns of wavelike changes occur relative to all polar categories, the patterns being sometimes regular and sometimes irregular. But such shifting back and forth repeatedly passes through, but never stops permanently in, any supposed static mid-point. Organicism seeks the middle of the road as compared with polar extremes, but also avoids any mere middle or every dead-center. In fact, any supposed middle must itself be organic, both remaining and changing at the same time. Just as there is no highest unchanging level such as "the universe as a whole," and no lowest level which does not also have a lower level, so there is nothing which serves as a middle which does not also function as other than a middle.

What about causation? Most philosophers demand some first cause, or uncaused cause. If organicism admits no completely highest or lowest levels of existence, how does it account for ultimate causation? It finds such causation, not in some extreme polar limits, but everywhere and in all events. To exist is to involve both caused causation and uncaused causation or, to use more common terms, determinism and indeterminism. The organicist view may here again be derived with aid from the Diagram of Types. Extreme determinism contends that whatever exists is caused to exist, and this without exception. No uncaused causes exist. Modified determinism admits that there are accidental effects. Extreme indeterminism holds that nothing which exists is caused to exist; it merely is. Whatever exists is self-existent, not caused by something else. For modified indeterminism, a thing must be before it can cause, but it does cause. God, for example, causes everything, but nothing caused God. Extreme dualism wants two independent realms, one consisting of caused causes (matter) and the other of uncaused causes (spirit). Modified dualism, accepting both caused causes and uncaused causes, conceives most things as resulting from both determinism and indeterminism. Extreme aspectism sees what is conceived as caused cause and uncaused cause as two apparent aspects of that which ultimately is neither caused nor uncaused, and is neither causer nor without result. Modified aspectism admits the existence of both caused causes and uncaused causes but as aspects dependent upon that which ultimately is neither. Organicism, accepting both determinism and indeterminism as ultimate, finds caused causation and uncaused causation present in every existent. To make clear how this can be is our next task.

Determinism and indeterminism, properly interpreted, are polar opposites, not contradictories. In order to show this, let us re-examine the nature of causality. Determinists are correct in asserting that each cause-effect situation involves complete determination of effect by cause in the sense that the effect is caused to be what it is entirely by its causes. That is, only its causes cause it. If anything else caused it, this something else would also be included among its causes. Furthermore, there is nothing in the effect which was not caused by its causes. Yet, even though this be true, it is also true that each effect is in some sense new and different as compared with its causes. The crux of the difficulty lies partly in the usual tendency to oversimplify what we mean by the cause and the effect. For symbolic convenience we often use the symbolism: $C \rightarrow E$ or $C = E$. Such symbolism tends to presuppose that cause and effect are merely simple or single or unitary entities. If so, then if they equal each other, or if the effect follows wholly from its cause, we have a kind of identity of cause and effect. But surely we do not intend that cause and effect should be exactly identical. In fact, when we examine more fully what we mean, we discover that each existing cause and effect is really a complex of causes and a complex of effects. Each effect is really the effect of a multiplicity of causal factors or influences from a number of different entities. Each effect is an entity which then functions as a cause of a multitude of influences upon many other different entities. Thus a minimum symbolization of the situation involves something like the following:

In so far as each effect is one effect, i.e., has some unity or whole-ness about it, it is substantially different from the multiplicity of its causes. This difference is not only a difference of the effect from each one of its causes taken singly, but also a consequence of the fact that it is one although they are many. That is, c^1 cannot be the sole cause of e, for c^2, c^3, c^4, and c^5 also are its causes. Likewise c^2 cannot be the sole cause of e since it must share such causation with the other causes. Likewise for c^3, c^4, and c^5. If e is the joint effect of the five c's, there must be something about it which is contained neither in any one of its causes taken singly nor in all of them collectively, because their collectivity involves a manyness, and an external re-latedness of each from the others, which does not exist in the effect. What was external in the causes has become internal in the effect. Thus although, on the one hand, the effect is completely caused in the sense that its nature is what it is because of its causes; yet on the other hand, there can be no causation without causes causing effects in such a way that each effect involves something which was con-tained neither in any one of its causes taken singly nor in all of them taken together as an externally related collection. This something in the effect which was not contained in its causes is, in a sense, uncaused. If being caused means that there is nothing in the effect which was not already in the causes, then this something, which was not in the causes, is uncaused.[11]

The effect, as an existing entity, in turn functions as a cause of other effects. In so far as its effects are a result of its causes, it is a caused cause. But in so far as its effects are a result also of it as uncaused, it is an uncaused cause. Thus, not only is determinism true, in the sense that each effect is caused by nothing but its causes, but also indeterminism is true, in the sense that there is something about each effect which, though entering into subsequent causation, did not exist as such in its causes. Dualists are mistaken in holding that caused causes and uncaused causes are essentially different. Rather, caused causation and uncaused causation are two polar aspects of every cause-effect situation. Modified dualism is mistaken in pushing un-caused causation and caused causation out to substantially different, if interacting, ends of the scale. Organicism contends that the most

---

[11] Something similar should be said about each cause having a multiplicity of effects where, again, the unity of a cause is destroyed through dispersion into its effects and is contained neither in any one of them singly nor in all of them sepa-rately, although, of course, the cause is also preserved in so far as its causality is carried over into its effects.

completely caused type of causation has an uncaused aspect to it, and the most completely uncaused kind of causation has a caused aspect to it.

The organicist conception of causality may be further clarified by the observation that, since there are levels of existence, there are levels of kinds of causes and levels of kinds of effects. "Whereas it

is common to seek the cause of the behavior of a particular kind of entity in antecedent entities of the same kind, organicists insist that it is equally important to seek such causes in entities of other kinds, including those which make up both higher and lower levels. The behavior of a cell is caused partly by its biological antecedents, but also by its molecular, atomic, electronic, etc., constituents and by its biological, social, terrestrial, solar, etc., environment." [12] When it is realized that each event or entity ("eventity" [13]) reflects the causal influences of an infinite number of levels, each is seen to be not only unique in some sense but also a product of "the whole world." However, unlike Leibniz' monads,[14] it does not mirror the world from its private point of view in accordance with a pre-established harmony, but rather it is an actual effect of all that is related to it causally. Each eventity is, in a sense, a product of the whole universe, though it is equally true that the universe is, in some sense, a product of it. To the extent that it is a product of a whole universe of causes other

[12] Archie J. Bahm, "Emergence of Purpose," *The Journal of Philosophy*, Nov. 6, 1947, pp. 633–634.

[13] Archie J. Bahm, "Emergence of Values," *The Journal of Philosophy*, July 15, 1948, p. 412.

[14] See pp. 184–185.

than itself, it is determined and unfree, but to the extent that it is also an uncaused cause of the universe, it is free. Freedom consists, not in complete absence of causation, but in self-causation.

Now, self-causation has two aspects. In so far as anything is uncaused it may be spoken of as self-caused, where uncaused means having no external causes, and self-caused means having internal causation. This involves the question of in how far the inner and outer aspects of anything are both parts of that thing. If my externals are mine (i.e., are parts of me or are internal to me), then is not the whole universe as my exterior also internal to me in the sense that it is my universe? In so far as any eventity is part of the universe, it is, to this extent, identical with the universe, and, thus, any self-causation of the universe and its self-causation are, in part, identical. If freedom consists in self-causation, then in so far as the self-causation of an eventity is identical with the self-causation of the universe, its freedom and the freedom of the universe are the same. But, since no eventity is ever wholly or merely identical with the universe, its own freedom is always restrained by, and always restrains, the freedom of the rest of the universe.

What about novelty? Emergentists are correct in asserting that genuine novelty occurs in the world. When an emergent emerges for the first time, however, not only are there new kinds of stability, structure, properties, capacities, functions, laws of behavior, and causal efficacy,[15] but also new manifestations of each of the polar categories of existence.[16] Since all categories of existence are essential to existence, no new existent can come to be without involving all of them in some new way. Furthermore, since there is something new about every cause-effect situation, all the categories are constantly being newly remanifest. Creationists are correct in claiming that each new effect is always a product of both higher and lower causes. But they are mistaken in claiming that there are highest and lowest levels which remain forever unchanged and unnew. Newer highest and lowest levels continue to emerge. Does all this mean that the universe is expanding at both ends, so to speak? Yes, but also no, for the opposite end of the new-old polarity is also always involved. "To be involves being both old and new. Each entity is always being created and destroyed, for to create is to destroy and to destroy is to create. Things are new because they become different. Things are old be-

[15] See pp. 215–217.
[16] See p. 240.

cause they remain the same. To become different involves becoming something which was not before and also ceasing to be something which was before." [17] Walt Whitman captures the idea when he says

I have heard what the talkers are talking, the talk of the beginning and the end.
But I do not talk of the beginning or the end.
There never was any more inception than there is now,
Nor any more youth or age than there is now,
Nor any more heaven or hell than there is now.

The universe cannot become new without becoming old. For "whenever anything that is new continues to be, its newness is less new than it was before its newness continued. Thus, continuity of novelty destroys novelty. Yet novelty is not completely destroyed through its own continuity. Rather, it is other novelty that destroys the old novelty. However, even continuity of novelty means that what is new remains through other times and it is the novelty of this otherness which eventually destroys the old novelty, even if no other kinds of novelty intervene." [18] Contrary to common opinion, even that which is past is new, in a sense, for as each new event happens and then ceases it is newly added to what is past. So whatever is past is such that it is true about it that it is constantly being joined by new additions to it as past. Also, contrary to common opinion, what is new cannot be entirely new, for every new thing must be exactly like all past novelties in being new, and novelty is as old as existence.

How does organicism compare with creationism and other views regarding which is more active, matter or spirit? For Boodin, spirit is active and spontaneous, matter passive and inert. But tradition also has it that spirit as unity is peaceful, unchanging, eternal, whereas matter is in motion. Plotinus, for example, held that the ultimate unity is eternally unchangeable. Since nothing can influence it, it is inert. Which of these views, then, is correct? Is spirit active or passive, spontaneous and initiative or inert, the source of "initia" or of inertia? For organicism, both these views are true, each in its own way. Just as spirit and matter (whole and parts) are two aspects of each existent, rather than two separate kinds of existents, so initia and inertia are two aspects of each existent, rather than traits of dif-

[17] Archie J. Bahm, "Organic Unity and Emergence," *The Journal of Philosophy*, April 27, 1947, p. 243.
[18] *Ibid.*, pp. 243–244.

ferent kinds of existents. Spirit and matter, and initia and inertia, consist of the inner and outer aspects of each existent, as Leibniz [19] and Bergson [20] have pointed out. To the extent that anything is pushed from the outside, it is mechanical or material. In so far as it itself is the origin of pushing, it is spiritual. Spiritualists and emanationists are correct in attributing both initia and eternality to spirit, but mistaken both in denying equivalent spirituality to lower-level entities and in asserting that there is some completely perfect spirit which has no exterior and thus no materialistic type of inertia. Materialists and emergentists are right in attributing both motion and inertia to matter, but wrong in denying equivalent materiality to higher-level unities and in asserting some lowest level of indivisible particles which, because indivisible, have no inner or spiritual nature. Those views which posit existents with pure spirituality (inner without outer nature) or pure materiality (outer without inner nature) are false. The inner and outer aspects of each existent are organically related. Wholes and parts are genuinely (though not wholly) independent of each other as well as dependent upon each other. To the extent that they are independent or external, each offers resistance (inertia) to the other and also serves as a source of causation (initia) for the other. A thing, as spirit, offers some resistance or inertia to its matter and its matter likewise to it as spirit. This fact forms the foundation upon which dualisms are built, but in so far as dualisms overlook the interdependence of spirit and matter as aspects of every existent, they, too, become false.

Do persons have souls? If soul means "whole," then yes. Every existent has its own kind of whole, so its own kind of soul. How is soul related to body? Soul and body are related as whole and parts. Is soul eternal? If eternal means duration without change, then so long as an existent persists as a whole, the same whole, it endures, as that whole, without change and is, in this sense, eternal. But since each whole of changing parts must also, after any change, become somewhat different (it is now a whole of somewhat different parts) it is temporal and not merely eternal. Where change is involved, the eternal and the temporal pertain to the inner and outer aspects of each existent, and thus soul, as the inner whole of each existent, is eternal, but, as dependent upon outer parts which change, is temporal. What happens to soul at death? As long as there is a whole of parts, there can be no death. But when there is no whole of parts,

---

[19] See pp. 184–185.
[20] See Ch. 11.

there is no soul, and thus no death of that which is not. Only in so far as a soul is temporal can it die.

Since there are levels of existence in which each existent participates, the whole or soul of each existent is complex and multileveled. It may cease to function effectively at one level and yet continue at others. The soul of Socrates no longer influences his bodily digestive processes. Socrates is dead. But Socrates still influences the minds of men today. Socrates still lives. In so far as there is a whole of this same Socrates, such whole or soul continues, as unchanged, eternally. But what about those who are now completely forgotten? Are their souls completely dead? No, for the whole of each entity includes both the whole of what it is and the whole of what it is not, in so far as these are organically related. That is, since part of what each existent is is that it is not what it is not, all of what it is not is involved in the whole of what it is. Now, in so far as any part of the rest of the universe continues both to be and to be not this existent, such continuing involves, even if negatively, the continuing of this existent. Thus, in this sense, old souls never die; they just fade away into increasing insignificance.

Criticisms

Criticisms of the author by himself seem inappropriate, not so much because others will not find much to criticize, but because all known criticisms should have been taken into consideration before presenting this view. However, one may object that the author is indiscreet not only in presenting his personal viewpoint as one among others which have received historical recognition, but also as superior to all of them. The reply to this criticism is double: first of all, the reader of an introductory text has a right to know where his author stands, and secondly, if an author holds a distinguishable type of view which he considers demonstrably superior and which is not held by others, he has not only a right but a duty to express such a view as part of the philosophical picture. As to whether it is demonstrably superior, the reader will have his own opinions, especially if a critical temper, which it is a major aim of this text to stimulate, has developed in him.

Another recognized difficulty will be found by many in the somewhat unfamiliar usages of matter and spirit, even though these usages have a long and well-established precedent in the history of metaphysics. Unfortunate popularizations of spirits as spooks and of God as a great personal magician have poisoned our minds concerning more general and, apparently, more legitimate meanings of these terms. Likewise, prevalence of materialism among mathematical conceptions of matter, especially as influenced by the separation of science and religion into two widely different categories, has partly destroyed more traditional conceptions of spirit and matter as unitary and pluralistic aspects of existence. The tremendous influence of materialistic presuppositions upon current scientific interpretations ("If it can't be measured, it doesn't exist.") has spread the conviction that all concern for immeasurable spirit is superstitious. But, the basic metaphysical problem of how to account for both unitary and pluralistic aspects of existence reappears persistently until it is solved, regardless of tastes in language. Perhaps it would have been wiser to discard the terms spirit and matter altogether and to start with a completely new terminology. However, it would then become necessary to translate all other theories (spiritualism, materialism, dualism, etc.) into this new language for comparative purposes. It is questionable whether the already complicated philosophical vocabulary should be further complicated by another language, simply for the purpose of avoiding certain contemporary distastes. Furthermore, organicism, as a philosophy of language, holds that organic relations exist between old and new languages as well as between old and new philosophies. If philosophical and linguistic progress is to be made, the necessary and useful aspects of both the old and the new need to be incorporated into newer expressions. A wholly new language, like a merely old one, would fail in this. When faced with the choice of adopting a wholly new term to represent a partly new meaning or of adding a partly new meaning to an old term, we find it normal to waver,[21] sometimes adopting a new term and sometimes modifying the old. Since, as semanticists point out, terms partly keep and partly change their previous meanings when they occur in each new context, it is difficult to see how we could do otherwise. In this context, where organicism is being compared with previous metaphysical views, it seems best to retain older terms for such comparative purposes.

Each of the types of metaphysical outlook has its own criticisms to make of organicism. All the other types discussed in this section on reality must claim that organicism has no ultimate substance and they will hardly be satisfied with the reply that each existent is in some sense substantial and that such substantiality is in some sense

[21] The term "waver" as used here is intended to be related to "the wavelike changes" referred to on p. 244.

ultimate. Monistic spiritualists and emanationists will claim organicism to be but a thinly disguised pluralism which is all the more dangerous because it claims to accept unity as ultimate. The organicist reply is that organicism is even more devoted to unity than monists, for it accepts a unity of unity and plurality which is superior, as a unity of existence, to mere unity, i.e., to that kind of unity which remains separated from (ununited with) all existing plurality. Although one might contend that pluralism is more devoted to unity than monism because it accepts more (a plurality of) unities, organicism is still more devoted to unity because it is concerned also with the unity of both unity of pluralities and a plurality of unities. Pluralistic materialists and emergentists will claim that organicism is a poorly disguised monism, all the more vicious because it speaks the language of pluralism. The organicist reply is that organicism is, in a sense, more pluralistic than materialism, for materialists recognize only one level of plurality, whereas organicism accepts a plurality of levels of plurality. Organicism, then, is at once more unitarian and more pluralistic than any of the other views because it presupposes organic relatedness between existing unity and plurality.

Spiritualists condemn organicism for holding that matter is equal in ultimacy with spirit, because they believe that it is "more reasonable to suppose that the world which we do not know is like that which we know," [22] when spirit (conscious experience) alone is known. Organicism gives a threefold reply: (1) Since conscious experience itself involves both unity and plurality, wholes and parts, spirit and matter, then, if the rest of the world is like conscious experience, it too should involve both unity and plurality, wholes and parts, spirit and matter. (2) Arguments from the known to the unknown should be based, not merely on likenesses, but upon both likenesses and differences. Since, within experience, different experiences are both like and different from each other, what is beyond experience, even if it were merely like experience, should also include both likenesses and differences. (3) Furthermore, what is beyond experience is, most probably, not just like, nor just different from, but both like and different from, experience.

Materialists also condemn organicism for admitting that spirit is equal in ultimacy with matter. Those materialists who accept both the principle of uniformity of nature and an empirical basis for science claim that, since empirical science interprets objects experienced

[22] See p. 187.

as consisting ultimately of material particles, we are warranted in inferring that the rest of the world, with which science has not yet dealt, is uniform with the part dealt with and is therefore material and not spiritual. Organicism makes another threefold reply: (1) Experience itself is not completely material and cannot be reduced to mere matter, if the fact of experienced wholes is admitted. So, if the rest of the world is uniform with experience, it, too, should involve unities, wholes, spirits, as well as matter. (2) Experience is not completely uniform, but includes nonuniformities, i.e., uniquenesses, as well. Therefore, even if the rest of the world were merely uniform with experience, it too should include both uniformities and nonuniformities or uniquenesses. (3) But the argument from the uniformity of nature is one-sided, for it needs to be balanced by the argument from the uniqueness of each individual—resulting in the organicist argument that the rest of nature is both uniform with experience and also uniquely different from experience, even as different experiences of a single scientist or of different scientists are both uniform in some respects and unique in others. Organicism, being antireductionistic, claims that a truly empirical philosophy of science, one which takes full account of both unitary and pluralistic aspects of experience, will succumb falsely neither to materialistic nor to spiritualistic extremes.

Final criticisms, to which the author can make no reply, will be made by the reader. Such criticisms are to be expected; since the experiences of the writer and the reader are different as well as similar, the most that can be hoped for is partial agreement and partial disagreement.

As a concluding note to the section on reality, one criticism which applies to the presentations of all of the views considered is that discussions have been too brief, concentrated, technical, and selective. Since the aim of this introductory text is primarily to give insight into the major problems, and then into some of the main types of solution, it may have succeeded in spite of such shortcomings. If the reader has found some hopeful clues toward a more satisfactory philosophy, he will search further in the original writings of the various thinkers and movements.

· 21 ·

Philosophy
of Organism

Alfred North Whitehead (1861–1947), English mathematician whose critical awareness of broader implications in technical scientific difficulties led him into metaphysics, became a Harvard professor of philosophy at the age of 63 and has become one of the most-quoted of recent philosophers. He has been rated as one of the six classic American philosophers.[1]

Whitehead, like most modern philosophers, was troubled by the problems inherited from the metaphysical dualism of Descartes [2] and the epistemological dualism (representative realism) of Locke.[3] However, these problems have increased in complexity and subtlety and in the varieties of forms which they have taken. They presented themselves to him, as a mathematician, in his attempts to apply mathematics to the physical world, i.e., the world conceived in terms of Newtonian physics. For Newton, continuous motion was explained in terms of three mutually exclusive classes of entities, points of space, instants of time, and particles of matter. This theory has "a trimness about it, with its instantaneous present, its vanished past, its non-existent future, and its inert matter." [4] It proved very useful.[5] But it failed to show how such supposedly ultimate discontinuities can account for experienced continuities—of extension, duration, and feeling. Since absolute space and absolute time and material particles are independent of each other, "if material has existed

[1] See Max H. Fisch, editor, *Classic American Philosophers.* Appleton-Century-Crofts, New York, 1951.

[2] See Ch. 13.

[3] See Ch. 3.

[4] Alfred North Whitehead, *The Concept of Nature,* p. 73. Cambridge University Press, Cambridge, 1920.

[5] See Alfred North Whitehead, *Science and the Modern World,* Ch. IV. The Macmillan Co., New York, 1925.

255

during any period, it has equally been in existence during any portion of that period. In other words, dividing the time does not divide the material. Secondly, in respect to space, dividing the volume does divide the material. Accordingly, if material exists throughout a given volume, there will be less of that material distributed through any definite half of that volume. . . . For the division of time functions, in respect to material, quite differently from the division of space. Furthermore, this fact that the material is indifferent to the division of time leads to the conclusion that the lapse of time is an accident, rather than of the essence, of the material. The material is fully itself in any sub-period however short." [6]

Difficulties inherent in trying to account for experienced value, purpose, and ideals, as well as physical continuities, in Newtonian terms, led Whitehead deeper into philosophy. If science, in attempting to interpret a dynamic world, has been misled to abstract only static concepts and to reduce the dynamic wholly to the static, how shall its mistakes be conceived and whence is the source of its error?

Whitehead early concluded that Newtonian physics involved two closely related fallacies: the "fallacy of simple location" and the "fallacy of misplaced concreteness." A thing is thought of as having "simple location" when its existence and nature are conceived as independent of all other things, except those to which it is directly related. The idea of simple location involves being "here in space and here in time, or here in space-time, in a perfectly definite sense which does not require for its explanation any reference to other regions of space-time. . . . In fact, as soon as you have settled, however you do settle, what you mean by a definite place in space-time, you can adequately state the relation of a particular material body to space-time by saying that it is just there, in that place; and, so far as simple location is concerned, there is nothing more to be said on the subject." [7] The notion of simple location involves "the concept of an ideally isolated system," [8] i.e., one which is free from causal dependence upon other parts of the universe. The idea of simple location is a "fallacy" because "every actual entity is present in every other actual entity. The philosophy of organism is mainly devoted to the task of making clear the notion of 'being present in another entity.' " [9]

6 *Ibid.*, p. 73.
7 *Ibid.*, p. 72.
8 *Ibid.*, p. 68.
9 Alfred North Whitehead, *Process and Reality*, pp. 79–80. The Macmillan Co., New York, 1929.

Not only is "a favorable environment . . . essential to the maintenance of a physical object," [10] but also "the environment enters into
the nature of each thing." [11] "Any physical object which by its influence deteriorates its environment, commits suicide." [12]

Faith in simple location involves the "fallacy of misplaced concreteness" because the actual concrete world is one of dynamic interdependence from which the idea of simple location can be obtained
only by a process of abstraction. This "error of mistaking the abstract
for the concrete" [13] lies at the root of most difficulties in philosophy
and science. Since all thought is abstractive, we are constantly in
danger of reducing the rich complex dynamic processes which we
experience to simple abstractions and then of mistaking these abstractions for realities. When we do this, we distinguish between
appearance and reality. "But we may drop the term 'apparent'; for
there is but one nature, namely the nature which is before us in perceptual experience." [14] "What I am essentially protesting against is
the bifurcation of nature into two systems of reality . . . ," [15] the
one actually experienced, the other inferred consequent upon abstractive processes, or "the nature apprehended in awareness and the
nature which is the cause of awareness." [16]

Whence the source of the errors of modern science? It is to be
found in certain traditional metaphysical notions. "All modern philosophy hinges round the difficulty of describing the world in terms
of subject and predicate, substance and quality, particular and universal." [17] Whitehead focused his criticisms upon the concept of
substance, especially as formulated by Descartes, namely, something
which requires nothing but itself in order to exist. Since actual entities cannot exist in isolation from, or even within, the universe, they
require everything else, a whole universe of things, in order to exist.
If substance is conceived as depending upon nothing else, it is an
example of the fallacy of simple location. Since the concept of substance has played such a fundamental part in the history of philosophy and science, the whole of philosophy and science needs to be
reconstructed along lines which avoid this fallacy. So, like Dewey,
Whitehead rejects the notion of substance. "I refrain from the term

[10] *Science and the Modern World,* p. 160.

[11] Alfred North Whitehead, *Nature and Life,* p. 13. University of Chicago
Press, Chicago, 1934.

[12] *Science and the Modern World,* p. 161.   [15] *Ibid.,* p. 30.

[13] *Ibid.,* p. 74.   [16] *Ibid.,* pp. 30–31.

[14] *The Concept of Nature,* p. 40.   [17] *Process and Reality,* p. 78.

'substance,' for one reason because it suggests the subject-predicate notion; and for another reason because Descartes and Locke permit their substances to undergo adventures of changing qualifications, and thereby create difficulties."[18]   "The simple notion of an enduring substance sustaining different qualities, either essentially or accidentally, expresses a useful abstract for many purposes of life. But whenever we try to use it as a fundamental statement of the nature of things, it proves itself mistaken. It arose from a mistake and has never succeeded in any of its applications. But it has had one success: it has entrenched itself in language, in Aristotelian logic, and in metaphysics."[19]

If substance is that which stands by itself, how is it related to qualities and how is change possible? A substance is a substratum of which we predicate qualities. "Some of the qualities are essential, so that apart from them the entity would not be itself; while other qualities are accidental and changeable."[20]   Since, in order to "be itself," a substance cannot change, to be a substance means to be unchanging. All change is external to substance, not in substance. Change must then be explained as an exchange of accidental qualities. If substance cannot really change, then can there be real change? The growing conviction that change is real throws doubt upon a doctrine which presupposes that reality consists ultimately of substances which are unchanging.

Although many other recent philosophers have directed their criticisms mainly at spiritual substances, or at God as the ultimate substance, Whitehead's scientific background led him to consider the mistakes of materialism,[21] with its concept of material substance, as most pressing. Much of the burden of Whitehead's *Science and the Modern World* consists in pointing out that both the genius and failure of European science in the seventeenth, eighteenth, and nineteenth centuries have centered around materialistic conceptions. "There persists throughout the whole period a fixed scientific cosmology which presupposes the ultimate fact of an irreducible brute matter, or material, spread throughout space in a flux of configurations. In itself such a material is senseless, valueless, purposeless. It just does what it does do, following a fixed routine imposed by external relations which do not spring from the nature of its being. It is this assumption which I call 'scientific materialism.' Also it is an assumption which I shall challenge as being entirely unsuited to

[18] *Ibid.*, p. 116.
[19] *Ibid.*, p. 122.

[20] *Science and the Modern World*, p. 77.
[21] See Ch. 16.

the scientific situation at which we have now arrived."[22] ". . . a thoroughgoing evolutionary philosophy is inconsistent with materialism. The aboriginal stuff, or material, from which a materialistic philosophy starts is incapable of evolution. This material is in itself the ultimate substance. Evolution, on the materialistic theory, is reduced to the role of being another word for the description of the changes of the external relations between portions of matter. There is nothing to evolve, because one set of external relations is as good as any other set of external relations. There can merely be change, purposeless and unprogressive. But the whole point of the modern doctrine is the evolution of the complex organism from antecedent states of less complex organisms. The doctrine thus cries aloud for a conception of organism as fundamental for nature."[23]

Having abandoned the concept of substance, Whitehead found himself faced with the unenviable task of reconstructing the metaphysical foundations of science. How should this be done? In general, the solution seems obvious. Replace static substances with dynamic events, independent substances with interdependent entities, ideas of isolated systems enjoying simple location with continuously interfusing systems mutually pervading each other and the whole universe. In detail, however, the task was not so easy. In order to cope with the problem, he found that he had to invent a new language, or at least new words which would express dynamic concepts without succumbing to the fallacies of simple location and misplaced concreteness. Since bifurcations appear also in modern conclusions concerning knowledge and its objects, value and fact, reason and emotion, the natural and supernatural, no reconstruction will be satisfactory unless all bifurcations can be eliminated.

In his search for solution, Whitehead retained the scientific ideal of a more inclusive generalization. His "method is mathematical because the author is aiming at a single Concept of the universe, in which the various ideas form a natural circle from which none can be excised without leaving a gap between principles involving the others—for each fundamental idea is metaphysical, i.e., expresses an ultimate factor relevant to everything that happens."[24] "Whitehead intended his fundamental concepts to be so inclusive in scope, and

---

[22] *Science and the Modern World*, p. 25.

[23] *Ibid.*, p. 157.

[24] Victor Lowe in *The Philosophy of Alfred North Whitehead,* edited by Paul Schilpp, p. 103. The Library of Living Philosophers, Vol. III, second edition, Tudor Publishing Company, New York, 1951.

so interlocked, as to overcome all its traditional dualisms. Subject and object, unity and plurality, teleology and causality, the mental and the physical, immanence and transcendence, value and matter-of-fact—these are united in every 'actual entity.' " [25]

Whitehead's reconstruction may be summarized by discussing his two fundamental kinds of being and the other basic concepts needed to explain them. There are "two ultimate classes of entities, mutually exclusive. One class consists of 'actual entities' . . . and the other class consists of forms of definiteness, here named 'eternal objects.' " [26]

"We must start with the event as the ultimate unit of natural occurrence. An event has to do with all that there is, and in particular with all other events." [27] "The actual world is a process, and that process is the becoming of actual entities. Thus actual entities are creatures; they are also termed 'actual occasions.' " [28] "Actual entities . . . are the final real things of which the world is made up. There is no going behind actual entities to find anything more real. They differ among themselves: God is an actual entity, and so is the most trivial puff of existence in far-off empty space. But, though there are gradations of importance, and diversities of function, yet in the principles which actuality exemplifies all are on the same level. The final facts are, all alike, actual entities; these actual entities are drops of experience, complex and interdependent." [29]

Eternal objects are unchanging forms. "These transcendent entities have been termed 'universals.' I prefer to use the term 'eternal objects,' in order to disengage myself from presuppositions which cling to the former term owing to its prolonged philosophical history. Eternal objects are, thus, in their nature, abstract. By 'abstract' I mean that what an eternal object is in itself—that is to say, its essence—is incomprehensible without reference to some one particular occasion of experience. To be abstract is to transcend particular concrete occasions of actual happening. But to transcend an actual occasion does not mean being disconnected from it. On the contrary, I hold that each eternal object has its own proper connection with each such occasion, which I term its mode of ingression into

[25] Victor Lowe in *Classic American Philosophers,* edited by Max H. Fisch, p. 415. Appleton-Century-Crofts, New York, 1951.
[26] *Process and Reality,* p. 239.
[27] *Science and the Modern World,* p. 151.
[28] *Process and Reality,* p. 33.
[29] *Ibid.,* pp. 27–28.

that occasion. Thus an eternal object is to be compounded by acquaintance with (i) its particular individuality, (ii) its general relationships with other eternal objects as apt for realization in actual occasions, and (iii) the general principle which expresses its ingression in particular occasions." [30] "But there are no novel eternal objects." [31] "An eternal object can be described only in terms of its potentiality for 'ingression' into the becoming of actual entities." [32]

How are actual entities interrelated? How can one event be itself, i.e., be different from other events, and still be in other events? Through "prehension" and "nexus." "Actual entities involve each other by reason of their prehensions of each other." [33] In preference to the term "apprehension," which is often limited to grasping of meaning through "understanding," "I use the term 'prehension' for the general way in which the occasion of experience can include, as part of its own essence, any other entity, whether another occasion of experience or an entity of another type. This term is devoid of suggestion either of consciousness or of representative perception." [34]

"The essence of an actual entity consists solely in the fact that it is a prehending thing (i.e., a substance whose whole essence or nature is to prehend). A 'feeling' belongs to the positive species of 'prehensions.' There are two species of prehensions, the 'positive species' and the 'negative species.' An actual entity has a perfectly definite bond with each item in the universe. This determinate bond is its prehension of that item. A negative prehension is the definite exclusion of that item from positive contribution to the subject's own real internal constitution. . . . A positive prehension is the definite inclusion of that item into positive contribution to the subject's own real internal constitution. This positive inclusion is called its 'feeling' of that item. All actual entities in the actual world, relatively to a given actual entity as 'subject,' are necessarily 'felt' by that subject, though in general vaguely. . . . An actual entity as felt is said to be 'objectified' for that subject. Only a selection of eternal objects are 'felt' by a given subject, and these eternal objects are then said to have 'ingression' in that subject. But those eternal objects which are

[30] *Science and the Modern World*, pp. 228–229.
[31] *Process and Reality*, p. 33.
[32] *Ibid.*, p. 34.
[33] *Ibid.*, p. 29.
[34] Alfred North Whitehead, *Adventures of Ideas*, p. 300. The Macmillan Co., New York, 1933.

not felt are not therefore negligible. For each negative prehension
has its own subjective form, however trivial and faint." [35]

Every event has both an intrinsic and an extrinsic reality, "namely,
the event as in its own prehension and the event as in the prehension
of other events." [36] Each involves two patterns, "namely, the pattern of aspects of other events which it grasps into its own unity,
and the pattern of its aspects which other events grasp into their
unities." [37] "Every prehension consists of three factors: (*a*) the 'subject' which is prehending, namely, the actual entity in which that
prehension is a concrete element; (*b*) the 'datum' which is prehended;
(*c*) 'the subjective form' which is how that subject prehends that
datum. Prehensions of actual entities . . . are termed 'physical prehensions'; and prehensions of eternal objects are termed 'conceptual
prehensions.' Consciousness is not necessarily involved in the subjective forms of either type of prehension." [38]

A significant consequence of Whitehead's theory is that self as subject is an emergent arising in and through process. In contrast to
those who hold that there must be a knower before he can have
knowledge, Whitehead conceives that which functions as prehender
as a product of prehending. "The feeler is the unity emergent from
its own feelings." [39] "An occasion is a subject in respect to its special
activity concerning an object; and anything is an object in respect to
its provocation of some special activity within a subject." [40] Each
actual occasion of experience is a subject, and the subjectivity of the
occasion came into being as the occasion itself came into being. "Actual entities 'perpetually perish' subjectively, but are immortal objectively. Actuality in perishing acquires objectivity, while it loses subjective immediacy." [41] Our deceased ancestors are still prehended
by us. Having perished as subjects, they remain objects. "Objects
are elements in nature which do not pass." [42]

Prehensions involve "emotion, and purpose, and valuation, and
causation," [43] and have a vector character. They involve direction,
aim, feelings of effectiveness, self-enjoyment, and satisfaction. "The
notion of life implies a certain absoluteness of self-enjoyment." [44]

[35] *Process and Reality*, pp. 65–66.
[36] *Science and the Modern World*, p. 151.
[37] *Ibid.*
[38] *Process and Reality*, p. 35.
[39] *Ibid.*, p. 136.
[40] *Adventures of Ideas*, pp. 226–227.

[41] *Process and Reality*, p. 44.
[42] *The Concept of Nature*, p. 143.
[43] *Process and Reality*, p. 28.
[44] *Nature and Life*, p. 25.

"The aim is at the enjoyment belonging to the process." [45] "Actuality is value." [46] "The organism is a unity of emergent value, a real fusion of the characters of eternal objects, emerging for its own sake." [47] Yet "value is in its nature timeless and immortal. Its essence is not rooted in any passing circumstance. The immediacy of some mortal circumstance is only valuable because it shares in the immortality of some value. The value inherent in the Universe has an essential independence of any moment of time; yet it loses its meaning apart from its necessary reference to the World of passing fact." [48]

The concept of prehension constitutes the core not only of Whitehead's metaphysical reconstruction but also of his epistemology. Whitehead is especially aware of the fact that problems of knowledge and reality cannot be treated adequately in isolation from each other. Dualisms of knower and known, knowledge and object, ideas and things are among the bifurcations of nature against which he revolts. "Our experience, so far as it is primarily concerned with our direct recognition of a solid world of other things which are actual in the same sense that we are actual, has three main independent modes, each contributing its share of components to our individual rise into one concrete moment of human experience. Two of these modes of experience I will call perceptive, and the third I will call the mode of conceptual analysis." [49] The two, called "presentational immediacy" and "causal efficacy," are involved in physical prehensions, the third pertains to conceptual prehensions and is related to the analytical character of the realm of eternal objects. "By 'presentational immediacy' I mean what is usually termed 'sense-perception.'" [50] It "is our immediate perception of the contemporary external world, appearing as an element constitutive of our own experience." [51] Thus Whitehead is in agreement with the common-sense notion [52] that we have a direct experience of real objects in the external world. "Qualities, such as colors, sounds, tastes, etc. . . . can with equal truth be

[45] *Ibid.*, p. 28.

[46] *Science and the Modern World*, p. 155.

[47] *Ibid.*, p. 157.

[48] Alfred North Whitehead, *Essays in Science and Philosophy*, p. 62. Philosophical Library, New York, 1948.

[49] Alfred North Whitehead, *Symbolism*, p. 17. The Macmillan Co., New York, 1927.

[50] *Ibid.*, p. 21.

[52] See Ch. 2.

[51] *Ibid.*

described as our sensations or as the qualities of the actual things which we perceive." [53]

Furthermore, in opposition to the views of Hume and Kant and the critical realists, Whitehead claims that we experience causes themselves or, as he puts it, we have "direct perception of causal efficacy." [54] "There is, in the mode of causal efficacy, a direct perception of those antecedent actual occasions which are causally efficacious. . . ." [55] "The synthetic activity whereby these two modes are fused into one perception is what I have called 'symbolic reference.'" [56] Symbols are concrete aspects of experience referring to actual things with which they are interrelated, for a symbol is simply one aspect of experience "eliciting consciousness" respecting other components of experience. "The second 'ground' for symbolic reference is the connection between the two modes effected by the identity of an eternal object ingredient in both of them." [57] "It belongs to the essence of each occasion of experience that it is concerned with an otherness transcending itself. The occasion is one among others, and including the others which it is among." [58]

Thus, by means of the concept prehension, Whitehead believes he has solved the many problems arising from bifurcation of sense data and thing causing the sensation, percepts from causes of percepts, symbols from what is symbolized, as well as moments of experience from eternal objects. It should be remembered that prehension is not peculiar to humans, but is common, in varying ways, to atoms and all other existing organisms.

We turn now to "nexus," or togetherness, among actual entities. "A nexus is a set of actual entities in the unity of the relatedness constituted by their prehensions of each other, or—what is the same thing conversely expressed—constituted by their objectifications of each other." [59] "The concept of an organism includes the concept of the interaction of organisms." [60] Actual entities are mutually immanent in each other. "A nexus can spread itself both spatially and temporally. In other words, it can include sets of occasions which are contemporary with each other, and it can include sets which are relatively past and future." [61] Although not all nexus are societies,

[53] *Symbolism*, p. 21.
[54] *Ibid.*, p. 39.
[55] *Process and Reality*, p. 256.
[56] *Symbolism*, p. 18.
[57] *Process and Reality*, p. 259.

[58] *Adventures of Ideas*, p. 231.
[59] *Process and Reality*, p. 35.
[60] *Science and the Modern World*, p. 151.
[61] *Adventures of Ideas*, p. 259.

"a Society is a nexus which 'illustrates' or 'shares in' some time of 'Social Order.' . . . A society is more than a set of actual entities to which the same class-name applies. . . . A society must exhibit the peculiar quality of endurance. The real things that endure are all societies. They are not actual occasions." [62] It is a mistake "to confuse societies with the completely real things which are the actual occasions. A society . . . enjoys a history expressing its changing reactions to changing circumstances. But an actual occasion has no such history. It never changes. It only becomes and perishes. . . . The society, in each stage of realization, then consists of a set of contiguous occasions in serial order. . . . Any society of this type may be termed a 'person.' . . . A 'personal' society need not be 'living' . . . ; and a 'living society' need not be 'personal.' " [63] "A tree is a democracy." [64] Finally, "the Universe achieves its values by reason of its coordination into societies of societies, and into societies of societies of societies." [65]

Having accounted for actual occasions and their nexus, Whitehead turns to the question: How did all this come about? Those who say that God created the world are left with the question: Who created God? Since, for Whitehead, "there is only one entity which is the self-creating creature," [66] he cannot be satisfied with "an entirely static God." [67] Yet, since the universe as a whole needs explanation, "we require God as the principle of concretion." [68] Since "God is that non-temporal actual entity . . ." [69] ". . . which enters into every creative phase and yet is above change, he must be exempt from internal inconsistency which is the note of evil. Since God is actual, he must include in himself a synthesis of the total universe. There is in God's nature the aspect of the realm of forms as qualified by the world, and the aspect of the world as qualified by the forms. His completion, so that he is exempt from transition into something else, must mean that his nature remains self-consistent in relation to all change." [70] "Analogously to all actual entities, the nature of God is

[62] *Ibid.*, pp. 261–262.
[63] *Ibid.*, pp. 262–264.
[64] *Ibid.*, p. 264.
[65] *Ibid.*
[66] Alfred North Whitehead, *Religion in the Making,* p. 102. The Macmillan Co., New York, 1926.
[67] *Process and Reality,* p. 526.
[68] *Science and the Modern World,* p. 250.
[69] *Religion in the Making,* p. 94.
[70] *Ibid.*, pp. 98–99.

dipolar. He has a primordial nature and a consequent nature. . . . One side of God's nature is constituted by his conceptual experience. This experience is the primordial fact in the world, limited by no actuality which it presupposes. It is therefore infinite, devoid of all negative prehensions. This side of his nature is free, complete, primordial, eternal, actually deficient, and unconscious. The other side originates with the physical experience derived from the temporal world, and then acquires integration with the primordial side. It is determined, incomplete, consequent, 'everlasting,' fully actual, and conscious." [71] "God, who is the ground antecedent to transition, must include all possibilities of physical value conceptually, thereby holding the ideal forms apart in equal, conceptual realization of knowledge. Thus, as concepts, they are grasped together in the synthesis of omniscience. . . . It is not true that God is in all respects infinite. If he were, he would be evil as well as good. . . . He is something decided, and he is thereby limited. He is complete in the sense that his vision determines every possibility of value." [72] "This ideal world of conceptual harmonization is merely a description of God himself. Thus the nature of God is the complete conceptual realization of the realm of ideal forms." [73]

But God is inseparable from the world. God's consequent nature is "God as really actual, completing the deficiency of his mere conceptual actuality." [74] "God's conceptual nature is unchanged . . . but his derivative nature is consequent upon the creative advance of the world." [75] "Each temporal occasion embodies God, and is embodied in God. In God's nature, permanence is primordial and flux is derivative from the World; in the World's nature, flux is primordial and permanence is derivative from God. . . . Creation achieves the reconciliation of permanence and flux when it has reached its final term which is everlastingness." [76] "It is as true to say that God creates the World, as that the World creates God. God and the World are the contrasted opposites in terms of which Creativity achieves its supreme task of transforming disjoined multiplicity, with its diversities in opposition, into concrescent unity, with its diversities in contrast." [77]

"In our cosmological construction we are, therefore, left with the final opposites, joy and sorrow, good and evil, disjunction and conjunction—that is to say, the many in one—flux and permanence, great-

---

[71] *Process and Reality*, p. 524.

[72] *Religion in the Making*, p. 153.

[73] *Ibid.*, p. 154.

[74] *Process and Reality*, p. 530.

[75] *Ibid.*, pp. 523–524.

[76] *Ibid.*, p. 529.

[77] *Ibid.*, p. 528.

ness and triviality, freedom and necessity, God and the World. In this list, the pairs of opposites are in experience with a certain ultimate directness of intuition, except in the case of the last pair." [78]

Criticisms

Although Whitehead's courageous attempt to reconstruct the foundations of philosophy and science along dynamic lines and in such a way as to avoid bifurcation of nature and the fallacies of simple location and misplaced concreteness marks him as a genius of first rank, critics can be found who claim that he failed on all counts. "He reaffirms the bifurcation of nature he had previously condemned. . . ." [79] While he was busy fighting bifurcation in some areas, it cropped up unawares behind him, so to speak, in his own presuppositions. "Whereas Whitehead criticizes mechanistic materialism for its bifurcation of nature into static substances and changing attributes, he, himself, also bifurcates nature but in a reverse form: dynamic substances (events, process) and static attributes (objects)." [80] "Whitehead's God has as his function, not the saving of the world from 'wreckage,' but rather the salvaging of Whitehead's metaphysical system from its pervasive and unresolvable bifurcation or dualism. . . . God, himself, is bifurcated." [81]

Many who admire Whitehead for getting process into reality condemn him for his failure to go far enough. His long experience as a mathematician embedded in him rationalistic ideals and habits too deeply to be discarded even when he aimed at reconstruction. Not only does he assert that "the essence of the universe is more than process," [82] but also persistent overtones of statements to the contrary leave the impression that eternal objects constitute the reality in the process. His admiration for Plato, the father of rationalism, reveals a lurking insistence upon the priority of the rational, despite his claim to having found roots for the dynamic aspects of his philosophy of organism in the thought of Plato. [83] His interpretation of the history

---

[78] *Ibid.*, p. 518.

[79] Victor Lowe in *The Philosophy of Alfred North Whitehead*, p. 103.

[80] Harry Kohlsaat Wells, *Process and Unreality: A Criticism of Method in Whitehead's Philosophy*, p. 11. King's Crown Press, New York, 1950.

[81] *Ibid.*, p. 174.

[82] Alfred North Whitehead, *Modes of Thought*, p. 137. The Macmillan Co., New York, 1938.

[83] See *Process and Reality*, p. 146.

of Western philosophy as consisting of a series of footnotes to Plato [84] contradicts the spirit of his assertions that each thinker is a unique series of actual occasions with its own unique value and importance.

This criticism is illustrated in what is perhaps the most serious defect in his system. He attempted to reconstruct dynamic reality in terms of a static logic. "Whitehead's method was in absolute opposition to the content on which he employed it. It was his uncritical acceptance of traditional method which led him to posit a dualism in nature. . . ." [85] "He might have gone on to develop a method adequate to deal with process in its own terms: that to deal with process in its own terms would have meant an attempt to discover a functional structure within, rather than an absolute and eternal 'reality' without, process." [86] Another way of expressing this criticism is that, although he fought the subject-predicate notions embedded in Aristotelian logic, he did so while thinking in a subject-predicate language and, in doing so, entrenched it even more strongly in the presuppositions with which he fought. For, although his *Principia Mathematica* is a work of major importance, it represents a "statification" of logic in terms of eternal objects—a going backwards from Aristotle to Plato—rather than a dynamization of logic, a result which might have followed from a fuller awareness of the contributions of Hegel and pragmatism. Whitehead tried to reconstruct an organic metaphysics without an organic logic.

Thus there seems to be a wavering between the reconstructed and the unreconstructable [87] Whitehead. His writings are rich in suggestiveness for thinkers of different persuasions who are able to quote, or misquote, his authority as support for their particular outlooks. The incompleteness of his reconstruction has led some to evaluate his thought as transitional. "In the absence of a major contemporary philosophy which is consistent at all points with the field theory as it is formulated at the present time, the process philosophy of Whitehead functions as an interim philosophy. . . ." [88] "The philosophy of organism is the ultimate intellectual achievement of the nineteenth century." [89] Whitehead helped to lead us into the twentieth century, but is by no means its culmination.

[84] See *ibid.*, p. 63.
[85] *Process and Unreality*, p. v.
[86] *Ibid.*, p. xi.
[87] No mind can wholly reconstruct itself.
[88] Howard M. Ham, "The Field Theory: A Foundational Concept in Modern Science," *The Iliff Review*, Winter, 1952, p. 18.
[89] Victor Lowe in *The Philosophy of Alfred North Whitehead*, p. 124.

Other criticisms, which reflect the peculiarities of the writer's point of view, will be reserved for the following section.

Comparison

This final section, presenting some likenesses and differences between organicism and the philosophy of organism, serves a triple function, namely, to clarify further both views and to criticize further the philosophy of organism. Organicism is similar to the philosophy of organism in many ways. Both aim to give primacy not only to the dynamic but to the organic conceived as consisting as a "union of opposites which is the ground of dualism." [90] "All these kindred dualisms [91] are here founded within each occasion of actuality. Each occasion has its physical [92] inheritance and its mental reaction which drives it on to its self-completion. The world is not merely physical, nor is it merely mental. Nor is it merely one with many subordinate phases. Nor is it merely a complete fact, in its essence static with the illusion of change. Wherever a vicious dualism appears, it is by reason of mistaking an abstraction for a final concrete fact. The universe is dual because, in its fullest sense, it is both transient and eternal. The universe is dual because each final actuality is both physical and mental." [93] Both are devoted to an overcoming of dualisms, by antibifurcationism on the one hand and by antireductionism on the other. Both agree that creativity involves the emergence of unique individuals, that each individual is unique, but that somehow each individual involves, and is involved in, every other individual, even if primarily in negative ways. Both agree that value is concrete and that whatever is concrete is value. Both find organic relatedness between experience and existence and the emergence of subjectivity within experience in response to objective causes—though organicism insists that objects, as objects, are also products of subjectivity. Both reject as inadequate some traditional notions of substance and subject-predicate logic, but in radically different ways.

Differences in reaction to the doctrine of the ultimacy of substance result in all-pervasive differences in the two systems. Choosing Descartes' definition of substance as that which stands by itself in-

[90] *Adventures of Ideas*, p. 245.
[91] See p. 240.
[92] The writer prefers "material" and "spiritual" to "physical" and "mental" in this passage, reserving the latter for narrower uses.
[93] *Adventures of Ideas*, p. 245.

dependently, Whitehead had to reject the notion of substance if he wished to adopt a doctrine of dependence or interdependence. Organicism accepts a more literal definition of "sub-stance" as that which stands under or remains through change. Whenever there is functioning there is that which functions, so whenever there is functioning there is substance. Having defined substance functionally, organicism keeps it as a category of organic existence.

This doctrine affects criticisms of subject-predicate notions of logic. Whitehead's rejection of substance caused, or perhaps was caused by, his studies in mathematical logic in which a matrix of variables is considered as prior to its values—as in algebra, when $x + y = z$ is considered fixed, whereas which particular numbers may be substituted in the formula is something entirely arbitrary and changing. Considering these forms and formulas as eternally fixed, Whitehead felt he could abandon the concept of substance with impunity. God, who, in his primordial nature, conveniently contains all eternal objects, remains changeless, serves as a true substance of the kind Whitehead rejected. Although God, who is an actual entity but not an actual occasion, cannot stand by himself in the sense that he is independent of the world of occasions, does stand by himself in the sense that he is dependent upon nothing above or beyond himself. Since there are no other gods with which God is interdependent, God remains the ultimate substance, the ultimate matrix, which conditions all predication.

Organicism, with its organic logic,[94] finds subject-predicate logic partly true, partly false. It is true to say that a predicate depends upon its subject, but it is also true to say that a subject depends upon its predicate. Subject and predicate are polarly interdependent. Whitehead, in his metaphysics, often makes organicistic statements (e.g., "It is as true to say that God is permanent and the World is fluent, as that the World is permanent and God is fluent."[95] But his logical notions seem to presuppose a matrix as always somehow superior to its values. His primordial nature of God seems to be a universal substance which achieves predication through ingression of eternal objects into actual occasions. Clarification of the organicist view of subject-predicate logic and language will be promoted by examining further differences between "actual entities" and "eventities."[96]

[94] See p. 239.   [96] See p. 247.
[95] *Process and Reality*, p. 528.

Each eventity has its substantial and functional poles. So long as there is functioning, there is that which functions and that which functions is substance and may properly be spoken of as subject. But in so far as that functioning has ceased, that substance which arose interdependently with that functioning has ceased also. Whereas the being of Whitehead's actual occasions consists entirely in its becoming,[97] i.e., in arising and perishing without endurance, organicism's eventities endure as long as there is any functioning which is appropriately attributable to the "same" substance. Eventities are like actual occasions in coming and going, but if actual occasions are conceived as without endurance, then, for organicism, there are no actual occasions. Events and duration constitute polar aspects of each eventity. Neither exists without the other. If "eternal" means duration without change, then, since there is an unchanging aspect to each eventity there is an eternal aspect to each eventity. But if that eventity has ceased completely, then there is no eternal aspect of that which is not. Eternality, like substantiality and subjectivity, arises internally to each eventity. It does not "ingress"—except in the sense that one eternality is like all other eternalities and thus participates in a universal eternality. But such a universal is organically (polarly) related to each particular eternality and thus is as much egressed as ingressed. Such a universal is itself a polar aspect of a long-range eventity and is a particular universal and is, to this extent at least, a particular, i.e., a particular kind of eventity. Whitehead's realm of eternality seems, despite his denials, to subsist externally to process, for he speaks of "ingression" of eternal objects, i.e., as if they entered from the outside, and of actual occasions as limitations upon possibilities (eternal objects),[98] i.e., as if such possibilities pre-existed to be imposed upon. Thus organicism and the philosophy of organism place eternality at opposite ends of an internal-external polarity.

Consequently, there is disagreement concerning "subjective perishing." For Whitehead, "actual entities 'perpetually perish' subjectively, but are immortal objectively." [99] For organicism, eventities, although "immortal objectively," are "immortal subjectively," for so long as there is a subject, it has not perished. No subject can be aware of its own finish. To be finished means that there is no longer a subject. So long as there is a subject, it remains unfinished and,

---

[97] See *Process and Reality*, pp. 34–35.
[98] See *Science and the Modern World*, p. 251.
[99] *Process and Reality*, p. 44.

thus, "immortal." Only when we stand outside another eventity can we say that it is finished. Even then, that which functions as the "it" in "it is finished" remains through this functioning, constituting an objective part of the unfinishedness of that which, in another sense, is finished.

Organicism thus involves a dialectic that is largely missing in Whitehead's system. And, despite his awareness of the inseparability in dualities, he neglected to arrive at an adequate analysis of the nature of polarity. Also, despite his awareness of levels and gaps between levels,[100] he ends, like Boodin [101] and Plotinus,[102] with some highest level, the primordial nature of God, which does not emerge. There is nothing higher than God, and God, though fluent in and through the world, never flows beyond itself. For organicism, the "world as a whole" is an eventity which passes beyond itself into another "world as a whole" inclusive both of it and something other than it. God, too, is organic, passing beyond itself to new levels of Godhood.

Thus organicism accuses the philosophy of organism of being not sufficiently polar, not sufficiently levelistic, not sufficiently dialectical, and, consequently, not sufficiently organicistic. Also, the philosophy of organism is too idealistic in the sense that "feeling," "prehension," and "envisagement"—terms drawn from the psychic aspects of experience—are preferred in expressing ultimate characteristics of existence. Despite his valiant efforts to achieve an organic philosophy —and we should not minimize the success of his actual achievements —Whitehead appears to organicism to retain tendencies toward a double reductionism, i.e., to reduce the being of actual occasions to becoming (arising and perishing without endurance) and to reduce the nature of actual occasions to eternal objects. Nevertheless, there is an organic relation between organicism and the philosophy of organism; that is, they are both alike and different. There is some basis both for those who prefer to see them as alike and for those who prefer to consider them as different.

[100] See *Adventures of Ideas*, p. 265.

[101] See Ch. 19. However, Whitehead is a sort of inverted Boodin, for Boodin's matter offers resistance to the activity of mind (God), whereas Whitehead's "matter" is dynamic, processual, and consists in actual occasions; whereas God, in his primordial nature, is eternal, thus resistant to additional possibilities of actualization (because it contains them all to begin with), and God's consequent nature is a product of process, i.e., dependent upon the activity of matter.

[102] See Ch. 17.

· 22 ·

Axiology

At the beginning of the third part of this book, it may be well to consider its subject, and to see how it is related to the first two parts. This third part deals with values, first, generally, in the present chapter, and then in relation to more particular problems, in the following chapters. Knowledge, reality, and values are three different aspects of the world as experienced, not three separate realms unconnected with each other. Knowledge of values is a special kind of knowledge, so all the difficulties inherent in the problem of knowledge beset us as we investigate knowledge of values. Values exist, so the existence of values is entangled in all of the problems which trouble us in attempting to understand the nature of existence generally. However, although values may thus seem to be subordinated to knowledge and existence, there is some justification for holding that values should have the preferred place in philosophical investigation, since the nature of knowledge and existence are investigated only because there appears to be some value in such investigations. If a person has no understanding of values, he can hardly understand the value of investigating either knowledge or existence. Since one's desire to understand knowledge or reality is a motivated desire, a value-desire, value is presupposed in all philosophical searching.

Experience is pervaded with values. Not only do all pleasures and pains, enjoyments and miseries, appreciations and dislikes, involve values; but also all evaluations, or judgments of value, entail values. Most standards for judging are value-standards. The language of each specialized field of endeavor is suffused with value-aspects, despite occasional denials that values are involved. Although it is clear to most that aesthetic objects involve beauty and ugliness as aesthetic values or disvalues, that standards of musical, literary, and other artistic criticism involve value-judgments, that religion is concerned with the conservation of values, many will doubt that ethics, soci-

273

ology, economics, political science, and the natural sciences all involve values. Although ethics concerns mores, duties, or rightness, which sometimes appear as if unrelated to values, a closer examination of ethical problems will reveal that rightness is so related to value that without value there can hardly be any rightness.

Sociology, if its task is to ascertain what is good for society, the nature of social progress, and plans for improving social welfare, presupposes some theory of the nature of goodness whenever it is ready to make evaluative judgments, or even when it judges that there are judgments which it is unwilling to make. If "progress" means "becoming more good," then knowledge of what such goodness is is necessary before progress can be understood. Economics, which has been defined as the "science of wealth-getting activities," involves value in its very definition, for "wealth" (formerly "well-th" as opposed to "ill-th") is just another form of "good-th" or "goodness" or, simply, "goods." A "drygoods store" specializes in handling certain types of goods. Political science, in so far as it is concerned with "the commonwealth" or "the common weal" or "public welfare," deals with another somewhat specialized area of values. The natural sciences, although sometimes claimed to be axiologically as well as ethically neutral, normally presuppose the belief that it is better to be than not to be scientific in dealing with scientific problems. Since the scientific attitude and method are better, or more valuable, than other attitudes and methods, science presupposes value. Life in all its phases, then, is suffused with value. We cannot understand life until we understand value.

"Axiology" is the technical name given to the science of value, or to that area of investigation concerned with the nature of value or goodness. The terms "value" and "goodness" are commonly used as synonyms, though occasionally writers prefer to make distinctions between them. Since the term "values" often is intended to include "disvalues" or both "positive and negative values," the reader must discover from the context which sense is intended. When the term "goodness" is used synonymously with "value," the same ambiguity persists; i.e., the term "goods" refers sometimes to "both goods and bads" and sometimes to "goods as opposed to bads." Furthermore, when something considered neither good nor bad is spoken of as having "neutral value," the term "values" is sometimes used to include both positive, negative, and neutral values but at other times refers only to positive values in opposition to both negative and neutral values. Axiology may be simply, if ambiguously, defined, then, as the science of goodness. Its basic problem: What is goodness? seems simple enough, but like the simple questions: What is knowledge? and What is reality? it also tends to become complicated as our comprehension of its various aspects increases.

Before proceeding farther, a distinction should be made between axiology and ethics, partly because there is considerable common-sense confusion concerning goodness and rightness, and partly because many reputable thinkers have deliberately identified them. A moment's reflection will reveal a need for differentiation, for, although some things, e.g., a mother's giving her child its breakfast, are both good and right, others are good without being right, while still others, some think, are right without being good. An example of the former is an inanimate object, such as an apple, a windstorm, a cliff; these may be good or bad but not right or wrong. An apple may be good to eat, in which case we call it a good apple, but we do not call it a right apple. The windstorm may blow down our house and we may say it was a bad windstorm, but even so we do not call it a wrong windstorm. Rightness and wrongness commonly apply to voluntary acts of persons. The apple and storm do not act from choice, so are neither right nor wrong, even though good or bad. An example of the latter may be found in the views of those who believe that moral standards determine rightness and wrongness regardless of whether the consequences are good or bad. If it is believed that one ought to "keep the sabbath" even though he loses his year's crops, then such sabbath-keeping is right even if bad. While not all ethicists hold this latter view, it at least illustrates that the meanings of the terms "right" and "good" are not synonymous. Axiology centers its inquiry upon the question: What is goodness? in contrast with ethics, which focuses its investigations upon: What is rightness?

The Kinds of Values

Whoever undertakes a thorough study of the nature of value is led, almost without exception, to distinguish between two basically different kinds of value, expressed in different ways by different investigators, but commonly called "intrinsic value" and "extrinsic" or "instrumental value." Intrinsic value is the value which anything has, or is, when its value is within itself. If anything has intrinsic value, such value depends upon no other thing for its existence as value. Intrinsic value is internal to that which has it. Extrinsic value is the value which anything has as a consequence of its relations to something else. If anything has extrinsic value, such value does depend upon the value of some other thing for its existence as value. As Titus puts it: "An intrinsic value is one which is sufficient unto itself. An intrinsic value is good in itself in that it does not depend on something else for its worth. An extrinsic value, on the other hand, is a means to the attainment of other things. An extrinsic value is a value because it is good for something or because it may be a means to an intrinsic value." [1]

It is this "good for something else" character of extrinsic values which causes them to be called "instrumental values." Instrumental values are those values which anything has in so far as it is good for, or useful to, something else. Intrinsic value is that value which anything has to the extent that it is just good, or good in itself, without necessarily being good for something else. Of course, one thing may have both intrinsic and instrumental value. Consider, for example, wheat. Wheat is judged to be good because it can be planted and grows well to produce more wheat. This additional wheat is good for making flour, which is good for making bread, which is good to eat because it is nourishing. Nourishment is good for health and strength and life. Each of these is good for something else. Does such a process go on endlessly? Or is there a termination to the series such that all of these goods will ultimately have ended in some ultimate good? Most axiologists agree that this is so, even though there is much dispute as to just what this ultimate end is. Many different views about such ultimate or intrinsic value will be discussed in the next section. By way of illustration, we may take the view that happiness is an end-in-itself, or an intrinsic value. If so, then the goodness of wheat, flour, bread, nourishment, and health all consist in their being instrumental to happiness. The resulting happiness is just good, or is good in itself, without necessarily being good for anything else. Now, of course, such happiness might also be instrumentally good, for if one's happiness causes another person to be happy, the first happiness was instrumentally good in producing the second.

If instrumental value depends for its existence as value upon its service to some intrinsic end, then without such intrinsic value no instrumental value could exist. Whether intrinsic value can exist without instrumental value is a matter of considerable dispute. The views of the disputants may be arrayed on the Diagram of Types. [2]

[1] Harold H. Titus, *Living Issues in Philosophy*, p. 297. American Book Co., New York, 1946.
[2] See p. 241.

At one extreme we find certain Vedantists [3] believing that intrinsic value (Nirguna Brahman) alone ultimately exists; all else, including all instrumental value, is illusion. At the other extreme, we find certain pragmatists, John Dewey [4] for example, carrying instrumentalism [5] so far as to deny, verbally, at least, the existence of intrinsic value. Dewey's apparent denial of intrinsic value flows, doubtless, from his identification of intrinsic with everlasting, an identification not made by those hedonists who locate intrinsic value in momentary pleasures. Extreme dualists who would grant existence to both intrinsic and instrumental values but would isolate them into two separate realms, the eternal and the temporal, have few persistent followers. Most axiologists prefer some modified view, accepting the existence of both intrinsic and instrumental value, though holding either that intrinsic value is primary whereas instrumental value depends upon intrinsic value, or that instrumental value is primary while intrinsic value is merely a result of and dependent upon instruments, or that both somehow interact in each new value situation. Organicism [6] not only asserts the existence of both intrinsic and instrumental values, but claims that nothing can exist without having both intrinsic and instrumental aspects. Thus, neither of these aspects, even though distinguishable as kinds of value, can exist in complete independence of the other. Sometimes the intrinsic and sometimes the instrumental aspects are of primary concern, but nothing that exists is, or has, purely intrinsic or merely instrumental value.

Intrinsic Values

If instrumental values are derived from intrinsic values, which they serve, the primary problem of the axiologist is to discover the nature of intrinsic value. Focusing our attention upon this problem, we may summarize the different varieties of views, in relation to the epistemological and metaphysical types discussed in Parts I and II.

[3] For example, Ram Pratap Singh, in his *The Vedanta of Śáṅkara, A Metaphysics of Value* (Bharat Publishing House, Jaipur, 1949), claims that Nirguna Brahman as the ultimate end-in-itself must be intrinsic value rather than beyond both value and disvalue, as most Vedantists hold.

[4] See his monograph, *Theory of Valuation*, published as Vol. II, No. 4, of *The International Encyclopaedia of Unified Science*, University of Chicago Press, Chicago, 1939.

[5] See pp. 159–162.

[6] See Ch. 20.

First, axiological theories may be classified according to the epistemological distinction between real and subjective. Axiological subjectivists treat intrinsic value as depending for its existence upon being experienced or appreciated, whereas axiological realists do not.

1. All axiological subjectivists believe that intrinsic value depends
for its existence upon a valuer. Those who are thoroughgoing subjectivists in epistemology and spiritualists in metaphysics naturally prefer
subjectivism in axiology also. However, many who are realists in
epistemology or materialists in metaphysics may still be subjectivists
in axiology. For example, representative realist John Locke [7] distinguished not only between primary or real qualities and secondary or
subjective qualities, but also spoke of values as "tertiary qualities"
since they are "even more subjective" than such secondary qualities
as color and sound. Although colors are subjective, we tend to agree
that a color exists, when we dispute about its shade, but we often
disagree entirely as to whether that which has color has goodness
or badness. Critical realists, subjective idealists, agnostics, positivists, intuitionists, and some pragmatists also tend to be axiological
subjectivists.

However, to say that value is subjective is not to say in what value
consists. Parker, who asserts that "values belong wholly to the inner
world, to the world of mind," [8] that "a value is always an experience,
never a thing or an object" for "things may be valuable, but they are
not values," [9] says that "the satisfaction of desire is the real value; the
thing that serves is only an instrument." [10] "Desire is the only basis
of value; value itself does not exist until desire is being satisfied." [11]
Evil consists in frustration of desire. If there were no desires, neither
good nor evil could exist.

Another completely subjectivistic view is hedonism—the view that
goodness consists in pleasant feeling, evil in pain or in some other
unpleasantness. For Aristippus, an early hedonist, "all pleasures are
alike, except in quantity." [12] "The greatest pleasures and pains are
those of the body, i.e., those that arise from a present stimulus acting
upon the senses of touch, taste, or smell." [13] However, there are

---

[7] See Ch. 3.
[8] DeWitt H. Parker, *Human Values*, p. 20. Harper Bros., New York, 1931.
[9] *Ibid.*, p. 21.
[10] *Ibid.*, p. 20.
[11] *Ibid.*, p. 24.
[12] Theodore De Laguna, *Introduction to the Science of Ethics*, p. 125. The
Macmillan Co., New York, 1914.
[13] *Ibid.*

pleasures of the mind, connected with memory, expectation, feelings of sympathy, etc. Later hedonists, such as Jeremy Bentham, developed a "calculus" of pleasures [14] in which intensity, duration, certainty, nearness, fruitfulness, purity, and extent were factors in pleasures to be taken into account in ethical choices. Greater intensity of pleasure versus longer duration of less intense pleasures may be balanced against each other. Although hedonistic ethics does not concern us here, it illustrates the type of view that holds that value is entirely subjective.

2. Among the varieties of realistic theories of intrinsic value, the following may be noted. Naive realism [15] accepts a thing as being really good if it appears to be good. When a naive realist judges a table to be a good table, he unreflectively fails to distinguish between its intrinsic and instrumental goodness and so considers the table itself to be a good. Since the distinction between a thing and its qualities is inherent in his language, he implicitly considers such value as a real quality which is part of the real table. Evil, likewise, really exists just as it appears in real things or situations.

Platonic realism [16] holds that goodness is an Idea, a universal, or an essence, which subsists prior to all existence and from which the goodness of all existing good things is derived. Each thing that is good depends for its goodness upon Goodness, for if there were no Goodness, nothing could be good. For Plato, further, the Idea of the Good is the supreme Idea, all other ideas, as well as all existing things created after their pattern, are good because they partake of Goodness. Such Goodness is entirely independent of the experiences of persons, but the experiences of persons must depend for their goodness upon the Idea of the Good. Evil is absence of good. There is no Idea of Evil after which bad things are copied. Evil increases in proportion to the distance of an existing thing from its perfect subsisting prototype or Idea, and thus from the Idea of the Good itself.

A third variety of realism holds that value is a genuine property of particular real things. "A thing is recognized as possessing goodness, not in terms of some quality of the immediate experience in which it figures, but in so far as it is fitted to call forth in our mind the judgment of approval." [17] It is that property of an object which

[14] See William Henry Roberts, *The Problem of Choice*, p. 148. Ginn and Co., Boston, 1941.

[15] See Ch. 2.

[16] See pp. 118–120.

[17] Arthur Kenyon Rogers, *The Theory of Ethics*, p. 14. The Macmillan Co., New York, 1922.

consists in its capacity to cause a value experience in the subject
which contemplates it. In this view, "we only repeat what common
sense and all action say, that value is resident within the object.
This is its location." [18] Evil, likewise, is the power in objects to produce displeasure in the subject. But, apart from this, what its nature is we cannot say. Moore says good "is simple, unanalyzable,
indefinable." [19]

3. Increasingly, wholly subjectivistic or wholly realistic views of
intrinsic value are giving way to a third conception according to
which value cannot exist without both subjective and objective factors.
One of these views, i.e., that of Perry, contends that the term "good"
applies to "any object of any interest." "That which is an object of
interest is *eo ipso* invested with value. Any object, whatever it be,
acquires value when any interest, whatever it be, is taken in it; just
as anything whatsoever becomes a target when anyone whatsoever
aims at it." [20] "In no case do we strive for, wish for, long for, or
desire anything because we deem it to be good, but on the other hand,
we deem a thing good because we strive for it, wish for it, long for
it, or desire it." [21] However, value does not reside in the desire, but
in the object. That is, it is the object which is good, even though its
being good originates in our interest in it. Perry is a realist [22] in
holding that real things are values or become values when they become objects of interest. Value, then, depends both upon real things
and upon some interest in them. Evil, however, is something Perry
has difficulty in explaining, for one cannot dislike an object without
being interested in it, and thus an object cannot be evil without also
being good. Evil, therefore, involves a real object in which we are
interested, but it is one in which we are interested negatively, i.e., we
want it *not*. [23]

[18] Leo Richard Ward, *Philosophy of Value*, p. 141. The Macmillan Co., New
York, 1930.

[19] G. E. Moore, *Principia Ethica*, p. 37. Cambridge University Press, Cambridge, 1903, 1948.

[20] Ralph Barton Perry, *General Theory of Value*, pp. 115–116. Longmans,
Green and Co., New York, 1926.

[21] Benedict Spinoza, *Ethics*, Part III, Prop. IX. Quoted in Perry, *op. cit.*, p.
116.

[22] See pp. 121–128.

[23] Cf. Perry, *op. cit.*, pp. 239–240.

Gotshalk propounds a "relational theory of value" [24] in which there is an objective component, a subjective component, and a relational component. The relational component consists of a "telic pattern . . . which originates in the subject but extends to the object, uniting it with the subject into a value situation. . . . Any telic pattern can be analyzed into two factors. There is always some drive, need, want, propensity, impulse, urge, desire, attention, interest, aim, purpose, or other telic factor. In addition, there is a vector, or a set of requirements, sent out to some quality, state, event, thing, or complex of these, actual or potential, past, present, or future." [25] Evil involves these same three components, except that the subjective component involves an "unpleasant affective quality" instead of a pleasant one. Gotshalk's treatment, although involving both subjective and objective factors, ends in a "triadic analysis." [26]

Organicism also accepts both subjective, objective, and relational factors, as does Gotshalk, but its solution is organic rather than triadic. It recognizes both subjective and real aspects as does Perry, but claims that the statements, "objects are good because we desire them" and "we desire objects because they are good," are both true, though sometimes the one and sometimes the other appears to be primary. But the organicist view is too complicated for extended presentation here. It can hardly be stated adequately apart from its treatment of both subject-object and appearance-reality as two somewhat different polarities, [27] which have been omitted from this text. Put briefly, experienced value involves, first, both subjective and objective factors, both feelings and something felt, both something that is mine and something that is not mine; though the ways in which these are involved is complicated by the ways in which desire-satisfaction, aim-goal, actual-ideal, higher-lower, value-fact, apparent-real, as well as means-end polarities function in various experiences. Experienced value involves, secondly, both apparent (experienced) and real (existing without depending completely upon experience) factors organically related; however, since existence is complex and a matter of levels, what is meant by such real aspects of value is not simply

[24] D. W. Gotshalk, "Outlines of a Relational Theory of Value," *Ethics*, April, 1949, pp. 181–189.

[25] *Ibid.*, p. 184. [27] See p. 243.

[26] *Ibid.*, p. 185.

locateable [28] in some specific real thing. If one asks whether intrinsic values exist in other real things, such as atoms or galaxies, the reply is that other eventities, being both like and different from human experience, are probably both like and different from it with respect to value. The problem of how to determine the nature of particular values, i.e., details of their degrees of subjectivity or objectivity or of appearance or reality, is a task for particular specialists, scientists, or other persons confronted with problematic situations and employing pragmatic methods. Evil, the other end of the good-evil polarity, is similarly complicated. "Evil appears in conflict of goods," [29] and goods are always in conflict.

Secondly, axiological theories may be classified according to the metaphysical distinctions between spirit and matter dealt with in Part II. Are all values spiritual (i.e., do they belong to wholes) or are there material values (i.e., those belonging to parts)? Since the present section deals only with intrinsic values, by material values here is meant not instrumental values, about which there is little dispute, but whether matter (parts) has intrinsic value.

Spiritualists [30] believe that all values are spiritual and, usually, that all spirit is good. Concerning evil, however, they differ; some deny its existence, some give it permanent but inferior status due to conflicts among goods, and a few seem inconsistently to accept evil spirits, or a single Evil Spirit. Emanationists [31] hold the same ideals, but admit that evil has a negative existence. "While the Good itself remains in complete unity," [32] evil consists in plurality. Evil is the absence of good. Materialists [33] deny ultimate reality to value, and account for its appearance in pleasures and pains as a temporary illusion, fortunate for those with pleasures, unfortunate for those with pains. Matter itself is neutral, or valueless.

Emergentists [34] agree that matter ultimately is neutral, but believe that when new units of organization emerge they become self-deter-

[28] We must avoid what A. N. Whitehead has aptly called the "fallacy of simple location" (see his *Process and Reality*, p. 208), though his conception of the non-simple is quite different.

[29] Archie J. Bahm, "Emergence of Values," *The Journal of Philosophy*, July 15, 1948, p. 414.

[30] See Ch. 15.

[31] See Ch. 17.

[32] Joseph Katz, *The Philosophy of Plotinus*, p. 30. Appleton-Century-Crofts, New York, 1950.

[33] See Ch. 16.

[34] See Ch. 18.

mining and free, and, thus, relatively self-contained wholes. Good consists in growth of emerging self-realization, whereas evil, for such emergents, lies in destruction and death. Dualists [35] treat values as spiritual, matter as neutral. Creationists [36] attribute goodness to God, but since spirit or organization permeates to the lowest level of existence, all existence is good or has goodness immanent in it. However, created units are not eternal. The inertness of matter, which resists the active persistence of emergent units, eventually destroys them. Evil consists in the uncooperativeness of matter with spirit. Both matter and evil remain ever-present in the universe along with spirit and good. For Vedantism, existence is ultimately valueless. Good and evil are merely illusions. For neutral monism,[37] likewise, existence, or substance, is neutral or valueless, except that it manifests itself through value aspects. However, much of the writing of Vedantists and neutral monists suggests, paradoxically, that ultimate neutrality is really better than good as an aspect; if independence is better than dependence, then neutrality is better than goodness.

Organicism [38] agrees that intrinsic value is spiritual; both good and evil are spiritual, good consisting in wholesome (spiritual) existence, evil existing as destructive conflict between such existing goods. There can be no evil without matter (plurality), but matter (plurality) in itself is not evil. Plurality of existents involves (1) a plurality of goods and (2) a plurality of conflicts among such goods. As new existents emerge, new goods emerge, but as new existents bring new conflicts, they also bring new evils. Evil is dependent upon good, for there can be no conflicts among goods unless goods already exist. But, also, good depends upon evil, for a good can come into existence only by coming into a world of other existents, and its coming as one more (adding to the plurality) adds one more set of conflicts (evils) to existence; so only if its evil can emerge can it come into existence as good.

Judging About Values

In addition to, although involved in, theories of the nature of intrinsic values, are views as to whether such values can be understood, compared, and standardized.

Can values be understood as scientists understand facts, or must values be grasped by nonscientific means? Is there a dichotomy between value and fact such that two different kinds of apprehension

[35] See Ch. 13.   [37] See Ch. 14.
[36] See Ch. 19.   [38] See Ch. 20.

are required? Extreme factualists assert that only facts, and not values, can be understood. For modified factualists, we understand facts, not only facts without values, but also facts about values. Values can be understood, but only to the extent that they are also factual. Extreme valueists would assert that only values can be apprehended, not facts. Modified valueists consider values as primary, facts as secondary; what good is a fact if it has no value? Extreme dualists recognize that we apprehend both facts and values, but by different means; e.g., we know facts, but intuit values. Modified dualists recognize that facts and values intermingle part of the time in our understanding. Extreme aspectists believe that understanding understands, and that the distinction between fact and value is insignificant, since understanding is always the same, regardless of what is understood. Modified aspectists feel that the distinction between fact and value is itself understandable, and that this distinction makes a genuine difference to our understanding. Organicists see fact and value as two interdependent aspects of each experience. Fact is not value and value is not fact; yet facts and values are never understood in complete independence of each other. For, although sometimes the one and sometimes the other predominates in our awareness, the very reason for wanting to be strictly factual is that it is better to be so, and no experience can be wholly emotional unless it is a fact that it is wholly emotional.

Can values be compared? Some thinkers assert that intrinsic values not only are immeasurable but also incomparable. Each is a unique whole, and there is no disputing about tastes because no two intrinsic values are alike. Yet we do make comparisons and, in fact, spend most of our time doing so. The comparative and superlative forms, better and worse, and best and worst, are among our most-used terms. The relative uniqueness of different values does not prevent comparison, for even unique values are alike in being unique, so we come naturally to adopt such terms as "more unique" and "most unique." If uniquenesses were incomparable, there could not be two of them; for two such would have to be alike (comparable) at least in being uniquely different.

If values appear to be comparable, even if only partly, then the question remains: In what ways? Answers will vary with different theories of the nature of intrinsic value. Also, if several kinds of intrinsic value exist, then there may be different kinds of bases for comparison. For example, hedonist Bentham [39] compares pleasures

[39] See p. 279.

with respect to intensity, duration, etc. A Hindu yogin feels he experiences greater intrinsic value as he approaches nirvana. Organicism believes both that intrinsic values are incomparable and equally (i.e., comparably) incomparable and that each is partly what it is as a consequence of its organic relations with all else. That is, as organic, a thing is both one and many, and exists in and through both one and many levels. In so far as anything exists more wholly at one level than at many levels, it is, in one sense, more intrinsic and, in this sense, a higher value. But in so far as a thing exists at many levels, the more levels it exists in, the more there is of it and the more highly complex (higher, in another sense) it is. Since some tension exists between the "one" and the "many" aspects of an existent, that existent with either the least disturbing tension or with that tension most suited to its vitality is best adapted and, in this sense, a highest value. Best adapted here refers to intrinsic value, though the relevance of instrumental value should not be ignored. Whereas, for the yogin, the higher the intrinsic value the more it is freed from the instrumental, for organicism, the higher in all senses retains the instrumental. Those existents which are both intrinsic and instrumental are higher than those which (if there were any) would be either purely intrinsic or purely instrumental. To be both is to have double value, for being instrumental means that more other intrinsic value is inherently involved. "No eventity can end completely except through other ends." [40]

Can values be standardized? Or, rather, do standards of value inhere either in values themselves, or in the nature of value-judgments, or both? In so far as values are incomparable, there can be no standards. But to the extent that they are alike or different, the possibility of being generalized about, and thus standardized, is implied. We must leave to later chapters discussion of kinds of standards for judgment (aesthetics), of obligations to judge by, and be judged by, standards (ethics), of the higher values and their relations to lower ones (philosophy of religion), and of socially-standardized values or mores (social, political, and economic philosophy). As such discussion proceeds, it will become increasingly difficult to disentangle intrinsic from instrumental values, for most of our common concerns with standards pertain to beliefs about standardized instruments [41] rather than to standards associated with intrinsic values. The relative dominance of monotheisms in both Western and Eastern cultures

[40] Bahm, *op. cit.*, p. 413.
[41] Refer, for example, to the work of the U. S. Bureau of Standards.

has promoted widespread acceptance of the emanationistic conception of a single ultimate Good, often called God, to which all other
values are subordinated. Consequently, the question of comparing
intrinsic values is left largely to gourmets and other aesthetes. Moral
concern over comparisons of possible alternative ultimate ends is
largely missing from our civilization.

Optimism and Pessimism

Whoever believes that life is worth while because it contains more
good than evil is an optimist. Optimists vary in outlook from those
who, like Leibniz, believe that God created this the best of all possible
worlds, to those who feel merely that there is an actual preponderance
of good over evil in life, or in the world. Pessimists think that evil
predominates over good. Materialists, believing that matter is utterly
neutral, and that finally all our values, which are temporary, will
cease, tend to be pessimistic when they dwell upon life's futility, but
may be quite optimistic if they appreciate what values they enjoy as
better than nothing. An extreme pessimist should, according to his
own philosophy, commit suicide, unless he fears that such action will
bring him a still worse fate. Pessimistic too are those who believe
either that God does not care about, or cannot help, the world's miserable condition. Some of those who believe the Devil will claim his
share to populate Hell have reason to be pessimistic. However, most
people are naturally optimistic, believing that somehow everything
will turn out for the best in the end.

Recently, the term "meliorism" has been added to axiological and
ethical vocabularies. A meliorist is one who believes that, though
there are both good and evil in the world, and though the outcome
may be uncertain, still it is possible to improve our lot if we try in
appropriate ways. James says that "pragmatism must incline toward
meliorism. . . . Take, for example, any one of us in this room with
ideals which he cherishes and is willing to live and work for. Every
such ideal realized will be one moment in the world's salvation. But
these particular ideals are not bare abstract possibilities. They are
pledges, and if the complementary conditions come and add themselves, our ideals will become actual things." [42] A meliorist, then,
believes not only that the fate of each man's values is partly under

[42] William James, *Pragmatism,* pp. 286–287. Longmans, Green and Co., New
York, 1907.

his own control but also that his power to increase such values is sufficient to make the effort largely worth while.

Happiness

Although not all types of view agree that happiness is the highest good, the concept of happiness plays such an important role in the life of each individual as well as in the history of value-theory that discussion of it can hardly be omitted here. Disputes as to what constitutes happiness may be illustrated briefly by comparing pluralistic and monistic views. Those pluralists who located intrinsic value in pleasures of the moment think of happiness as consisting of an innumerable series of happy moments. Monists, who place intrinsic value ultimately only in God or Brahman, picture happiness as a single, eternal, happy moment which is merely now, without beginning or end or change of any kind. All lesser moments are forgotten, blotted out, for memory of them would bring, by comparison, only a regret that they could not have been better, a regret which would spoil the perfection of ultimate happiness. Organicism, accepting some truth from both pluralistic and monistic types of view, adds its concept of levels and dynamic adaptation. As many recognize, happiness involves a kind of mystical aura over and above particular enjoyments. Happiness is felt as a kind of unitary whole which can neither exist apart from each pleasant moment nor yet be reduced to any one of them or to all of them taken collectively. Lives devoted completely to momentary pleasures usually remain unhappy. Some who appear to have few pleasures still seem to maintain happiness.

For organicism, happiness involves both particular satisfactions and also some over-all enjoyment. Happiness depends upon both "getting what one wants" and "wanting what one gets." Whereas orientals seem to stress appreciating what they have rather than striving for more, and westerners seem to emphasize going after more rather than appreciating what they have, organicism recommends that fuller measures of happiness can be found to the extent that striving and appreciating become more organically balanced and more closely adapted to life's natural rhythms of anticipation and repose. Perfect satisfaction, that which would leave one so completely satisfied that he would never want anything else, would leave him dead. Those satisfactions which demand endurance or recurrence, which prompt desire for more, are richer than those which quench all desire completely. True happiness then combines both satisfaction and interest in living, both appreciating what one has and wanting more, both achievement of goals and hope for improvement. Each moment of happiness, as inner, is eternal, like God's now; each, as outer, contains promise of future reward. Both inner and outer aspects are essential to higher happiness, and the quality of happiness is greater as conflict between the inner and outer decreases.

Happiness is personal and private, but it may also be social and public. There are happy peoples, as well as happy people. A person's happiness somehow increases when he shares in, and is not shut out of, his people's happiness. There are levels of happiness; and one who can somehow hope that the universe itself is happy, and that the universe is happy through him as well as he through the universe, may attain a richness of happiness which, by comparison, makes his merely private happiness seem poor. Lonely happiness is hardly happiness at all. Yet, also, whoever has nothing but some universal happiness to enjoy, who has no happiness that is primarily his own, he too has but a thin share. Variations are to be expected, but one who participates in many levels of happiness has both a better chance of being happy and greater possibilities for richer happiness.

· 23 ·

Aesthetics

What is beauty? and What is art? are the two basic questions investigated by aestheticians. Naturally involved also are problems concerning the nature of ugliness, the inartistic, the neutral, and what standards, if any, may be used in aesthetic judgment.

Whether these questions are trivial or basic is a matter of some dispute. In a society which magnifies business, science, and technology, the artist is considered of peripheral importance and, by many, as being merely a useless parasite. Even among philosophers, metaphysics and epistemology have tended to pre-empt the primary roles. But the view of those who consider aesthetics the basic science needs to be heard. Beauty, they point out, is an intrinsic value. The goal of life is to achieve its intrinsic values. All else—business, science, technology, even philosophy—are instrumental means, not the ends themselves. The goals are to be found in those experiences in which the ends of life are immediately apprehended, and what are these but aesthetic experiences?

If religionists assert that in religion, not in art, are these goals to be found, attention is shifted to a different controversy. If religion is concerned with immediate enjoyment of intrinsic value, then it, too, is aesthetic and there is no fundamental difference between the religious and the aesthetic; in fact, the religious is then simply one kind of the aesthetic. The great joy reported to attend the beatific vision, of coming face to face with God, of achieving nirvana, or the other however different descriptions of the ultimate goal of religious experience, is claimed by some aestheticians to be an epitome of aesthetic experience. But, their point is, this is aesthetic and not merely religious. Their case may seem stronger when religion is conceived, not as identical with aesthetics, but as a mundane affair of sterile rituals and incredible creeds, of hypocritical morality and ecclesiastical cantankerousness. Then, says the romantic type of artist, religion is a very poor means to achieve aesthetic ends. Those who specialize in aesthetic experiences often believe that they reach immediately what some theists can promise only in some far-off heaven. Or, if they subscribe to immanentalism, then God, as beauty, appears to man directly in each experience of beauty. Consequently, the clutter of ecclesiastical institutions is irrelevant, except when, through the beauty of cathedrals, of ceremonial pageantry, of choral anthems, and of inspired oratory, they contribute to the aesthetic whole. Although it may be true that there is much that is trivial in art, the artistic itself is not trivial. And although the uninitiated may be unable to distinguish the trivial in troublesome techniques or what they misunderstand in cubistic experiments from the tremendous in aesthetic ecstasy, the true artist knows.

Turning from the contention that aesthetics is important because it most closely approaches intrinsic value, we may consider another claim, namely, that aesthetic experiences are the most widespread, if not, indeed, all-pervasive. Aesthetics, according to this view, is a universal science. Although the case here is not so clear, acquaintance with it may broaden our vision of the extent and importance of this field of study. If there can be no experience without an emotional, affectional, or value aspect, and if there can be no experience without objects of experience, and if, as Santayana [1] maintains, any intrinsic value treated as an object is aesthetic, then every experience is aesthetic, either positively, negatively, or neutrally, in some degree. If this be true, then the aesthetic is not a separate kind of experience, but is an aspect of every experience. Although experiences vary from those which appear to be wholly aesthetic to those in which the aesthetic seems to be entirely ignored, all are aesthetic to some extent. Aesthetics, then, is a universal science.

Opposed to this view, however, is that of aestheticians who believe that the aesthetic is something rare, something extremely precious, something reserved for people of taste. These aestheticians, sometimes called "aesthetic aristocrats," reject the democratic view that each person, including infants and dullards, has his own share of aesthetic experiences. What this something rare is is a matter of disagreement, just as is that which democratic aestheticians consider common to all experiences. The existence of these disputes must be taken into account in any attempt to define aesthetics. Except for their rather general agreement that aesthetics is concerned with

[1] See George Santayana, *The Sense of Beauty*. Charles Scribner's Sons, New York, 1896.

beauty and art, definers differ in handling the problem: shall they first define aesthetics and then discuss varieties of views within the limits of this definition, or shall they first discuss the various views— each one of which will have its own definition of aesthetics—and then try to derive a definition common to all? The problem: What is aesthetics? is itself still an unsolved problem for aestheticians.

Beauty

Can beauty be defined? "A definition that would really define must be nothing less than the exposition of the origin, place, and elements of beauty as an object of human experience. We must learn from it, as far as possible, why, when, and how beauty appears, what conditions an object must fulfill to be beautiful, what elements of our nature make us sensible of beauty, and what the relation is between the constitution of the object and the excitement of our susceptibility." [2] That is, as a scientist, the aesthetician has to observe aesthetic data, formulate hypotheses about them, and test these hypotheses by applying them to other similar data. What kinds of data does he seek? If he limits his investigation to beauty in the fine arts, then he concerns himself with music, painting, sculpture, drama, literature, dancing, etc. If he finds beauty in photographs, costumes, cookery, or tatooing, then he must extend the range of his investigation. If he sees beauty in stars, ocean waves, flickering fires, and pleasant smiles, these too become part of his data. Which hypotheses shall attract his attention or arise in his intuition may well be a consequence of fickle circumstance. Today, however, it is usual in aesthetics, as in most sciences, for beginners to examine some of the many hypotheses which have become famous in the long history of attempts to formulate answers. What are some of these views?

Theories of beauty, like theories of knowledge and value, may be grouped according to their subjective or realistic emphases. Realists, exemplified by naive realists,[3] believe the beauty of a painting to exist on the canvas just where it seems to be, and to remain there whether anyone sees it or not. Platonic realists,[4] following Plato, who held that the Good, the True, and the Beautiful were the three highest Ideas, consider beauty a subsistent universal quality upon which each particular beautiful thing depends for its beauty. Some theists, fol-

[2] *Ibid.,* p. 14.
[3] See Ch. 2.
[4] See pp. 118–120.

lowing Plotinus,[5] consider beauty a cosmic expression of divine perfection, the beauty of physical things being but a shadow of the divine.[6] Greek idealizations of beauty as harmony, proportion, and measure, as illustrated in "the golden section,"[7] and as typified by contemporary attempts to interpret beauty mathematically,[8] picture beauty as independent of, and prior to, our appreciation of it. This view leads to the doctrine that knowledge of beauty is a kind of insight into reality, some claiming that music is a universal language which all may understand, others holding that aesthetic insights give us unique intuitions of what is, nevertheless, rational or real. Realists often seek beauty in pattern, form, balance, symmetry, rhythm, and ratio, because these seem more easily identified with "the real."

For subjectivists, like Hume,[9] beauty exists not in things themselves but only in the mind. For Hume, beauty depends upon utility. Others see beauty in pleasant sights and sounds or in other immediate satisfactions. Carritt, for example, holds that "beauty is found in what is expressive of feeling,"[10] "that all beauty is expressive,"[11] and that "if the artist's aim is admitted to be self-expression, then all expression is beautiful. . . ."[12] "For Schiller, the genesis of art is to be sought in the play-impulse, and play for him is the expression of superfluous energy. 'The beast *labors*, when a want is the incitement of its activity, and it *plays*, when profusion of vigor is the incitement, when life is its own stimulus to activity.'"[13] Whenever expression occurs for its own sake, detached from animal needs, enjoyed as undistracted contemplation of idealized objects for their own sake, beauty becomes pure and unadulterated by practical pressures.

Both realism and subjectivism tend to appear in modified forms. Implicit in most realisms is acceptance of the existence of beauty also in experience, even if such experienced beauty continues to depend upon its real source. Subjectivisms often include realistic aspects,

[5] See Ch. 17.

[6] This view is illustrated in Castiglione's *The Courtier.*

[7] See Herbert S. Langfeld, *The Aesthetic Attitude*, pp. 224 ff. Harcourt, Brace and Co., New York, 1920.

[8] See George D. Birkhoff, *Aesthetic Measure.* Harvard University Press, Cambridge, 1933.

[9] See Ch. 5.

[10] E. F. Carritt, *What is Beauty?* p. 87. Oxford University Press, London, 1932.

[11] *Ibid.*, p. 99.

[12] *Ibid.*, p. 95.

[13] D. J. Bronstein, Y. H. Krikorian, and P. P. Wiener, *Basic Problems of Philosophy*, p. 430. Prentice-Hall, New York, 1947.

without admitting primacy to them. Santayana, for example, says that beauty "is pleasure regarded as the quality of a thing"[14] or "is pleasure objectified."[15] Sometimes it is difficult to decide whether sensuous beauty, for example, is subjective or real, since the line between the subjective and the real is not clear. Extreme realists consider sensations, which are dependent upon sensory end organs carried about by the beholder, as subjective; but extreme subjectivists think of them as attached to the external bodily mechanisms which serve as external limitations upon the free flow of the imagination. Extreme dualism requires two different kinds of beauty: real beauty, harmony of physical structure, for example, existing without appreciation, and subjective beauty, such as the wild fantasms of dreams which could not exist elsewhere. Modified dualism, although admitting these two different kinds, claims that both the real and the subjective cooperate in practical beauties; the laws of nature and human intuition combine creatively, for example, in cathedral construction. Organicism believes that subjective and real factors coexist in all experiences of beauty, even though some experiences seem more obviously subjective while others appear more real. Romanticism and realism are both legitimate types of aesthetic theory in their constructive aspects, but false to the extent that each denies the truths expressed by the other.

Classification of theories of beauty in relation to the theories of reality (spirit-matter or unity-plurality) discussed in Part II is both easy and difficult. For those who consider beauty almost identical with goodness, the classification is so nearly like that given for goodness[16] that it need not be repeated here. But with respect to those who do not identify beauty with goodness, i.e., who treat it either as evil, or neutral, or at best as a minor species of the good, the variations multiply and involve more detail than can be dealt with here. However, considerations pertaining to the relative importance of unity and variety remain close to the heart of aesthetic discussion. Preference for unity appears in the expressions of those aestheticians who characterize beauty as involving peacefulness, repose,[17] restfulness, calmness, completeness, perfection. Variety or plurality is preferred by those who stress interestingness, vivacity, vitality, attractiveness, ar-

[14] *Op. cit.*, p. 52.
[15] *Ibid.*, p. 49.
[16] See pp. 282–283.
[17] See Ethel Puffer, *The Psychology of Beauty*, Ch. III. Houghton Mifflin Co., Boston, 1905.

restingness. However, more prolonged analyses of experiences of beauty usually reveal that perfect unity results in monotony while mere variety consists in chaos. Beauty involves both unity and variety, however these may be named. In Parker's words, "the unity is a unity of the variety and the variety is a differentiation of the unity" and "the variety is of equal importance with the unity, for unity can assert itself only through the control of a multiplicity of elements." [18]

These words, giving equal stress to both poles of the unity-variety or identity-difference polarity, well express the organicist viewpoint, though Parker more consistently prefers identity-in-difference to identity-and-difference in his interpretation of the nature of beauty. Both views agree that the unity-variety relationship is not merely static but also dynamic. Organicism emphasizes the fact that experiences of beauty are tending always toward either more unity or more variety. To be beautiful, an object must remain interesting, must contain more and more of what it takes to attract and hold interest. Yet each new point of interest must not absorb the whole of one's attention, otherwise the beauty of the object as a whole will disappear. The new needs to be incorporated into the retained interest in the larger whole. If it cannot be so incorporated, then the beauty of the whole is lost. If it can be, then the whole is enriched. If nothing new is added, however, the whole eventually becomes so monotonous and boring that its beauty disappears because it lacks power to retain interest in it. To remain beautiful, an object must continue to provide new varieties of interestingness, and yet somehow contain them altogether in a satisfying whole.

An explanation of ways in which this dynamic character of beauty is grounded in physical and metaphysical bases has been ably pointed out by Dewey. "There is in nature, even below the level of life, something more than mere flux and change. Form is arrived at whenever a stable, even though moving, equilibrium is reached. Changes interlock and sustain each other. Wherever there is coherence there is endurance. Order is not imposed from without but is made out of the relations of harmonious interactions that energies bear to one another. Because it is active, order itself develops. It comes to include within its balanced movement a greater variety of changes. Order cannot but be admirable in a world constantly threatened with

---

[18] DeWitt H. Parker, *The Principles of Aesthetics,* second edition, p. 70. Appleton-Century-Crofts, New York, 1947.

disorder—in a world where living creatures can go on living only by taking advantage of whatever order exists about them, incorporating it into themselves. In a world like ours, every living creature that attains sensibility welcomes order with a response of harmonious feeling whenever it finds a congruous order about it. For only when an organism shares in the ordered relations of its environment does it secure the stability essential to living. And when the participation comes after a phase of disruption and conflict, it bears within itself the germs of a consummation akin to the aesthetic." [19] "Because the actual world, that in which we live, is a combination of movement and culmination, of breaks and reunions, the experience of a living creature is capable of aesthetic quality. The live being recurrently loses and reestablishes equilibrium with its surroundings. The moment of passage from disturbance into harmony is that of intensest life." [20]

To have decided whether or in how far beauty is subjective or real and whether or to what extent it involves unity and plurality is only a beginning. Among other problems confronting definers of beauty we may mention only a few. What parts are played by sensation, pattern, meaning, reason, emotion, symmetry, balance, and harmony?

Although some say that all beauty is sensuous, even limiting sensuous beauty to the two aesthetic senses, sights and sounds, thus excluding the possibility of beautiful odors or beautiful flavors, others not only include the latter and all other types of sensation, but also say that "there is no function in our nature which cannot contribute to this effect." [21] However, to say that all kinds of sensation may contribute to experiences of beauty, and that some must, are two different statements. For, if there can be beautiful dreams or beautiful thoughts, experienced without perceptual ingredients, then sensation is not necessary to beauty.

Although some contend that "beauty consists in certain patterns in things," [22] most will agree that there is more to beauty than form, for this view would rule out all possibility of "formless beauty." If there are beautiful colors or beautiful ideals which involve no pattern, then "pattern, while usually present, is not necessary. But, also, pattern is

[19] John Dewey, *Art as Experience*, pp. 14–15. G. P. Putnam's Sons, New York, 1936.

[20] *Ibid.*, p. 17.   [22] Carritt, *op. cit.*, p. 72.

[21] Santayana, *op. cit.*, p. 53.

sufficient in that a pleasantly felt organic unity may consist entirely of pure pattern, without sensory or significant ingredients." [23]

Must beauty express [24] meaning? If there are meaningless forms or colors, which are yet beautiful, then beauty can be experienced as if it had no meaning. However, most experiences of beauty involve meaning. Some beauties appear to consist entirely of meanings, as in the case of mathematics which, "rightly viewed, possesses not only truth, but supreme beauty—a beauty cold and austere, like that of sculpture, without appeal to any part of our weaker nature, without the gorgeous trappings of painting or music, yet sublimely pure, and capable of a stern perfection such as only the greatest art can show." [25]

Is beauty rational or irrational, intellectual or emotional? Rationalists tend to emphasize the rational nature of beauty. For Leibniz, the beauty of music is due to an unconscious arithmetic involving numerical ratios between harmonious tones. For Herbart, aesthetics is an exact science which concerns the relations between elements which are immediately pleasing but which have nothing to do with ideas or feelings. However, intuitionists, who see beauty in the unique, unanalyzable, ineffable, deny that aesthetic taste can have anything to do with reason. Furthermore, there are those who say that "from the aesthetic experience both thought and emotion are ruled out." [26] Finally, organicism believes that beauty involves both reason and emotion.

Can beauty exist without symmetry or balance or harmony? Must there be contrast, rhythm, hierarchy, dominance, evolution, and climax? [27] Are there degrees of beauty or is each beauty absolute? Can beauty and ugliness exist together in a single experience or object, or must an aesthetic experience be wholly beautiful or wholly ugly? These and hosts of other questions confront the aesthetician, and thus the reader, in so far as he has made aesthetic problems his own. In addition, the aesthetician faces various problems involved in relating beauty to specific arts (beauty of sculpture versus beauty of dance), to aesthetic types (the sublime, the grand, the charming, the

[23] Archie J. Bahm, "Beauty Defined," *The Philosophical Review*, September, 1947, p. 583.

[24] See Santayana, *op. cit.*, Part IV, "Expression."

[25] Bertrand Russell, *Sceptical Essays*, p. 73. W. W. Norton, New York, 1928.

[26] Max Schoen, *Art and Beauty*, p. 153. The Macmillan Co., New York, 1932.

[27] Some of these concepts are treated by Aram Torossian, *A Guide to Aesthetics*, Ch. VI. Stanford University Press, Stanford, 1937.

pretty, the cute, and the picturesque [28]), and to movements (surrealism, impressionism, classicism, etc.) in art.

Art

"To understand art means to find an idea or definition which applies to it and to no other activity . . . and our understanding will be complete if our idea includes all of the distinguishing characteristics." [29] But, unfortunately, the term "art" has many different meanings, and the aesthetician must decide upon which of these he is investigating, if he is to avoid confusion. Five different meanings, ranging from broader to narrower, are: (1) Art is anything that is artificial, as distinguished from natural, or man-made in the sense that it involves intentional human intervention. (2) Art is anything skillfully produced or the skill of production. In this sense, no distinction is made between arts and crafts, for all crafts are arts in this sense, e.g., the art of making bread, the art of love making, the lost arts, the liberal arts, etc. (3) Art is anything that is ordinarily termed "fine art," though what is to be included under this term continues to be controversial. (4) Art consists in painting and sculpture or graphic and plastic art in contrast with music, poetry, drama, ceramics, etc. When we say, "She is studying art and music," the art referred to is intended not to include music. On the other hand, art in the previous sense may include drama, dancing, photography, etc. (5) Finally, some narrow the term art to include only those things possessing especially valued qualities or possessing them only in a superlative degree. "This is a famous painting, but it's not art." Although any of the last three meanings may become the focal point of an aesthetician's interest, the third, art as fine art, is the broadest and most usual area of his investigation.

Is art subjective or real? Some say that art is real and exists independently of artists and appreciators. Paintings, statues, buildings, landscapes, and vases are art objects and all of them together constitute existing art. Those works of art located in museums or galleries, for example, are art works whether they are being appreciated or not. Archeologists who discover buried temples, beautiful necklaces, or other artifacts, uncover art which has continued to be art even though hidden and unappreciated. This realistic view is the

[28] Cf. *ibid.*, Ch. XV, or Louis W. Flaccus, *The Spirit and Substance of Art*, Part IV. F. S. Crofts and Co., New York, 1926.

[29] Parker, *op. cit.*, p. 2.

natural, common-sense, or naive view of the locus of art. Art consists in those works which can be pointed to, handled, and bought and sold in art shops. Without works of art, such realists hold, no real art would exist.

Subjectivists, on the other hand, see art as subjective. "Art is primarily a creative activity on the part of the artist." [30] "Art is not a quality of things but an activity of man. . . . strictly speaking, pictures, statues, and the like are not art at all but works of art; and art is not a quality discernible in them but an activity of man,—the activity, namely, of which such things are products." [31] Croce "denies, above all, that art is a physical fact" and asserts "that art is vision or intuition." [32] Artistic creation takes place in the activity of the artist's mind. The process of putting on a canvas what the artist has in mind Croce calls "extrinsication," not creation, for the actual painting adds nothing but extrinsication to the artistic intuition already created in the artist's mind.

Organicists agree with Dewey in holding that "art denotes a process of doing" and that "every art does something with some physical material, the body or something outside the body, with or without the use of intervening tools, and with a view to production of something visible, audible, or tangible," [33] or perceivable through some other sensory end organ. In fact, fine art exists fully only when three factors are organically related: 1. A producer, creator, or artist who desires, intends, attempts—and partially succeeds—to express somewhat unique feelings in an objectified form with some technical skill. 2. A consumer, or appreciator, who perceives beauty or ugliness expressed in an object. The experiences of the producer and consumer need be only similar. The consumer's awareness of the artist's technique and skill is not necessary. The producer and consumer may be the same person. 3. An instrument or work of art which involves material elements influenced by intended activity of a producer and actually producing perception in a consumer. With hairdressing or aesthetic dancing, the producer's own body is the material instrument in which training, practicing, and "keeping in shape" are means of molding it as an aesthetic instrument or work of art. For organicism,

[30] Sheldon Cheney, *A Primer of Modern Art*, p. 9. Liveright Publishing Corp., New York, 1939, 1945.

[31] Curt J. Ducasee, *Philosophy of Art*, p. 15. Dial Press, New York, 1929.

[32] Benedetto Croce, "The Breviary of Aesthetic," *The Rice Institute Pamphlet*, December, 1915, p. 229.

[33] Dewey, *op. cit.*, p. 47.

art depends for its fullness upon organic interaction of creative activity and instruments for reproducing appreciation. Our desires for reappreciation motivate our creating of works of art, and the making of these works stimulates new varieties of appreciation which in turn modify creation. Croce is mistaken in limiting art to intuition, even though there can be no art without intuition, for what the artist intuits is usually modified in the process of molding his instrument. Both what the artist wants to express and the resistance or suggestiveness of the instrument as the artist works with it organically interact upon each other in a dynamic evolutionary unity. "The process of art production is related to the aesthetic in perception organically." [34]

Is beauty essential to art, or may art be ugly, e.g., not just accidentally but deliberately horrifying? Can there be meaningless art, formless art, unsensed art? Must art imitate? Is each object unique or is a reproduction of an original yet art? Is technique more important than the theme expressed? Must art be communicable or communicated, or may there be purely personal or private art? May art be useful or does utility destroy artistic value? Are some arts superior to others, or more artistic than others; e.g., is painting better than music? Is there a supreme art, superior to all others? Do all of the fine arts exist already or will more new fine arts come to be? These and many other questions constitute problems for the scientist who seeks to define art.

Standards

If "an art work is the expression of a unique experience by a unique mind," [35] then there can hardly be any standards for comparing what is unique and incomparable. But some think that "when we judge that an object is beautiful we demand the agreement of others. The judgment, 'This is beautiful,' does not merely mean that I who judge, who so judge, take pleasure in the picture. It implies that all other persons of good taste ought to take pleasure in it and judge it to be beautiful, and that if they do not they are guilty of bad taste. A judgment of taste claims to be valid for all men." [36]

Between aesthetic agnosticism and aesthetic absolutism range many varieties of views concerning the nature of aesthetic standards. Modi-

---

[34] *Ibid.*, p. 49.

[35] Schoen, *op. cit.*, p. 33.

[36] Walter T. Stace, *The Meaning of Beauty*, p. 33. G. Richards and H. Toulmin, London, 1929.

fied agnosticism, although claiming that aesthetic experience is ultimately ineffable, admits that we can and do try to share and compare, even if unprecisely, our feelings. Modified absolutists, although accepting as foundational the fact that true art implies true standards for art, explain that human frailties prevent us from grasping the truth about art as it is; consequently we should be wary about expecting too much success in judging art. Dualists claim that some aspects of art, such as size, shape, and harmonious proportion, can be standardized, even absolutely, whereas others, such as emotional quality and imaginative significance, are utterly undiscussable. Artistic criticism should pertain only to the former.

Modified dualism, recognizing both unique and common ingredients as intermingling in some aesthetic experiences, accepts courageously the task of untangling what is judgable from what is not. Extreme aspectism sees aesthetic experience as being neither incomparable nor comparable because the distinction between comparable and incomparable is an illusory one. Modified aspectism considers aesthetic experience as both comparable and incomparable, since it is such that it manifests itself through both common and unique aspects. Organicism agrees that each aesthetic experience involves both unique and common aspects and that any recognizable similarity or difference between aesthetic experiences may serve as a basis for comparison, regardless of whether it be a shape or a feeling. Thus there may be as many kinds of aesthetic standards as there are kinds of discernible similarities and differences.

Standards may occur with respect to (1) the work of art. We sometimes appreciate an object for the quality or rarity or purity of its materials, the skills and difficulties involved in its production, and its durability, size, or age. We often judge art relative to (2) the artist's purpose. Was his theme a good one, original, unique, significant, or representative? Did he have great depth of insight? Was he fitted for his task? Did he choose the most appropriate medium? What audience did he have in mind? Art works are evaluated according to (3) the artist's success. Did he succeed in expressing what he wanted to express? Was his technique well-used in such expression? Was his achievement appropriate to his age, skill, background, experience? How did this achievement compare with his earlier successes, or with works of other similar artists? Finally, we discover standards relative to (4) the consumer's experiences. Do I like it? Is it what I expected? Does it measure up to what critics have said about it? Is it more beautiful than other works of the same kind? Does it fit in with my other interests (e.g., would I like to have it in my living room)? Answers to these and hundreds of other questions face the aesthetician when he seeks to establish standards. Then, in addition, come three other questions: Are some standards for judging the excellence of art better than other standards? Is there some standard for judging standards? Is there a supreme standard?

·24·

Ethics

No matter how unfamiliar the reader may have been regarding epistemology, metaphysics, or axiology, surely in taking up ethics he is in familiar territory. The term "ethics" is used more often than the term "philosophy" itself. However, if he is like most others, he will have associated the term with negative commands, such as: Thou shalt not, Don't do this, or You mustn't do that. Since the term is associated with frustrating or inhibiting situations, it is one concerning which he has developed somewhat definite opinions. Since people dislike irritations, they commonly react to ethics as something essentially evil and something which, ideally, we could better do without. However, there is another side to the picture, the positive, in which, once it becomes clear, ethics is seen as something which we not only cannot be without, but also as something we should not wish to dispose of, even if we could. Since ethics is involved in choice, we cannot be without ethics unless we can forego choice. Furthermore, it would be difficult for us to choose to be completely without choice, for such choosing itself would be a choice; ethics, thus, deals with another kind of presupposition and is another kind of all-pervasive science, at least as pervasive as our choices.

Before proceeding very far, we need to recognize a common distinction, i.e., that between theory and practice, as it relates to ethics. Most of us are more familiar with ethical practices than with ethical theories. We are often told what not to do without being told clearly why. The whole realm of commands, taboos, mores, moral codes, laws, and authoritative demands, whether related to parents, police, courts, legislature, church, scriptures, clergy, teachers, employers, or friends, pertains to ethical practice. But why? Ethical theories, explanations of why we ought to act in certain ways, also may be derived either from authoritative commands or by means of scientific attitudes and methods. Each culture has its own traditions as to how ethical demands come to be. Many, though not all, theistic traditions associate rightness with divine commands. However today, where scientific ideals predominate, the field of ethics, too, has become an area for scientific investigation.

Ethics, then, is a science. As such, its task is to investigate all phases of ethical practices, as well as existing ethical theories, to discover, in so far as it can, more adequate hypotheses as to the nature of such ethical practice. One's hypothesis is better if it more satisfactorily accounts for the facts of experience than other theories. One test of adequacy is, of course, whether or not it fits with other theories which one holds, in metaphysics, epistemology, and axiology, for example, as well as in physics, psychology, sociology, and theology. Since ethical data are as fundamental as any, it is as necessary for physics and metaphysics to square themselves with ethics as it is for ethics to fit itself into physics and metaphysics.

The aim of an ethical scientist, then, is not to begin either by commanding or by presupposing commands, except perhaps the self-imposed demand that he be scientific, but to begin by treating ethical phenomena as data for consideration. Such a scientific adventure requires an open mind. If the reader has more definite opinions in this area, and if this means that his mind is already more fully made up, i.e., is less open-minded, then it may be more difficult for him to be scientific. This too is a matter about which he will have his own opinion. Varieties of readers, as the writer sees them, range somewhere between two types of extremes: those who accept standards which they refuse to question and those who insist upon denying the possibility of ethical standards altogether. Most thinkers will, however, reject both absolute moral tyranny and complete moral anarchy; thus they find themselves deeply involved in the problem of whether morality is primarily absolute or relative, as well as in such issues as whether it is real or subjective, social or personal, universal or local, eternal or temporary, certain or, at best, probable.

Other problems with which we as ethicists are concerned include: What are rightness, rights, duty, obligation, oughtness, responsibility, justice, punishment, conscience, virtue, and wisdom? What part do intentions play in determining rightness? Can obligations be standardized and, if so, how? How are customs, public opinion, laws, contracts, authority, self-realization, and God related to morality? Can practical moral problems be solved generally, or do specific problems in business, marriage, politics, education, race relations, war, and religion require separate treatment? Does ethics include etiquette or do we have two separate fields of investigation? Although ethicists may differ regarding which problems should be considered most fundamental, all agree that each of these problems is involved in ethics in one way or another. Since some will include still other problems, and since the precise boundaries between ethics and other fields have not been agreed upon, the question: What is ethics? is itself not completely answered.

Although ethical theories may also, like those in axiology and aesthetics, be classified by means of a subjectivism-realism scale and in relation to metaphysical types, ethicists more commonly seem concerned about whether ethical principles are absolute or relative. This concern cuts across the subjectivism-realism scale, however, for some absolutists (certain theists, for example) believe their principles to be prior to, superior to, and in this sense exterior to man (realistic), whereas others locate them within man's own absolute nature (subjective). Some relativists believe rightness to be relative to mores pre-existing in the social environment (realistic), whereas others see it as relative to each person's momentary interests (subjective). Is stealing, for example, always wrong, or sometimes right and sometimes wrong? "According to the absolutists there is but one eternally true and valid moral code. This code applies with rigid impartiality to all men. What is a duty for me must likewise be a duty for you." [1] Critical minds will quickly discover an ambiguity here. Does the absolutist's view mean that all men have exactly the same duties regardless of circumstances, or are duties absolute only if circumstances are the same?

Extreme absolutists maintain that all are the same regardless of circumstances. "The ethical relativist consistently denies, it would seem, whatever the ethical absolutist asserts. For the absolutist, there is a single moral standard. For the relativist there is no such standard. There are only local, ephemeral, and variable standards." [2] That is, "the very same kind of action which *is* right in one country and period may *be* wrong in another." [3] Relativism, too, is involved in ambiguity; for a view which holds that rightness which is relative to particular societies might still be quite absolutistic in the sense that it is held to remain exactly the same for all individuals within each society. To say that each person may have his own standard is more

[1] Walter T. Stace, *The Concept of Morals*, p. 1. The Macmillan Co., New York, 1937.
[2] *Ibid.*, p. 11.
[3] *Ibid.*, p. 9.

relativistic than to say that each society may have its own but each individual must not. To say that a person may have different standards for different kinds of occasions is even more relativistic than to say that each person may have his own standard so long as he uses it consistently in all kinds of occasions. Extreme relativism, if it admits that there are any ethical standards or principles at all, must hold that each particular situation has its own unique set of them. Like all extreme views, extreme relativism contradicts itself; for at the same time that it denies that any principle can apply to all situations it implies that it itself is a principle which does apply to all situations.

Extreme views usually become modified. Although western history is replete with heroic battles against extreme ethical absolutisms, a battle which is still going on, nowadays "relativism has run riot, become insane." [4] Modified absolutism considers some absolute principles as primary, though their application in particular situations is relative; e.g., what is actually right for me now in the face of my peculiar problem holds for all others faced with the same problem, even though no others are so faced. Modified relativism considers the uniqueness of particular situations as primary, yet also recognizes that, to the extent that all situations of the same kind have something in common, such common elements may provide a basis for empirical generalizations which then probably apply to still other similar situations.

Extreme dualism is that view which claims the existence of two kinds of standards, the absolute and the relative, which are in no way related. Such a dualist might hold, for example, that Thou shalt not kill is absolute, whereas Which set of Canasta rules shall we use for our game tonight? is relative. Modified dualism, beginning with both absolute and relative standards, recognizes that both are applicable in some practical situations. That one ought not to kill, for example, may be absolute, but what one ought to do in order not to kill may be quite relative to the particular situation. Extreme aspectists would hold what is hardly intelligible to most of us: rightness is neither absolute nor relative but it merely appears so from the viewpoints of those who cannot penetrate its true nature. Modified aspectists see absoluteness and relativeness as two aspects of rightness, each of which expresses the nature of rightness, though in opposing ways.

Organicism again rejects the negative and accepts the positive in the foregoing views. "Neither relativism nor absolutism, as an ex-

[4] *Ibid.*, p. ix.

treme or exclusive theory, meets the world's needs."[5]   Yet both stress aspects inherent in every ethical situation.   If absolute-relative means the inside-outside aspects of ethical circumstances, then in so far as a situation is unique its rightness is also unique, or inside it, or absolute, and to the extent that it is like other situations its rightness is not unique but universal or outside it or relative to other situations also.   Extreme absolutists mistake the universal for the absolute because they concern themselves solely with the absolute as the inside of the universe, which has no outside, but they fail to be concerned with the absolute as the inside of any ethical situation which does have an outside.

Extreme relativists, in mistaking rightness of a particular situation as wholly inner, are, in a sense, even more absolutistic than the absolutists.   Since, as organicists believe, the rightness of any ethical situation involves both its rightness relative to itself and its rightness relative to other situations, rightness has both absolute and relative aspects.   Absolutists fail to the extent that they make rightness wholly relative to the universe; relativism is false to the extent that it restricts rightness as absolutely intrinsic to the particular situation.   Of course, as experience shows, sometimes the inner and sometimes the outer aspects seem to predominate.   Cultures and personality types may be interpreted, and their ills diagnosed, in accordance with their devotion to inner or outer aspects of ethical ideals.

Rightness

The concepts rightness and wrongness lie close to the core of ethical thinking.   As pointed out previously,[6] many ethicists, when confronted with the problem of how to relate rightness and goodness, have decided to define them independently.   A similar problem faces ethicists regarding the relation of rightness to duty, responsibility, oughtness, justice, virtue, and wisdom.   Does each of these terms represent an independent concept or should some be defined in terms of others?   For example, should rightness be defined in terms of oughtness (as Immanuel Kant seems to do) or oughtness in terms of rightness?   One's answer to this question will determine which ought to be considered first.   Since, for organicism, each of many organically related terms must be defined partly in terms of the others, it makes

---

[5] Melvin Rader, *Ethics and Society*, p. 122.   Henry Holt and Co., New York, 1950.

[6] See p. 275.

little difference with which we begin. The concepts of rightness and wrongness are as basic as any. Following a pattern set by Drake,[7] we will compare thirteen prominent theories of the nature of rightness and wrongness. Surely the reader is already somewhat familiar with all of them.

Acts are right because they are in accord with custom. "Right and wrong . . . are only other names for customary and contrary to custom." [8] "Conduct is moral which conforms to the customs of the group." [9] The term morality comes from the Latin *mores* meaning "customs." Since distinction is often made between "mores" and "folkways," [10] and since nonconformity to folkways may be considered queer, but not wrong, a stricter definition of this view is that acts are right because they conform to the mores.

Acts are right because the group approves them. Whereas "custom" ordinarily means something established, fixed, unchanging, if a group unanimously agreed to violate a custom, its action would be wrong, according to the customary theory, whereas it would be right according to the group-approval theory. In fact, it is argued, the reason why customs acquire and maintain their sanction is that the group approves them. Thus group approval is considered a more ultimate basis of rightness than custom.

Acts are right because they are legal. "Rights are the fruits of law and of the law alone. There are no rights without law, no rights contrary to law, no rights anterior to the law." [11] In complex societies, not everyone can participate in forming group consensus. Democracies have found it necessary to establish legislatures empowered to enact laws on a majority-opinion basis. So long as there are disputes as to what the group opinion is, there must be some specific means for determining what such opinion is. Only an official legislature, supported by authority to enforce its decrees, can be relied upon to provide definite principles for the guidance of conduct. Laws differ from customs in that laws become effective from date of enactment, or some other specified date, whereas customs involve

[7] See Durant Drake, *Invitation to Philosophy*, Ch. XXV. Houghton Mifflin Co., Boston, 1933.

[8] Theodore De Laguna, *Introduction to the Science of Ethics*, p. 73. The Macmillan Co., New York, 1914.

[9] Joseph A. Leighton, *The Individual and the Social Order*, p. 14. D. Appleton and Co., New York, 1926. Used by permission of Appleton-Century-Crofts.

[10] See Charles Horton Cooley, Robert C. Angell, and L. J. Carr, *Introductory Sociology*, pp. 89–97. Charles Scribner's Sons, New York, 1933.

[11] Jeremy Bentham.

time for their development, during which time there must be considerable uncertainty. Laws, in providing specific penalties, also give some indication of how wrong an act is, since, for example, it is less wrong to overpark than to murder. Laws are stable in comparison with mere public opinion, which may fluctuate ficklely in response to effective propaganda. Law, then, is claimed to be the only dependable basis of rightness.

Acts are right because they are according to contract. Laws and legislatures, customs and public opinion, are hardly self-sustaining, but rest upon something more fundamental. The rightness of laws passed by legislatures rests upon the right of the legislature to pass laws. Where did this come from? From a constitution, which is a contract by people with each other to abide by such laws, regardless of temporary opinions to the contrary. Thomas Hobbes in his *Leviathan,* and Jean Jacques Rousseau in his *Contrat Social* present different versions of the ideal that men once lived in a "state of nature" without rights or rightness until they discovered that they could survive more happily if each would surrender certain of his natural rights and thereby gain certain political rights. This contract was, in itself, the origin of rights and of rightness. Cabot defends what he calls the "agreement" theory and defines an agreement as "a declaration of intention arrived at in view of an understanding of the facts by the various tendencies within a person or two or more persons." [12] Rightness consists in keeping one's agreements, wrongness in violating them. One can even make an agreement with himself (e.g., new year's resolutions) which bring into being rightness regarding one's own personal behavior with respect to himself. Where there has been no contract, there can be no wrong.

Acts are right because they are successful. The term "success" may be applied to a number of different theories which are alike in this respect, namely, that rightness rests upon expediency. In the words of the Greek, Thrasymacus, right is acting in "the interests of the stronger." [13] Militarists know that "might makes right." Pragmatists sometimes join James in saying that "the 'right' is only the expedient in the way of our behaving." [14] Despite differences in their interests

[12] Richard C. Cabot, *The Meaning of Right and Wrong,* p. 47. The Macmillan Co., New York, 1936.

[13] See B. Jowett, *The Dialogues of Plato,* Vol. III, Third Edition, p. 15. Oxford University Press, New York, 1892.

[14] William James, *Pragmatism,* p. 222. Longmans, Green and Co., New York, 1907.

and motives, the proponents of these views agree that rightness consists in success, wrongness in failure. The reason why customs, group opinion, law, contract, etc., may seem to determine rightness is that someone was successful in establishing such customs, opinions, legislatures, or contracts. One also has to succeed in keeping them going, or rightness even according to them will disappear.

Acts are right because conscience commands them. The significance of this view depends partly upon how conscience is conceived. According to one conception, conscience is an innate faculty fully present at birth though not fully developed. Some speak of it as "the still small voice of God" implanted in the soul. If one obeys its commands, he will never act wrongly. However, according to another more recent conception, conscience is an acquired product of conditioning. It consists of that fear of evil consequences which accompanies inhibitions. Those who accept this view, however, seldom define rightness merely in terms of conscience.

Acts are right because an authority commands them. This theory is one of the most commonly practiced of all theories. Children come into contact with it early in their lives through conflict with parental authority. Why is it wrong for Johnnie to help himself to the cookie jar? Because mother says so. Teachers, preachers, policemen, and the like also often seem arbitrary in their decisions, but nevertheless determiners of rightness in specific situations. In an army or a dictatorship, the command of the superior officer is always right. In some religions, a Bible, a Church, or a God is the final authority. If God commands, what he commands is right. Why? Because he commands it. Although difficulties may beset those who seek to compare alleged authorities, once an authority is accepted, then the theory works well provided the authority speaks on all, or almost all, ethical matters.

Acts are right because they promote self-realization. Whoever proposes a self-realization theory must first determine what he means by self, and by its realization. Divergent conceptions of self result in different conceptions of self-realization and, thus, of rightness. Aristotle, for example, spoke of a person's "potentialities," which were thought of as fixed within certain limits, in accordance with his doctrine that each species has an unchanging nature. Behavior which is conducive to the realization of one's potentialities is right, and conduct destroying one's potentialities or opportunities for realizing them is wrong. Many current views which prefer dynamic to fixed concepts of personality also interpret rightness in terms of self-realization, though they more commonly speak of personality development. Rightness, for these views, consists in such conduct as leads to a wholesome personality, wrongness in what thwarts healthy growth.

Acts are right because they produce good results. All the foregoing theories, although failing to make "good results" basic to their theories, really presuppose them implicitly. For if group welfare is believed to depend upon conformity to mores, is not this welfare a more ultimate basis of rightness? Group approval determines rightness only because approval means what the group considers good. Law and contract determine rightness only because people believe that it is good to form a contract and to abide by legislation. It is not merely success which determines rightness, for if one succeeded in killing, torturing, crippling, or otherwise wronging himself, he has succeeded, but surely this is not what is meant by success; success really means success in producing good results. Conscience can determine rightness only if it helps us to avoid evil and achieve good. An authority commands us rightly only if his commands produce good results; it is wrong to obey the authority of the Devil because obedience to such authority will bring evil results. Self-realization is right only if one realizes his good potentialities, not if he realizes his potentialities to produce evil. Thus, the basis for all theories, it is claimed, is reduced to good results. However, this still leaves the question: good results for whom? Five answers to this question will be considered: for others, for one's self, for God, for the best people, and for the most people.

Acts are right because they produce good results for others. Right consists in acting for the benefit of others, wrong in acting for one's own benefit. Altruism is right because egoism is wrong. Self-seeking is selfish and selfishness is the root of all evil. The cure for this evil is to pursue the opposite course: love others and promote their good.

Acts are right because they produce good results for oneself. It is natural to seek survival and happiness—for oneself. Whatever helps this is good and right; what prevents it is bad and wrong. Giving to others is wrong if it harms oneself, though giving to others may be good if, thereby, one's own self is benefited. There are many varieties of egoism or individualism depending upon how the nature of self is conceived. Those who conceive self narrowly, have a narrow conception of what is best for themselves. Others who believe that their children, their community, their nation, or even mankind, are parts of themselves, have broader and more complicated conceptions of what is good for themselves.

Acts are right because they produce good results for God. Some hold that since God, although superior in power and goodness, is not perfect, the future of goodness and badness in the cosmos still hangs in the balance. If our helping God will improve our cosmic situation, then goodness will prevail to a greater extent. Our acts are right to the extent that they serve God and ultimate goodness, wrong to the extent that they detract from the goodness of God. On this theory, God, too, may be a moral being with power of choice, who, himself, could choose wrongly, even though perhaps he never does. God, too, on this theory, could act wrongly if he should act not to produce good for himself, whereas on the authoritative theory (acts are right because God commands them) there could be no wrong for God, unless he had first commanded himself and then disobeyed his own commands. The good-results-for-God theory presupposes a God who can be benefited by our action, in contrast with a perfect God who can be helped by nothing.

Acts are right because they produce good results for the best people. Aristocrats who believe that some people are better than others often sanction class systems in which the lesser serve the greater in the interests of the greater. Frederick Nietzsche's famous doctrine of the "Superman" epitomizes the ideal that the weaker ought to serve the stronger, that slaves deserve to be slaves and masters masters, that superiority is naturally and deservedly superior to inferiority. Many who despise Nietzsche still advocate eugenics programs which compel sterilization of the unfit and approve other differential rights for geniuses and morons. One difficulty with this view has to do with the establishment and justification of some criterion for determining who are the best people. Whereas some advocate racial or caste distinctions, others idealize religious (the elect), educational, economic, or political types of superiority.

Acts are right because they produce good results for the most people. Utilitarianism, acclaiming "the greatest good for the greatest number," has been widely heralded as the ethical foundation for democratic forms of government. Although this was a radical theory in the days of monarchies and divine right of kings, today it is commonly accepted as part of the supposedly self-evident groundwork of democratic practices. The democratic form of government is considered right because it is believed to produce the best results for the most people. Difficulties encountered by this view include trying to decide who constitute the most people, and what is right with respect to minorities or individuals, whose welfare happens to be not in accord with that of the majority.

All of the foregoing theories have been stated in a streamlined form. Whoever holds one of them probably would modify the theory in explaining precisely what he means by custom, success, God, or good results. Furthermore, most ethicists also point out that not all acts, but only voluntary acts, are right or wrong. That is, the foregoing views probably would be modified so as to include only intentional acts: acts are right, for example, which are intended to be customary, intended to conform to group approval, intended to be legal, etc. Those ignorant of their obligations or of the consequences of their actions can hardly be held blameworthy, unless they have deliberately rejected opportunities to become informed. In such cases, the deliberate rejection is considered wrong rather than the ignorant act itself. Although ethicists still debate whether, as Socrates said, "No man can do wrong voluntarily," most will agree that he can do no wrong other than voluntarily.

Perhaps, at this point, the writer should confess his own view of rightness, even though it involves a conception of self likely to be misunderstood without the supplementary treatment in later chapters. "Acts are right because they are intended to produce the best results for one's self in the long run." [15] Since one's self and others are organically related, what is best for oneself cannot be adequately determined apart from what is best for others. Those presupposing a logic of external relations naturally think that what is best for oneself involves no good for others. Those who base their thinking upon internal relatedness, who therefore believe that oneself and others are ultimately identical (my Atman and your Atman are both Brahman), conclude that what is good for others is good for oneself and what is bad for others is bad for oneself. [16]

Acceptance of organic logic implies the conception that what is best for oneself and what is best for others are interdependent. Since our dependence upon, and independence from, each other vary from time to time, so the extent to which we ought to take each other into consideration in right action fluctuates. To the extent that we are unrelated, we rightly ignore each other. In so far as our interests are identical, what is best for each is best for all and none can act

[15] Archie J. Bahm, "Rightness Defined," *Philosophy and Phenomenological Research*, December, 1947, p. 266.

[16] For details, examine the "Ahimsa" doctrine of Jains and Hindus.

rightly without thereby aiming at that which is best for all. To the extent that we are genuinely antagonistic, we rightly oppose each other, though feelings of opposition usually falsely obliterate awareness of underlying identities, even as ecstatic love momentarily blinds us to persisting differences. Normally, no one is completely unrelated to, or identical with, or opposed to, all others. Most of our life is occupied with choices involving fluctuating notions of the relative interdependence of our selves and others. The situation is complicated by the fact that we differ in insight, foresight, and comprehensiveness of vision. We are given to misunderstanding each other and are easily insulted when misunderstood. Since this is so, it may pay us to look to history's moral lessons for guidance.

The golden rule is a simple formula distilled from the ethical struggles of many cultures. That it works well in most situations has been demonstrated time and again by empirical tests. Unlike the aluminum rule [17] (Don't let others do to you what you wouldn't do to them) or the silver rule [18] (Don't do unto others what you would not have them do unto you), the golden rule (Do unto others as you would have others do unto you) strikes closest to the core of human nature. It really involves what should be called "the platinum rule" (Do unto others as others would have us do unto them [19]), for this is what we would have others do to us.[20] If the reader is sceptical about the value of the golden rule because he has seen it fail, then one may question whether he has given it a fair trial. Some, who have rejected theological or other foundations upon which they believed the rule to rest, have unnecessarily rejected the rule itself. A rule which is to be found in so many cultures, even in the presence of conflicting theologies, may well rest upon a broader empirical foundation than those theologies themselves. The following simple experiment may reawaken interest. Give your own answer to three questions: "(1) Do you prefer to be liked or disliked? (2) Which people do you like, those who like you or those who dislike you?

[17] See Thomas V. Smith, "In Accentuation of the Negative," *The Scientific Monthly*, December, 1946, p. 465.

[18] *Ibid.*, p. 464.

[19] See *ibid.*, p. 463.

[20] Confucian ethics contributes an insight often overlooked in the West, i.e., justice demands that unequals should treat each other as unequals. For, if father and son were to treat each other as equals, then a father ought to respect his son in exactly the same way as he wishes to be respected, i.e., as a father. But ought a father respect his son as a father? No. He should treat his son as he would like to be treated if he were his son.

(3) Then, if others answer Questions 1 and 2 as you did, what must you do to them in order to get them to like you?" [21]   Human nature seems so constructed that one who seeks what is best for himself in the long run can hardly find what he seeks without obeying the golden rule. "Furthermore, one must not merely pretend to be seeking the welfare of others, but must seem to them to be seeking their welfare." [22]   "If you merely pretend to like others, the most you can expect, according to the golden rule, is that others will pretend to like you." [23]   Thus, actually, wise self-interestedness demands some genuine altruism.

Intentions

Ethics, some say, is the science of choice, or "is the search for principles to guide choice." [24]   Choice exists only when one is faced with alternatives—alternatives which are good, bad, or indifferent. Here values are presupposed, as well as awareness of them as alternatives, and some kind of decision or voluntary selection of them. Since decision cannot occur without intention, the problem: What is intention? confronts the ethicist as basic, and most troublesome. Although everyone knows from firsthand experience what intentions are, his unreflective beliefs about them may be disturbed by considering some of the complications involved. The line between intended and unintended action, although sharply drawn by dualists, becomes more difficult to distinguish as certain questions are considered. Is each intention separate and distinct, or do our intentions overlap and intermingle with each other? Is unintended action always wholly unintended or may it be partly intended? Can a person's action ever be wholly unintended and still be his own action?

Some suggest that accidental or unconscious responses may be wholly unintended. Sometimes behavior produces results beyond what was intended or different from what was intended. We often say that "we didn't mean to" cause effects even when we admit we intended to act. Some distinguish between conscious and subconscious selection, the latter being considered unintentional. At times we feel that we have to choose what we do not want, i.e., feel forced

[21] Archie J. Bahm, "That Good Old Golden Rule," *Your Life*, March, 1941, p. 16.

[22] Bahm, "Rightness Defined," p. 268.

[23] Bahm, "That Good Old Golden Rule," p. 16.

[24] William Henry Roberts, *The Problem of Choice*, p. 24.   Ginn and Co., Boston, 1941.

to intend what we do not wish to intend. Turning to intended action, we face similar questions. Is intended action only partly intended or may, or must, it be wholly intended? When we do not care how the action comes out, are we intending? That is, do we escape intending when we intend to do nothing about it, or when we intend not to intend? Surely our action cannot be intended so long as we are unclear or feel unsure as to the outcome? We often assent half-heartedly or with mental reservations or, at times, when we are half asleep. Degrees of intention sometimes seem correlated with intensity of enthusiasm. However, if this were so, then glandular factors, for example, which fluctuate in their influence upon emotional responsiveness, might constitute the primary difference between intended and unintended action. Whether an action should be considered wholly intended may depend upon (1) whether it is the intention of the whole person, and (2) whether it results in action.

1. Some seem to believe that a course of action is wholly intended as soon as one's mind is fully made up, or when his conviction about it and his commitment to it are felt as complete. But does "complete" mean complete for the moment (implying intention to reserve the right to change one's mind later) or complete for a lifetime (until death do us part) or forever (for time and eternity) without reservation? Is it possible for one's intention to be so complete that it can never be changed regardless of changing circumstances, or is every intention subject to change?

However, others seem to think that a course of action can never be wholly intended unless his whole person is actually committed to it. A person is complex, too complex to keep all of his interests in mind at once. At those times when a particular interest occupies our whole attention, all others tend to be forgotten. So we sometimes say that a person's true intentions are not always those which he asserts with honest conviction, but what he would say if he understood himself more clearly. Can a man truly intend to do what he will later regret? Do we not excuse the willful damage of children and the insane and forgive evil doers when they see the light, repent, or regret? However, the problem of what a whole person is cannot be disentangled from differing metaphysical views of self. If an omniscient God knows one's true self, then one's true intentions are what God knows them to be. Or, if a self is conceived as God's creation, ultimately its intentions are what God intended its intentions to be, wholly or partly. Or, if self is thought of as identical with intentionless Brahman, then all intention, choice, and wrongness is illusory. If self consists merely of a particular momentary self-awareness, then one's whole self may easily be committed to an intention; but then each such self and its intentions can make no claim upon, or can justly place no blame upon, previous momentary selfs, and ethics becomes a rather senseless, or at best aesthetic, phase of life's self-deceit.

Organicism, with its conception of self as both momentary and enduring, as both conscious and unconscious, as both private and social, as both local and cosmic, as both completed and yet incomplete, and as involving both intended and unintended action, concludes that, on the one hand, in so far as there is a whole of one's self there is a sense in which one's whole self is involved whenever one intends, but that, on the other hand, in so far as one's self is incomplete (at many levels) and in so far as his knowledge both of his self and of the consequences of his action is always incomplete, no particular intention can be the intention of his whole person. In this second sense, one could not act as a whole unless this were his only act and unless his whole self were consumed, or consummated, in it. The very conception of intention involves a view of futurity which implies that one's present self is incomplete. Can one be wholly committed unless he commits his future also? Can this be done? Yes, for we do this constantly. The intention to marry, for example, involves the intention to have whatever other intentions become needed to carry on married life. One can hardly live without intending to take risks; i.e., to commit one's future self in present choice. In fact, every choice involves something of a commitment of this kind. Furthermore, in a sense, the whole universe intends through each of my intentions and, in a sense, my present intention exists only as mine now. But the explanation of whether an action is wholly intended cannot be reduced to either one of these senses alone. If ethical action can be understood only if we first understand the nature of intentions, ethics is, indeed, a complicated science.

2. Some think that an action is wholly intended only if it ends in action. In fact, some claim that unless one acts upon his intention, he has not really intended. However, those who distinguish between overt and covert action may assert that intention is itself a kind of covert action. The situation is complicated further by the fact that there are degrees of action. One might intend to act, if such action requires no trouble, without intending to take the trouble to act. Or, one might fully intend to act if an appropriate opportunity arises, even though it never does. Or one may begin an action which he

does not continue, or he may continue up to the last step without completing it. Is action enough, or must an action be carried out exactly as intended before it is wholly intended? At this point we may raise again the question, What is the relation of rightness to action or to intention? Some think that only actions can be right or wrong, not intentions. Others believe that only intentions are right or wrong, not actions ("As a man thinketh in his heart, so is he"). Still others, including organicists, relate rightness to both. For organicism, since intention and action are organically related, one does not fully intend until he acts, and his action is not fully his unless he intends it. Each intention is an incipient action and, so long as a person is conscious or has control over his intentions, his action, even his act of being, is partly intended.

Two other questions may be raised about whether action is wholly intended. 3. Since each action involves consequences for which one is responsible, and since one may or may not be willing to accept his responsibility for these consequences, some believe that an action is wholly intended only if one intends to accept the consequences willingly. 4. Since both intention, action, and willingness to accept consequences may be thought of either as free or determined, some claim that action is wholly intended only if it is wholly free in each of the three respects. But discussion of these must await our next two topics: responsibility and freedom.

Responsibility

One reason why intentions play such an important part in ethical discussion, it is claimed, is that without them there could be no responsibility. That there is responsibility in some sense or other is agreed by all, judging from the fact that all societies have mores involving punishment for violation, and that all of us at times judge others, or ourselves, to be or not to be to blame for certain consequences. Responsibility is a core concept, some say "the" core concept, of ethics. What, then, is responsibility?

At least five factors enter into our conception of responsibility, as the writer understands it. 1. A person is usually considered "responsible for any effect of which he is believed to be the cause." [25] To say that someone is responsible is to say that he, and not something else, is the cause of his effects. This implies that responsibility pre-

[25] Wilbur M. Urban, *Fundamentals of Ethics,* p. 400. Henry Holt and Co., New York, 1930.

supposes that the responsible being is in some sense an uncaused cause. Since many will challenge this conclusion, further discussion of it will be necessary, but this must wait until we consider the nature of freedom in the next section. 2. "Responsibility means," further, "the acceptance of one's act as his own . . . ," [26] or of recognizing that he himself is the cause. Or, as we say sometimes, one is a responsible person if he is capable of recognizing himself as the cause once the matter is drawn to his attention; others are said to be irresponsible. 3. However, a person may be able to recognize himself as the cause and still be unable to do anything about remedying the evil which has resulted. If one has deliberately caused a $50,000 damage but has only ten cents in assets, then, although he is responsible for the damage, he cannot be held responsible for repayment of the loss. One is not responsible, in this sense, unless he has the capacity to rectify harmful consequences. 4. Since one may have the capacity (i.e., the means—in the foregoing example, $50,000) to remedy the results and yet be unwilling to do so, one can be said to be responsible, in this fourth sense, only if he willingly accepts as his own the task of removing such ill effects of his own action as he can. 5. Finally, since each person is social and since society involves mores or established standards regarding what a person's responsibilities are under certain circumstances, one has such responsibilities as are assigned to him as a citizen. "A person may be held responsible even if he will not accept the consequences of his acts voluntarily." [27]

Even when all of the foregoing five senses or aspects of responsibility are accepted by ethicists, many questions remain to be answered before the nature of responsibility can be understood. How do responsibilities originate? To whom is one responsible? For what is one responsible?

1. In so far as one is responsible for whatever he himself causes, such responsibilities originate in himself as an uncaused cause. One cannot answer the question of how responsibilities originate unless he can answer the question of how he himself originated. Here we are deep in the metaphysical problem of how an uncaused cause can originate, so we have to call upon our metaphysical conclusions to help settle our ethical questions. One gets his responsibilities by being himself. Furthermore, to the extent that one is responsible for whatever he intends, i.e., by accepting himself as a free causal

[26] Edwin T. Mitchell, *A System of Ethics*, p. 305. Charles Scribner's Sons, New York, 1950.
[27] *Ibid.*, p. 294.

agent, his responsibilities originate in his intending. One cannot be what he is as an intending being without thereby being responsible. One cannot even intend not to intend without being responsible. To be a person is to be responsible. Also, if he is responsible to the extent that he has the means to remedy evils, then this responsibility originated where these means originated. One who inherits an estate inherits responsibilities. Fourthly, if one's responsibilities include only those which he is willing to accept as his own, then such responsibilities originate in his own willingness. Therefore, as ethicists, we must ask how willingness originates. Finally, since one has socially assigned responsibilities which others regard as his whether he accepts them or not, these originate in his society. Discussion of whether a group may itself be an uncaused cause must await the chapter on Social Philosophy. Certainly socially assigned responsibilities are at least partly acceptable to him; otherwise he could not accept himself as a responsible member of his society. To the extent that he intentionally accepts group membership he also involves himself in some intention to accept the responsibilities it attributes to him. Thus these responsibilities also have a personal origin.

2. To whom is one responsible? Although social practice has tended to convince us that our responsibility is always to others, even only to others, or to God, even only to God, there is a very fundamental sense in which one is responsible first of all to himself. If one wants to survive happily and if one's own actions may promote or prevent this, then one is responsible to himself. Why? Because his own wants (which are part of him as an uncaused cause) contain also the ground, or basis, of his action. If one does not care whether he lives or not, then he is not himself or is "beside himself." In his desire to live is inherent not only the source but also the goal of his responsibility. He is responsible because his own life is worth while —is an intrinsic value. He has responsibilities to others only because they, too, are intrinsic values which are not completely independent of him. Since each person is himself inherently social,[28] he cannot be what he is, and be the intrinsic value that he is, and be the goal of responsibility that he is, apart from other persons. One who thinks he can do without all other persons has, in terms of his own thinking, no obligations to them. But how does anyone fare when he denies that he has duties to others. He loses all rights, as we shall see later. To the extent that each person is organically related to others, he owes

[28] See Ch. 26.

it to himself to promote their welfare as his welfare and he is, thereby, responsible to them as well as to himself precisely because he is responsible to himself as a social being.

So far as God is concerned: if God is an intrinsic value not independent of us, then we are responsible also to God, because we are responsible ultimately to ourselves. Has God no responsibilities? Or is God all-responsible? If God were the only intrinsic value, then God would be both the only source of responsibility and the only being to which we could be responsible, and, like Spinoza,[29] we should have to admit that the only responsibilities which we have are those wherewith God is responsible to himself. But if each person is also an intrinsic value, then God has responsibilities to persons, since, as personalists[30] believe, persons and God depend somewhat upon each other.

3. For what is one responsible? For intrinsic value, since things which are, or have, intrinsic value, may perish. Responsibility, then, presupposes intrinsic value in at least three ways, since responsibility not only arises from it and is indebted to it, but also is obligation for it. It is true that, in a sense, one is responsible only for what he causes, intends, can remedy, willingly remedies, or is asked to remedy by society—whether for self or others. But is it not also true that one is responsible for more than he causes, intends, can remedy, etc.? Between possible minimums and maximums of responsibility which one may choose to assume, ought one to accept as little as possible, or as much as possible, or how much? One who dislikes responsibilities because he feels them as external restraints will seek to accept as little as possible. The proposal that he ought to do more than he ought to do will seem absurd. But if it is recognized that responsibility implies entailment of intrinsic value and that, in a sense, the more one is responsible the greater is his value, both instrumentally and intrinsically, since these are organically related, then assumption of responsibility comes to be conceived as a privilege and, to a certain extent, as a right. If enjoyment of intrinsic value is the ultimate goal of life, and if assumption of greater responsibility involves one in greater intrinsic value, then what one most wants to do is to accept his maximum of responsibility.

Part of the secret of the marvelous powers attributed to Jesus may be found in his willingness to accept more responsibility than he

[29] See Ch. 14.
[30] See p. 185.

needed to, more than others were willing to accept—i.e., responsibility for "the sins of the whole world." Such willingness was, and always will be, marvelous.[31]   Any person who is unwilling to accept the blame for the consequences of his action is spiritually sick, and he can be healed only by faith that accepting such blame is best for him in the long run.   The Calvinist doctrine, that only those can be saved who are willing to be damned eternally for sins for which they were not wholly responsible, has a core of truth in it.   For only by being willing to assume more responsibility than one needs to accept can he acquire greater intrinsic value than he otherwise has any right to.   One cannot love deeply without being willing to accept blame for more ill than one would want to happen.   Great joy in mother-hood is justified when, and because, it brings with it an intuitive will-ingness to bear responsibilities for the mistakes of children—results which a mother very much does not want and tries to prevent.   How-ever, although there may be great wisdom in bearing a maximum of responsibility, this does not mean that we should take away from others such responsibilities as they need.   One can be selfish about assuming responsibility for others (as exemplified in "smother love").   Since life is dynamic, how much one should be responsible for will vary from time to time and will depend upon the kinds of circum-stances into which he happens to come.

How is responsibility related to rightness and wrongness?   Are one's acts right or wrong only if, or to the extent that, one is respon-sible?   If responsibility is complicated, do its complications permeate rightness and wrongness?   If, for example, one's responsibilities de-pend partly upon his nature and circumstances and partly upon his willingness to accept responsibility, does the nature of rightness and wrongness also fluctuate with variations in these?   If rightness and wrongness depend not only upon intentions, responsibility, but also upon freedom, are these three separate conditions of ethical action, or merely three aspects, different ways of looking at the same thing?

Freedom

Many think that acts are right or wrong only if the actor chose to act of his own free will.   Accidental or coerced action is unfree and thus not wrong.   Such a view presupposes freedom of choice

[31] For an excellent interpretation, see Fritz Kunkel, *God Helps Those* . . . Ives Washburn, New York, 1931.

and involves the ethicist in the problem of freedom. In a way, this is a very simple problem, for everyone knows what freedom is. Yet, like so many other concepts which we have examined, it develops amazing complexity as we pursue our examination of it. A first thing to note, of course, is that the term "freedom" is used in many different settings. For example, we speak of freedom of will, political freedom, and metaphysical freedom. Discussion of the many kinds and levels of social and political freedom will be left to later chapters. Although the ethicist is concerned primarily with freedom of will, he soon finds that his ethical problem cannot be solved adequately apart from metaphysical considerations. No ethical view is complete until it is demonstrated to be metaphysically possible, just as no metaphysical view is adequate until it works in ethics.

Freedom consists in being able to do what one wants to do. However, six different conceptions of what this statement means need to be examined.

1. Probably the most common conception of freedom is the negative one: freedom consists in absence of restraint. Either one is bound or free, held or let go, tied down or let up, imprisoned or let out. Since whatever restricts one makes him unfree, whatever relieves him of restrictions brings him freedom. Whoever feels himself imposed upon tends to idealize freedom as complete absence of limitations upon his action. Then it is that he dreams of the proverbial "south sea isles," where one is supposed to be freed from all need of labor as well as of all duties and responsibilities. Unfreedom here is conceived as a purely external matter. Only what frustrates (outer) one's self and its wants makes one unfree; one's own self and its wants (inner) have nothing to do with unfreedom.

A moment's reflection, however, should reveal the inadequacy of this view. We also recognize that we have inner restraints, such as debilitating indigestion, forgetting, fear, and inhibitions. When we do not have sufficient energy or knowledge or confidence to do something, then we recognize that we are not free to do such. Here freedom is still conceived as absence of restraint, though the conception is expanded to include inner restraints. Here, further, freedom may be thought to include freedom from inhibition and freedom from conscience. If we reflect farther we may note that our wants themselves make us unfree. Sometimes we become slaves to habit, to habitual wants. We spend so much time filling some wants that we are prevented from satisfying others. When this is the case, some of our wants frustrate others and so make us unfree. In fact, whenever we have freedom of choice, i.e., have several alternatives all of which we want but only one of which we can have, we are bound to be frustrated regarding all but one of them. A person faced with a decisive choice, between two alternatives, both of which he dearly wants, suffers cruelly. When the price is great and the alternatives evenly balanced, he wishes he did not need to choose. Here he desires, not freedom of choice, but freedom from choice. To need to choose when one does not so wish makes him unfree. Thus, choice may either increase or decrease one's freedom. Those who conceive freedom in terms of unlimited choices see only one side of the picture.

The other side, carried to extremes in some forms of Hindu, Jaina, and Buddhist thinking, is that desire itself is the root of all evil. If evil occurs whenever desires are frustrated, then if there are no desires, there can be no evil. Therefore, if desires for what we cannot have cause our unfreedom, the only way to achieve complete freedom is to get rid of all desires. The yogin aims at complete extinction of desire. The whole source of unfreedom is conceived as inner, not outer. This view is, indeed, about as reasonable as its opposite, i.e., that the source of freedom is outer, or consists entirely of removal of external restraints.

In fact, external restraints not only may be means to freedom, but some external limitations are always present where freedom is possible. The same prison walls which incarcerate a murderer also protect him from a vengeful mob. Or, as we shall see in discussing social and political philosophy, laws that restrain one's actions are necessary to maintain the possibility of one's own freedom to live in a lawful society. Each social restriction may be a means to freedom as well as to unfreedom, just as one's own inhibitions may help one to avoid harmful effects. A well-developed and readily obeyed conscience gives many people a superior sense of freedom. Since neither absence of restraint nor absence of desire satisfies most thinkers as constituting the core of the nature of freedom, most of them have looked elsewhere for a solution of this problem.

2. Since determinism has played such a large part in modern science, and since freedom and determinism have long been considered contradictory, freedom easily became identified with indeterminism. Either a thing is caused or uncaused, determined or undetermined— entirely or partly. Where complete determinism prevails, it is believed that there exists no indeterminism and thus no freedom, and, consequently, no ethics in the usual sense of the term. However, faith in freedom and rightness is naturally too strong to be downed

so easily. Some persons who insist on at least partial indeterminism believe they have found a solution in dualism.[32] Much of the reason for the success of dualism is that it has been able to subscribe to both determinism and indeterminism by attributing determinism exclusively to matter, indeterminism exclusively to spirit. As long as science restricted itself to matter, and religion to spirit, faith in freedom of will was safe. This view has persisted and is widespread today. However, since, except in popular thinking, dualism has been almost entirely outmoded, most ethicists have sought elsewhere for solution. When the physicist, Heisenberg, announced his "principle of indeterminacy," many ethicists immediately grasped it as proof of their faith that freedom is inherent in the structure of the universe. But if this hope is premised upon the view that determinism and indeterminism are contradictory, then, other ethicists think, it is still searching in the wrong direction. The next three views we shall consider presuppose the conception that determinism and indeterminism are opposites, not contradictories.

3. Freedom is often conceived as self-determinism or self-causation. So long as one's causes are part of his own self, he is self-caused and, thus, free. Here the issue is one of outer versus inner determination, rather than of determinism versus indeterminism. This idea is supported by the language commonly used regarding political liberty, in which freedom is spoken of not as freedom from government but as freedom of peoples to govern themselves. The statement that "one is free when he is able to do what he wants to do" does not imply that one's wants are not determined, but only that the source of determination lies inside the self. Since there are many different views of the nature of self, and thus of what lies inside of it, so this conception of freedom is really many different conceptions. To say that acts are free when they are the result of one's own character or "to the extent that they are the result of enduring and significant tendencies within ourselves" [33] still does not tell us much about such tendencies. According to this conception, as well as to those which follow, freedom is consistent with complete determinism, in contrast with the preceding conceptions which presuppose them to be incompatible.

4. Age-long reflection upon the nature of self has led to the discovery that it is not simple, but consists of higher and lower aspects.

[32] See Ch. 13.
[33] Roberts, *op. cit.*, p. 297.

The search for self-realization has brought many thinkers to the conclusion that one's true self is his higher self, and that what one really most wants is to realize his true self. Freedom then comes to be conceived as submission of the lower to the higher part of self. Wants may be an expression of either part of the self. When conflict between such wants arises, and when the lower desires predominate over the higher, then one's higher, or true, self is enslaved by his lower and less real self. Freedom consists in subordination of the lesser to the greater, or surrender of the unreal to the real self.

Although debates continue concerning what constitutes the higher self, some well-known examples may be cited. If God both knows and wants what is really best for a self, then one who wants to do what is really best for himself will want to do what God wants him to do. Freedom, then, consists in submission of one's own will to the will of God.

If the universe is ultimately rational, and if reason is a safer guide to the good than irrational emotion or violent and erratic passion, then one is free to achieve the good only to the extent that he wants to be, and can be, reasonable. Freedom, then, consists in letting one's own mind be governed by the rules of logical validity. If, however, as romanticists maintain, the universe is ultimately irrational, and if spiritual intuition or divinely inspired impulse alone can direct us to intrinsic values, then freedom consists in submission to impulse and riddance of rule by illusory logic. Finally, if being reasonable consists, not in conformity to logical forms, but in choosing the best among alternatives, then even a worshipper of reason can be free only if he submits his will to wanting what is best. Submission, then, of lower to higher self, or self-determination by one's higher or better self, is the core of freedom, according to this conception.

5. Still another conception claims that freedom consists in willingness to accept oneself as a cause, agent, or originator of action. Here the issue is thought of, not in terms of presence or absence of restraint, not in terms of presence or absence of causation, not in terms of outer or inner causation, not in terms of lower or higher causation, but in terms of accepting or not accepting oneself as a responsible cause of consequences. According to this conception, each person not only is caused but causes. To the extent that he considers himself merely a transmitter of causes, he is an irresponsible mechanism who is neither to be blamed nor praised for the consequences. But to the extent that he considers himself as an individual, as an agent, as a prime mover, or as himself a cause, he himself becomes worthy of both credit and

blame. In fact, selfhood itself arises only through a willingness to accept oneself as a self; so one is free to be only if one wills to be, and one is free to act, or to be an actor, only if he wills his acts to be his own. So, although one is caused to be what he is, he is not free to be anything other than an effect unless he willingly accepts himself as something original, as an originator of consequences. For this conception, freedom cannot arise without entailing a willingness to be responsible and without some risk of being responsible for some unforeseeable results.

6. Organicism, although rejecting each of the foregoing as insufficient by itself, accepts each as making some positive contribution to a more adequate conception of freedom. Whatever restrains or limits one makes him unfree when it makes him less able to do what he wants to do, but the same limitation may function also as a means to greater freedom when it makes him more able to do what he wants to do. Inhibitions, for example, do not of themselves make us more unfree, for they also make it possible for us to act where these inhibitions are required. Freedom of choice and freedom from choice are equally true types of freedom. One of the best ways to get what one wants is to want what one gets, but, always, part of what one gets is more wanting. Stoic "acceptance of the universe" is wise, if not carried too far, for one can hardly accept the universe unless he accepts his own desires as part of it. The ideal of complete extinction of desire, however, brings one no freedom, except freedom from freedom, or freedom from existence itself. One is not able to get what he wants unless he wants, just as he is not able to get what he wants unless he gets. But if, when he gets what he wants, he does not want what he gets, then both his wanting and getting have been in vain. Of course, since we seldom either get all we want or want all we get, life is partly vain. Yet to the extent that we do get what we want or want what we get, what we get is all gain.

Indeterminism, too, plays a part in the organicist conception of freedom. Unlike dualism, however, which attributes determinism and indeterminism to two unrelated substances, matter and spirit, organicism conceives them as aspects of each person, even if related to the material and spiritual aspects of each person.[34] Self-determinism also pervades organic conceptions of freedom, though only if a more-complex-than-usual conception of self is intended. Since one's self is both one and many and exists at many levels, the line between the

[34] See pp. 244–250.

inner and the outer, between self and not-self, is itself organic. "Because we conceive ourselves differently at different times, what it takes to make us feel free will likewise differ from time to time." [35] And "any shift in feeling from opposition to identification involves a shift in feeling from unfreedom to freedom." [36] If duty is conceived as externally imposed, more duties seem to make one more unfree; but when duties are thought of as inner demands, then one's most important duty consists in what he most wants to do. Submission of lower to higher interests also increases organic freedom, though which interests are higher and which lower is conceived in terms of dynamic and rhythmically fluctuating aspects of polar categories of personality. Willingness to accept oneself as a cause constitutes another aspect of organic freedom. Speaking of self as subject, we may say that "every human being is subject and object at the same time. . . . If he is subject, or a living being, he must act; if he is object, he is acted upon." [37] "Who affirms life must agree to the fact that he must be the subject of his own behavior and the object of all the results of that behavior. More than that, he is also co-subject of the behavior of greater collective subjects, such as the family, class and state, and he is co-object of the reactions which fall upon these collective objects, such as epidemics, wars, financial crises and the like." [38] He who, because he blames others for his predicament, refuses to act, thereby willfully destroys his own freedom to act. But he who accepts full responsibility for his acts, even though others caused him to be the kind of actor he is, acts as a free agent. Freedom arises from acceptance of oneself as a cause rather than from repudiating one's causes, or from wanting to be responsible rather than from fearing and fighting responsibility. All these, then, absence of restraint, indeterminism, self-determinism, submission, and agentism, participate in the organic conception of freedom. Everyone knows what freedom means, or does he?

The aim in summarizing these six views of freedom is to throw further light upon the nature and complexity of ethical problems. Although drawing out the ethical implications of each of the foregoing views is too extensive a task to undertake here, the discussion should help us to become both more critical and more tolerant about ethical

---

[35] Archie J. Bahm, "Freedom is Fitness," *The Scientific Monthly*, August, 1946, p. 135.

[36] *Ibid.* See further.

[37] Kunkel, *op. cit.*, p. 13.

[38] *Ibid.*, p. 18.

assertions. If, as many think, acts are right and wrong only in so far as they are intended, and if "action is wholly intended only if wholly free," [39] then if action is never wholly free, is any act ever wholly right or wholly wrong? Surely we are hardly in a position to be very dogmatic about rightness and wrongness until we have become more clear as to what we mean by freedom.

Rights

Ethics is concerned not only with rightness, but also with rights. This matter is more often associated with political and legal philosophy, since people seem to be more concerned about their legal than their moral rights. Socially, a right is something which others owe us, whereas rightness is often thought of as what we owe others. "A right is the minimum claim upon the services of others, as a duty is the minimum claim of others upon ourselves." [40] Although ethicists do not often discuss them, many troublesome questions arise concerning rights: Does oneself later in life have any rights owed by oneself earlier in life? Do animals, unborn babies, or God have rights? Are rights and duties exactly correlative, or do some kinds or degrees of duties carry no reciprocal rights? Does assumption of increased responsibility increase or decrease one's rights? What happens to our rights when others do not do their duties? Can a person rightfully be deprived of his rights? Is each right equal to every other right, or are some rights more important than others? Do all people have equal rights, or do some people have a right to differential treatment?

Justice

What is justice? Of many different conceptions, two types predominate. These are commonly called distributive justice and retributive justice. Distributive justice has to do with whether people have equal shares of both rights and duties. "The essence of justice is impartiality. This means the resolute exclusion of all considerations not truly relevant to the issue in question." [41] But does it mean that all persons have equal rights and duties? People are alike, but people are also different. Do not people have a right to differential treatment in so far as they are different, just as much as they have a right to

---

[39] See p. 317.   [41] *Ibid.*, p. 302.
[40] Roberts, *op. cit.*, p. 252.

similar treatment in so far as they are alike? Does a child have the same duties as a parent? If rights and duties are correlative, does a person with increased rights (e.g., one who acquires more property) thereby have correlatively greater duties? Is justice always social, or does one face the problem of doing justice to each of his own many interests?

Punishment

Retributive justice pertains to equality of repayment for damage. If one has harmed another, does he owe him a like amount of good in return? The history of retribution is a wild and furious tale, but not without obvious progress. Although we now despise the "eye for an eye" conception of justice, a look at its predecessors reveals it to have been a great improvement. Primitive ideals of vengeance often required twenty enemy lives for one lost by the clan, or the life of a slave as the price for his bruising his master. Limiting retributive demands to "a tooth for a tooth" was probably the greatest step forward ever taken in the history of justice. Since paying back equally meant paying back exactly, this involved payment in kind. How can one pay for an eye, except with an eye? However, mankind gradually realized the inadequacy of this view. Although a cow for a cow might make restoration, a person without a cow could not, and a person who had already lost both eyes might then gouge eyes with impunity. Furthermore, the retributive loss of a second eye was not only an evil (adding evil to evil does not produce good) but its loss by the second person really did no good for the first. Therefore, substitute payments were considered acceptable—a view which became more feasible as property increased. Justice prevailed when the injured was repaid an equivalent in other acceptable goods or services, a factor contributing somewhat to "justified" servitude, slavery, and serfdom.

However, since different goods and services are never quite equal, in the opinions of the different parties, the problem of justice became more complicated. Since, like "the widow's mite," a small amount means proportionately more to a poor man than to a rich one, equality is a matter not merely related to property, but involves how important it is relative to its owners. Since the same dollar has different values to people of different economic classes, for example, justice cannot be done without recognizing inequalities. Greater inequalities relative to distributive justice tend to involve greater inequalities relative to retributive justice. Consequently, ethical thinkers are pressed to reformulate ideals of justice on other planes, or in terms of other principles. Two types of attempts are well known.

According to the first, exact justice can be maintained only if one has either a just and powerful God or a Law of Karma to rely on, as well as other lives to live in which the balances can somehow surely be restored. According to the second, which may or may not be associated with the first, no amount of wisdom can calculate "each jot and tittle" of justice, especially when there is no clear proof that anyone has any rights at all in the first place. Justice then comes to be conceived as a matter of reciprocity, not so much regarding property as attitudes. The golden rule is the supreme principle of justice because it is the primary principle of reciprocity: act toward others as you would have them act toward you if you were in their place. Justice, here, presupposes dialectical ability—i.e., ability to see oneself as one is not and what is not oneself (others) as if it were oneself; and the ability to rise above a merely one-sided view of a two-sided situation. This is not easy, and yet, for many of those who do so, it turns out to be by far the easier solution to the problem of justice. Punishment takes on some entirely different colors, for now one has to evaluate how he thinks he should be punished if he were in the culprit's shoes. Then he will be able to think of more reasons why he is not to blame. Although even the most honest and successful attempt to take the position of the other may fail to achieve perfect exactness, since two different people may actually evaluate themselves differently, this method probably most closely approximates such perfection of justice as is open to human beings, and it is, some Christians think, God's first, or second, law.

But, even so, the problem is not settled, for, as we shall see in the chapters on social and political philosophy, it is seldom that only two people are involved. Since others in one's family, community, and nation have a stake in one's welfare, they too may have rights in what seems to be a private affair. Theories of punishment now propose rehabilitation as the primary goal. If penalties are themselves evil, and if multiplying evils does not produce good, then each punishment situation is looked upon as an opportunity for increasing good rather than evil for all concerned. All this indicates that the golden rule, even if indispensable, is not enough, unless one can somehow put himself in the shoes of multitudes in his society as well as in those of the other person directly involved.

No matter how much we may be interested in justice, justice is never the whole of any ethical situation. Apparently the problems facing ethicists continue to become more difficult as we penetrate more deeply into them. If we can find no simple principle, then what? Another view holds that there can be no easy solution to ethical problems, so none should be expected. Each problem, with all its complexities and uncertainties, must be dealt with individually. Preconceived solutions, no matter how ingenious and satisfactory on previous occasions, cannot be expected to work in similar, yet also different, situations. Does this mean that all principles are useless? Does this mean that it is hopeless to consider ethics as a science seeking general principles? No, for, in so far as different ethical situations are alike, generalizations based upon their common elements may be possible. Rather, this view holds, all known principles regarding rightness, intentions, responsibility, rights, justice, punishment, and the like, which are relevant to a situation, need to be brought to bear; yet, in addition, unique aspects of each situation, including some unique ways in which the various principles apply to the situation, require consideration also. Even then probably few solutions can ever be completely satisfactory. Looked at in this way, the problem of how to solve ethical problems is itself an ethical problem. Being faced with an ethical problem is itself an evil, so there is some justification for people not liking ethics. But unless one can figure out a way to avoid them, he is stuck with them. One result of becoming aware of the complicatedness of ethics should be that a person comes to expect that he cannot get all that he thought he had coming, i.e., that he does not really have a full right to all of his rights, or, rather, that he does not have quite as many rights as he thought he had.

Virtue

Much misunderstanding occurs relative to virtue, because narrower and specific meanings often are mistakenly attributed to this term when broad and general meanings are intended. Narrowly speaking, for example, a virtuous woman is one living strictly within accepted sex codes. But broadly speaking, virtue is ability to act rightly. Each of the various theories of rightness will, consequently, have different conceptions of the nature of virtue. For example, if acts are right because God commands them, then virtue consists in ability to keep God's commands. However, if one's acts are right because they produce the best results for himself, then whoever has this ability is thereby virtuous. Virtue, then, is neither a peculiar kind of ethical trait which only a few attain nor a characteristic of only certain kinds of behavior. It is an aspect or factor in every ethical situation.

Of course, emphases upon the use of the term virtue differ in the thought and language of different ethicists. Since Plato and Aristotle have played an important role in western philosophy, it is common for western ethicists to discuss their views of virtue and, especially, of the cardinal virtues. "Plato's list has at least the merit of simplicity. It contained only four—Wisdom (or Prudence), Courage (or Fortitude), Temperance (or Self-Restraint) and Justice (or Righteousness). Plato, and Greek moralists in general, thought of these as cardinal, not only because in one form or another they are universally valued, but also because they are fundamental and irreducible, being those qualities of character on which all others hinge." [42] "Aristotle, who followed immediately after Plato, was led to a considerable expansion of the list. Anything like a complete list would include, among others, such desirable qualities as the economic virtue of thrift; the specific virtue connected with the sex life, called chastity; and the peculiar social virtue of loyalty in its manifold forms." [43] Following Aristotle further, "An examination of the particular virtues reveals that each is a mean between the two vicious extremes of defect and excess. Courage is the mean between cowardice and foolhardiness. Liberality lies between stinginess and prodigality, temperance between harsh asceticism and dissipation. Magnificence is a splendid quality that in excess becomes bad taste or ostentation; in defect, shabbiness." [44]

In addition to such "practical" virtues as the foregoing, Aristotle advocated as superior certain "theoretical" virtues, the chief of which was the disinterested pursuit of truth, which is satisfied only in contemplation of truth for its own sake without hint of practical use. Aristotle's ideal is surpassed in purity of impracticality by that Hindu ideal in which yogic virtue consists in ability to achieve nirvana by discarding all illusion of distinction. As philosophies differ regarding which goals of life are primary, e.g., other-worldly or this-worldly, so they naturally differ as to which virtues are considered primary.

Organicism not only accepts Aristotle's doctrine of the mean between extremes but carries it farther in two directions: 1. Between his practical and theoretical virtues there is also a mean. The ability to seek this mean is also a virtue. In other language, since instru-

[42] Urban, *op. cit.*, pp. 333–334.
[43] *Ibid.*, pp. 334–335.
[44] Roberts, *op. cit.*, pp. 162–163.

mental and intrinsic values are equally necessary aspects of existence, the virtuous man devotes himself to both, not to either the one or to the other exclusively or primarily during his lifetime.[45]   2. Since one may go to an extreme in seeking the mean between extremes, organicism claims that being virtuous involves being not too virtuous in any one way, i.e., involves the ability to pursue a mean that is somewhere between an extreme mean and a mere extreme.[46]   In pursuing the virtue of liberality, for example, one may find that his aiming to be liberal will cause him to be more stingy at some times and more prodigal at others.   Or the same trait, such as "penny-pinching," which may be a virtue in a poor man turns into a vice for a rich man who thereby becomes a miser.   Since life is dynamic and variable, a basic virtue, according to organicism, is adaptability.

Although we have been speaking of virtue as any ability to act rightly, we should recognize that most uses of this term connote also that such abilities are somewhat enduring.   A virtue is not merely a momentary or accidental ability, but a character trait.   Usually only one who has many rather stable abilities for acting rightly is spoken of as a virtuous person, as a righteous character, or as a good man. Ethics, some think, is the science of character-building, or of virtue.

Ideals

It is common to speak of having high ideals.[47]   What is an ideal, and when is it high?   An ideal is something which has not been, but supposedly can be, realized, and which, because it has not yet been realized, is aimed at or serves as a goal, or end, of our action.   Now, in so far as ends are identified with intrinsic values, in contrast with

---

[45] See pp. 275–277.

[46] See pp. 243–244.

[47] This discussion of ideals and of ethical idealism introduces a third basic type of meaning of the terms "ideal," "idealism," "real," and "realism."   According to the first type of meaning, i.e., that pertaining to theory of knowledge, ideas are subjective, or mind dependent, whereas real things are independent of minds and ideas.   Those who hold that objects of knowledge are subjective are called subjectivists or subjective idealists, whereas those holding that objects of knowledge are real are called realists.   According to the second type of meaning, i.e., that pertaining to metaphysics or theory of reality, the real, or ultimate reality, is that which "most is," or which cannot be reduced to anything more ultimate. The view of those metaphysicians who believe that mind or ideas are most ultimate is often called "idealism," though the term "spiritualism" seems more suitable because somewhat less confusing.   The term "realism" is seldom used to

means, which serve as instrumental values, ideals come to function as if they were as-yet-unrealized intrinsic values which, therefore, have some claim to realization. If an ideal is thought of as an intrinsic value, it appears to be an end-in-itself which does not yet actually exist but which, as we say, ought to exist.

Some ethicists have concluded that all ideals involve obligations, whether they be ideals for self, social, or cosmic realization. However, such ethicists seem to presuppose certain conceptions, which have not been universally accepted, regarding actuality and potentiality, and of the priority of ideals as potentialities over men as actualities. The nature of ethical ideals can hardly be arrived at apart from a solution of the metaphysical problem concerning the relative priority of the ideal and the actual. Platonic idealists [48] consider ideals as primary and as patterns which any attempt at actualization ought to conform to.

However, emergentistic pragmatists believe that actuality is primary and "that ideals grow out of the life of every day as leaves grow out of the life of the tree. I am not attempting to minimize the importance of ideals. They help to determine human destiny. They will serve that destiny better if they are seen to be what they are, expressions of the very life they aim to command." [49]   According to this view, ideals are means to human ends, rather than ends-in-themselves. Ideals control us, and should control us, but only up to a certain point. When they become tyrannical and destructive of human ends, they should be discarded. The nature of all ideals may be summed up in the words of Jesus: "The sabbath was made for man, not man for the sabbath." As needs change, so will ideals, for

name metaphysical types, for all metaphysicians are concerned with the metaphysically real and specific types have other names such as "materialism" or "dualism." According to the third type, "ideals" are goals yet to be realized, or actualized, and those who consider goals worth striving for are called idealists, in contrast with realists, who believe that we should accept things as they are without wasting time pursuing illusory values. Or, more specifically, an idealist is one who devotes himself rather completely to pursuit of ideals, especially distant ideals, or who considers ideals as oughts which compel him to follow them. An idealist, in this sense, believes that ideals are what make life worth while, whereas a realist, in this sense, thinks that ideals are unreal or deceptive and to be avoided as distracting us from the actualities of living. Some thinkers are idealists in all three senses, others in some or none.

[48] See Ch. 9.

[49] Max Otto, *The Human Enterprise*, p. 70.   Appleton-Century-Crofts, New York, 1940.   See also his *Things and Ideals*, and *Science and the Moral Life*.

"the ideal itself has its roots in natural conditions." [50]   But, also, "ideals change as they are applied to existent conditions." [51]

This leads us to the organicist view, which holds not only that the actual and the ideal mutually influence each other in ethical behavior, but also that both the actual and the ideal are primary, each in its own way. Organicists think that emergentistic pragmatists, on the one hand, are correct in holding that actual persons in actual situations exist prior to their ideals, which arise from awareness oɾ something lacking, as projected conceptions of what it would take to make up the deficiency. Each actual person is an intrinsic value and his ideals are instrumental values, i.e., means to furthering himself as an intrinsic value. But, also, each person is a product partly of the ideals of his parents and of a whole history of cultural ancestors. As such, he is a means to the fulfillment of their ends. He is their ideal come to realization, even if quite imperfectly. Yet, on the other hand, organicists think that Platonic idealists are right in holding that ideals ought to be realized, but wrong in thinking that the source of such oughtness should be located in ideals as independent realities. The actual person who has ideals is the primary intrinsic value whose value is, nevertheless, incomplete in whatever way it may be supplemented by realizing its ideals. Ideals ought to be realized by a person because he has actual need for supplementation. It is his need for realizing ideals that constitutes their oughtness relative to him. It is his actually existing intrinsic value and also his actually existing incompleteness which constitutes the source of their value both as means to his ends and, when realized, as ends-in-themselves.

Ideals may be considered as ends-in-themselves in two ways: first, by their participation in the actuality of the person who further actualizes himself through realizing them in and as himself, and, secondly, by their becoming actualized. Or, first, as potential intrinsic values and, secondly, as such potential values actualized. Sometimes these actualized values have a kind of independence from the actuality which idealized them. For example, persons wanting children have an ideal. They recognize themselves as incomplete without children. When one's children arrive, they are one's own children; they are one's own self, as wanting to be a parent, realized in a way which could not be realized without children. But children, them-

[50] John Dewey, *A Common Faith*, p. 48. Yale University Press, New Haven, 1934.
[51] *Ibid.*, p. 50.

selves, are not only means to their parents' ends. They are ends-in-themselves which are, in many respects, quite different from the ways in which they were idealized by their parents. Children and parents are, thus, both ends-in-themselves and means to each other's ends.

Kant was right in asserting as a "categorical imperative" that we should "so act as to treat humanity, whether in your own self or in any other, in every case as an end, never as means merely." [52]   That people should use each other as means is all too obvious. With respect to ideals, we may supplement Kant, following Otto and other pragmatists, by saying that we should treat ideals, whether our own or those of others, always as means, never as ends merely. That people should use ideals as ends is all too obvious. External morality, whether imposed on us from the outside, or whether worn by ourselves or by others on our outsides, is really immorality. Only when ideals, inspired by inner needs, re-inspire inner efforts toward greater intrinsic value, does the organicistic ideal about the nature of ideals itself become realized.

If one has a high ideal, what makes it high? Each of the various theories of value and of rightness will have its own conception, and these cannot be reviewed here. But all agree, surely, that what is higher among ideals (which are values) will depend upon which are the higher values.

If ethical idealism and realism are opposites, each tends to consider the other as low relative to itself. According to realism, in this sense of the term, we ought to accept things as they are and not waste our efforts in pursuit of illusory values. Ugliness and evil are permanent parts of existence. If we desire to know the truth about things, and if things are actually dirty, then we ought to want to see them as dirty and we ought not try to hide or minimize the dirt by believing that somehow underneath things are really clean. Reform efforts are largely useless since either the dreamed-of values cannot be achieved or they will turn out to be different than expected. Now, although it is true that realism often leads to scepticism, cynicism, and pessimism, the easy conclusion, that only ethical idealists devote themselves to values, whereas realists sink spinelessly into dross preoccupations, is hasty. Realists are actualists. That is, they accept present and existing values as the best possible. They believe, thus, that this is the best of all possible worlds and that we are foolish not to recognize it

[52] Theodore M. Greene, *Kant, Selections,* p. 309. Charles Scribner's Sons, New York, 1929.

as such. Intrinsic values are at hand, and awareness of admixture of intrinsic evil should not cause us to run fearfully away into a dream world, an ideal world, of a future that can never come. The future, when it comes, will be like today, with its own admixture of evil. Therefore, as honest, courageous, responsible ethicists, let us face the evils of our day. Although Americans like to think of themselves as practical realists and of orientals as spiritualistic idealists, the reverse, actually, is also true. For one cannot be a "go-getter" unless he dreams of a better future. On the other hand, those Chinese, for example, who believe that "the way to do is to be," and who are content with what is, rather than clamoring for what is yet to be, are more realistic, in this sense, than idealistic. American materialists are extremely idealistic in the sense that they think that they can, and ought to, make the world better by their own efforts.

Organicism sees both realism and idealism as persisting in all of us in varying degrees. When either is carried to extremes, absurdity appears. Logically, one cannot be realistic without also being idealistic, for he must at least idealize realism—or have faith that realism itself would be an improvement over the idealism which actually prevails. Practically, he cannot be a good realist unless he recognizes the reality of those ideals which actually function in present life. Logically, also, one can hardly be an idealist without also being something of a realist, for idealism claims that we must submit to the actuality of ideals. One ought to face the fact that misery automatically generates ideals which then determine our behavior as realistically as the misery itself. Since life is inherently purposive, one cannot be fully realistic without recognizing that hope for elimination of ideals from actual life is itself unrealistic.

Wisdom

"Wisdom is not synonymous with knowledge. A man . . . may be a 'walking encyclopaedia' and yet be a moral fool." [53] A wise man not only knows what the goals of life are, and how to attain them, but he actually attains them, not just occasionally, but habitually. Mere knowledge of what one ought to do is not an end-in-itself, but the doing of what one ought to do is. A wise man may, at times, be uncertain as to what he ought to do, but he is no longer troubled about whether he ought to do what he ought to do. He willingly does

[53] Harold H. Titus, *Ethics for Today*, p. 204. American Book Co., New York, 1936.

whatever he ought because oughtness arises out of intrinsic values which are inherently self-justifying. Wisdom has to do with the ability to use one's other abilities to best advantage. Thus it is the supreme virtue, not only because it involves all other virtues, but because it consists in the ability to integrate them effectively with each other in practical living. Wisdom exists only in living well, not in a mere promise to do so. The proof of the wise man's know-how is his actual enjoyment of the intrinsic values constituting the ends of life.

· 25 ·

Philosophy
of Religion

For some strange reason, our culture has failed to develop a common term, such as science of religion, or religionology, to name the scientific investigation of the nature of religion, even though it has adopted such terms as theology (science of God), bibliology (science of the Bible), hymnology (science of hymns), etc., and, in specialized scientific fields, such terms as psychology of religion, sociology of religion, pastoral psychiatry, etc. The term "philosophy of religion" has persisted in our language as the name for scientific study of religion.

The general problem of the religious scientist is to discover the nature of religion, and his more specific tasks involve investigating the various characteristics and problems of religion, whatever they turn out to be. In pursuit of his general aim, he has, as a scientist, to examine all of the various religions and the things, activities, institutions, or beliefs which are called religious. Thus he must study the major religions, such as Christianity, Brahmanism, Buddhism, Mohammedanism, Shintoism, Taoism. He must study also primitive religions such as animism, and prehistoric religions such as the Egyptian, the Mesopotamian, the Celtic, the Mayan, etc., and their various subdivisions and sects which seem endless in number. Since Confucianism, Jainism, Communism, and Humanism are claimed to be religions, these, too, must be investigated. If rain-making, prostitution, church finance, trances, medical missions, and the like, are considered essential parts of some religions, all these constitute data which must be examined.

One dilemma which the religious scientist faces, as do all scientists, has to do with where he shall mark the boundaries of his investigation. Is religion so all-pervasive that he must investigate everything? Or is religion clearly distinguishable from the non-religious? If he begins with certain preconceptions about the matter, has he not already prejudiced the outcome? Is atheism, for example, a kind of religious outlook which denies the existence of God, or is it a nonreligious belief? Without settling this question for the reader (he may want to do this for himself), we may with profit examine and compare various viewpoints concerning both (1) What is religion? and (2) theology.

What Is Religion?

"When we think of religion, probably a group of things will come to mind, such as churches, prayers, sermons, songs, collections, creeds, and rituals, people sitting together quietly. But evidently these things are not religion." [1] For some religions do not have them, or at least not all of them. Many claim that belief in God, belief in spirits, or belief in supernatural power is necessary to religion. But religions which reject such beliefs do exist. Some persons think that sacred doctrines, sacred scriptures, sacred places, and sacred days are essential. Yet others do not. Some assert that faith in miracles, in divine revelation, and in personal immortality form the core of religion. Others deny this.

Each specific suggestion offered tends to be colored by the point of view of the sect, the religion, or the culture of the person making it. A problem facing everyone seeking to be scientific about religion, or about any cultural matter, has to do with how he can rise above his culture in order to see in religion what is common to the viewpoints of all the various other cultures. One can do this conveniently only if his own culture has developed, dialectically, a cultural trait encouraging the rising above one's own culture. Although the writer hopes that he has been able to do this, he cannot rightly assert his own conclusion as the ultimate truth for philosophy of religion. Much progress is being made at present in this field because of the tremendous stimulation to thinking due to rapid increase in the availability of ideas of different cultures to each other. Many different kinds of definition of religion must be recognized as having some claim to consideration. Although the description of religion given here obviously will be colored by the writer's own views, he must admit that the question: What is religion? is still a question, and may always be a question confronting scientists seeking to explore this field. Efforts to explore the inner nature of religion are hampered

[1] G. T. W. Patrick, *Introduction to Philosophy*, Revised Edition, p. 36. Houghton Mifflin Co., Boston, 1935.

by uncertainties as to where the boundaries should be drawn between what is inside and what is outside religion.

Nevertheless, considerable light may be thrown upon problems dealt with in philosophy of religion by examining certain questions: Is belief in God essential to religion? Is religion true? How did religion originate? Is worship essential to religion? What is salvation? In what sense are religious values higher? Are religious and scientific knowledge incompatible?

1. Is belief in God essential to religion? When stated in this form, the question must be answered in the negative. Many religions are explicitly atheistic. The Jains, for example, who take their Ahimsa doctrine, Thou shalt not kill, so seriously that when they go walking they carry a brush to remove insects from their path, disbelieve in God. Also many, if not most, Buddhists, Vedantists, Confucianists, Marxists, and Humanists,[2] are avowedly atheistic. Most primitive religions, although believing in many gods, have no conception of God. The belief in a single personal deity (whether as the Hebrew Jahweh, the Christian God, or the Mohammedan Allah), which has played such an important role in western civilization, has not been so widely shared by other peoples of the world. In some religions, Absolutistic Vedantism, for example, God (Içvara) is accepted as part of the system, but is subordinated to impersonal Brahman so that, ultimately, God, too, is illusory.

It is common, in discussions about the nature of religion, to say, "I didn't mean that one must believe in a single God who is a person. I mean that one may believe in spirits of any kind." Polytheisms, henotheisms, duotheisms, deisms, and pantheisms, as well as personalistic theisms, are all religious. How the discussion will go from here depends upon whether agreement can be reached about the meaning of the term "spirit." If spirit means any nature power, then sparkling stones have spirits, and the distinction between what is religious and nonreligious seems to disappear. If spirit means something not natural but supernatural, then problems involved in distinguishing between natural and supernatural become primary. However, since no distinction is made between natural and supernatural in some religions, and since the distinction is hard to draw in those which do make it, this suggestion is not very fruitful. For if there is a God,

[2] For the writer's interpretation of Humanism, see: "Varieties of Humanism," *The Standard,* April, 1951, pp. 333–337; "Humanism—A Religion for Scientists," *The Scientific Monthly,* April, 1946, pp. 310–315; D. D. Runes, *Dictionary of Philosophy,* pp. 131–132.

it is natural that there should be a God, and such a God not only has his own nature and follows it naturally, but is naturally related to the world and its nature.

If supernatural means merely a higher nature involved in nature, then the distinction loses much of its supposed significance. But if belief in God, in spirits, or in the supernatural is not essential to religion, then what is? Some conclude, even more generally, that one must at least believe in some higher power, to which man is subordinate. This conclusion seems sufficiently general to win wide approval. However, many think it too general to be significant, whereas others resent the view that man is subordinate to anything. The writer sees each individual as both unique in some sense and superior to all else in this sense, and also subordinate to all else in whatever respects other things are unique in their own ways. In whatever sense one feels himself part of a larger whole, not just instrumentally, but also somehow intrinsically, he may be said to be religious. Whenever one is aware of his duty to himself as involving a duty to realize further some higher intrinsic value in which he actually partakes, he is religious. Does this view apply to all religions?

2. Is religion true? We shall interpret this question, not as inquiring whether each doctrine of each religion is true, but as asking whether there is something genuine with which religion deals and whether this something is subjective or real. Instead of reviewing all epistemological problems and theories as they bear upon religious knowledge, we shall simply summarize a few typical views. These will be divided into western and eastern approaches.

a. Western realists interpret the question: Is religion true? to mean: Is there some religious reality existing external to the knower? Religious knowledge is true to the extent that it faithfully reveals that reality. For many realists, God not only is a real object (epistemologically) but is the most real being (metaphysically). For such realists, religious knowledge is held to be most true, not in the sense that the knower always succeeds in knowing the truth (for God may be essentially unknowable to man), but in the sense that it aims directly at what is most real. Since naive realism is the view we naturally first acquire, we should expect widespread prevalence of naive realistic views of religious objects. If there is a heaven, then heaven is a real place, and if God is a person, then he is a real person.

Western subjectivists, on the other hand, tend to hold either that religion is false or that it has subjective truth. (1) All religion is superstition, some think, and, like bad dreams or childish ideals, should be dispensed with as persons and cultures mature. Others, like Browne, although regarding religion as false, consider it natural and possibly necessary for human survival. Says Browne: "By the word faith we mean that indispensable—and therefore imperishable— illusion in the heart of man that, though he may seem a mere worm in the earth, he nevertheless can make himself the lord of the universe. By the word religion, however, we mean one specialized technique by which man seeks to realize that illusion." [3] (2) Religion, for Santayana, is the poetry which we believe.[4] The need for believing is inherent in human nature and represents a true demand which the dismissal of religion as mere illusion cannot satisfy. If prayer, for example, expresses a soul's sincere desire, and if it is true that one ought normally to have such sincere desire, then one ought to pray and have faith that prayer is answerable. Of the various kinds of prayer—those of petition, of communion, of confession, of thanksgiving, of meditation, of concentration [5]—each may be regarded as revealing a different kind of personal need. Freud, similarly, sees religion as an expression of need felt by fearful individuals searching to return to the "safety of the womb." Thomas, likewise, finds a subjective basis for religious truth in his analysis of personality as having normal needs for some measure of security, esteem, fellowship, and adventure.[6] The desire for security finds satisfaction in different ways, depending both upon one's actual needs and how he conceives them. Earlier concerns for crops, progeny, health, protection from animals, etc., made these needs focal in religious endeavor. As scientific agriculture, gynecology, hospitals, and guns have gradually modified these needs, religious efforts have tended toward concentration upon hope for immortality, or more enduring security. Men who are ignored or despised by their fellows may still satisfy their desire for esteem by feeling recognized as worthy by an unseen superior power. In a world of love and hate, those lacking in human companionship

[3] Lewis Browne, *This Believing World,* pp. 29–30. The Macmillan Co., New York, 1926, 1935.

[4] See George Santayana, *Reason in Religion.* Charles Scribner's Sons, New York, 1905.

[5] See Edwin E. Aubrey, *Religion and the Next Generation,* Ch. 6. Harper Bros., New York, 1931.

[6] See William I. Thomas, *The Unadjusted Girl,* Ch. I. Little, Brown and Co., Boston, 1932. See also Elmer Pendell, *Society Under Analysis,* pp. 232–236. The Jaques Cattell Press, Lancaster, 1942.

may still need, and seek, fellowship with, and to be loved by, God. Although religion is not noted, especially in an age of formalism,[7] for promoting adventure, many religions express subjective truth, by promising a rebirth, in which all things become new.

Between realistic and subjectivistic extremes are to be found several other varieties of religious epistemology. There are dualists who hold that some supposedly religious objects are real whereas others are unreal (e.g., God is real, the Devil unreal). There are sceptics and agnostics who doubt or deny the possibility of knowledge of religious objects. There are pragmatists who prefer an experimental attitude, claiming that the truth about religious objects is subject to empirical verification, a matter depending partly upon the will and skill of the experimenter. There are organicists who believe that all objects, including religious objects, have both realistic and subjectivistic aspects, such that the existence and nature of God, for example, cannot be either wholly explained nor wholly denied either on realistic or subjectivistic bases alone. But something so all-pervasive in the experiences of mankind should not be lightly dismissed just because difficult to explain or because so many easy explanations have proved inadequate or false.

b. Turning to eastern views, we find not only most of the western types, but also an emphasis largely missing in the West. In addition to seemingly endless kinds and degrees of realism regarding spiritual beings, there are many interesting and informative varieties of subjectivism. Absolutistic Vedantists, for example, turn inward in search of religious reality. They agree that all of the gods, and even God (Içvara) himself, are illusory (Maya). The ultimate reality is to be sought after, not as an objective reality, but as a subjective reality. Since one's own inner soul (Atman) is God (Brahman), one cannot deny the existence of God without denying the existence of one's own self. However, although whatever we seek after functions as an object of our search, if and when we find Brahman, we will find that it is subject, not object, and thus that although there is a true goal of religious knowledge, it is unknowable as object, because it is essentially a subject freed from all objectivity.

Buddhists, although they differ among themselves as to their ultimate preferences, are usually interpreted as denying reality to both the objective and subjective realms. Not only God, as an object of

[7] See Charles Horton Cooley and others, *Introductory Sociology*, pp. 406–414. Charles Scribner's Sons, New York, 1933.

knowledge, but Atman itself, as subject of knowledge, is as transitory and unreal as apparent objects. However, even though thus doubly atheistic, Buddhism is one of the world's oldest, most widespread, and most profound of religions. But it is beyond the power of the writer to expound here the subtleties involved in finding satisfaction through faith in the ultimate reality of the unreal—not in Buddha, the historical person, but in Bodhi, "Enlightenment." Nor is it possible to explore here the probable consequences of further intermingling of western and eastern ideals of religious knowledge into a more organic view. But to the question: Is religion true? we must answer that, despite all disputes, surely there is something genuine to dispute about.

3. How did religion originate? Answers to this question will differ depending upon how religion is conceived. Yet, also, how religion is conceived will depend upon how it is believed to have originated. Like other chicken-and-the-egg questions, this one may never yield a sure answer. Nevertheless, scientists of religion can hardly keep from examining the arguments put forth for and against the various hypotheses which have appeared from time to time. For convenience, we may divide views into those locating the source of religion outside the individual and those locating it inside, though the line is often hard to draw.

a. Externalists seek the origins of religion in something outside the person, either in the perilous environment, in society, or in some cosmic spirit. Browne repeats an old doctrine when he says: "In the beginning there was fear; and fear was in the heart of man. . . . Earth and sea and sky were set against him; with relentless enmity, with inexplicable hate, they were bent on his destruction." [8] Durkheim claims that the force or power which religious beliefs have over individuals originates in society. Religion is nothing but "the sentiment inspired by the group in its members." [9] Whether established unconsciously through childhood awareness of the greater wisdom and power of their elders (even of departed ancestors) or by the intentional guidance of wise leaders or crafty self-interested rulers or priests, "a religion is a form of belief providing for an ultra-rational sanction of that large class of conduct in the individual where his interests and the interests of the social organism are antagonistic and

[8] Browne, *op. cit.*, p. 27.
[9] Emile Durkheim, *The Elementary Forms of Religious Life*, p. 229. The Macmillan Co., New York, 1915, 1926.

by which the former are rendered subordinate to the latter in the general interests of evolution which the race is undergoing." [10]

Another well-known view holds that some cosmic power caused both men and their religion. Although many of these thinkers find religion's chief sustaining power in men's fears—of hell, the Devil, or of God (for these thinkers, if there were nothing to fear, there would be no need for religion)—others feel that God is either good or, at least, neutral toward men. By far the vast majority of those in the West who consider themselves religious, at least today, believe that God is good and that religion has its origin in the goodness of God. As a consequence, these thinkers insist that belief in God is essential to religion. "Religion is not merely faith in an impersonal principle of conservation, but confidence in the 'Friend behind phenomena' who cares for us and who has the power and the will to carry our efforts to victorious ends." [11] Exactly how God originated and sustains religion is disputed by these thinkers. Some believe that God, in creating man, implanted not only soul, conscience, and free will, but also a "yearning after righteousness" in man's body. Some believe that the human animal, born a dumb brute, may be inspired (in-spirited) upon hearing the "good news" that he has a "higher calling," and that religion, which now originates in individuals by missionary education, was inspired first through specific revelations to especially favored holy men. Some are unsure as to whether religious virtue has its source in God's grace, or in individual free will, or in an historical racial contract such as Jahweh made with Moses and his people. But all of these views join in believing that, since the aim of religion is to help the individual to adjust to something outside himself, religion had its origins, whether in the environment, in society, or in God, in something external to him.

b. Internalists discover the sources of religion within human nature itself, somewhat as subjectivists locate the object of religious knowledge inside the self. But here, again, conflicting views of the nature of self result in numerous varieties of theories of origin. Recalling James' distinction between "tough-" and "tender-minded" persons,[12]

[10] Benjamin Kidd, *Social Evolution,* p. 103. The Macmillan Co., New York, 1894.

[11] D. Miall Edwards, *The Philosophy of Religion,* pp. 152–153. Richard R. Smith, Inc., New York, 1930.

[12] William James, *Pragmatism,* p. 293. Longmans, Green and Co., New York, 1907.

some think they discover the source of religion in tender-minded feelings of inadequacy in the face of demands by a world too big for them to grapple with unaided by superior power. Tough-minded men need no religion. But many others think that tough-mindedness is a more promising source in which to seek the subjective origins of religion. For example, some hold that religion arises only because the biological instinct for survival is so strong in some that it grows demandingly into a faith in survival after the death of the body. Or, for example, the Vedantist claim that reality itself lies hidden so deeply in the core of self that it cannot be discovered without courage to abandon all possessions, desire, friends, and even all ordinary knowledge and certainty. According to this view, lack of wisdom is due in part to karma and part to lack of courage to face one's own inner reality. Since Brahman is Atman, the real self underlying the apparent self, one must seek the sources of religion by turning away from outward appearances and inward toward reality. Typical Vedantists think that Westerners hide from themselves by devoting themselves to objects—whether they be scientific, mechanical, financial, artistic, or religious. Ritualism, which some take to be the core of religion, is here despised as a mere excrescence, to be sloughed off as one approaches the goal. Such a search for freedom from ignorance takes courage of the most tough-minded sort.

c. In addition to internalists and externalists there are those who recognize "the two sources" [13] of religion, one inner and one outer. Although some thinkers tend, dualistically, to separate religious activities into two somewhat incompatible kinds, those of the heart, which can in no way be formalized, and those demanding ritualistic conformity, others, including organicists, see religion as involving an interaction between the inner and the outer that requires constant mutual readjustment between them. Religious needs have a double source (as well as a double means of satisfaction), but it is out of the dynamic interactions between the two that religion, seen in larger perspective, arises. The religious task is sometimes mainly to inspire confidence and sometimes to promote humility. Religion is, inherently, neither merely self-condemning nor self-condoning. But its larger task is to satisfy the need for feeling safe in the face of persistent conflicts between the demands, and variations in demandingness, of the inner and the outer. Growth in the faith that the pressing conflicts between these two have a sufficiently satisfactory resolu-

[13] See Henri Bergson, *The Two Sources of Morality and Religion.* Henry Holt and Co., New York, 1935.

tion, even if a dynamic one, is not made easier by accepting the organicist view, namely, that there are, not one, but many levels of both inner and outer among the sources of religion.

4. Is worship essential to religion? The answer to this question depends, of course, upon what is meant by worship. Since, as is not commonly remembered, the term "worship" is an abbreviation of "worth-ship," it refers to values, or to what is or has worth. Worship, then, is an appreciative attitude toward, or an actual enjoyment of, values. The question: Is worship essential to religion? must be answered in the affirmative if we accept this broad meaning of the term. However, since many identify worship with ceremony, or ritual, we are involved in the further question: Is ritual or ceremony essential to religion? This one is not so easy to answer, partly because (*a*) rituals may be found in most, if not all, religions at some state or in some form and (*b*) most new adherents to any religion tend naturally to interpret their instructions more formalistically than originally intended and (*c*) ritual, if this means merely form, may be found anywhere one chooses to look, for even the succession of the seasons may be interpreted, as by certain Taoists, as a cosmic ritual. Nevertheless, since ritual often is explicitly condemned as evil, to the extent that it detracts from the ultimate goal, one would be unsafe in generalizing hastily that ritual is essential.

However, inherent in the foregoing is a somewhat more basic question: Are religious values primarily intrinsic or instrumental? When we worship, which do we value, ends or means? Our answer will depend partly upon what we, personally, get out of worship. If we stand on the outside and observe others perform what are, to us, meaningless acts, or if we are compelled to conform uncomfortably to local ceremonial customs, we tend to conclude that religion consists entirely of means to dubious, evil, or nonexistent ends. The more religion seems to consist of means without ends, the more useless, stupid, and vicious it seems to be. But when we ourselves enjoy the ends, the intrinsic values themselves, then we find whatever means we have used to be fully justified. The ends justify the means, here as elsewhere. The ardent seeker who, having tried different ways, has found only one which worked, is likely to tell others about what he has found to be "the way." Men of broader experience, however, who have succeeded by many different ways, may be able to suggest variety.[14] Of course, for those who consistently fail to achieve the

[14] E.g., "the four paths." See, for example, S. C. Chatterjee, *The Fundamentals of Hinduism*, Chs. 9–12. Das Gupta and Co., Ltd., Calcutta, 1950.

end, the means come to seem of primary practical importance. When devotees persist in dealing merely with means, the original ends may, even, be entirely lost from sight.

However, the problem of the importance of ritual cannot so easily be disposed of. The foregoing discussion has left untouched the question as to whether rituals, as symbolic means, can be separated completely from immediate enjoyment of religious ends. If rituals carry us to the end, then, in our enjoyment, we may be unable to distinguish clearly means from ends. What does it matter if, in enjoying ends, we do not clearly distinguish them from means? But when rituals do not bring us to our goal, then any mistaking of means for ends further separates us from such ends. Whenever ritual objects are taken to be ends-in-themselves, then we become idol worshippers. But when, functionally transparent, they conduct us to our ends immediately, they themselves seem to embody such ends. For those who are alive religiously, means and ends (ritual and enjoyment of intrinsic values) interact organically, although worshippers naturally waver somewhat in irregular rhythms regarding the degrees to which religious symbols transport them to, or obstruct them from, their goals. Religious services, like other works of art, succeed or fail in proportion to their yielding enjoyment or leaving us with the feeling of frustration, of promise unfulfilled, of great instrumental effort which has been good for nothing. Worth-ship, then, is essential to religion, and so is ritual as some form of means; yet ritualism, the mistaking of means for ends, is religion's greatest enemy.

5. What is salvation? Salvation is commonly thought of as pertaining to the saving or conserving of what is good. One seeks to be saved so that his good, i.e., his own intrinsic value, will not perish. However, if self is considered evil, then one can "save his life only by losing it." Investigators of the nature of religion find, not only an apparently endless variety of doctrines as to how to conserve what is good, but also a controversy about whether salvation refers merely to the saving of pre-existing values or also to the creation of new values. Since some Humanists, for example, maintain that an important part of the religious task is to make this a better world in which to live, and mean by "better" a world with both some of the old and many new and as-yet-uncreated values (both instrumental and intrinsic), they consider creation, and not merely preservation, of values as central to religious endeavor. Now either the meaning of the term "salvation" needs to be stretched to cover creating as well as preserving or a new term is required to cover both. If the mean-

ing of the term "salvation" can undergo expansion in this direction, carried farther in the following, then one may well conclude that salvation is essential to religion; if not, then not.

A third aspect of salvation, which is at least as important as the first two, is consumption. This is symbolized, for example, by the third aspect of the Hindu trinity or trimurti (i.e., Vishnu, Brahma, Siva; creator, preserver, destroyer), where destruction means actualization of, or perfect realization of, values. Some values can be consummated only by being consumed. Just as one can actualize his potentialities only by destroying those potentialities as mere potentialities, so he can reach his goal only by coming to the end of his journey. The only way one can consume the intrinsic value of living a lasting life is by living it day by day. One can, in another sense, save his life (continue to live) only by losing it (consuming it minute by minute and month by month). If heaven means enjoyment of intrinsic value, and if each day has its own intrinsic value to be enjoyed, then those days which are unenjoyed are lost heavens. He who would seek salvation, in this sense, then will care not for the morrow, but will seek to save each day's value from loss. He must save by consuming, for what is not consumed is lost.

These three aspects of salvation, creation and re-creation, preservation, and consummation, receive different emphases by different persons, sects, and cultures. When all three are recognized, then attempts to relate and evaluate them complicate the religious problem. Some, such as Vedantists, seek to rise above the three aspects by idealizing nirvana as an intuitive grasp of all three at once without distinction. At other times, the three are conceived, like "gunas," as each taking its turn at "having the upper hand." Organicism, considering all three as inherent in every value situation, finds salvation difficult to conceptualize and institutionalize; yet it believes that all three are present in each life lived naturally, i.e., not drawn too far toward creative, preservative, or consumptive extremes.

6. In what sense are religious values higher? Debates regarding whether religion deals with all values or with only the higher values usually end in uneasy agreement that it is more profitable to limit the meaning of the term "religion" to the higher, though debate continues as to what precisely shall be meant by "higher." Although "the higher" means something which is "up" or above, and thus, superior or super, a question remains as to whether this implies, as many think, that religious values are essentially supernatural.

If, as is common in cultures dominated by a logic of external relations, superiority is preconceived as implying separation of the inferior from the superior, then the view that a self can become higher than itself is unintelligible. What is above or superior to man's nature is supernatural. Although the higher values are higher than man, he must still continue to struggle toward them. If, for example, God is considered the highest value, then man should strive toward God as an ultimate goal, but the most that he can hope for is to approach, or be near God, for he can never become God. The natural, or lower, cannot, logically, become the higher, or supernatural, no matter how hard it tries. Atonement, which means "at-one-ment," is interpreted as "near-to-but-not-at-one-with." In cultures permeated by a logic of internal relations, on the other hand, all ultimately is one, so the distinction between the natural and supernatural is considered unreal or illusory. The higher values are thought of in terms of "one's own higher nature" rather than in terms of "higher than one's own nature." The religious quest comes to be conceived primarily as an emphasis upon the higher within one's own nature, rather than as a fruitless pursuit of that which is other than self. If one can realize, with Samkara, that "Atman is Brahman" or, with Jesus, that "I and my Father are one," then the religious task is greatly simplified. Since there is no rift between higher and lower, or between supernatural and natural, it is, indeed, natural for man to seek that which is his own higher or greater value, whenever he is not distracted by those values which are lower.

There is no mystery about questing for higher values for anyone who understands the nature of growth, for growth, whether it be growth in plants, or persons, or societies, involves a giving up of a lesser and more primitive status in order to achieve a higher and more fully developed state. Just as a seed must become other than it is, merely as a seed, in order to become what it really is, as a plant, so a self cannot achieve its own fullness or wholeness (holiness) without losing itself (its lesser self) in the process of finding itself (its higher self). If losing one's life in order to save it is so natural, one wonders whether those who make what is natural seem extremely mysterious are not, even if unwittingly, enemies of religion.

However, even though there be no deep dichotomy between lower and higher values, nevertheless, if higher values are better than lower, ought one, in seeking the better, abandon the worse? That is, once religious insight arises, ought one devote himself wholly to the religious and to withdraw all his interests in lower and lesser values? Two kinds of answers may be worth considering.

a. The first has to do with whether the higher can exist independently of the lower and whether there is only one highest or many equally high values. One of the most prominent of historical tendencies, apparently, has been one in which preference for the highest over the higher has come to seem as necessary as preference for the higher over the lower—for, logically, even the merely higher, being still lower than the highest, is still essentially lower and should be shunned. Consequently there arises a demand for purity and perfection. Perfect purity is possible only if the self can be purged of all contamination with the lower. He who, having set his course upward, looks back longingly "is not worthy of entering the kingdom of heaven." However, a contrary tendency, which also persists historically, claims that each intrinsic value is incomparable as a unique end-in-itself and thus is equally the highest in its own way and in its own right. Any attempt to subordinate each supreme value to any single supreme value is wanton destruction of multitudinous supremacies. Individualistic romanticists often contemptuously condemn as stupid the stagnating attempt to sterilize all highest values but one. It is true that one should seek the highest values, but no one value is so high as to absorb or negate the intrinsic supremacy of all other highest values.

For organicism, both these tendencies contend for ultimate truths, but each mistakenly denies the other's truth. Even when the higher is thought of in terms of the more inclusive, and the highest in terms of most perfect unity, that which includes both higher and lower is more inclusive than that which includes merely the higher, and the highest can be the most perfect unity only if it includes, rather than excludes, all of the varying degrees from highest to lowest. Furthermore, since there are many intrinsic values, and many levels of intrinsic value, religious endeavor aims at the highest value only when it seeks to include all existing diversity within its scope. Organic holiness consists not in sterile purity of soul but in dynamic integration of soul and body, of self and environment, of individual and society, of man and cosmos. For organicists, mere atonement is not enough; for the unity of at-one-ment with at-many-ment is a higher at-one-ment than that in which the one remains separated from the many; and there is more unity in many at-one-ments than in only one at-one-ment.

Although extreme individualism is as false as extreme totalitarianism regarding religious values, the intrinsic value of each unique self has a kind of highestness which totalitarian proponents deny. Each man has a kind of double (really multiple) dignity. On the one hand, each person, as unique, has a kind of supremacy over all else, a kind of intrinsic value which nothing else can have. On the other, each also has a kind of cosmic dignity through participating in the uniqueness of cosmic unity. It is true that "Atman is Brahman," but it is also true that "Brahman is Atman" or that the universe is, in a sense, as truly subordinated to the self as the self is to the universe. But also both self and universe are, in a sense, subordinated to their mutual interdependence in such a way that both their independence of, and their dependence upon, each other retain ultimacy. To totalitarians, all this seems unduly arrogant or self-assertive. To extreme individualists, the same appears as a weak and halfhearted totalitarianism.

But, organicists feel that this doctrine of the double dignity of man involves a double humility. For, in order to enjoy attainment of atonement with a highest cosmic intrinsic value, one must also thereby acquire cosmic humility; while in order to enjoy his own unique and, thus, in a sense, isolated, intrinsic value, he must humbly accept his isolation. However, since one cannot be at-one with the universe unless the universe is also in some sense at-one with him, his humility must extend in two directions. He must not only be willing to say "I accept the universe," but also to say what may be even more difficult, "I accept myself." If the seeker after atonement humbly does the latter, then he commits himself to a willingness to be, or to try to become, something with which the universe can be worthily at-one. It is in the acceptance of this double affirmation that organicism finds religion's higher goal. Religious traditions are correct in believing that the individual can achieve his own higher goal only through submission, but tradition has too often neglected to recognize the need for double submissiveness. However, since there are not just two, but many levels of self-existence, so religion involves not just a double, but multiple dignities, humilities, and submissions. Back-sliding, too, becomes multiple—but surely all this is beyond the concern of the reader. Some justification for this presentation may be found in considering the second answer.

b. To the pressing question: Ought one devote himself unreservedly to religious values? one must raise a counter-question: Can one? The answer to both questions will depend partly upon how religious values are conceived. If, as in all growth, one must develop first through lower stages before he can advance to the higher, then should one make religious growth exceptional and seek to escape from the lower when there is no escape? For any beginner in growth, the next higher stage is genuinely higher and, no matter how much lower than the highest, is the primary goal at that stage. If the primary goals of infants, adolescents, adults, and the aged are genuinely different, then the crushing of all ideals into the framework of a single creed must be condemned. Although one can hardly be expected to put his creeds on and off like clothes, yet, like clothes, one's creeds may be expected to vary somewhat in proportion to his stage and to fit better when "tailored to fit." Although most people may have to be satisfied with "store-boughten" creeds, those religions which provide a greater selection of sizes and shapes promise to fare better. Single-creed religions tend either to idealize a goal too high or a God too distant for beginners to understand, or to stagnate with such childish hopes that those who gain in growth must abandon the doctrine altogether. The Hindu example, which provides not only many paths but also four stages of life, might well receive wider consideration. Only at the fourth stage, after retirement, does one normally devote his attention wholly to atonement with cosmos. But success at this stage is to be expected only by those who have already succeeded at previous stages.

Not only individually, but also historically, creedal adaptability is essential for healthy religious growth. If one lives in a static society enjoying rural simplicity, which is sufficiently served by simple and long-standing creeds, then he should seek either to be satisfied with his heritage or to migrate to a more complicated setting. If one lives in a metropolis, one teeming with creedal variety and troubled by creedal turmoil, then he may find it necessary to do considerable religious "window shopping" and "trying on" of various garments before selecting a most suitable fit. Again, religious ideals are like motor cars: if one is no mechanic, he had better buy a standard make or one for which he can find easy access to repairs; but if one has experimental ability, and pride in personal craftsmanship, no mere stock car will satisfy; some, of course, will want "the latest model" while others will prefer the sturdier and more economical virtues of earlier models.

Possibilities for growth from lower to higher have an inherent danger, namely, that those persons who grow up will develop contempt for the values present in the stages left behind and, by implication, for those persons still at home in lower stages. Just as in music, one grows to appreciate symphonies only by advancing beyond the thrills of baby's rattles, but becomes a snob when symphonic idealizations prevent rattle appreciation, so, in religion, one grows to higher types of sainthood only by leaving behind Santa Claus types of religion, but becomes a snob when he declares that a Santa Claus type of religion has no value whatsoever. The religious universe is all the richer for having both, and many other, types; but it becomes poorer to the extent that each condemns the other and mistakes such condemnation as somehow adding to its own virtue.

In what sense, then, are religious values higher? They are, primarily, those constituting one's own higher self and as such are naturally sought after when known about. Yet, in so far as the highest is conceived as inclusive of, rather than as exclusive of, those which are lower, one may put away but not despise childish things. Many a person will recognize that there are higher values to which he himself will never attain, but he should not be led into thinking that only these, which are higher than himself, are religious. Those who teach that "the religious" is unattainable preach a doctrine of despair which makes religion itself a thing of lesser, or lower, value. Religious values are higher either because enjoyed as higher (for one knows them when he gets them, not by comparison with others who do not have them, but by an inner satisfaction which no one else can describe to him) or steadfastly hoped for with some feeling of assurance that they can be realized. Relative to this latter alternative, as someone has said, "the only real atheist is the quitter."

7. Are religious and scientific knowledge incompatible? As usual, we are faced with a variety of views. Typical dualists, of course, say "Yes, religious and scientific knowledge are different in kind and have nothing at all to do with each other." However, most types of view consider them compatible, even if in different ways. Those who claim that all true knowledge ultimately is religious consider scientific knowledge as nothing if not religious or as subordinate to the religious. Compatibility is achieved here through subordination of science to religion. Those who believe that only scientific or factual knowledge is reliable claim either that all alleged religious knowledge is mere opinion or superstition, or that there are facts about religion

but that factual knowledge about religion is really scientific. Compatibility is claimed here because religious knowledge is either denied altogether or treated as a part of scientific knowledge. Finally, there are those who say that knowledge is knowledge and that tagging some as scientific and other as religious adds nothing to knowledge for, ultimately, knowledge is neither scientific nor religious. Compatibility exists because knowledge is inherently compatible with itself, and incompatibility does not arise simply because a differentiation of knowledge into religious and scientific aspects appears.

Organicism considers religious and scientific knowledge as partly compatible and partly incompatible. Denying both extreme dualism and extreme aspectism, it sees a scientific aspect to all knowledge as well as a religious aspect of all knowledge. The same conclusion, e.g., that people treat each other as they are treated, may be considered either as an empirical generalization or as a divine revelation, and either as an interesting bit of useful knowledge or as a mystical expression of eternal justice. Neither of these aspects can be reduced to the other, and the presence of one aspect does not exclude the presence of the other, though, of course, our attention often is concerned primarily with one or with the other.

Although previously science had to fight for recognition, through persecutions, inquisitions, martyrdoms, today there is much persecution by scientists of those who value religious knowledge. In our age of science there is much sneering at religion by those who are unscientific about religion. But, if the test of truth is experimental workability, then should we not put our religious beliefs to experimental test? Unfortunately, Western civilization, especially since it became permeated with the dualistic spirit of Descartes, has developed a cultural schizophrenia, believing that science and religion pertain to completely different worlds, the one testable, the other not. This prejudice has so closed the minds of many that they are not even open to experiment regarding anything called religious.

Prayer, for example, may be experimented with easily; and many no longer pray because their experiments with prayer ended in failure. But how scientific were such experiments? Persons who train for some specialized scientific fields expect tedious repetition of failure after failure under skilled guidance before achieving some success; yet many of these same persons toss prayer aside after a single trial without ever consulting an expert on the subject. "Gimme" prayers, those in which one asks for what he cannot have and does not deserve, naturally end in failure. "If one has advanced beyond the Santa Claus stage of prayer he will be asking for the secrets of transforming personality . . . ,"[15] instead of magical disruption of the world. Many prayers rightfully aim at "conviction of sin," i.e., at convincing oneself that he has a wrong attitude which must be changed if he would be happy. When one suffers because he is too proud for his own good, prayer may reduce his suffering more effectively than a fight. At other times, when one suffers because he lacks confidence, prayer may bolster his faith and give him courage enough to go on. But without willingness to be experimental, or to act upon one's prayerful decision, prayer itself remains ineffective. The story is told of a Negro slave who, after praying for liberty for seven years without answer, realized that he himself must act with confidence if his prayer was to be effective. With his eyes fixed on the North Star, he prayed with his legs, and lo and behold his prayer was answered. Too few "scientific" Americans are willing to try out and test seriously the claims of the various religions.[16]

If one may be scientific about religious matters, then may he be religious regarding scientific affairs? If religion pertains to the higher values and if scientific knowledge leads men toward these higher values, then science functions as a religious instrument. But, further, scientific knowledge may itself be a religious value. It "takes us out of ourselves and puts us into relations with wide ranges of facts. Thus it can fairly be said to enlarge us."[17] The grandeur of the cosmic grasp which appreciation of scientific knowledge can give may be experienced as genuinely higher. Whereas those who see religion and science as in opposition expect decline in religion with increase in science, others see growth of science as providing increasing opportunities for religious appreciation. Some fear that, as scientists become more and more specialized and devote themselves to the intricacies of trivial techniques, fewer and fewer of them are destined to enjoy science as religious; however others, more hopefully, believe

[15] Ernest M. Ligon, *The Psychology of the Christian Personality*, p. 191. The Macmillan Co., New York, 1935. See also the works of Fritz Kunkel, *Let's Be Normal, What Happens When We Grow Up, God Helps Those . . . , Character, Growth and Education, Conquer Yourself, In Search of Maturity.*

[16] For an example of one who tried out all of the principal Hindu sects and Christianity and Islam, see Swami Nikhilananda, *The Gospel of Sri Ramakrishna*, Ramakrishna-Vivekananda Center, New York, 1942.

[17] William H. Roberts, *The Problem of Choice*, p. 265. Ginn and Co., Boston, 1941.

that unsuspected clues to cosmic magnificence, and opportunities for religious appreciation, will be found in heretofore undiscovered trivia.

We conclude our inquiry into religion without attempting final definition. The foregoing seven questions and summaries of types of answers are intended as suggestive of the types of problems with which philosophy of religion deals. Although, surely, further success is possible in understanding and defining religion, seeming success will be specious if the dynamic nature of religion is neglected, for "the great religions are movements not positions, processes not results, growing revelations and not fixed traditions. Religion is a journey rather than a destination." [18] And if religion consists in living enthusiastically,[19] then it may forever escape the confines of any definition.

Theology

Although it may be that "a man does not need to believe in God in order to worship," [20] since many consider theology the core of religion, we can hardly pass on without considering it further. Whether or not theism is essential, it certainly has played a large part in religion. One of the most striking aspects of theology is the enormous quantity of the "various ideas of God." [21] Although the path of history is strewn with cast-off gods, "the procession of the gods has been an advance and not a retreat." [22] "The gods are a splendid company. It is a great pity that they are not better known. 'He who knows only one, knows none.' " [23] "The cross-fertilization of religions is bound to produce strange hybrids. . . ." [24] "Periodically, belief in gods or God has had to reconstruct its object. . . . As knowledge

[18] John Clark Archer, *Faiths Men Live By*, p. 6. The Ronald Press, New York, 1934.

[19] "Enthusiasm is a beautiful Greek word, *entheos einai*, meaning 'in-God being.'" Gustav E. Mueller, *Discourses on Religion*, p. 170. Bookman Associates, New York, 1951.

[20] Henry Nelson Wieman, *Methods of Private Religious Living*, p. 19. The Macmillan Co., New York, 1929.

[21] Walter M. Horton, *God*, p. 1. Edward W. Hazen Foundation, Haddam, Conn., 1937.

[22] Gaius Glenn Atkins, *The Procession of the Gods*, p. 5. Harper & Bros., New York, 1930.

[23] A. Eustace Haydon, *The Quest of the Ages*, p. 72. Harper & Bros., New York, 1929.

[24] Charles Francis Potter, *The Story of Religion*, p. 583. Simon and Schuster, Inc., New York, 1929.

increases we are able to get a better idea of God, and the succession of new definitions is evidence that this has been done." [25]

Distinction should be made between popular theisms and technical theology. "For many the idea of god is undefined. That god is real such persons devoutly believe. But precisely what he is or what he is like they have never tried to determine. . . . Thus they *use* god more than they think about him." [26] Jesus himself, "the greatest psychologist of all times," [27] was a theist, but not a theologian. So far as we know, he offered no arguments for the existence of God, no metaphysical interpretation of his attributes, no logic-tight definitions. But, then, he did not need to. "Jesus believed in God as readily as he believed in the sun. He believed that he had as immediate experience of the one as of the other." [28] Perfect certainty concerning theological technicalities is not necessary to achieving religious goals. The person in crisis is more concerned about assurance of effectiveness than about niceties of doctrinal consistency. For many ministerial students, theological training involves great disillusionment. Critics rightly question whether ably constructed theories are functionally successful.[29] Since St. Thomas Aquinas' abstruse conceptions [30] are seldom understood by average parishioners, there is considerable wisdom in Roman Catholic concentration upon the more functional sacraments and the use of saints and their visible representations to achieve practical satisfactions—especially since, for example, "the doctrine of the Holy Trinity is a strict mystery." [31] Nevertheless, it is our purpose here to have a look at some theological views.

In a sense, we have already had, in Part II, a review of theological types. In contrast with those who consider theology a separate and

[25] Max C. Otto, *The Human Enterprise*, p. 321. Appleton-Century-Crofts, New York, 1940.

[26] Horace T. Houf, *What Religion Is and Does*, revised edition, p. 137. Harper & Bros., New York, 1935, 1945.

[27] Fritz Kunkel, *In Search of Maturity*, p. 12. Charles Scribner's Sons, New York, 1943.

[28] Eugene G. Bewkes and others, *Experience, Reason and Faith: A Survey in Philosophy and Religion*, p. 180. Harper & Bros., New York, 1940.

[29] Stephen Lee Ely, *The Religious Availability of Whitehead's God*. University of Wisconsin Press, Madison, 1942.

[30] E.g., *On Being and Essence*.

[31] W. Wilmers, S.J., *Handbook of the Christian Religion*, translated from the German by James Conway, S.J., p. 196. Benziger Brothers, New York, 1891. Reprinted by permission of the copyright owners.

superior science,[32] we have included theology as a part of metaphysics. Each metaphysician has had to deal, in one way or another, with the problem of the existence and nature of God. For dualistic Descartes, God is an uncreated substance distinct from matter and spirit as created substances. For neutralistic Spinoza, God or Nature alone exists, all else being attribute or mode of God. For spiritualistic Leibniz, omniscient God functions of necessity as the creator of this the best of all possible worlds which functions freely in accordance with the principle of pre-established harmony. Other spiritualists, such as Royce, equate God with the Absolute, while personalists consider God as a cosmic companion of finite spirits. Materialists either deny the existence of God or explain him as made of matter, or accept his functions while claiming theological terminology obsolete. Emanationistic Plotinus and multitudes of Neoplatonic fellow travelers hold that God's ultimately perfect ineffability emanates imperfection, though he himself does not degenerate in the least. Emergentistic Alexander finds God becoming manifest in recent and contemporary evolutionary processes as that ideal which human minds have generated as the higher goal toward which they strive. Creationistic Boodin sees God as the cosmic womb in which matter becomes organized into newer levels of existence in accordance with eternal principles. Organicism finds God an organic unity, both one and many, both remaining and changing, both eternal and temporal. Although these and the multitudes of other conceptions cannot be reviewed here in any detail, this reminder may serve to refer the reader back to previous chapters, if he is in a mood to reconsider those summaries.

More fruitful, perhaps, will be some mention of characteristics which have been attributed, from time to time, to God: omnipotence, omniscience, omnipresence, transcendence, immanence, eternality, perfection, infinity, omnibenevolence, justice, love, personality, first cause, and final cause. Only some of these can be considered.

Why should God be considered omnipotent or all-powerful, and what is involved in such omnipotence? In western history, Jahweh, or Jehovah, the God of Mt. Sinai who contracted with Moses to free his people from bondage to the Egyptians and their gods, proved himself equal to the task. He had great power, greater power than other gods, and thus he came to be thought of as supreme over them whenever conflict arose. Later Hebrew prophets expanded their concep-

[32] See Jacques Maritain, *An Introduction to Philosophy*. Sheed and Ward, London, 1930.

tion to consider him controller over other nations and, gradually, of all creation. Then, consequently, being conceived as having power over all, he came to be considered all-powerful. However, as a result of the influences of Greek developments in logic flowing into the mainstream of Christian thought, the term "all" came to have precise meanings interpreted in terms of Aristotelian logic. When these interpretations were read back into Hebrew passages, the results were different and difficult. Whereas God had been merely sufficiently powerful enough to overcome awesome obstacles, now God became considered subject to the laws of logic. If "all" means "without exception," then an all-powerful God can do anything without exception. There is nothing which such a God cannot do. If this be so, then can God make a stone so big that he himself cannot lift it, can he annihilate himself completely, can he change the past, can he do the impossible? If any of these are things which he cannot do, then, strictly speaking, he is not all-powerful in this sense. Awareness of such incapacities is hard on the faith of literalists with Greek-trained minds. Of course, all-powerful may be interpreted differently: e.g., "can do anything possible," or "has all the power that there is," or "can do anything he wants to do (it being impossible for him to want to do anything he cannot do)." However, this line of thought tends to make us aware of how dependent theology is upon semantics and logic and tends to direct our attention away from reality to the nature of meanings and the difficulty inherent in thinking adequately. These difficulties have led some to abandon theology, others to surrender rational theology or to supplement it with revelation, while still others have given up the idea of an unlimited God. McConnell [33] and other personalists [34] have accepted the idea of a limited God, one limited in power, in freedom, and in knowledge. Most conceptions, examined closely, reveal either some limitations or some irrational paradoxes. Even St. Thomas, for example, thought God, though omnipotent in the sense of involving all the potentiality of created beings, as impotent in the sense that he is powerless to be changed or to change himself.

Turning to omniscience, does "all-knowing" mean: all that happens exactly when and as it happens; all that could possibly happen even though it does not happen; all that has happened but not all that will happen; all that has and will happen, or everything all-at-once or

[33] Francis J. McConnell, *Is God Limited?* The Abingdon Press, New York, 1924.
[34] See p. 185.

eternally? If all of God's knowledge is eternal, how can he have temporal knowledge; i.e., knowledge of things that happen as they happen? If he knows the latter, then he must have some new knowledge. If God's knowledge is completely perfect, then he is unable (powerless) to learn anything. Can he then have no knowledge of learning? If there is knowledge of error, does God also know error, or does he know only the truth? If he knows all, must he not know error also? If there are many kinds of knowledge, clear and vague, discursive and intuitive, deductive and pragmatic, does God know through all these ways? Can God have experimental knowledge without experimenting? Can God have knowledge of novelty unless there is something genuinely new for him? Is God's knowledge rational, irrational, or suprarational? Does he reason, decide, believe, hope, desire? Or does perfection imply ignorance of knowing processes? Does God know what it is to desire, without he himself desiring, what it is to be frustrated, without his being frustrated, what it is to have unactualized ideals without being imperfect? Can he know exactly as we know unless he is exactly as we are with all our limitations? If God is not ignorant, at least in some sense, how can he know what it is to be ignorant? If different epistemologies [35] conclude differently concerning the nature of knowledge, must there not be as many different theories about the nature of God's knowledge?

What about omnibenevolence? If God is all-good, how can evil be explained? Does "all-good" mean that he can do no evil? If so, then is he powerless to cause evil? If he cannot cause evil, then he cannot cause everything, unless evil is nothing. The perennial paradox—how can a good God, who knows all that can be done and who can do anything he wants to do, still permit evil to exist—has given endless trouble. To many, it seems that either he wants evil (and thus is not omnibenevolent) or cannot prevent it (and thus is not omnipotent). Apologists generally conclude that either evil is unreal or that there can be no good without evil. Thus, according to this view, although God is powerless to prevent all evil, his goodness causes him to create a world of suffering because only by this means can the greatest good be achieved. Just as a salad is more tasty with vinegar and pepper—evils in themselves—so life can be freed from unbearable monotony, boredom, and dead desirelessness only by introducing evil. The superior benefits of freedom of choice are possible only if one is free to make mistakes. Of course, there are those

[35] See Part I, "Knowledge."

who prefer to attribute evil to a Devil, but this divides God's power with an evil being. Is the battle between evil and good (symbolized by Armageddon) a real one in which God's power is really challenged, or does God's omnipotence make the supposed battle against the Devil merely a sham? Is it possible for the Devil to do good? If one serves the devil well, is this doing good? Is it then sometimes good to do evil and evil to do good? Can one do what is good for God without doing what is evil for the Devil? Can one do good without doing evil? If there can be no good without evil and if the Devil causes evil, then is not the evil which the Devil causes a necessity without which good could not exist? Puzzles like these lead many to reject theology in favor of simple revelation. Others put God "beyond good and evil," as some conceive Brahman, while still others prefer God as a finite companion, limited in power, but committed to do the best he can in a real struggle against real evil. "For Brightman it is more important to save God's benevolence, his infinite goodness, than it is to preserve his omnipotence." [36]

Is God eternal, unchanging, perfect, or growing, developing, progressing? If God is eternal, is he timeless, i.e., nontemporal, and thus unrelated to time? Or does "eternal" mean "everlasting," i.e., enduring through each and every time? Should we believe that God's work was perfect from before the beginning (involving complete monotony for God) or that God "has more to do than he has yet done, and so is capable of growth"? [37] Is God an unmoved mover or a self-creating creativity? [38] Is God free to choose (and thus able to make mistakes) or completely determined in his actions? If God is perfect, is he free to choose the imperfect? Is he free to make erroneous judgments and then suffer evil consequences? Is God immanent or merely transcendent? If immanent, is he immanent in each and every moment and place and is he dependent upon such moments and places for something for him to be immanent in? Is God a person, a distinct personality, or merely an impersonal principle (first cause, ground, necessary being, highest good), or perhaps an impersonal principle which appears as personal only in persons? If the latter, is God present only in selected persons (Jesus, avatars, bodhisattvas)

[36] W. H. Werkmeister, *A History of Philosophical Ideas in America*, p. 338. The Ronald Press, New York, 1949.

[37] Edgar S. Brightman, *The Problem of God*, p. 11. The Abingdon Press, New York, 1930.

[38] Alfred North Whitehead, *Religion in the Making*, p. 92. The Macmillan Co., New York, 1926.

or equally present in all, such that God has no other hands but our hands with which to handle things here and now, no personality other than our personalities in which to express himself in this or that place or time or way? Does God express himself in only one way, or is the truth about God like a "spectrum, as if the light from some Object had been refracted through a prism composed of various historic cultures and schools of thought . . . and had cast upon a screen a rainbow image, extending through a range of different wave lengths"? [39] Regardless of our answers to all of these questions, we can hardly dismiss them as trivial because, like other aspects of religion, they are rooted in "the deep needs within the living organism." [40] "The God in man is a task as well as a final fact, a problem as well as a possession." [41]

Before leaving theology, let us consider some arguments for the existence of God. Although, obviously, different conceptions of God will require different kinds of arguments, perhaps we should review some that have come to be well-known. 1. One of the most common is a causal argument or argument from the apparent necessity of a first cause, or prime mover. Nothing happens without a cause. The universe exists, and thus must have had a cause or creator. 2. Teleological arguments rest on the evidence of law, order, design, plan, purpose, evolution, value. If there is law, there must have been a lawgiver. If there is order rather than chaos, someone must have been responsible for the order. If the world has pattern or design, there must have been a designer, just as there could be no watch without a watchmaker. [42] The world is purposive—at least there are purposes in the world—and purpose involves working toward an end; thus there must be a goal or final cause or God. Evolution, once considered as evidence against the existence of God, is now more often appealed to as a support, for if evolution is progressive, obviously it must be heading somewhere and since this goal is unknown to us, there must be a God who knows. Since evolution is progressive, there must be a peak of progress, a goal toward which evolution is progressing, a supreme value which is God.

[39] George P. Conger, *The Ideologies of Religion*, p. 1. Round Table Press, Inc., New York, 1940.

[40] Houf, *op. cit.*, p. 17.

[41] S. Radhakrishnan, *Indian Philosophy*, Vol. I, p. 209. George Allen and Unwin, Ltd., London, 1927, 1948.

[42] See Frances Mason, *The Great Design*. The Macmillan Co., New York, 1934. See also Archie J. Bahm, "Teleological Arguments," *The Scientific Monthly*, May, 1944, pp. 377–382.

3. Many moral arguments have been advanced. The concepts of duty and obligation imply responsibility for justice. If, as is obvious, justice is not always done in this life, there must be another; and thus there must be a God to see it through. 4. Revelational arguments say that even man's ignorance presupposes the truth that he is ignorant, and some truth implies a whole of truth. If such a whole of truth is not available to man, even through reason, then it can come only through special revelation. There is plenty of evidence of revelation, whether through the Bible, the Church, or Jesus, that God exists. 5. Empirical arguments often appear to be the most conclusive. Some confess to an immediate and direct acquaintance with God. The chief difficulty here is that so few seem to be able to acquire this experience. 6. Historical arguments point out that people always and everywhere have believed in God. Although this is not deductive proof, the persistent and widespread survival of such a belief is surely some evidence, for such uniformity and endurance could hardly happen without some cause. 7. Ontological arguments, although highly technical, are given great credence by some theologians. One formulation is as follows: the existence of a perfect being follows from the idea of a perfect being because the idea of perfection implies existence. Descartes argued that, since he is an imperfect being having an idea of perfection (i.e., a perfect idea), and since an imperfect being could not produce anything perfect, there must be a perfect being which produced it. 8. Tychists sometimes argue that even on the basis of pure chance in an infinite time all possibilities can (or must) be actualized. If it is possible that God should exist, then sometime, even if not now, God must exist. 9. Finally, there is a "synthetic argument." Although none of the classical arguments, taken singly, may be conclusive proof of the existence of God, all of them together provide a preponderance of evidence which can hardly be ignored.[43]

In addition to the foregoing arguments intended to prove that God exists, there are others aimed at convincing us that we should believe that God exists, even in the absence of positive proof. 1. For those who are unable to understand the proofs and who must rely upon others for guidance, the thing to do is to seek the best advice they can get from those who are best qualified to give such advice, i.e., from theologians. Theologians say God exists, therefore one should believe. 2. Pascal, a French Catholic sceptic, is famous for his wager.

[43] William K. Wright, *A Student's Philosophy of Religion*, p. 371. The Macmillan Co., New York, 1922.

Even when "reason cannot help us . . . it is like a game in which heads or tails may turn up. . . . Let us weigh the gain and the loss in wagering that God does exist. If you wager that he does, and he does, you gain all; if you wager that he does, and he does not, you lose nothing. If you win, you take all; if you lose, you lose nothing. Wager, then, unhesitatingly, that he does exist." [44]   3. More convincing, in an age of experimental science, are various pragmatic arguments. Beliefs in God not only have worked successfully for multitudes and have survived for centuries, but they can be tried out and tested by each individual for himself. If one is happier believing that there is a God who cares enough for him to assure him eternal life, then he ought, as a simple practical matter, to believe that which makes him happier.

[44] Blaise Pascal, *Pensées*, quoted in Albury Castell, *An Introduction to Modern Philosophy*, p. 36. The Macmillan Co., New York, 1943.

·26·

Social
Philosophy

For more than half a century people have been asking whether social phenomena can be treated scientifically. Despite continuing disagreement, more and more effort is being made to apply scientific methods and attitudes in attempts to understand group affairs. Social science has come to stay. But what difference is there between social science and social philosophy? The difference is one of degree. Social philosophy concerns itself with the more general questions: What is society? What is a group? What is culture? Social science busies itself primarily with detailed evidence concerning more specific problems. Since social sciences have only recently separated from philosophy, its specialists continue to be more conscious of their philosophical problems than specialists in those sciences which became independent long ago. However, "when splitting off from philosophy in order to become scientific, the social sciences took a bad moment to imitate the natural sciences. They did so just before the natural sciences themselves began to undergo major changes. The result is that many social scientists pride themselves on being natural scientists or regret that they cannot be, whereas the science they emulate or would like to emulate became obsolescent fifty years ago."[1] Doubtless social science will mature and, as it is already doing, develop methods peculiarly suited to its problems.

An initial problem of the social philosopher and social scientist alike is where to mark out the boundaries of their joint investigation. Difficulties involved in dealing with this problem include the following: Different metaphysical theories, for example, result in different conceptions of the nature of groups and their place in existence. Investigators with conflicting preconceptions concerning the nature

[1] Lewis White Beck, "The 'Natural Sciences Ideal' in the Social Sciences," *The Scientific Monthly*, June, 1949, p. 386.

of existence will bring these to bear in interpreting the nature of groups. Also, divergent views of the nature of science or philosophy will involve conflicting ways of framing the limits and nature of the investigation. Likewise, varying psychological, ethical, religious, mathematical, biological, etc., conceptions bear upon how sociologists picture their problem. Of course, we must ask whether a social scientist should begin by accepting and adjusting to conclusions in all other fields or whether he should examine his own subject matter first and then draw out the implications of his own conclusions for the other fields. Probably the best answer is "both." That is, it is just as important for metaphysicians, biologists, psychologists, etc., to take into consideration the established conclusions of social scientists as is the reverse. Our placing social philosophy toward the end of this book does not mean that it is any tail-end investigation. One may as well start his philosophical career by investigating social problems, for these are as significant as any. Whether there is more danger of developing ineradicable biases from which he cannot free himself as he expands his conceptions in the light of other areas is doubtful, for this danger exists no matter what the starting point.[2]

Two of the most general social problems have been selected here as constituting the core of social philosophy: What are groups? and What is culture? Involved in these are questions concerning the interrelations and relative primacy of individuals and groups and culture.

Groups

For our purposes, a group involves two or more persons consciously associating or interacting, directly or indirectly. Omitting such questions as: Does a group disappear when one of the two persons goes to sleep or directs his attention elsewhere? and In how far do groups depend upon physiological, biological, and psychological bases for their existence and nature? [3] we may note that groups involve consensus or agreement of some sort. Even groups of antagonists must agree that they disagree and that fighting is worth while in dealing with their disagreement. Although attitudes may seem a flimsy basis upon which to build stable social structures, they are almost as per-

---

[2] An example of an introductory philosophy text emphasizing social problems is George R. Geiger's *Philosophy and the Social Order*. Houghton Mifflin Co., Boston, 1947.

[3] See L. L. Bernard, *Introduction to Sociology*, Parts I–III, for treatment of some of these bases. Thomas Y. Crowell Co., New York, 1942.

sistent as the people who have them. Although some groups obviously are temporary, even momentary and casual, we may gain greater insight by examining more stabilized types of groups.

Following Cooley,[4] we may distinguish between primary and nonprimary association. Primary groups, which consist of relatively intimate, face-to-face, unspecialized associations, are called primary because (1) "they are fundamental in forming the social nature and ideals of the individual" and (2) they "are springs of life, not only for the individual, but for social institutions."[5] Without primary association, with its ideals of individual worth and its tendencies to develop ideals of group loyalty, lawfulness, and freedom,[6] human nature could not develop in the biological baby nor could other more complex and specialized groups arise with stabilized sentiments and habitualized attitudes of agreement in the individuals who form their basis. "This humanizing of the animal drives is perhaps the greatest service performed by the primary group,"[7] partly because it gives the child something that he does not have at birth which makes both his remaining life and nature possible, and partly because the whole existence of society depends squarely upon the standards of value he develops there. Nonprimary groups, those where association is more specialized, partial, and impersonal, are possible only because the ideals developed in primary groups become extended gradually as the individual grows in awareness of the values of larger and more specialized groups to his own welfare. Both in the history of the race and in the life of each person there develops wider ranges of "we-feelings." Historically, "human association has grown out of the old primary group that enclosed it in the beginning until now we find it organized in communities, regions, states, nations and finally the world market."[8] Individually, the infant grows through expanding his feelings of identity with parents, playmates, neighborhood, school groups, community, state, nation, and mankind. He who cannot grow up to cooperate within the limits of local consensus is imprisoned, asylumed, exiled, or killed.

Nonprimary, or secondary, association has some tremendous advantages, which "may be summed up as those resulting mainly from specialization, impersonality, reach, and continuity."[9] Specialization

---

[4] Charles Horton Cooley and others, *Introductory Sociology*, Chs. IV, XV. Charles Scribner's Sons, New York, 1933.

[5] *Ibid.*, pp. 55, 59.

[6] *Ibid.*, pp. 60–68.

[7] *Ibid.*, p. 59.

[8] *Ibid.*, p. 193.

[9] *Ibid.*, p. 215.

and division of labor result in richer varieties and greater quantities of complicated and skillfully produced goods and services; e.g., not only economic (farm, factory, mine, store, bank) but also educational, religious, political, medical, recreational, and the multifarious special branches of these. Impersonality "simplifies decisions and cuts through complexities" [10] by standardizing our contacts in such a way that interactions between people become habitual and automatic rather than remaining a continuously difficult series of adjustment problems. Reach means that we can share the fruits of distant peoples and feel at home in a larger world. Continuity refers to perpetuation of institutionalized values and functions from generation to generation, so that persons born today enjoy a much richer heritage than primitive peoples.

But "secondary association is partial association. It is association narrowed down by special purpose, by communication at a distance, by rules, by social barriers, or by the casual nature of contact. This means that under such conditions associating personalities present only special facets of themselves to one another. They cannot meet as whole persons." [11] Such association suffers from certain dangers which "lie chiefly in the social illiteracy of the narrow specialist, in the functionary's tendency to disregard human values, in the inertia of great organizations, and in the resulting readjustment lag." [12]

Increasing stress upon specialization magnifies both specialization in partiality rather than in wholeness and in regard to interdependence of people. The more wholly a person devotes himself to his specialty, the more he cuts part of his personality off from association with others. Even in the same university, different specialists often cannot understand each other's language. Furthermore, "it is a fatally short step from the impersonal to the inhuman. . . . Large organizations have an inertia much greater than primary groups. . . . The lag between need and readjustment tends to be longer." [13] Thus, although expansion of personality profits greatly by extension and growth in efficiency of secondary groups, the benefits are bought at a price. A person's confidence that he is valued as an end-in-himself tends to decline as increase in nonprimary association decreases the proportion of time spent in intimate, face-to-face, whole-personality association. Consequently his sense of loyalty, fair play, devotion to others tends to decline and the wholesome feelings that come from belonging tend to be replaced gradually by disregard not only for

[10] *Ibid.*, p. 216.   [12] *Ibid.*, p. 215.
[11] *Ibid.*, p. 214.   [13] *Ibid.*, pp. 217–218.

local mores but even for all morality in general. Human nature becomes dehumanized. Of New York high school seniors, "one out of twenty will at some future time be found in a hospital for the insane."[14] "In the future we may expect to meet an ever-increasing degree of social and individual disorganization."[15] These trends make us more fully aware of our "interdependence. More than ever before men's lives are at the mercy of their fellowmen," which makes more difficult the "problem of how to locate responsibility."[16] Before we can do this, we shall have to understand more fully the nature of the relations between persons and groups.

Unfortunately for those who desire ready understanding of individual-group relationships, there are many varieties of outlook upon the world and life involving different explanations. Although we have not and cannot here draw them out, it should be easy to see that each of the different metaphysical theories discussed in Part II have implications bearing upon this problem. For example, among spiritualists,[17] personalists consider individual persons as metaphysically primary and, consequently, groups as secondary and completely dependent upon persons; Hegelians, on the other hand, subordinate individuals to the state as a higher level of dialectical being which is closer to the Absolute and, thus, more real. Emergentists[18] consider groups as later and less-real emergents than persons, while creationists[19] find the higher and the lower or, in this case, groups and individuals, both influencing and molding each other and thus, in a sense, equally real.

For convenience, in this and the following chapters, we shall summarize social philosophies into three groups: Those preferring to believe that the individual is real and that groups are unreal will be called "individualistic." Those tending to consider the dependence of persons upon groups greater than dependence of groups upon persons, and thus groups more real than persons, will be called "totalitarian." Organicism,[20] of course, claims that individuals and their groups are interdependent and thus both real, in some degree, each in its own way. "The organic view stresses both the unity of the

---

[14] William F. Ogburn and Meyer F. Nimkoff, *Sociology*, p. 214. Houghton Mifflin Co., Boston, 1940.

[15] Mabel A. Elliott and Frances E. Merrill, *Social Disorganization*, p. 16. Harper Bros., New York, 1934.

[16] Harold H. Titus, *Ethics for Today*, p. 419. American Book Co., New York, 1936.

[17] See Ch. 15.   [19] See Ch. 19.

[18] See Ch. 18.   [20] See Ch. 20.

whole and the peculiar value of the individual, explaining each by the other." [21]   Although it is difficult to find actual examples of societies in which either of the extreme views is carried out fully and consistently, it is easy to discover philosophical statements that idealize such extremes.

Individualism, exemplified by "rugged individualism," tends more or less consistently to follow the ideals inherent in metaphysical pluralism—the many are more real than the one.   Individuals are more real than groups.   Persons are substantial causes, whereas groups are merely epiphenomenal effects.   Totalitarianism, exemplified by "Fascism," accepts ideals implicit in metaphysical monism—unity is more real than plurality.   Individuals are less real than their groups, even as their groups are less real than still higher and more unified beings, such as the State, the Race, or God.   Individuals derive their minute and finite substantiality from higher powers in which they live and move and have their being.   Organicism, holding that a thing is what it does (substantiality existing only so long as there is functioning), believes that both individuals and groups are somewhat substantial, that both function causally, that each influences and determines the other and, therefore, each has some degree of reality.

Individualists, as a consequence of idealizing independence, conceive each man's goals in terms of self-interest, his responsibility as only his own, his ability to succeed as primarily internal.   The great man is self-reliant, defiant, unpliant.   He is likely to reject charity as a sign of weakness and believes that the sources of genius are located only within persons.   Totalitarians, on the other hand, believe that a man's significance consists primarily in his being a means to higher ends.   Something superior, which has brought him into being, is responsible for his fate and provides all that is needed for his welfare.   He must accept his lot, for if he rejects it he is as something powerless rejecting the source of his power.   The great man is wholly devoted to his cause, is a willing servant selflessly trusting that to which he ought humbly submit, achieving greatness in proportion to the greatness of his cause and his service to it.   Genius exists in those selected by the higher power to fulfill its will, whether by divine inspiration, or by accident of fate.   Organicists see men's goals as their own, although partly suggested by and partly fulfilled through group action.   Men are social animals whose nature and goals arise out of their interaction with each other and who grow by submitting

[21] Cooley, *op. cit.*, p. 71.

to the pull of ideals calling for self-realization through group participation. The great man is adaptable, sometimes defiant, sometimes devoted, depending upon whether submission or assertion promises the greater value. Genius consists in ability to reconcile opposites, to survive through adaptation—sometimes to inner, sometimes to outer, demands. Intelligence is neither merely an individual hereditary I.Q. nor a product of racial or cultural superiority alone, but is a consequence of the integration of both. Education can increase the intelligence of some more than others, partly due to differences in heredity and partly to differences in teaching methods. Groups, too, are more or less intelligent, depending upon whether their members survive happily. Intelligent individuals make good use of their groups while intelligent groups make good use of their members for the benefit of their members.[22]

For individualists, each personality is an integral unity which normally remains such unless infected by evil influences from the outside. What desire he has is purely a personal matter. He is naturally good, so all badness arises from external interference. Consequently he desires freedom, conceived as absence of all external restraints. For totalitarians, the source of personality integration resides ultimately in the higher, holier, and perfect unity of the totality. Therefore one can mature properly only by submitting to the molds, the mores, the disciplines which have been graciously provided and without which the individual remains as nothing. Non-conformity in social affairs constitutes a crime, just as sin consists in refusal of the individual to submit his will to the will of God—for only thus can he "be made whole." The freedom to be desired is freedom from individual willfulness, from selfish desires, from the illusion that an individual is something which can stand by himself. For organicism, personality integration and disintegration have both inner and outer sources. "The individual and the social environment . . . are constantly creating each other."[23] Consequently, integrity depends upon dynamic interaction.

For example, children desire to become firemen or policemen because their social environment provides these as exciting ideals or

[22] John Dewey has expressed organicistic ideas concerning intelligence in individual-group affairs as well as anyone. See, for example, Ch. VII of Joseph Ratner's summary and selections, *Intelligence in the Modern World, John Dewey's Philosophy.* The Modern Library, New York, 1939.

[23] L. L. Bernard, *Introduction to Social Psychology*, p. 270. Henry Holt and Co., New York, 1926.

models. "By means of this process of imitation we use the personality materials of others in building up our own personalities." [24]
But, also, the kinds of personalities which these children grow up to
be then come to serve as models for others, models influenced by
whatever peculiarities the individual himself contributes as he grows
up interacting socially. If satisfaction of desire is good and frustration
evil, then one should seek to have only those desires which can be
satisfied. If a person wants what his group cannot give him or if
his group cannot or will not give him what he wants, then he is
frustrated. But if an individual wants what his group has to give or
if his group gives him what he wants, then he is free, for freedom
involves fitness [25] of desires to possibilities for satisfaction. A person
"is free or unfree in proportion as he does or does not find himself
in the midst of conditions conducive to full and harmonious personal
development." [26] Social "freedom can exist only in and through a
social order, and must be increased by all the healthy growth of the
latter." [27] Although the desires of persons can be modified somewhat
either by personal will or by social decision, the degree to which
either can occur beneficially will depend upon whether persons believe they will get more satisfaction as a consequence. Societies, too,
survive and prosper only to the extent that they satisfy the needs of
those who depend upon them. Groups rightly derive their freedom
to control individuals from the needs of individuals for the benefits of
such group service.

Culture

What is culture? Culture consists in those "capabilities acquired
by man as a member of society," [28] in contrast with those derived
through biological heredity or endowed by the physical environment.
One's cultural heritage centers around habitual attitudes and behavior-patterns, especially those pertaining to individual-group interaction. Sociologists commonly distinguish between folkways, mores,
and institutions as representing ascending degrees of enforcement of
behavior-patterns upon individual conduct. "Folkways" are "the

[24] *Ibid.*, p. 333.
[25] Archie J. Bahm, "Freedom is Fitness," *The Scientific Monthly*, August, 1946,
p. 135.
[26] Cooley, *op. cit.*, p. 74.
[27] *Ibid.*, p. 75.
[28] E. B. Tyler, *Primitive Culture*, seventh edition, p. 1. Brentano's, New York,
1924.

spontaneous, unpremeditated, common ways of acting" [29] without any obvious pressure from group sources. The mores include all kinds of conduct considered necessary to the welfare of the group, but enforced largely by group opinion, whereas these become institutionalized when groups establish "authorities whose special business it is to enforce them." [30] Groups cannot exist without some stability of structure, and human beings cannot exist apart from groups. "One can no more organize his personality independently than he can be born without a mother." [31] A person's cultural ingredients are part of what he is. But, on the other hand, "it is in the individual and nowhere else that the institution is to be found. . . . The individual is always cause as well as effect of the institution." [32]

Culture with its natural stability is a necessary condition of human nature and thus basically beneficial. But certain serious problems arise consequent upon the natural opposition of stability to change. An institution, by its very nature, is something established, fixed, unchanging. Yet, as students of history know, new problems arise, from changes in climatic and geographical conditions, discoveries of new lands, inventions, borrowing from other cultures, etc. Whenever new problems and attitudes meet old patterns and habits, there is conflict. "When the socially accepted habits prove inadequate to the new situation, the old equilibrium is destroyed. Then it is that the social structure tends to become disorganized." [33] This conflict and disorganization has serious consequences for integrity of personality. When the culture upon which one depends for his nature is disorganized, he becomes disorganized. Not all personal disorganization is due to cultural conflict. Much is caused by illness, overstimulation, and the "revolt of youth" involved in incomplete transfer of cultural ideals from one generation to the next. But more important, from a more general point of view, is the disorganization caused by cultural conflict—resulting in "marginal" men. "The marginal personality is most clearly portrayed by those individuals who are unwittingly initiated into two or more historical traditions, languages, political loyalties, moral codes, or religions," and who, because he "is identified with both groups, experiences the conflict as an acute personal dif-

---

[29] Cooley, *op. cit.*, p. 89.

[30] *Ibid.*, p. 94.

[31] Ellsworth Farris, *The Nature of Human Nature*, p. 279. McGraw-Hill Book Co., New York, 1937. By permission of the publishers.

[32] Cooley, *op. cit.*, p. 404.

[33] Elliott, *op. cit.*, p. 5.

ficulty or mental tension." [34] Responses of individuals and groups to
difficulties inherent in cultural conflict vary somewhat in accordance
with the social philosophies they bring to bear in trying to deal with
them.

Those who consider the permanent, the eternal, the substantial, as
more real, and thus more right, tend to believe that change to something new is bad and that the tormented individual who succumbs to
the temptation to try out the new is weak, immoral, evil, sinful.
Others who, either because they are more adaptable or because they
have been ousted from status in the old order, come to praise the new
just because it is new, sometimes reject as bad all that is old. Between these extremes are varieties of views concerning the true nature
of social change and how to react wisely to it. Organicism, finding
cultural change more or less normal in the development of both
persons and civilizations, considers Cooley's "cycle of institutional
development" [35] a helpful interpretation:

"We may roughly distinguish four periods of institutional organization: (1) incipient organization, (2) efficiency, (3) formalism,
(4) disorganization," [36] followed by (5) either disintegration or reorganization. The first period consists of coming to awareness that
a group adjustment problem exists, a tentative seeking for adjustment,
and the beginnings of the rise of institutional forms. When these
become successful in meeting the problem, i.e., when personality
works "hand in hand with the institution" because it satisfies personality needs, the second stage—efficiency—has been reached. But since
the fixity of institutional forms does not readily respond to changes
when new personality needs arise, they gradually drift into "formalism"—a period when they compel obedience to the law for its own
sake rather than because there are benefits from obedience, and "intolerance goes very naturally with formalism." [37] When this occurs,
persons naturally revolt against the tyranny of the mores, though not
without a price. When some do and some do not conform, members
of the group condemn each other as immoral and innocently suffer
from each other's unjust condemnation. The power of group morality declines and personalities lack guidance which can be confidently
relied upon. Such disorganization is miserable and results, eventually, in disintegration, when all but stubborn diehards reject the

[34] Everett V. Stonequist, *The Marginal Man*, pp. 3–4. Charles Scribner's Sons,
New York, 1937.

[35] Cooley, *op. cit.*, p. 407.   [37] *Ibid.*, p. 409.

[36] *Ibid.*, p. 406.

old and outworn institution. However, if the need which the institution arose to serve in the first place still persists, then the group will grope again for a new institution to serve this need. Often institutions become only partly disorganized, so that reorganization is a partial process. Those who suffer from the stresses and strains of cultural change without knowing what is happening often are bitter, either against particular individuals, against group morality in general, against God, or even against life itself.

However, when the nature of social change is understood and its phases detected, people can more readily adapt themselves to the difficulties as they arise. Instead of feeling that one must merely submit helplessly to social ills, men come to believe that they may lessen the periods of disorganization and extend periods of efficiency by consciously attending to difficulties and their solution. Scientific investigation and enlightened social legislation may help detect and eliminate some unnecessary ills. Social and cultural planning can become vital tools of societies conscious of their power to modify or eliminate social evils. However, mores concerning whether societies should assume more self-control are themselves subject to formalism, etc., and so citizens must endure those conflicts which are involved in reorganizing institutionalized ideals concerning self-control of cultural change. Today is not without its voices pointing out the "next steps in moral evolution" and "principles which need to be brought up to date." [38] But "when anyone proposes to change the mores, he must remember that the change must be brought about by individuals who are trained to conform to the present mores. . . . Reform must not only begin with the existing situation; it usually involves the sacrifice of one or two generations as the result of the transition from one moral consensus to another. . . . If one is to advise the average individual in terms of his own welfare, the answer is quite clear: 'Be not the first to take up the new, nor last to put the old aside.' " [39]

[38] Titus, *op. cit.*, p. 421.
[39] Willard Waller, *The Family,* revised by Reuben Hill, pp. 592–593. The Dryden Press, New York, 1951.

·27·

Political
Philosophy

Although differences in political theory flow naturally from differences in more general social philosophy, additional difficulties arise in attempting to understand the nature of political philosophy itself. One of these is the fact that it has become customary to distinguish, even if not sharply, between political science studies and courses in government, the latter stressing the actual structures of existing governments, whereas the former tends to include generalizations about the nature of government, which are based upon comparisons of such governments. Whether these generalizations are scientific or philosophical is a matter of considerable dispute, but it appears that political scientists tend to be more fully aware of their involvement in philosophy than most specialists. Another difficulty grows out of the fact that lines between social, political, and economic philosophy, ethics, and philosophy of law, are not only indistinct and broad but subject to various interpretations by accidents of personal interest or professional tradition. Finally, political scientists, too, have their own typical insights which are not always fully taken into account by more general social philosophies. This failure may be due, in part, to the unsavory connotations that suffuse current meanings of the terms "politics" and "politician," which prejudice us against admitting that the professional politician has anything worth contributing to intellectual insights.

However, if we open our eyes and ears enough to consider the conclusions of philosopher T. V. Smith [1] who, after a term of practical legislative experience, came to appreciate and defend the functions of professional politicians, we may discover a contribution by

[1] See Thomas Verner Smith, *The Legislative Way of Life*, University of Chicago Press, 1940, and *The Promise of American Politics*, University of Chicago Press, 1936. See also Chester C. Maxey, "A Plea for the Politician," *The Western Political Science Quarterly*, September, 1948, pp. 271–279.

politicians to philosophical understanding which is commonly over-looked. In governmental systems based on geographical representation, single representatives are called upon to do an impossible job, i.e., to represent fairly multiplicities of antagonistic interests among their constituents. This requires, on the part of him who would be successful, a promise of much more than can possibly be fulfilled and a vacillating response to changes of public opinion. From the point of view of absolutists, such apparent fickleness seems dishonest, corrupt, immoral; but from the standpoint of those who feel that satisfaction of the desire for political peace, even at the cost of some comparatively minor disappointments, is important, the functions of the professional compromiser, both with regard to his antagonistic constituents and to his antagonistic colleagues in the legislature, fulfill a great need. Although, of course, far from all legislators are free from special-interest loyalties or from self-interested grabbing, yet, when the need for compromise becomes imperative, unswervingness becomes detrimental to political health. The philosophies of those who make discoveries from practical political experience have something to contribute to the philosophical picture, which those persons who deduce their political theory merely from other aspects of social philosophy, or from theology, metaphysics, or aesthetics, are likely to miss.

Although the primary function of government is social control, what is meant by this term tends to be limited to those types of control which have become institutionalized; control by mores, folkways, public opinion, primary group ideals, and the like, is generally referred to social psychology. More particularly, "the political" pertains to constitutionalized government, though, of course, de facto governments are governments also. Since no group (except temporary, casual, or primary groups) can exist without some established system of social control, government is an essential aspect of practically all human life. Without government, civilization could not exist. Students may find that starting with philosophy of government or law is as good a way as any to be introduced into philosophical problems. Although, obviously, political philosophy is neither all of philosophy nor even the most important part of it (no essential part can be the most important part, for essentials are, as essential, equally important), it is as easy for epistemologists, metaphysicians, aestheticians, etc., to underestimate the role of government as it is for political philosophers to overrate it.

Sovereignty

Summarizing under sovereignty, hierarchy, law, and revolution some of the major problems confronting political philosophers, we may begin by asking the basic question: What is sovereignty? Sovereignty pertains to self-control. However, since what self-control is depends upon what self is, different views of the nature of self result in differing theories of the nature of sovereignty. Since people commonly recognize both individual sovereignty and state sovereignty, or group sovereignty, and since there are various kinds and levels of groups, we have to deal both with problems concerning relations between individual and group sovereignty and problems involving the relative sovereignty of different groups.

If we draw out the implications of individualism, totalitarianism, and organicism [2] for individual-group relations, certain types of political philosophies naturally appear. Individualists, who assert that individuals are real and groups unreal, naturally think of sovereignty as individual self-control and of freedom as absence of control by others. The typical individualist fears political control because he believes that liberty and government are antithetical—the more he is controlled by his government the less he controls himself. His ideal naturally becomes "that government governs best which governs least." Government is inherently evil and should be tolerated only when necessary. Such a view is most consistently represented by anarchism, though recent and contemporary Republicanism acclaims adherence to this slogan.

Totalitarians, who idealize wholeness, tend to find in some cosmic principle, such as God, the ultimate locus of political control. Only God is truly sovereign, so the ideal government is some form of theocracy, in which the goal of government is to help men to do God's will, and where individual self-assertiveness constitutes a sin punishable, perhaps, by eventual exile into hell. However, when the totalitarian spirit imbues the minds of men whose philosophical focus is limited to more earthly systems of control, it tends toward what we have recently come to call fascism—illustrated by Italian fascist doctrine: "For fascism, society is the end, individuals the means, and its whole life consists in using individuals as instruments for its social ends. . . . Individual rights are only recognized in so far as they

[2] See pp. 371ff. for previous discussion of these terms.

are implied in the rights of the state." [3]   In so far as the individual
is opposed to the state, the individual has no rights, so any attempt
on the part of persons to assert them are rightly suppressed. The
only freedom that individuals have is the freedom to profit from the
interest of the state in their welfare, just as the theocratic sinner finds
true freedom only when he freely chooses to surrender his will to the
will of God who cares for him.

Organicism opposes the extremes of both individualism and totalitarianism because it rejects as false all overemphasis upon "the antitheses, society versus the individual." [4]   Mutual dependence of persons
and groups means that each controls the other somewhat. Ideals of
government, then, must be framed neither in terms of complete absence of control by groups nor of complete control by groups, but
in terms of the most healthy types of organic functioning. To the
extent that an individual can mature normally only by identifying
himself with groups, he depends upon these groups and their control
over him for providing him with "opportunity for right development." [5]   To the extent that an individual feels identified with his
group, group-control is a form of self-control. The more he controls
himself through controlling his group which in turn controls him, the
more he has self-control of this kind. Freedom, in such circumstance,
is not freedom from group control, but freedom to control himself
through the medium of his group. However, in so far as he is also
not identified with a group, the more it controls him against his other
interests, the more unfree he becomes through such control. Thus
his problem is, not one of rejecting all group control or all individual
independence, but in seeking that balance of control and lack of control by groups which most nearly corresponds with his actual needs
and nature as a member of such groups.

These needs vary, both historically, because of changing circumstances influencing civilization, and in the life development of each
individual. Children and the aged are usually more dependent in
certain respects, whereas the more vigorous of the mature may be
capable of more independence in these same respects. The ill, the
insane, the poor, and the illiterate often are more dependent than

[3] Alfredo Rocco, *The Political Doctrine of Fascism.* Translation in *International Conciliation,* October, 1926 (No. 223). Published by Carnegie Endowment for International Peace.

[4] Charles Horton Cooley and others, *Introductory Sociology,* p. 71. Charles
Scribner's Sons, New York, 1933.

[5] *Ibid.,* p. 73.

the healthy, wealthy, and wise. Organicists expect changes in degrees, kinds, and methods of social control, both in society at large and in the desires of persons to make good use of their groups. Although it is true both that men make history and that history makes men, organicists believe that men can make themselves somewhat better by helping make better men make better history. Even though certain amounts of formalism [6] and cultural lag are to be expected, experimental modification of governmental-control systems may suggest means for adjusting such controls more sensitively to changing needs for group self-control. That government governs best which governs most nearly in accordance with the wishes of the governed. Government is neither something to be feared nor something to be completely submerged in, but is a tool to be used to best advantage. For organicists, the paradox of liberty is no paradox, for "without such regulations it is easy to see that freedom would be still more restricted." [7]

What is democracy? "It is both a set of high ideals and a variety of imperfect practices. . . . As a form of government, democracy cannot long sustain itself unless it is suckled and nourished by a social milieu favorable to it. Thus understanding of democratic political ideals presupposes insight into the philosophy underlying the democratic way of life." [8] But there are disagreements as to what this underlying philosophy is. Some totalitarians, holding that all are equal in the sight of God, claim to be democratic because they assert that each should be treated with equality before the law. However, "in rejecting democracy Fascism rejects the absurd conventional lie of political equalitarianism." [9] Thus political totalitarians tend to be anti-democratic. Individualists, on the other hand, are more likely to acclaim democratic ideals conceived, however, in terms of individual liberty, i.e., complete absence of social control. If laissez faire means freedom from control, then it means freedom from government, rather than freedom through government. The ultimate ideal, from this point of view, is anarchy—each man being equally free from government. However, in actual practice, this means that stronger individuals are free to enslave other individ-

[6] See discussion, p. 376f.

[7] William Henry Roberts, *The Problem of Choice*, p. 308. Ginn and Co., Boston, 1941.

[8] Archie J. Bahm, "Democracy Defined," *School and Society*, Aug. 23, 1947, p. 135.

[9] Benito Mussolini, *The Doctrine of Fascism*, p. 14. Vallecchi, Firenze, 1935.

uals without group interference. Thus, unrestricted anarchy begets tyranny, not of a group over individuals, but of some individuals over others. Therefore, the democracy idealized by individualists is unrealistic because it tends to disappear in actual practice.

Organicism, seeking a system in which democracy will be practicable and thus more easily practiced, conceives democracy as a system of collective self-control. It opposes both anarchy, in which persons are uncontrolled, and tyranny, in which individuals do not share in the control. Democracy prevails to the extent that each individual shares in the consensus and is controlled by the power of the consensus exactly as much as he needs to be. Although, in practice, no one can get all he wants, whether through or apart from government, it is possible for people to adapt their desires, and the capacities of governments for serving these desires, to each other more effectively. Since men are equal in some respects and unequal in others, no government is highly democratic unless it responds sensitively to both the equalities and inequalities among men. Sovereignty is always incomplete. Capacities for different kinds of sovereignty vary. A good democracy will seek to promote fitness of varying capacities for sovereignty to varying opportunities for sovereignty, and vice versa. For example, voting qualifications based upon demonstration of insight into group nature and group needs would be more sensitive than those based upon reaching twenty-one years of age, something automatically achieved by moron and genius alike. Since some persons are capable of more sovereignty through groups because they are capable of more interdependence with others, a political system becomes more democratic to the extent that it provides more freedom through government for these persons, as well as more freedom from government for those with lesser capacities of this sort.

Hierarchy

Shifting attention from individual-group relations to group-group relations, we may note that no political philosophy is adequate until it somehow has accounted for the relations of different governments to each other, especially since the problems involved in group-group relationships seem to be becoming both more complex and more important as history proceeds. Not only do we have more levels of organized government extending over larger and larger geographical areas (family, community, state, nation, world) but also increasing varieties of specialized interests which have become politically incorporated, not only within specific groups (state, nation, world) but crossing to boundaries of, and interacting with the functions of, governments of different levels. Problems arise concerning the relative autonomy of such groups, how sovereignty should be distributed among them, and what principles should be applied in dealing with conflicts between them. Some of the bitterest fighting has occurred over questions, for example, of "states' rights versus national rights" and, now, of "national sovereignty versus world government." Again we find that men are divided. Clues to their divisions may be discovered in their basic political philosophies.

In any political hierarchy, the totalitarians naturally consider the highest group supreme in political power, lower groups having been delegated only that power needed in performing certain specific functions for the supreme authority. The lowest official serves merely as a minor representative of the highest power. Individualism reverses this doctrine by insisting that (if groups have any political power at all, because voluntarily delegated to them by individuals) lower groups, those closest to the individual in degree of intimacy or geographical area, naturally are prior in political power to those less intimate or more distant. "A man's home is his castle"—a sacred precinct rightly defended with arms against all intruders. However, presumably, it is his wife's castle too, and his children's, though men differ as to whether other members of their families are considered separate individuals or part of their private property. Some are more dictatorial at home than abroad, and others who practice political tyranny are democratic at home. Students of human nature can find plenty to fascinate them in examining the curious mixtures of relative dictatorial-democratic policies of those who entertain varying views of family rights versus community rights, community rights versus state rights, state rights versus national rights, and national rights versus world rights. An individualist who, for whatever reason, happens to identify himself with his state, and who ardently defends the sovereignty of his state against that of his nation, can often be embarrassed by pointing out both his lack of loyalty to his underlying individualism (as opposed to statism) and his lack of patriotism. Individualists who begin to admit that there are levels of groups and that groups have some, even if delegated, sovereignty soon find themselves in difficulties, theoretical and practical, which help to convince them that as more levels of groups come to exist more evil is bound to result. Since each higher-level group merely adds its burden of law and taxation (i.e., more loss of liberty), such higher levels are to be consistently repudiated—unless they appear to have some negative value, i.e., prevent further destruction of individualism.

Organicists accept a hierarchy of political groups as a natural development because they recognize the multiplication of governments as a normal consequence of the growth of human interests—as people become increasingly interdependent on larger and wider scales. If all political systems are democratic (i.e., are systems of collective self-control efficiently fitted to the needs of persons), then more and higher levels of government may function as means to additional freedom for those capable of participating in them. However, as always, the dangers involved in the tendency of groups to control individuals more than they want to be controlled may also multiply as levels of government increase. The problems inherent in the fight against both too much tyranny and too much anarchy recur at each new level. It is much more difficult to maintain democracy at many levels than at only one or two (though not as difficult for those genuinely inspired with democratic ideals as nondemocrats think). But, so long as the kind of freedom and welfare achieved at higher levels of interdependencies results in more benefit than evil, organicists will consider the trouble worth while.

However, in addition to levels of democracy, there should be also democracy of levels. That is, since each level represents a stable area of interest of individuals, each embodies a part of those individuals. When governments of different levels compete with each other, their competition may be detrimental to individual sovereignty. For, if one level should exercise such control over other levels as to hamper their more efficient exercise of self-control, this one level becomes, to that extent, a tyrannical hindrance to individual sovereignty. Each level of social control should be maintained if, and because, it functions as a better means of self-control than other levels. Democracy of levels exists to the extent that each level of government serves the various needs of individuals for such multi-level sovereignty as they desire. Troubles arise from conflicts between levels for disproportionate parts of the needed political power. Evils of formalism and disorganization, or of cultural lag, which tend to become more serious in the larger secondary groups, become even greater where there is friction between the cultural inertia of two larger levels of government. Additional difficulties come from the fact that, if democracy must account both for equalities and inequalities, then democracy of levels involves recognizing some degree of equality for all levels of government and, at the same time, such differences as are involved in the actual differences in the kinds of control they are called upon to exercise. Furthermore, these relative equalities and inequalities also change from time to time, both historically and in the life growth of each individual—this latter being influenced somewhat by the relative effectiveness of educational induction of persons into larger social freedoms. But, if persons are really interdependent, at many levels, they can hardly ignore their own needs for self-control through many levels, i.e., some sort of hierarchy, of government.

In the foregoing, we have neglected to mention the political philosophy of the dualist who, believing in two realms of existence, the material (civil) and spiritual (ecclesiastical), must have two systems of government, one for control over men's natural interactions and one for government of their supernatural relations. The difficulties inherent in metaphysical dualism [10] appear here all over again, perhaps in an aggravated form. For, difficult as it is to explain the interaction of separated souls and bodies, even more difficulties are added in attempts to explain the relative superiority of power when there is conflict between civil and religious authority. Those who have their distinctions between the secular and sacred clearly marked off may, with relative ease, "render unto Caesar the things that are Caesar's and unto God the things that are God's," but, for most dualists, any authority responsible for clarifying such distinctions is likely to be either a civil or an ecclesiastical authority, but not both, for if there were some authority over both, their dualism would break down again. Usually dualists abandon their strictness of view by considering either their ecclesiastic authority superior, in which case they surrender their political dualism as ultimately inferior to a theocratic totalitarianism, or hold that their civil system is superior in political power, no matter what non-political power churches, whose political status is something determined by legalized incorporation by the civil state, may have. Organicism accepts the view that, in so far as there are some religious functions best served by ecclesiastic organizations, there are some phases of control which rest solely with such organizations, but, like all specialized agencies, these find their origin, nature, and purpose within an organic society upon which they depend as much or more than such society depends upon them, and which, thus, have their control functions conditioned by all other kinds of control functions organic to such society.

[10] See Ch. 13.

Law

What is law, and how is it related to government? Political law pertains to established rules of dealing with control situations which are considered binding upon citizens, and such that violation is punishable by appropriate penalties. But which is primary, government or law? If governments have power to enact laws, whence comes this authority? In constitutionally established governments, such authority comes from a constitution which is itself a primary legal document providing what powers a government shall have. But from what does a constitution derive its authority? A written constitution is merely a piece of paper unless there is willingness on the part of citizens and their governments to support it effectively by guiding their actual behavior in accordance with it. Of course, there are de facto governments coming into existence by military force, but these, too, can remain effective only so long as people are willing to support them and to tolerate them at any cost, in preference to rejecting them.

Law and government are organically related. No government can last long without law and no law can endure effectively without enforcement. Each depends upon the other. Both are primary, each in its own way. Except for temporary lags, both arise together and cease together. Sometimes our concern focuses more upon the failure of a government to adhere to its constitutional limitations, and at others we are more troubled about the failure of a constitution to provide a government with as much authority as is needed to deal with actual welfare problems. In addition to these two most serious concerns, i.e., about governments extending their powers or neglecting their responsibilities unconstitutionally, and about constitutional obsolescence, most of our political attention is occupied with changes in governments (elections or coups) and with changes in legislation and legislative enforcement. The term "law" covers both governmental enactments and enactment of government.

What is the purpose of law? Either a governing power must deal with each specific control situation as it arises, or it must develop some general principles for dealing with control situations in so far as they can be grouped into kinds. To the extent that situations remain the same, if a problem of one kind has been solved rightly at one time, this solution can then serve for all other problems of this same kind at other times. The use of legal precedent is justified, to the extent that previous decisions were wise and the situations remain the same. However, since both these ifs are questionable, legislators, policemen, judges, and prison authorities are plagued constantly with the problem of the applicability of general laws to specific situations. On the one hand, many control problems are the same in many respects. Therefore, what is good in one situation is good in another and justice demands sameness in treatment. But, also, each problem is in some sense unique, and thus each requires specific consideration. However, in so far as law enactment is concerned, it is possible to consider only the general similarities, for legislators themselves can hardly be on hand to consider each case separately. If they were, then law would become less necessary. But if laws can be concerned only with the general, then attention to the unique aspects must suffer, unless provisions are enacted for dealing with such unique aspects. The situation is complicated by the fact that persons administering laws may have interpretations of the meanings of the words used in legislation different from those originally intended. In fact, both administrators and legislators may differ among themselves as to the precise meanings of terms, making the nature of law dependent upon matters of semantics.

In complex societies, the need for division of labor in performing governmental functions tends to create a separation of powers among legislative, administrative, and judicial agencies with results harmful as well as beneficial, since some friction naturally develops between these different agencies. When powers are separated, some theory of their relative importance is involved. Political philosophers with totalitarian temperaments insist that one of the three, the legislature, the administration, or the judiciary, is primary, and the others subordinate, though different totalitarians can be found to disagree as to which is primary. Individualistic-minded philosophers, who have consented to endure government as a necessary evil, tend toward equal distribution of powers with a system of checks and balances among mutually restrictive, semi-autonomous branches of government. Organicism sees different branches as organically related, i.e., partly independent and partly dependent, each influencing the others and being influenced by them. Difficulties involved in fulfilling the purposes of law, i.e., trying to deal with specific situations by means of general rules, recur in each of the three branches:

Law enactment, even in systems committed to representative government, is entangled in the problem of what kinds of distribution of representation is best. Shall the legislative body consist of one, two, or many houses? Shall representatives be elected on bases of geographical area, population area, political organization of areas, economically well-integrated areas, caste, economic class, racial or national culture area, educational strata, special-interest groups, or social function? If the latter, which functionaries, e.g., farmers, merchants, teachers, physicians, ministers, bankers, etc., deserve the greatest proportion of representational power, or, if all functions are treated equally, how shall the obvious differences between some of them be justified? If there is more than one house, how shall power be distributed between them? Since, over long periods, there tend to be shifts in population, education, caste, political organization, and social function, how shall reapportionment of representation be accomplished? Since each person is in some sense a "whole person," whereas division of representational power tends to represent him in "fractions," the problem of regaining organically unified representation is fraught with continuing difficulties.

If we turn to the problem of sensitiveness of legislative representation to changing needs and opinions, then problems pertaining to the relative merits of regular elections versus elections when needed must be dealt with. Since governmental stability and adaptability tend to be contrary to each other, our philosophy must help us decide on one or the other, or induce us to put forth the effort needed to devise a new system. Shall people vote directly upon issues and for their representatives, or indirectly, through parties which are committed to a more or less consistent legislative policy? To what extent shall decisions by lower-level legislatures and higher-level legislatures affect each other when the problem, though belonging primarily to the lower house, also definitely belongs to the higher? Since the number of laws come to be so great that not even lawyers can keep up with them, at what point do we get too many laws, and what principles should determine how we shall let up after that?

For those persons concerned with the perpetuation of democracy, organically conceived, the problem of discovery and maintenance of majority rule is a basic one. "Since the principle of majority rule cannot be maintained long unless some system is devised to shift power from a dwindling majority to a growing minority, the rights of minorities must be fully protected. . . . The rights of real majorities are safe only if elections are uncoerced. This means that men must have opportunity to think for themselves, to express themselves freely, and to run for political office without jeopardizing their essential welfare. Regular elections must be provided for, and freedom from fear must be assured participants. Failure to want to guarantee civil liberties is one of the gravest dangers to the democratic ideal." [11]

Law enforcement is complicated by many sorts of administrative problems, all of which involve solutions in terms of certain philosophical outlooks. Different kinds of laws, e.g., pertaining to property ownership, taxation, fraud, violence, health, education, corporate responsibility, traffic ordinances, civil rights, etc., may require different kinds of specialists in enforcement. As these multiply, their interrelations result in problems requiring further legislation. Furthermore, there may be many distinct steps in law enforcement—e.g., informing citizens concerning laws, detection of violation, apprehension of violaters, custody of violaters until trial, appearance for court trial, conduct during trial, administration of punishment, transportation of criminals, imprisonment, release, parole, and rehabilitation—each step involving specialists and requiring legislation concerning the distribution of their duties and appropriate penalties for dereliction of duty.

How these problems arise depends partly upon whether the political system is based primarily upon a party system (with "to the victor belong the spoils" ideals) or to a civil service system (in which party activity may be prohibited). Although the interpretation of the law is a function delegated specifically to the judiciary, no administrator can avoid acting upon some philosophy of law interpretation; otherwise, the policeman would not always know when to make an arrest. However, while administrators must be partly judges, judges must administer control, at least over order in their courtrooms; and judges may declare legislation unconstitutional, self-contradictory, or inadequate, and thus force legislation, whereas administrators must provide salaries for both legislators and judges if their services are to continue. Thus, when powers are distributed, an organic relation—semi-independence and semi-dependence—continues to exist among the branches.

Law interpretation is perhaps the aspect of government least understood, not only by citizens, but also by legislators and administrators, at least as American society exists today. Even among judges and lawyers conflicting views prevail as to the function of those appointed interpreters of the law. Some are literalists, insisting that the letter of the law must apply. Others prefer more liberal interpretations, holding that the spirit or intent of the law is what must

[11] Bahm, *op. cit.*, p. 137. Also see Edwin Mims, *The Majority of the People*, Modern Age Book, New York, 1941, for an able account of the significance of the principle of minority rights.

be determined. Inherent in this controversy are views as to whether law is primary and, thus, something to which the citizen must submit, or whether the individual person is primary and, thus, something which the law is designed to serve. Since there are differences, also, in the views of judges and legislators, at times legislation intended literally is interpreted by liberal judges, whereas at others legislation intended liberally is interpreted by literal judges, sometimes with disastrous results.

Differences in more basic ethical theory (does rightness rest upon rights or rights upon rightness?) produce disagreements among lawyers, judges, jurymen, between higher and lower courts, as well as among legislators, policemen, wardens, and parole officers. Those easily fatigued by political intricacies may resort to short cuts: monastic isolationism, helpless submission to fate, chronic griping and self-pity, or day-dreaming about south sea isles where no political problems exist, or about utopias where everything is worked out to perfection. But people who are realistic enough to believe that problems can be solved only by working at them, and who reject dictatorial methods, still not only have to put forth effort in their endless grappling with their problems but also have to deal with them in terms of some philosophical perspective, clearly or confusedly defined.

Philosophies of law interpretation are complicated further by the fact that, since a crime is a violation of a law, the more laws we have the more criminals we tend to have. Repeal of any law would prevent conduct contrary to it from being a crime. Therefore, in a sense, our legislators are responsible for all crimes. However, some law is necessary, so legislators must keep clearly in mind the basic purpose of law enactment, if they are to produce more good than bad results. When legislators keep in mind the basic functions of law, they are more likely to allow some flexibility in interpretation by providing for minimum and maximum penalties, suspended sentences, indefinite sentences, and provisions for prevention, correction, and rehabilitation, etc., based upon judicial discretion. Judges, also, if they subscribe to correctional rather than retributive philosophies of justice, are inclined to delegate decisions regarding the methods of reforming criminals to prison and parole officers, especially when these include competent psychiatrists and social workers. When a judge is called upon to dispense justice in a political system suffering from multiplicities of cultural lag, a basic humane philosophy often serves the cause of justice better than an intricate knowledge of the letter of the law. The difficult job of deciding whether an individual has vio-

lated a law or whether a law has violated the individual is aggravated
by the fact that violations differ considerably in the seriousness of
their consequences, and that, moreover, laxity or undue severity in
enforcing some laws may produce disrespect for all law. A judge's
philosophy is of tremendous importance to his society.

Revolution

Since all societies, sooner or later, have to deal with the problem
of whether political changes shall be evolutionary or revolutionary,
gradual or abrupt, no political philosophy is adequate until it has
expressed principles pertaining to political transformation. Many
peoples today, in the United States, France, Russia, etc., are indoctrinated with political ideals born in historical revolutions. For example, the Declaration of Independence of the thirteen United States
of America, July 4, 1776, proclaims "that whenever any form of government becomes destructive of these ends, it is the right of the people
to alter or abolish it, and to institute new government, laying its
foundations on such principles and organizing its powers in such
form, as to them shall seem most likely to effect their safety and
happiness. . . . when a long train of abuses and usurpations . . .
evinces a design to reduce them under absolute despotism, it is their
right, it is their duty, to throw off such government, and to provide
new guards for their future security." However, "prudence will dic-
tate that governments long established should not be changed for
light and transient causes." If governments fail, for whatever reason,
to provide for gradual readjustments of distribution of power, taxation, or welfare, to meet changing needs, then revolution may be
expected.

Political philosophers have to consider whether anything can or
should be done to influence political processes toward either evolutionary or revolutionary steps. Of course, whether an event is the
one or the other depends upon whether it is considered a large or
small change, and this is partly a matter of point of view. From the
viewpoint of a totality, there can be no revolution short of changing
the totality into something else, which is impossible for a true totality.
From the point of view of any individualist, his coming into a power
that he formerly did not have, or his losing any which he previously
had, is revolutionary. For organicists, there can never be a complete
revolution, for something must remain through every change, and
selves of multilevel social organization may change at one or more

levels but never at all levels at one time. Revolution is always relative.

But every change is, in a limited sense, a revolution. When some readjustment becomes necessary, those who refuse to make small changes help to create a situation which will result eventually in larger changes, so reactionism tends to cause and justify radicalism. Likewise, however, radicalism tends to justify reactionism, for when some are so avid and hasty for changing to the new that they recklessly destroy old values, it is obvious to conservatives that such destructive evil needs to be destroyed. Organicism seeks to prevent both radicalism and reactionism because both of these, in trying to destroy each other, destroy some values. Organicism aims to be both conservative of proved values and progressive in achieving such new values as can be grown organically into changing social situations. Totalitarians say we ought never to revolt against anything except revolution itself. Individualists believe they should revolt whenever they can profit by revolution. Organicists are willing to revolt only when evolutionary methods break down.

When we are faced with revolution as a fact, then what do different philosophies recommend? If the revolution is conceived as a threat to the totality, revolutionaries are suppressed without compromise. If there is no threat to the totality, it is possible for totalitarians to look on both sides with equanimity. If individualists stand either to lose or gain all by revolution, they feel they ought either to suppress revolutionaries or to be revolutionaries accordingly. Organicists seek to make the best of a bad situation by partly submitting and partly preventing, trying to save both old and new values, i.e., to turn even a revolution into an evolution. If revolutions have a natural history,[12] organicists are likely to be mistakenly persecuted by both radicals and reactionaries during their respective reigns of terror. When a revolution has been accomplished, they will want to help pick up the pieces and heal the wounds as soon as possible.

But since it appears possible to prevent revolution by promoting appropriate evolution, organicists are committed to the attempt both to understand and to plan for political change, because this appears less costly in the long run, both in lives, personality problems, and in instrumental and cultural values. When political planning becomes a primary problem, again the various philosophies naturally advocate different solutions. Totalitarian temperaments want to plan every-

[12] Mabel A. Elliott and Frances E. Merrill, *Social Disorganization*, pp. 716–721. Harper & Bros., New York, 1934.

thing and to have a single master plan. Individualists can hardly consistently plan anything except to prevent political planning. Organicists recognize both that planning has its limitations and that planning is a fundamental need. To the extent that individual welfare can be improved by planning, planning should receive individual support. But "our obligation to obey the state endures only so long, and extends only so far, as it is achieving its purpose." [13] Beyond this, "resistance to the state" [14] and to state planning becomes a duty. Once planning becomes accepted as an appropriate political function, then problems concerning the distribution of planning functions arise. If, for example, there are three branches of government, should each have its separate planning agency or should there be one general planning office for all phases of government, or should some planning be done by both each branch and a general office? Some kinds of changes (e.g., changes in number of automobiles manufactured) can be planned more effectively than others (changes in population). Not all geographical areas, cultural areas, higher or lower level governments, or individuals can participate with equal willingness in planning attempts. Technological changes do not influence all parts of society uniformly. Needs for planning and skills or insights of persons serving as planning officials vary considerably. All in all, the job is difficult.

Democratic forms of government promise, as of today, to serve as the best means for promoting adaptation through evolution rather than through revolution, though even the various kinds of democratic forms suffer differently from cultural lag. When people are indoctrinated with ideals that are either too totalitarian or too individualistic, these extremities naturally reflect themselves in democratically arrived at decisions. Furthermore, some democratic systems may increasingly fail in practice to achieve democratic ideals. The fact that citizens are democratic at a national level is no guarantee that they will want to be democratic at a world level. People who are willing to undertake responsibilities for maintaining democratic practices in a small group where the task is not too difficult may surrender helplessly when the task becomes more complex, intricate, and exhausting.

Probably the most serious problems facing democratic peoples today are (1) how to extend democratic ideals and practices to

[13] Roberts, *op. cit.*, p. 321.
[14] *Ibid.*, p. 320.

more levels of government, especially the world level, and (2) how to adapt the mechanisms of government to the needs and facilities of rapidly advancing technological conditions. Whenever a need for developing a more complicated and sensitive system of governmental control is frustrated, because a theoretically amendable constitution becomes, in fact, impractical to amend, conditions ripen for both increased suffering due to technological maladjustments and for more dissatisfaction with the established system. Advocates of Technocracy [15] have pointed out many contemporary failures to make use of technological resources to improve human values, but, in doing so, they have ignored some of the more basic values involved in using democratic procedures to achieve improvement. Failure of Technocrats to be democratic in no way relieves democrats of responsibility for failure to evolve adequate technical planning in response both to needs and abilities for newer means of self-control. To the extent that changed technological conditions produce problems requiring political decisions in which people are controlled without sharing in the control, technological progress, in the hands of technically incompetent democrats, becomes an enemy of democracy. If democratic systems neglect to plan for more sensitive instruments of collective self-control, they are in danger of becoming totalitarian. Too much resistance to such collective planning may result in undemocratic planning. To prevent democratic evolution is to promote revolution.

[15] See Howard Scott and others, *Introduction to Technocracy*. John Day Co., New York, 1933.

· 28 ·

Economic
Philosophy

If economics, as a science, is concerned with wealth, its nature, origin, and ownership, then the economic philosopher must examine the presuppositions and other general characteristics of economic investigation. He will, among other things, have to compare different theories of the nature of wealth, how it originates, what constitutes ownership, and principles determining right distribution of property. He can hardly stop short of considering the different views concerning the nature and relative significance of the factors involved in production, consumption, and exchange in determining the nature of wealth and how it should be distributed. Since wealth is a necessary condition of human existence, no one can arrive at a completely adequate philosophy until he has not only developed an economic outlook, but has fitted it satisfactorily into the rest of his philosophy.

Since the consideration of economic problems contributes its own characteristic concerns as to what is important, one is hardly justified in merely deducing his economic philosophy from his metaphysics, epistemology, axiology, or other phases of his philosophy. A study of economic theories may be as good a way as any to be initiated into philosophizing and into the difficulties involved in trying to decide between conflicting views. A history of economic thought can be a good introduction to philosophy, though like any other introduction through special fields, such as ethics, epistemology, or philosophy of education, it may fail to lead the student into sufficient comprehensiveness of vision and interest.

Since economic philosophy is so intimately related to political philosophy, specifically, and social philosophy, more generally, sooner or later one must deal with the controversy, "Which is more important, the political or the economic?" Of course, different theories of the nature of wealth and of government may arrive at conflicting conclusions concerning such relative importance. But, also, opposed presuppositions concerning their importance naturally have a bearing upon how wealth and control are conceived. Those who believe that production, consumption, and ownership of wealth are determined primarily by the established system of social control tend to think of government as primary, wealth as secondary, in importance. On the other hand, those who see that a man's power to participate in government depends upon his economic circumstances can give good reasons for holding that economic factors are the primary determinants both of the individual's ability to participate in government and of the kinds of government that are likely to prevail.

But, as in every other area of thought, one can mistake his initial assumptions and conclusions for primary ones. Those who accept an economic interpretation of history as the sole basis, rather than as one basis, are in error, just as much as those who take the religious, the epistemological, the metaphysical, the aesthetic, or the political, etc., as the only basis. All essential conditions of existence are equally essential, for if any one were missing, existence would cease. However, it is true that sometimes one and sometimes another becomes more significant, so far as purposes of change and control are concerned, and, as a consequence, we are not without grounds for considering one or the other as relatively more important at different times. In any organism, different kinds of growth naturally take place differently at different times and under differing circumstances, but, if the organism continues to live, each essential factor continues to exercise its necessary influence upon the whole structure and whenever its particular contribution is neglected or weakened, the whole becomes weaker and in danger of disorganization.

Wealth

If economics pertains to wealth, then its basic philosophical question is: What is wealth? Derived from "weal" or "well," the science of wealth pertains not only to "wellth" but also "illth," not only to goods but also to evils. Consequently, economics rests upon axiology, for one can hardly understand production, consumption, and ownership of goods unless he first understands something about the nature of goods and goodness. The first job of the economic philosopher, one often overlooked by superficial students, is to achieve an adequate theory of values and disvalues, both intrinsic and instrumental.[1]

[1] See Ch. 22.

Since different axiological presuppositions permeate each economic philosophy, some controversies can be understood, and some problems, both theoretical and practical, can be solved, only by specific attention to axiological premises. Not only does the economist need to distinguish between intrinsic and instrumental values, and to develop satisfactory theories concerning each, but he must not forget these conclusions when he becomes absorbed in the complexities of the details to which he must devote himself.

On the other hand, anyone inductively seeking an axiological theory in the first place can hardly ignore economic values as part of his data, lest he arrive at a hasty and inadequate generalization. Not all economic philosophers agree about this. Some insist that the definition of economic value should be deduced strictly from the definition of value in general. Other specialists limit their conclusions about economic value to data drawn from purely economic investigations, lest wider considerations carry them too far afield. Organicists are committed to remaining unsatisfied with either axiological or economic conclusions until their interdependence becomes clear.

Of the many distinguishable kinds of value, our discussion will be limited to four: intrinsic value, instrumental value, economic value, and price. In addition to the difficulties involved in tending to confuse, or to fail to clarify the distinctions between, intrinsic and instrumental value noted in Chapter 22, there are others inherent in the distinctions between instrumental value and economic value and between economic value and price. Also, of course, these difficulties have influenced theorists to draw different conclusions about these distinctions as a consequence. Hasty axiologists may lump price and economic value together for convenience, whereas economists may feel no need for distinguishing between intrinsic and economic value.

One economist speaks as follows: " 'Value' is a term that has many meanings. In ordinary speech it is commonly attributed to anything that is of use in the satisfaction of wants. In this sense there are not only economic but also political, social, aesthetic, ethical, and religious values of life. The meaning which all such values have in common is perhaps best expressed by such words as 'worth,' 'esteem,' 'usefulness,' or 'utility.' But while economic values is a species that belongs to this broad genus of want-satisfying goods, it is something more than mere utility." [2] If we interpret "utility," or "want-satisfying

---

[2] William H. Kiekhofer, *Economic Principles, Problems, and Policies,* third edition, p. 410. D. Appleton-Century Co., New York, 1946. Used by permission of Appleton-Century-Crofts.

goods" to mean "instrumental value"—there are many who define the term more narrowly—then the distinction between the capacity of things to serve as instruments leading to satisfaction and the actual satisfaction is ignored, even if implied. Since not all economic products, for example, actually produce satisfactions which they could if circumstances permitted, and since subjective factors influence the actual satisfactions (intrinsic values), it is a mistake either to identify or to equate utility imputed to an instrument with the intrinsic value actually experienced. This mistake then tends to be carried over into all other aspects of economic theory dependent upon basic value investigations.

However, our concern here is more with the nature of economic value and price, and with the consequences of confusions regarding them. "In economic literature, unless qualifying adjectives are used, 'value' usually means 'exchange value,'"[3] though also "economic values may be thought of as existing antecedent to exchange."[4] The problem of potential versus actual economic value can hardly be solved adequately apart from solution to the more general problem of the interrelations between actuality and potentiality, but most economists today, like most other specialists, especially those who happen to have developed antimetaphysical biases, have to limp along with puzzling and embarrassingly inadequate value theories.

What is economic value? "Scarcity is the earmark of an economic good—scarcity, that is, relatively to demand."[5] Air, though an instrumental value essential to life, has no economic value unless its supply can be limited. But also "value may be defined as the power of a good to command other goods in exchange."[6] Three "conditions go to make up the value of anything—utility and scarcity"[7] and, although this is often omitted from formal definitions—exchangeability. Now, since both scarcity and exchangeability are functions of multiplicities of factors, economic theorists need to decide whether economic value is a fixed and stable property of goods or something fluctuating dynamically in consequence of variations in their conditioning factors. Those economists who subscribe to a static meta-

[3] *Ibid.*, p. 411.

[4] Ibid., p. 410.

[5] F. W. Taussig, *Principles of Economics*, Vol. I, second revised edition, p. 5. The Macmillan Co., New York, 1919.

[6] Lewis A. Froman, *Principles of Economics*, p. 14. Richard D. Irwin, Chicago, 1940.

[7] *Ibid.*

physics in which eternal intrinsic values are stable, in which the utility of an instrument is consequently fixed, may simply deduce, in principle, if not in practice, what the exchange value and fair price of a utility should be. However, whether influenced by the development of dynamic kinds of metaphysics or whether by discovering dynamic complexities in economic phenomena (which have metaphysical implications that may not be understood), economists today tend to be aware of the temporary and fluctuating nature of economic values. Awareness of this dynamic nature promotes emphasis upon investigation into the factors of production, consumption, and exchange, as together determining the actual or potential economic value of a commodity.

The persistent pursuit by economists for understanding these factors is of inestimable service to mankind. In so far as man is an economic animal, a man cannot understand himself until he understands economics. But today, many economists, like too many other scientists, suffer from "scientism," a tendency both to interpret science too narrowly (too materialistically and too mathematically) and to assume that science, so interpreted, is all-sufficient in interpreting reality. Materialistic scientists tend to believe that the proper way to satisfy man's natural desire for certainty is to analyze phenomena mathematically. Economics, a field in which so many phenomena are easily and necessarily subjected to statistical analyses, offers a natural field for those so inclined. The development of price as a symbol of value, and the relative ease with which such symbols can be manipulated mathematically, has tended to convince those who believe that reality can be captured only in mathematical correlations that economics is not only an exact science but, even, the basic science.

What is price? "While the exchange value of a good could be expressed in terms of every other good for which it might be exchanged, money serves as the most convenient common denominator. Accordingly price is exchange value expressed in terms of money. The fact that we can reduce all exchange values to money prices enables us to compare values of the most diverse sorts." [8] This view exhibits both the values of economics in developing a very useful kind of exactitude and the viciousness of overdoing a good thing—for it is false to say that we can reduce all exchange values to money prices, since not only were there exchanges before money was invented but, also, people often exchange priceless favors. Neither intrinsic, nor

[8] Kiekhofer, *op. cit.*, p. 411.

instrumental, nor even economic values can be represented exactly by any price, not only because some economic values are priceless, but especially because the introduction of money and other price-mechanisms into economic processes itself becomes a factor (a multiplicity of factors) influencing both the nature of the process and, consequently, the nature of economic and other values. Nevertheless, the facility with which price fluctuations lend themselves to price analysis makes it irresistible for some to jump to the conclusion that price itself is the locus of economic value, and to define economics as "the science of price." [9]

Not all economists succumb to such extremes, however. "On the contrary it is the great defect of the price theory of economic value and the great embarrassment of orthodox economic thinking that price makes economic value seem very much more definite and quantitative than it is." [10] "The quantitative certainty of price is an illusion, the very illusion from which economic thinking is now struggling to free itself." [11] Organic relationships exist between price and intrinsic values. Not only is there some hierarchical relationship between intrinsic values, instrumental values, economic values, and prices,[12] but there exists also a reverse hierarchy in which price-tags influence our conceptions of economic value, utility, and intrinsic value. People sometimes actually experience greater enjoyment when consuming higher-priced goods which have been deliberately marked up.[13] Catering to class consists partly in convincing customers that a higher price must mean greater value. Although some think that "the economist is not concerned with ends as such" because "economics is entirely neutral between ends," [14] others believe that the economist cannot escape being involved in the nature of ends because "price as we say 'sets a value' on goods and services" [15] in such a way as to determine what some of our ends shall be. Although it is true that the problem of the nature of human ends is not the economist's primary concern, it is false to say that economics is neutral, for it both

[9] Clarence E. Ayres, *The Theory of Economic Progress*, Ch. I. University of North Carolina Press, Chapel Hill, 1944.

[10] *Ibid.*, p. 226.

[11] *Ibid.*, p. 225.

[12] See diagram in Kiekhofer, *op. cit.*, p. 412.

[13] Cf. Thorstein Veblen, *The Theory of the Leisure Class*, esp. Chs. 5 and 6.

[14] Lionel Robbins, *An Essay on the Nature and Significance of Economic Science*, pp. 24, 25. St. Martin's Press, New York, and The Macmillan Co., London, 1948.

[15] Ayres, *op. cit.*, p. 226.

grows out of and determines human ends.   To ignore these facts is to shrink and shirk some of the economist's functions and to limit falsely both his scientific, philosophical, and practical tasks.

Varying views as to the extent of these functions result in disagreements concerning the relation of economics to politics, or of wealth to control.   For, the shrinking of economic philosophies induces those persons, who think they, as specialists, are free from larger obligations, to try to justify a kind of ivory-tower existence; otherwise, they could not be neutral.   On the other hand, awareness of organic interdependence of prices and political power leads to concern, both about the responsibilities of economists for explaining the influence of economic processes upon the nature and duties of government, and about the need for conscientiousness regarding political control over the effects of economic processes upon human welfare.   In a day when technological advances, not only in productive areas, but also in complicated exchange systems, have become the principal determinants of men's predominant desires, a shirking of responsibility for preventing or removing evils due to economic causes is like a neglect to diagnose a disease, which will take its toll in greater discomfort when its aggravated consequences can no longer be ignored.   "If economic value means anything at all, its meaning is that of a gradual and continuous realization of a more effective organization of the technological life process." [16]

Before leaving the problem of wealth or value altogether, perhaps it is well to look at some theories of the origin of economic value. Totalitarian types of philosophy hold that economic value as well as all other types of value originate in the totality.   Theistic totalitarians derive their theory of economic value ultimately from their theology. Political totalitarians see "one great social unit as dominating the valuation process through authority. . . .   On the other hand, the extreme individualist begins with the assumption that individuals are independent and virtually unrelated, the individual appearing as a non-social atom, acting freely and higgling with other individual atoms according to the force of self-interest." [17]   Historically, individualism's theory of value has been associated with hedonism [18]—the view that since value consists in pleasures and pains, economic mo-

[16] *Ibid.,* p. 228.
[17] Lewis H. Haney, *Value and Distribution,* p. 20.   Appleton-Century-Crofts, New York, 1939.
[18] See pp. 278–279.

tives have their sole basis in these pleasures and pains—and, consequently, with the labor theory of value: ". . . the quantity of labor commonly employed in acquiring or producing any commodity is the only circumstance which can regulate the quantity of labor which it ought commonly to purchase, command, or exchange for." [19]

Various difficulties with labor theories of value have given rise to a long history of attempts to modify but retain hedonistic bases for economic values. An outstanding result of this is the marginal utility theory which is based upon the law of diminishing returns: "The greater the quantity of the matter of property a man is already in possession of, the less the quantity of happiness he receives by the addition of another quantity of the matter of property, to a given amount." [20] Value is not inherent in products. "It is relative to wants, and too much of a good brings disutility. Utility decreases as the quantity increases. There is thus a difference between total utility and degree of utility, the degree of utility of successive units decreasing while the total utility increases." [21] "Labor once spent has no influence on the future value of any article." [22]

Increasing awareness of the factors of production, i.e., land, labor, capital, and management, however, reduces the significance of labor as the sole cause of economic value. Laws of supply and demand were discovered which operated naturally, impersonally, automatically, to determine price and value, and, consequently, economics became an independent, self-sustaining, natural science. The marginal utility theory developed into an equilibrium theory which, as one recent writer puts it, is based upon "a frankly dualistic position in philosophy. . . . 'forces' tending toward 'equilibrium' seem to be strictly consistent with the concept of two realities, mind and matter—man and his environment. Just so, the concept of value as an equilibrium between demand and supply is defensible only on the assumption of the reality and independent importance of mind and matter. . . . Values arise out of this process of adjustment. . . ." [23] Whether dualistic or materialistic or deistic, "in this view economic order is an

[19] Adam Smith, *The Wealth of Nations*, Book I, Ch. VI.

[20] Jeremy Bentham.

[21] Lewis H. Haney, *History of Economic Thought*, revised edition, p. 535. The Macmillan Co., New York, 1911, 1920.

[22] William Stanley Jevons, *Theory of Political Economy*, p. 159. The Macmillan Co., New York, 1871, 1931.

[23] Haney, *Value and Distribution*, p. 41.

automatic equilibrium of naturally opposing forces. Competition of
buyers forces prices up. Competition of sellers forces prices down.
The 'normal' price—the point of equilibrium—is the point at which
these forces cancel. Thus 'normal price' means competitive price." [24]
As these ideals have worked in practical American politics, it was
held that a depression and the uncomfortable phenomenon of business cycles can be cured only by a "return to normalcy," in which
independent and automatic economic processes are freed from all
external interferences.

However, another school of economic thought, unfortunately called
"institutionalism," because it holds that institutions or cultural factors
of all sorts influence economic processes, points out that constant interference or interaction between economic and other processes is
also natural and normal. "In analyzing the structure and functioning
of the economy, the cultural economist makes use of the principle of
interrelatedness. According to this principle no part of the economic
system can be adequately explained until its relations to the rest of
the system have been fully explored. Each aspect of the economy
must therefore be analyzed within the context of the cultural whole
within which it functions." [25] Accepting the "doctrine of organic
unity," [26] institutionalists deny "the automatic organization of our economic system. . . . Since men practice coercion rather than competition, since great and small power differentials make absence of economic conflicts between political equals the exception rather than the
rule, the basic situation premised by standard theory does not exist." [27]
Whereas previous theory held that money is a "mere convenience for
facilitating exchange," [28] institutionalists demonstrate the many ways
in which "money is also much more than that." [29] "An awareness of
the capacity of institutions to change is an awareness that the rules
of the economic game may be changed. . . . Economic conflicts thus
take place on the political field as well as in the market place." [30]
Consequently, economic science and social philosophy cannot be

[24] Clarence E. Ayres, *The Problem of Economic Order*, p. 55. Rinehart and
Co., New York, 1938.

[25] Allan G. Gruchy, *Modern Economic Thought*, p. 24. Prentice-Hall, New
York, 1947. Reprinted by permission of the publisher.

[26] John S. Gambs, *Beyond Supply and Demand*, p. 24. Columbia University
Press, New York, 1946.

[27] *Ibid.*, p. 15.

[28] John Stuart Mill, *Principles of Political Economy*, Book III, Ch. VII.

[29] Gambs, *op. cit.*, p. 18.

[30] *Ibid.*, p. 23.

separated without falsification of both. "The two must be organically related." [31]

Ownership

What is ownership? Ownership is a status of owning. If a thing is one's own, then he owns it. Since ownership thus pertains to self, different views of self yield opposing ideas of ownership. Since individualists conceive selves as wholly separate existences, they consider ownership to be exclusive. If a thing is yours, then it is not mine. Totalitarians see selves as submerged parts of a totality, more owned than owners, but owners nevertheless. If anything is God's or the state's, then it is yours as much as mine. Organicists, who see selves as social, hold that ownership is inclusive as well as exclusive. Some things are yours alone, but others, many others, are ours. Both joint ownership and exclusive ownership are ownership. Individualists fight multiplication of levels of groups because each new level of group ownership subtracts from what each individual can own exclusively. Totalitarians reluctantly participate in multiplied levels because each level of ownership detracts from the completeness of ownership by the whole. Organicists welcome new levels of ownership when and if they increase the amount of ownership by individuals.

What is distribution? Wealth may be distributed either by dividing it or by sharing it. Individualists want to divide it. They abhor socialism because sharing the wealth means, for them, dividing what they have and giving some to others. Thus, when one shares the wealth he loses unless he was very poor to begin with. Totalitarians feel that more wealth owned by the totality means more wealth owned by individuals through sharing ownership of the totality. Organicists seek to share much more wealth through joint ownership, for the more one shares, or shares in, the more wealth he owns, whenever such ownership is better for him. Organicists are unwilling to set up an unalterable plan for distribution because even the principles for evaluating just distribution are themselves subject to evolution.

The problem of distribution becomes more complicated with the emergence of each new owning group. Complications entail consideration of relative readjustment of shares of ownership between new and old groups, in accordance with criteria which are at least as difficult to come by as those related to distribution among individuals.

[31] Eric Roll, *A History of Economic Thought,* revised and enlarged, p. 556. Prentice-Hall, New York, 1946.

Criteria are even more difficult to achieve when the group is a higher-level group which itself is in process of growth and readjustment. Efforts to establish criteria are plagued also by tendencies which need restraining, such as: wanting to own more, or less, than one (either individual or group) has capacity for owning; devoting too much or too little of one's (either individual or group) efforts to economic functions; considering persons or groups too much or too little either as owner or owned (for persons and groups serve also, in a measure, as economic resources or instrumental values); condoning too much or little private versus public ownership; depending too much or little upon each particular significant criterion for distribution; setting maximum or minimum limitations on individual incomes too high or low; being too exacting or loose about preciseness of distributive justice; conceiving ownership too simply or complexly; and insisting too much upon experimentalism [32] as against traditionalism in ownership systems.

Perhaps some consideration is needed, before leaving economic philosophy, of capitalism and communism. Although interpretation and evaluation of actual governmental systems, such as the United States and Soviet Russia, is quite outside the scope of this philosophy text, readers may feel a bit more comfortable if some comment is made, especially since organicism claims that organic relations hold between theory and practice. Meaning by "communism" any philosophy committed to preference for collective as against individual ownership, extremely idealized as insistence upon complete collective ownership, and by "capitalism" any philosophy favoring individual as against collective ownership, we may observe that neither the United States nor Soviet Russia embodies these doctrines in a completely consistent manner.

The Constitution of the United States, aiming to "promote the general welfare," nowhere commits itself either to capitalistic or to communistic interpretations of property ownership. It provides that Congress shall have power to dispose of "property belonging to the United States" (Article 4, Sec. 3). Never without some government ownership, the United States has, since 1914, undergone rapid socialization of economic functions, establishing at least twenty-eight new federal

---

[32] Extreme experimentalists often overlook the facts (1) that the experiment of maintaining a tradition is a kind of experimentalism and that support of a tradition of experimentalism is a kind of traditionalism and (2) that experimentalism is itself an experiment (one who considers experimentalism itself as an experiment is, in a sense, more experimentalistic than one who does not).

corporations in the eight years, 1929–1936, for example.[33]   Not only are governmental agencies still multiplying, but, what is commonly overlooked, the system has long been gradually shifting from individual to private enterprise, where the great bulk of the wealth and income is owned by private corporations.[34]   This shift to corporate ownership, which is a kind of group ownership, has become recognized as providing such superior economic advantage for its members that pyramiding of corporations and monopoly have become illegal in some instances.   Token attempts at trustbusting, public subsidization of little business, and legalization of labor unions as rightful collective bargaining agencies, imply recognition that the failure of individuals to compete as equals against corporations is threatening a collapse of the system.   The citizens of the United States could elect to adopt communistic policies under their Constitution, but present sentiment reveals very little inclination to do so.

The Constitution of the Union of Socialist Soviet Republics is explicitly communistic: "The economic foundation of the USSR consists of the Socialist system of economy and Socialist ownership of the implements and means of production, firmly established as a result of the liquidation of the capitalist system of economy, the abolition of private ownership of the implements and means of production and the abolition of exploitation of man by man."   Yet "alongside the Socialist system of economy, which is the dominant form of economy in the USSR, the law allows small private economy of individual peasants and handicraftsmen based on individual labor and excluding the exploitation of the labor of others.   The right of personal property of citizens in their income from work and in savings, in their home and auxiliary household economy, in objects of domestic and household economy, in objects of personal use and comfort, as well as the right of inheritance of personal property of citizens, is protected by law" (Articles 9 and 10).

The extent to which individual enterprise prevails in practice in the Soviet Union is not commonly known in the United States.   Evolution in both theory and practice has taken place and may be expected to continue.   If Soviet policies are to be interpreted in terms of Marxist doctrine, then the present "dictatorship of the proletariat" is to be followed by a "withering away of the state" because "the

[33] See list in William F. Ogburn and Meyer F. Nimkoff, *Sociology*, pp. 763–764.

[34] Cf. *Final Statement* of the Temporary National Economic Committee, March 11, 1941, p. 9.

state" is "the organization of violence for the suppression of some class" [35] and in a "classless society" there are no classes to suppress. Although Marxism assumes that, when the evils of capitalism are done away with, everything will automatically turn out for the best, in the absence of any blueprint for either actually achieving demise of the proletarian state or as to how people will go about achieving "the free development of each," [36] conflicting theories as to future policy may be expected. If absence of "the state" means absence of all government, then the Marxist goal is still a kind of anarchism which even the most anarchistic of American individualists have, in practice, abandoned.

Organicistic doctrine holds that what is best in the way of government ownership as well as in governmental control is a matter that has to be worked out experimentally, and is something that changes from time to time, but that the extremes of no government (and thus no government ownership) and complete government ownership are alike both undesirable and impractical. Neither communism, in its extreme form, nor capitalism, in its extreme form, nor dualism, in its extreme form, will work. By "dualism" here is meant a politically established economic system based upon two classes, capital and labor, each distinct and independent of each other. Although laboring and managerial functions are distinguishable, organic relations between them seem to preclude considering them as completely independent agencies. Managing is a kind of labor and one can hardly labor without managing something, especially in more intricate systems. However, what precisely these relationships should be and what exactly should be accepted policy regarding individual versus group ownership is something which cannot be predetermined once for all. Organicism is committed to experimentalism, even to experimenting with experimentalism. The best kind of economy—both in theory and in practice—has not yet been fully worked out. Accepting the doctrine of "an open future," such that the future will really be somewhat different from the past, we should expect to continue to experiment with different forms of economy, adopting whichever seems best suited to particular times and places, yet keeping always open to and alert for newer possibilities, and newer necessities, as newer factors enter actually into functional determination of economic conditions.

[35] Nikolai Lenin, *The State and Revolution.*
[36] *The Communist Manifesto.*

·29·

Philosophy
of Education

Although it has been left to the last, philosophy of education is unsurpassed in importance as an area of philosophical investigation. If each person has been molded, either creatively or destructively, formally or informally, by educational policies, little can be more significant to his self-knowledge than insight into the philosophies underlying these policies. The relative importance of philosophies of education as compared with other phases of philosophy will depend upon how narrowly or broadly education is conceived. Some, who interpret it wholly in terms of local, mechanical, stimulus-response events, may consider education to be little more than a somewhat complicated and intimate example of mechanistic behavior. If the individual is held to be an eternal soul, education may be designed to test its fitness for, and to prepare it for, eternal life, or to purify it by helping to free it from the evil temptations of bodily existence. If the individual is considered a member of a species with specific but limited innate potentialities which deserve development, realization of these potentialities becomes the educational goal. If the individual is conceived as a growing organism with not only innate capacities but also with the ability to acquire new potentialities, educational goals come to include development of both inherited and acquired capacities.

In addition to those philosophies that limit the scope of education to individuals, there are those which treat education as primarily a social process, a means whereby a group or culture perpetuates itself, either exactly or with variations, through fashioning new citizens to carry on its existence, much as a body must have new cells to replace old ones if it is to survive. Still others find education to be an interactive process between persons and their groups, understandable only by insight into the nature of both as they influence and modify each other. However, the foregoing conceptions are still too narrow for those who propose the following. Dewey appears willing to expand philosophy of education to include all philosophy when he says that "philosophy may even be defined as general theory of education." [1] Since all fields of philosophical investigation have their significance ultimately only in terms of their bearing upon individual development, philosophy of education is inadequate when it stops short of considering all of the factors influencing the individual. Finally, we may lift our eyes to glimpse the cosmic nature of education. "Education is a world-process; it is the world at work developing a man into the fullness of his stature." [2] Education may be looked upon as part of the process whereby nature, for naturalists, or God, for theists, molds itself through creating mankind, in which it is immanent, and through which it expresses itself as personal.

We shall not here propose limitations upon how extensively education should be conceived. Each view deserves its hearing. Two dangers, however, need to be avoided. The first is the inclination of those persons who derive their educational philosophy solely from a study of educational practices, without considering its relation to other philosophical fields. Secondly, there is the tendency of philosophers whose primary interests lie in other fields to deduce and recommend a philosophy of education without having considered all the relevant facts, which can be observed and generalized only by those persons actually acquainted with practical teaching difficulties. This latter is especially serious when the philosopher is satisfied with sectarian assumptions and convinced of their exceptional truth. Whoever is able to evade both dangers may find in philosophy of education a most suitable starting point for induction into broader philosophical studies.

Contributions

Risking the second danger, we may point out some of the contributions which each philosophical area and its conflicting viewpoints make to the problems constituting philosophy of education. To be fully adequate, a philosophy of education has to decide between all the major issues which have been raised in this book. "Since knowledge is the stock and trade of education, it is easy to understand that a philosophy of education must be based on an adequate considera-

[1] John Dewey, *Democracy and Education*, p. 383. The Macmillan Co., New York, 1916.

[2] Herman H. Horne, *The Philosophy of Education*, p. 259. The Macmillan Co., New York, 1904.

tion of epistemology." [3] Whether one considers the aims of education to lead primarily to reflective (think before you act) or unreflective (good habits or automatic reactions) knowledge, or how much of each, will make a difference in his teaching methods. Likewise, whether one favors subjectivism or realism, rationalism or empiricism, dogmatism or scepticism, and exact or intuitive knowledge, will largely determine his goals and methods. The educator has to decide how far he shall emphasize "intellectual training" versus "character building," [4] or knowledge of facts versus valuational attitudes. He will have to deal with the problem of which is more important: "first-hand experience" or "second-hand experience." [5]

Turning to metaphysics, "nearly all arguments to settle fundamental conflicts in educational practice, if continued long and penetratingly enough, will be found to have an important source in the fact that the parties to the argument differ in their metaphysical assumptions." [6] Spiritualists must emphasize the spiritual, materialists the material, dualists both separation and interaction between spirit and matter. Those who consider the spiritual as higher than the material must teach how to subordinate flesh to spirit, whereas those who see spirit as emerging from matter must instruct how best to create, nurture, and evolve higher spirits. If spirit and matter are independent, some will separate sacred and secular education in different schools, but if they are interdependent, only limited separation seems possible. If there are two worlds, the natural and the supernatural, instruction fails if it does not take both into account. If only nature exists, the educator's duty is to dispel superstitious illusions about the alleged supernatural. If the next life is more important, education must be directed toward preparation for it, but if this life is all, one must seek to learn how to get all his enjoyment here.

"The importance of theory of values will probably be much more readily accepted by educators than will the importance of theory of knowledge or a theory of reality." [7] Some will emphasize ends and others means. Some will see values as subjective and primarily a matter of attitude, others as objective and, thus, to be sought after outside of self, while still others accept the more difficult job of inter-

[3] John S. Brubacher, *Modern Philosophies of Education*, p. 53. McGraw-Hill Book Co., New York, 1939. By permission of the publishers.

[4] See Michael Demiashkevich, *An Introduction to the Philosophy of Education*, Chs. V and VI. American Book Co., New York, 1935.

[5] *Ibid.*, p. 168ff.   [7] *Ibid.*, p. 76.

[6] Brubacher, *op. cit.*, p. 24.

relating each to the other. Some teach optimism, even too much optimism (e.g., "Pippa Passes"), some pessimism, even too much pessimism (e.g., Schopenhauer's attitude toward women), whereas others are either neutral or melioristic. The sciences of aesthetics and ethics contribute to educational goals by helping decide how to appreciate, discriminate, evaluate, and how to choose between right and wrong, both in general and in specific situations. The absolutist and relativist, egoist and altruist, aristocrat and utilitarian, all face different tasks as educators. The influences of religious, social, political, and economic philosophies upon educational philosophies are even more obvious. Individualists must train for self-reliance, how to succeed competitively, how to maintain one's rights. Totalitarians must teach self-control and submission to the will of God [8] or "silent obedience to authority and joy of responsibility" [9] to the state. Organicists must show when it is best to assert oneself and when to accept one's lot.

Controversies

If we turn from philosophy of education, understood in terms of contributions of different philosophical fields, to the actual controversies embittering contemporary American teachers and school administrators, we find a snarl of confusion and misunderstanding coming to focus in the opposition of two uneasy groups of alliances under the banners of "progressivism" versus "essentialism." Not only do fights about supernaturalism versus naturalism,[10] reflected both in conflicts over parochial versus public school support and in public school policies, continue, but they become sharpened around problems of curriculum planning and teaching methods guided by different assumptions concerning whether human nature is primarily static or dynamic and whether the primary sources of educational development lie inside or outside the learner.

This latter controversy is, perhaps, the basis for the others, though it cannot be isolated. Externalists believe that the individual begins

[8] "Without God, the Catholic maintains there is no ultimate purpose in life, no ultimate purpose in education." William McGucken, *The Philosophy of Catholic Education* (quoted in Stella Van Petten, *Introduction to Philosophy of Education*, p. 243. University of Chicago Press, Chicago, 1947).

[9] George Frederick Kneller, *The Educational Philosophy of National Socialism*, p. 141. Yale University Press, New Haven, 1941.

[10] Treated by Alexander Meiklejohn in *Education Between Two Worlds*. Harper & Bros., New York, 1942.

as practically nothing, or, at most, as a simple soul or blank tablet or empty cabinet waiting to be furnished. All that happens to the developing person, either for good or ill, comes from the outside. Those who conceive the external as ultimately static and perfect, either as an eternal God or a completely rational nature, believe the task of the educator to be that of molding the individual securely into the righteous pattern of the universe. Truth is known, at least in part; so the educational aim is to discipline the recalcitrant person into conformity with pre-existing truth. Those who believe the external to be dynamic, still see the individual as a subordinate member of a group which nurtures him and protects him and therefore should mold him for his own good. Internalists, on the other hand, tend to believe that human nature is essentially good and that if left alone it will develop naturally, wholesomely, and happily. Evil appears either in the way of temptations of the flesh, the illusion of material reality, the frustration of desires, or tyrannical control. If a person is thought of as an eternal soul whose perfection is assured unless it yields to external evils, the job of the educator is to help to protect the sacred spirit by aiding its flight from the world to monastic or yogic asylum. If souls have static potentialities which must flower into perfected actuality before they can reap their reward, then not flight from the world but stubborn and steeled resistance to it is the educational goal of those who would pass a fitness test before entering heaven. If personalities are conceived as dynamic centers of cosmic creativity, then each must blossom in its own way, so then originality, not uniformity, should be encouraged by educators. In extreme form, this latter means that a child should always do exactly as he pleases without anyone's inhibiting his actions. The disastrous attempts of those misled by such extreme individualism are too well known to need comment here.

Pressures of practice bring educational philosophy closer to organic conceptions, wherein the sources of growth are recognized as both inner and outer and such that development can take place only through interaction between inner and outer. This view is represented best by Dewey and his "progressive" followers, though a plethora of misunderstandings has resulted more in confusion and heated tempers than in enlightened practices. Says Dewey: "The history of educational theory is marked by opposition between the idea that education is development from within and that it is a formation from without; that it is based upon natural endowments and that education is a process of overcoming natural inclination and substituting in its place habits acquired under external pressure." [11] "In its contrast with the ideas both of unfolding of latent powers from within, and of formation from without, the ideal growth results in the conception that education is a constant reorganizing or reconstructing of experience." [12] "To imposition from above is opposed expression and cultivation of individuality; to external discipline is opposed free activity; to acquisition of isolated skills and techniques by drill, is opposed acquisition of them as means of attaining ends which make direct vital appeal; to preparation for a more or less remote future is opposed making the most of opportunities of present life; to static aims and materials is opposed acquaintance with a changing world." [13]

Although Dewey was apparently seeking a middle path, the fight in his time was primarily against the static and externalized extremes. When his fight began to prove effective, many different kinds of disgruntled teachers, from the lazy to the vicious, jumped on his band wagon and, although they did not wreck it, succeeded in making it seem so silly that it no longer appears in many places under the name "progressivism." Dewey warned that "there is always the danger in a new movement that in rejecting the aims and methods of that which it would supplant, it may develop its principles negatively rather than positively and constructively." [14] Too rapid expansion of the progressive movement resulted in trying to "teach old dogs new tricks" when too many teachers were incapable of reconstructing their whole life outlook and keeping up with day-to-day drudgery at the same time. The occasion offered opportunity for many crackpots to seize upon misunderstandings to promote many varieties of radicalism—rejecting all discipline, all preparation, all essential skills, all demands for cooperation—which made much educational practice a farce, all in the name of "progressivism." The failure of "progressives" to fight with complete success on both fronts has brought sufficient entrenchment of misunderstanding to warrant abandonment of the name in many places. But the fight continues and, in Bode's words, "If democracy is here to stay, then the spirit of Progressive education can never become obsolete." [15]

[11] John Dewey, *Experience and Education*, p. 1. The Macmillan Co., New York, 1938.

[12] Dewey, *Democracy and Education*, p. 89.

[13] Dewey, *Experience and Education*, pp. 5–6.

[14] *Ibid.*, p. 6.

[15] Boyd H. Bode, "Is Progressive Education Obsolete?" *School and Society*, Sept. 29, 1947, p. 416.

However, recent excesses have caused many varieties of opponents of "progressivism" to gather together as "essentialists," all claiming that it is "the duty of educators to develop in the young the fundamental attitudes, appreciations, skills, and information, the value of which has stood the test of the history of civilization and which therefore can be regarded as constant, unchanging fundamentals in the education of man, citizen, and world inhabitant." [16] "Convinced of what are the essentials of education, he firmly and resolutely insists that the child experience them. If he does not believe that the whole curriculum should be prescribed, he at least believes that a considerable part of it should be. In the traditional curriculum he finds certain classics in literature, mathematics, religion, history, science, and others whose value is independent of the place and time they are studied. These, educated men must know. They are essentials. They must be learned even though their significance is not made clear in the fulfillment of some present purpose. Till such occasion arises later, they are to be learned and stored away." [17] However, many disagreements exist among "essentialists" as to precisely what are the essentials and which are the frills. The reader must seek elsewhere for fuller accounts of essentialists and their continuing controversies with both the progressives and the varieties of radicals. Enough has been said, surely, to illustrate the significance of philosophical issues in educational practices.

The foregoing general considerations leave untouched many more specific areas where philosophical differences determine disagreement. Shall education be primarily vocational or primarily liberal and what, then, constitutes a liberal education? [18] Should public schools be considered specialized institutions aiming solely at "preparing" for living in the future, or thought of as integrative agencies in which the current happiness of the child "living today" is the primary concern? [19] Should educational responsibility pertain only to intellect or also to emotions; only to facts or also to attitudes; only to understanding or also to appreciation; only to subject-matter or

[16] Demiashkevich, *op. cit.*, p. 147.

[17] Brubacher, *op. cit.*, p. 336.

[18] See Everett Dean Martin, *The Meaning of a Liberal Education*. W. W. Norton and Co., Inc., New York, 1926. Also Archie J. Bahm, "What is a 'Liberal Education'?" in *School and Society*, July 26, 1947, pp. 63–64.

[19] For Thomas Verner Smith, ". . . education becomes not a preparation for life but apprenticeship in the process of living." *The Democratic Way of Life*, p. 199. University of Chicago Press, Chicago, 1926, 1939.

also to problem-solving adaptability; only to attendance records or also to wholesome personality; only to "passing on the wisdom of the elders" or also to "learning for oneself"; [20] only to individual resourcefulness or also to social cooperation. How much of one's education should be formal and how much from the school of hard knocks? Should educational opportunities, standards of achievement, and teacher-attentiveness be equal for all or do morons and geniuses deserve special consideration? Does education aim primarily at peace and contentment or at motivating desires and ambitions, at faith in mankind or at distrust with existing conditions, at dogmatic faith or at doubt and disillusionment? [21]

Ought children be taught to believe that the world owes them a living, or that each is somehow responsible for the welfare of the whole world? Can one get enough education in early years to last a lifetime or does each age or stage involve its own level of development before readiness for dealing with problems is possible, and require its own kind of schooling which cannot be achieved at earlier ages? Is the training in democratic living acquired at home or kindergarten sufficient for all later groups or must the educator reintroduce his pupils to the duties of citizenship at each new level of public achievement? How specific shall the school's responsibility be regarding preparation for marriage or job, readjustment after divorce, unemployment rehabilitation, keeping teeth clean, or psychiatric hospital parole? Finally, who is responsible for a person's philosophical development and to what extent should people be encouraged to devote themselves to general knowledge as compared with specific skills, problems, prides, and embarrassments?

All these, and more, are questions not only for the professional philosopher of education, but questions which every teacher and student, every administrator and voter, must settle if he is to be freed from confusion. A man cannot understand himself fully until he has gained some insight into the different philosophies of education. Only if he can reconstruct the policies of those persons who have

[20] "A half-truth won for ourselves is worth more than a whole truth learned from others." S. Radhakrishnan, *Indian Philosophy*, Vol. I, p. 553. George Allen and Unwin, London, 1931, 1948.

[21] "The process of education is a process of disillusion. Things are not what we thought. We are not what we thought. The values of life change with the journey. What seemed important becomes unimportant. What seemed unreal becomes momentous." John E. Boodin, *The Religion of Tomorrow*, p. 158. The Philosophical Library, New York, 1943.

guided his own upbringing will he be able to understand fully how he came to be as he is. The influences of philosophy of education are all-pervasive, observable not only elsewhere, i.e., in childhood experiences, school board meetings, educational textbooks, but at each moment of experience, such as in the reading of this book, chapter, or sentence.

· 30 ·

Where to from Here?

It is indeed questionable whether a concluding chapter of an introductory textbook has any right to draw conclusions. Since the viewpoint of the author is that philosophizing can end with a last chapter or last page no more than it could have begun with the first of any book, the following paragraphs will be devoted to suggestions for the future.

Those who believe that the definition of a subject comes better at the end than at the beginning of an introduction may now be encouraged to reflect upon the conception which they have developed and to compare it with earlier statements by rereading the first chapter. It is hoped that philosophical problems, attitudes, methods, activities, conclusions, and effects have been illustrated, though, obviously, in varying degrees of completeness. Although acquaintance with areas of problems and types of conflicting conclusions has been emphasized, to the neglect of attention to methods of pursuing philosophical activities, which can become familiar only through participation in actual give-and-take or Socratic discussion-type processes, the importance of the philosophical attitude has also been paramount.

The student who entered upon this type of introduction to philosophy expecting to find "the truth" already wrapped up in a neat package waiting to be handed him has been deeply disappointed. Students often say about philosophy that "this isn't like anything I ever had before," because it aims directly at challenging them to think for themselves. Although, of course, reflective thinking has occurred elsewhere also, seldom is the purpose to insist upon reflection so persistently pursued. When a person is encouraged to seek sympathetic understanding, first with one and then another and another of partially plausible views, and then he sees each, in turn, refuted by telling arguments, he naturally becomes confused. The difficulty lies partly in a false preconception that truth is simple and without multiple or opposing viewpoints, partly in naive faith that one's own outlook is consistent simply because it is one's own, and partly in the expectation that philosophy, too, is best taught by indoctrination which is to be regurgitated in examinations exactly as prescribed.

The demand that a student re-examine himself, and the discovery that all is not well in his own intellectual house, produce a disturbance and a bewilderment that lasts throughout a large part of the course. Once a student accepts the challenge, however, that it is only right that he earn his beliefs by his own efforts, instead of expecting, as his birthright, vicarious solution to his problems, he comes gradually to realize that the responsible job of philosophizing, for himself at least, is his own. When he seriously discovers that the first hasty reaction to mounting doubt and disbelief, namely, that "You can't believe anything," is itself a belief, he normally turns from intellectual fretting to intellectual sweating, if he is equal to the task. Only then is the first essential of the philosophical attitude achieved, namely, one must be troubled, perplexed, wondering about problems that are worth being worried about. One must himself experience the pangs of doubt, uncertainty, suspended judgment and a willing weariness in persistent reflection before he can appreciate fully the philosophical attitude.

But, also, he has not arrived until he has achieved considerable measure of what contemporary scientists like to call objectivity, i.e., faith in the belief that the ability to compare beliefs without fully believing them is the most superior belief—for purposes of intellectual reflection. This willingness to be tolerant of all beliefs, dogmatic about none, is not easy to come by, especially since a bias against bias does not cease to be bias. An unprejudiced attitude may be deliberately, but not completely, acquired.[1] He who would be philosophical is in constant danger of forgetting to reflect about the subjectivity of the desire to be objective. Finally, one understands the philosophical attitude only when he himself has accepted the necessity for speculation or for trying out various alternative hypotheses— a need arising naturally out of his willingness to face philosophical problems as his own. The writer's presentation of his own philosophy in this text may be taken, not so much as an attempt to convert readers, as a willingness to be objective, i.e., as an unwillingness to pretend that he has no viewpoint. His speculations, as well as his criti-

[1] See John Grier Hibben, *A Defence of Prejudice*. Charles Scribner's Sons, New York, 1911.

cisms of other views, may be taken as an example of the kind of effort he would have the reader make, both in attempting to attain the philosophical attitude and in pursuit of his own intellectual salvation.

In advising students what to do next, one is faced with the fact that such advice must be particular, not merely general, for where one should go next will depend upon how far he has come, where he stands, and where he desires to go and is capable of going. Risking superficiality, we may classify readers into the bored, the irritated, and the challenged.

For the bored, especially for those forced to endure a required course while subscribing unquestioningly to the philosophy that "philosophy bakes no bread," and for whom "bread" is the sole aim of education, advice is futile. Few of them will have read this far and, for those who have, the best advice is to drop the matter as quickly as possible. They are not in a mood for accepting recommendations and are likely to remain unimpressed either by warnings that their refusal to philosophize involves a kind of philosophy which falsely assumes that philosophies are innocent of practical costs and consequences or by warnings against temptations to "seek profits" in philosophy.

Although philosophy and profits are usually considered unrelated, there are two ways in which they are connected. First of all, though philosophy has so far been relatively free from business-type racketeering, the persistent and widespread need which people have for philosophical security offers a wide-open field for vicious exploitation. Exhorting the selfish not to exploit philosophy because, as has happened in psychology,[2] commercializing it would bring a bad name to a good thing, is more likely to arouse than to quiet interest. However, fortunately for philosophy, so long as religious and health cures offer much easier fields for quacks, philosophy remains unlikely to be troubled. Secondly, when one discovers that "practicality is inevitably shortsighted,"[3] and consequently profits foreshortened, a business man may, if he is able, try to profit by farsightedness. He rightly turns to economists, physicists, psychologists, sociologists, and the like, for broader outlooks. But, if he learns his first lessons well enough, he will realize that these fields, too, suffer from a measure

[2] E.g., Dale Carnegie's *How to Win Friends and Influence People.* Simon and Schuster, New York, 1936.

[3] George Russell Harrison, *Atoms in Action.* William Morrow and Co., New York, 1939.

of shortsightedness which can be cured only by a philosophical, or over-all, look. An awareness that contemporary big business and fascist and communist philosophies beget economic policies and business practices which both revolutionize outlooks and defeat competitors still practicing under older philosophies may cause some reconsideration of whether or not there are long-range profits derivable from investment in philosophy. Those persons wise enough to do this are not in need of much advice, and are not to be found among the bored.

The irritated—especially those already comfortably committed to a sectarian dogma and who squirm at each embarrassing question raised as to a painful thorn thrust mercilessly into their intellectual flesh—they too should run away as quickly as possible, back to the cover of their creed, the womb of their thought, the satisfaction of their unreflective security. Such words are not intended as facetious, at least not for those who have felt no signs of intellectual awakening after so much prodding. Those who have neither ability nor willingness to think for themselves should be troubled no more than necessary. Philosophizing is risky business, since one can become insane from too much philosophizing, i.e., from more than he can handle, as well as from too much of anything else. There are times, if one is too old or too young or too heavily laden with other problems, when pressure to philosophize becomes an evil. Only a devil would demand of anyone more than he can give. However, in dealing with the irritated there exists also a contrary problem. Narrow dogmas inspiring dogmatic minds are seldom innocent. Those who recognize their inability to philosophize are safe enough. But others, whose unwillingness or inability to appreciate the values of philosophical tolerance makes them even more zealous persecuters of all opposition, can hardly be warned, but merely warned against. The intolerant rightly seek sanctuary in sectarian schools, for only there can they be guaranteed freedom from disturbance of previously settled patterns of beliefs. Whoever graduates from a public college without having his mind changed somewhat owes apology to himself, his parents, his college, and his state. For, what is the purpose of college education if not to make one grow and, thus, to change? He who has not changed has not grown. Parents, paradoxically, want their children to grow (become different) and yet, somehow, remain the same. Today, at least, we are more likely to find the irritated among parents than among their children.

Finally, the challenged, especially those who have awakened to a compelling need for solving these tremendous problems for themselves, may wish advisement, so the remainder of this chapter is for them. Yet they, too, differ with respect to their needs, abilities and desires, in how much they have been challenged and how much more challenge they want, in how much insight they have achieved and how much more insight will be required to satisfy them, and in how far they remain bewildered or have regained (if they ever lost) confidence in their philosophical abilities. Surely the completely confused and those who are already on their way out of confusion will want different kinds of help. It is impossible, consequently, to advise all in the same way. All that can be done here, after noting further differences, is (1) to warn of some typical dangers and (2) to suggest possible sources for further help.

As for these differences, even some of those who have been challenged must be advised frankly to turn to some established pattern and to draw from it their guiding theories. Others may be encouraged to become extremely radical; for, once convinced that he must learn everything for himself, a person often has to go all-out in rejecting the hampering past. This, although a seemingly needless extreme to onlookers, is a path which some must follow. Whenever extremist temperaments undertake philosophical reconstruction, nothing less than a final realization of the extreme emptiness resulting from a complete house-cleaning will convince them of a need for a return to philosophy, much as many anti-religionists have found happiness only in a return to religion.[4] However, their distrust of the past and intolerance of any suggestion that does not meet wholeheartedly the demands of their inner sense of truthfulness may too easily be mistaken for cantankerousness. Nevertheless, like the intolerant demands of other dogmatists, a dogmatic insistence upon seeing absolutely everything first by oneself may be a vicious handicap to social harmony. About the only advice that may be taken by those who have become supercautious about satisfying the demands of their inner honesty is that they try not to be too persistent in pestering either friends or enemies with their private problems. Not only is thinking a "dangerous trade. It is also a troublesome one, as the thinker while he is thinking is apt to be an unsocial nuisance

[4] See Henry C. Link, *The Return to Religion*. The Macmillan Co., New York, 1936.

to his family and his friends, and in consequence to himself." [5] Finally, for those whose future calls for further floundering in uncertainties, the writer can only extend his best wishes, for the job of finding a way out of a personal muddle is one that each person must somehow do for himself.

Dangers

The typical dangers confronting the seeker for satisfactory philosophical insight are many. Chief among them is the expectation that a vision of the way out can come all at once or easily and, consequently, a willingness to succumb to hasty generalizations, especially to the generalization that no satisfactory solution is possible. Few who have been deeply stirred by awareness of philosophical variety can ever be fully or permanently satisfied with either a first new insight or any ready-made theory. Since each famous philosopher is a person whose conclusions were produced partly by the peculiarities of his own life and circumstances, few should expect to find their own intellectual needs exactly fulfilled in achievements of others. This leads us to the danger of hero-worship and consequent authoritarianism. Hero-worship is not, in itself, an evil, but, in many cases, a genuine good. He who would pursue his own quest for truth may do well to emulate one who has successfully gone before. "Vicarious integration of personality" [6] may be useful for beginners, but only up to a certain point. Beyond this point, when the job of integrating a unique personality becomes a unique job, continuation of hero-worship involves mistaking a means for an end.

Related to this is the danger of narrowness, due either to sectarianism or specialization. Since, especially for those who are eager and anxious, it is easy to mistake a part for the whole of truth, just because it is discovered to be truth, those for whom a path through sectarian or specialized channels is the only way, or the easiest way, are particularly in danger of stopping unknowingly far short of their goal. There is a similar danger that one will conclude too soon that attitude, or method, or activity, or conclusions is all that matters. Especially those who expect to find their salvation by listening to

[5] W. A. Sinclair, *An Introduction to Philosophy*, p. 149. Oxford Univ. Press, London, 1944.

[6] L. L. Bernard, *Introduction to Social Psychology*, p. 333. Henry Holt and Co., New York, 1926.

others, or, even better, to the great others, may conclude that philosophy consists in the history of philosophy and that he who knows this history has thereby already worked out his own philosophy.[7] One can hardly arrive at a satisfactory system of philosophy without having sufficient acquaintance with the achievements and mistakes of the past, in order to profit from them; yet philosophical pedantry may possibly be mistaken for philosophical salvation. A different danger which lies in wait for those who reject historical assistance is the succumbing to morbid self-examination.

Also, there are difficulties involved in assuming that one can stop living while he philosophizes. Since confused thinking tends to beget confused living, one may well give, like Descartes,[8] some preliminary consideration as to how best to provide for untroubled living while devoting oneself to troubled thinking. Then, of course, if one can succeed somehow in isolating himself from practical cares for pursuit of more efficient reflection, there remains the danger that he shall have built himself an ivory tower from which he can never quite come out.

As one approaches his final philosophical goal, two more dangers await him. When one has sought so long with perpetual open-mindedness for the truth, he is likely to think that the truth which he finds is open-minded truth. But the very reason for one's seeking truth is to enable him to close his mind against error. If one has persistently striven for objectivity and unprejudicedness, he tends to believe that his long-hoped-for prize actually embodies the complete absence of prejudice which he had idealized it to have. But the search for certainty is a search for prejudice, because only when one can prejudge what will be or ought to be can he be really certain. The aim of philosophy is to end philosophizing, so whoever succeeds in reaching this goal ceases, thereby, to be completely philosophical. The last danger which we shall mention is the same which tempts any winner of a rare prize: "This is the best yet, and I am, therefore, 'holier than thou.'" It is indeed doubtful whether anyone has arrived at philosophy's final goal until he has been humbled enough by the process to be willing to let others have "superior" philosophies, so long as his is sufficient for himself.

[7] See further, A. J. Bahm, "In Defense of Philosophy," *School and Society,* Feb. 16, 1946, p. 115.

[8] See René Descartes, *Discourse on Method,* especially Part III.

Sources

Suggestions for possible sources of further help will be limited to other courses, further readings, and philosophical societies.

Most of the readers for whom this book is intended, i.e., American college students, are already aware of other courses in their college's department of philosophy. No general advice can be given as to which course should be taken next, except that it should, if possible, be closest to one's present interests and that it should not be over one's head. General courses in the history of philosophy and logic are as fundamental as any, but the specific needs of particular students may lead them first into aesthetics, philosophy of religion, ethics, or philosophy of science.

However, some non-philosophical courses may be even more important than strictly philosophical courses. For if one's philosophy aims at comprehensiveness and at a kind of wholeness of which the subject-matters of the various sciences, for example, are parts, then must he not attend to these parts before he can become ready to conclude concerning the whole? If each of the physical, biological, psychological, and social sciences, and literature, language, and the fine arts, have something fundamental to contribute to human outlooks, a person short-changes himself if he fails to seek to understand the basic insights they have to offer.[9] However, since so many of those who begin to search for the insights of special sciences become so absorbed in these pursuits that they fail to return to more comprehensive philosophizing, often mistaking the outlook of the particular specialist for an all-sufficient over-all philosophy, there is great danger here.

Attempts to remedy the excesses of extreme specialization occur in general education courses, which aim both to survey the major contributions of each field and to integrate, or at least interrelate, their findings. In a day when people take pride in being scientific rather than philosophical, we find philosophy being taught under many different names. General, comprehensive, and integrative courses often aim, whether clearly or confusedly, to express philosophical outlooks. A student's philosophical growth may be served better by such a course than by a specifically philosophical course, especially if the person teaching philosophy happens himself to be a narrow specialist

[9] For suggestions, see A. J. Bahm, "A Proposed College Curriculum," *Bulletin of the American Association of University Professors,* Autumn, 1946, p. 548ff.

in one field or school of philosophical thought. A chief danger of general courses is the failure of their instructors to have achieved the philosophical maturity necessary to expound the major philosophical issues and movements, and their implications. But where there are good instructors, any course can be highly philosophical. A course in the humanities, for example, should be nothing if not philosophical. Courses in social science, natural science, history of civilization, world literature, and orientation may have philosophical content and implications.

In addition, some instructors teach philosophy under such titles as "History of . . ." (e.g., history of social thought, history of political theory, history of educational principles), "Comparative . . ." (e.g., comparative religions, comparative economic systems, comparative political philosophies), or, of course, "Philosophy of . . ." (e.g., philosophy of education, philosophy of science, philosophy of history). Also such titles as "Principles of . . ." or "Theory of . . ." may signify philosophical content or aim. The terms "literature" and "foreign language" (including courses interpreting foreign cultures) are ambiguous enough to cover philosophical literature and philosophical aspects of foreign cultures. Needless to say, it is wise to consult the instructor and previous students concerning the probable philosophical aspects of such courses.

Further readings may be of many sorts: 1. The timid student may wish to try another introduction. Some standard texts similar to this one are: H. H. Titus, *Living Issues in Philosophy;* Durant Drake, *Invitation to Philosophy;* W. S. Gamertsfelder and D. L. Evans, *Fundamentals of Philosophy;* G. T. W. Patrick, *Introduction to Philosophy;* George R. Geiger, *Philosophy and the Social Order;* Roy Wood Sellars, *Principles and Problems of Philosophy;* David A. Major, *An Introduction to Philosophy;* C. E. M. Joad, *Guide to Philosophy;* Clifford Barrett, *Philosophy;* Hunter Mead, *The Types and Problems of Philosophy;* Abraham Edel, *The Theory and Practice of Philosophy;* E. S. Brightman, *Introduction to Philosophy;* G. W. Cunningham, *Problems of Philosophy;* G. P. Conger, *A Course in Philosophy.* 2. Excellent variations from systematic-survey texts are: Max Otto, *The Human Enterprise;* Wm. E. Hocking, *Types of Philosophy;* Irwin Edman, *Four Ways of Philosophy.*

3. Various attempts at making selections from the writings of different types of authors include: R. E. Hoople, R. F. Piper, and W. P. Tolley, *Preface to Philosophy, Book of Readings;* J. H. Randall, J. Buchler, and E. U. Shirk, *Readings in Philosophy;* D. J. Bronstein,

Y. H. Krikorian, and P. P. Wiener, *Basic Problems of Philosophy;* B. Rand, *The Classical Philosophers;* R. T. Flewelling, *Things That Matter Most;* D. S. Robinson, *An Anthology of Recent Philosophy;* T. V. Smith, *Philosophers Speak for Themselves;* T. V. Smith and Marjorie Greene, *From Descartes to Kant.*

4. No interested student should neglect the history of philosophy. Those who seek the gentlest beginnings may start with: Will Durant, *The Story of Philosophy;* H. E. Cushman, *A Beginner's History of Philosophy.* 5. Standard histories include: Alfred Weber, *History of Philosophy;* A. K. Rogers, *A Student's History of Philosophy;* Frank Thilly, *History of Philosophy;* B. A. G. Fuller, *History of Philosophy;* George Boas, *The Major Traditions in European Philosophy;* Bertrand Russell, *A History of Western Philosophy;* W. Windelband, *A History of Philosophy.* 6. Some may prefer to begin with particular periods, such as the Greek, medieval, the modern, or the contemporary: John M. Warbeke, *The Searching Mind of Greece;* W. T. Stace, *A Critical History of Greek Philosophy;* Charles M. Bakewell, *Sourcebook in Ancient Philosophy;* Milton Nahm, *Selections from Greek Philosophy;* Henry Osborne Taylor, *The Mediaeval Mind;* E. Gilson, *The Spirit of Mediaeval Philosophy;* J. H. Randall, *The Making of the Modern Mind;* Alburey Castell, *An Introduction to Modern Philosophy;* D. D. Runes, *Twentieth-Century Philosophy.*

7. Many will want insight into special fields: (*a*) Epistemology: W. A. Sinclair, *Introduction to Philosophy;* Bertrand Russell, *The Problems of Philosophy;* W. P. Montague, *The Ways of Knowing.* (*b*) Logic and scientific method: John Dewey, *How We Think;* Alburey Castell, *A College Logic;* A. M. Frye and A. W. Levi, *Rational Belief;* Roger W. Holmes, *The Rhyme of Reason;* W. H. Werkmeister, *An Introduction to Critical Thinking;* Lionel Ruby, *Logic, An Introduction;* Morris Cohen and E. Nagel, *Introduction to Logic and Scientific Method;* Harold A. Larabee, *Reliable Knowledge;* C. W. Churchman, *Elements of Logic and Formal Science;* Columbia Associates, *Introduction to Reflective Thinking;* E. A. Burtt, *Right Thinking.* (*c*) Philosophy of Science: A. G. Ramsperger, *Philosophies of Science;* A. C. Benjamin, *An Introduction to Philosophy of Science;* W. H. Werkmeister, *A Philosophy of Science;* A. D. Richie, *Scientific Method;* C. E. M. Joad, *The Philosophical Aspects of Modern Science;* James B. Conant, *On Understanding Science.* (*d*) Metaphysics: W. B. Marvin, *Introduction to Metaphysics;* J. S. More, *Rifts in the Universe;* D. W. Gotshalk, *Structure and Reality;* Paul Weiss, *Reality;* F. H. Bradley, *Appearance and Reality.* (*e*) Axiology:

DeWitt H. Parker, *Human Values;* R. B. Perry, *General Theory of Value;* W. H. Urban, *Valuation, Its Nature and Laws.* (*f*) Aesthetics: DeWitt H. Parker, *The Principles of Aesthetics;* E. F. Carritt, *What is Beauty?;* Aram Torossian, *A Guide to Aesthetics;* H. S. Langfeld, *The Aesthetic Attitude;* D. W. Gotshalk, *Art and the Social Order;* L. W. Flaccus, *The Spirit and Substance of Art;* John Dewey, *Art as Experience;* E. F. Carritt, *Philosophies of Beauty;* Melvin Rader, *A Modern Book of Aesthetics.* (*g*) Ethics: Wm. H. Roberts, *The Problem of Choice;* H. H. Titus, *Ethics for Today;* W. T. Stace, *The Concept of Morals;* W. M. Urban, *Fundamental of Ethics;* Melvin Rader, *Ethics and Society;* E. T. Mitchell, *A System of Ethics;* D. S. Robinson, *Principles of Conduct;* Charles H. Patterson, *Moral Standards;* Philip Wheelwright, *A Critical Introduction to Ethics;* T. V. Smith, *Constructive Ethics;* R. A. Tsanoff, *Ethics;* Max Otto, *Things and Ideals;* T. E. Hill, *Contemporary Ethical Theories.* (*h*) Philosophy of religion: H. T. Houf, *What Religion Is and Does;* E. S. Brightman, *A Philosophy of Religion;* D. M. Edwards, *The Philosophy of Religion.* (*i*) Comparative religions: A. E. Haydon, *The Quest of the Ages;* Lewis Browne, *This Believing World;* J. C. Archer, *Faiths Men Live By;* Charles Francis Potter, *The Story of Religion;* G. G. Atkins, *The Procession of the Gods;* E. D. Soper, *The Religions of Mankind;* George F. Moore, *History of Religions,* two vols.; G. P. Conger, *The Ideologies of Religion.* (*j*) Social philosophy: Charles H. Cooley, *Human Nature and the Social Order;* George H. Mead, *Mind, Self, and Society;* C. A. Elwood, *A History of Social Philosophy.* (*k*) Political philosophy: G. E. G. Catlin, *The Story of the Political Philosophers;* F. W. Coker, *Readings in Political Philosophy;* J. A. Leighton, *Social Philosophies in Conflict;* T. I. Cook, *History of Political Philosophy.* (*l*) Economic philosophy: Eric Roll, *A History of Economic Thought;* L. H. Haney, *History of Economic Thought.* (*m*) Philosophy of education: John S. Brubacher, *Modern Philosophies of Education;* John Dewey, *Experience and Education;* E. D. Martin, *The Meaning of a Liberal Education;* M. Demiashkevich, *An Introduction to the Philosophy of Education;* A. Meiklejohn, *Education Between Two Worlds.*

8. It is dangerous to neglect other cultural areas: (*a*) India: Rabindranath Tagore, *Sadhana, The Realization of Life;* M. Hiriyanna, *The Essentials of Indian Philosophy;* S. Radhakrishnan, *Indian Philosophy,* two vols.; S. Dasgupta, *A History of Indian Philosophy,* four vols. (*b*) China: Lin Yutang, *My Country and My People;* Fung Yu-lan, *A Short History of Chinese Philosophy.* (*c*) America:

H. G. Townsend, *Philosophical Ideas in the United States;* W. H. Werkmeister, *A History of Philosophical Ideas in America;* P. R. Anderson and M. H. Fisch, *Philosophy in America;* M. H. Fisch, *Classical American Philosophers;* T. V. Smith, *The Philosophic Way of Life in America;* J. L. Blau, *Men and Movements in American Philosophy;* Herbert Schneider, *A History of American Philosophy.*

9. Encyclopaedias and dictionaries: Hasting's *Encyclopaedia of Religion and Ethics;* Baldwin's *Dictionary of Philosophy and Psychology;* D. D. Runes, *Dictionary of Philosophy.*

10. Journals: (*a*) General: *The Journal of Philosophy, The Philosophical Review, Journal of the History of Ideas, Mind, Philosophy.* (*b*) Special fields: *Ethics, Journal of Aesthetics and Art Criticism, Review of Metaphysics, Philosophy of Science, Journal of Social Philosophy* (publication discontinued), *Journal of Symbolic Logic, British Journal of Philosophy of Science, The Hibbert Journal* (religion), *Review of Religion, Journal of Religion.* (*c*) Journals representing movements or schools of thought: *Philosophy and Phenomenological Research, The Personalist, Philosophical Studies, Analysis, The Thomist, The Modern Schoolman, The New Scholasticism.* (*d*) Oriental and world-wide journals: *Philosophy East and West, The Philosophical Quarterly* (Indian).

Philosophical societies are not designed, ordinarily, to help beginners, unless they be local college or community groups and many of these depend for their existence and continuance upon the particular efforts of devoted persons. Philosophical problems often are so intimate and personal that they can be dealt with best in informal gatherings which may carry on until a person's problems get a thorough going-into. However, although there is some danger that philosophical interests will suffer from attempts to formalize and regularize student philosophical meetings, some notable exceptions exist. Nevertheless, beginners may gain help from knowing about the existence of various kinds of philosophical societies. Larger universities offering doctoral work in philosophy usually have a society of interest primarily to its professors, graduate students, majors, and other qualified persons from related fields.[10] Many states have state societies.[11]

---

[10] E.g., Boston University Philosophical Society and the University of Michigan Acolytes.

[11] E.g., Georgia Philosophical Society, Indiana Philosophical Association, Missouri State Philosophy Association, New Mexico Philosophical Society, West Virginia Philosophical Society, Wisconsin Philosophical Association, The Creighton Club (New York), Philosophy Section of the Michigan Academy of Sciences, Arts and Letters, Philosophy Section of the Ohio College Association.

Six regional groups exist [12] and there are national,[13] international,[14] and world-wide [15] organizations.   In addition to geographically organized societies, some have been established by those interested in special fields,[16] and for promoting particular movements.[17]   Although beginners are not eligible for membership in larger societies, usually, two possible uses may be made of them by students.   Each society holds an annual meeting at which visitors may attend most sessions where papers are read and discussed.   If one can avoid wasting time listening to those papers which are too specialized and technical for his purposes, he may profit considerably from observing contemporary philosophers at work expounding and criticizing their views.   A second possible use is to obtain information about where or whom to consult concerning a particular problem, if such help is desired.   Experts in particular fields often welcome the interest of outside students and may be persuaded to become visiting lecturers or to enter into correspondence.

Professional Possibilities

Perhaps some suggestions are in order for those who happen to be considering majoring in philosophy.   To these it seems appropriate to pass on the advice which DeWitt H. Parker gave to the writer when he sought assurance of the wisdom of his entering upon graduate work in philosophy: "Don't, unless you have an independent income."   To this may be added, "or unless you 'have to' because philosophical problems clamp such a hold upon you that they will not let you go

12 Eastern Division, Western Division, Pacific Division—all of the American Philosophical Association—and Southern Society for Philosophy and Psychology, Southwestern Philosophical Conference, Mountain-Plains Philosophical Conference.

13 E.g., American Philosophical Association, Indian Philosophical Congress, British Mind Association, British Institute of Philosophy.

14 E.g., Inter-American Congress of Philosophy.

15 Fédération International des Sociétés de Philosophie, which sponsors International Congresses of Philosophy.

16 E.g., American Society for Aesthetics, Philosophy of Science Association, Metaphysical Society of America, Association for Symbolic Logic, Philosophy of Education Society.   Also, some specialized societies have philosophical sections. The American Association for the Advancement of Science has a Philosophy of Science Section.   The American Academy of Political and Social Science constantly deals with philosophical topics.

17 E.g., American Catholic Philosophical Association, Association for Realistic Philosophy.

until you have solved them." There are some who say, with Luther, "Ich kann nicht anders" (I cannot do otherwise). These, no one can stop. But for those misguided youths who think that philosophy teaching is a soft job consisting in pointing out student stupidities, or that philosophy teachers constitute a superelite looked up to by all, or that propagandizing for sectarian doctrines is something that can be gotten away with (except in sectarian schools), rude shocks await. Although the teaching of philosophy "bakes enough bread" to support more than a thousand teachers in American colleges, it is not enough to warrant the vocationalizing of philosophy for any but those who have a burning interest in it. Yet, for whoever finds further pursuit of philosophizing a vital necessity, the teaching of philosophy may become the happiest of professions. Like most other phases of teaching, however, the contemporary prospect is that the activities of teaching themselves, rather than financial returns, will constitute the largest part of the reward.

To the inevitable question, "What can I 'do' with philosophy besides teaching it?" some answer must be given. Something so all-pervasive as philosophy must have connections with vocations outside the limited one of teaching in philosophy departments. This is true, but since few smooth paths have been clearly marked out in contemporary vocational customs concerning how to buy and sell philosophical services, those interested must be willing to blaze a trail and risk the consequences of enormous adjustment problems. For those thus interested, many other fields of teaching, first of all, may be indicated. In fact, some may find other fields even more suited to their own philosophical interests than departments of philosophy, for, increasingly, within such departments there is a tendency to specialize, in logic, in aesthetics, or in certain periods of philosophical history. If one has to specialize anyway, or wishes to specialize, he may find himself more at home teaching aesthetics in an art department, logic in a mathematics department, philosophy of history in a history department, political philosophy in a political science department, social philosophy in a sociology department, philosophy of science in a physics department, philosophy in literature in a language and literature department, epistemology or axiology in a psychology department, the writing of philosophical ideas in a journalism department, etc.

It is even possible to profit greatly by philosophical training for teaching in strictly vocational schools, such as those devoted to social work, agriculture, business administration, engineering, and law.

Nowhere, surely, does a philosophy get a clearer testing than in specialized application in technical situations, and nowhere, doubtless, is there greater need for insight into general implications of what is happening in particular circumstances than in places where technical policy is being determined. Social work is saturated with awareness of the consequences of conflicting philosophies. Many local agricultural problems are pervaded with world-wide significance, as the United States Department of Agriculture has sometimes recognized, by its conducting schools of philosophy for agricultural leaders. Philosophy of business, intermingled with business psychology and management problems, has to be taught, directly or indirectly, in business colleges. Engineering training, commonly criticized today for the narrowness of its scope, needs among its teachers men who understand the needs for such technical training and who can alike both criticize and reply to critics concerning the general scope of engineering. A position of national leadership awaits the engineer who is competent both as an engineer and as a philosopher and who can speak up for his fellow-engineers, if not for his fellow-philosophers, and represent their virtues truthfully and convincingly. Although many lawyers are petty men seeking selfish advantage, a great lawyer is nothing if not a philosopher and interpreter of conflicting philosophies.

To the question, What can I do with philosophy? then, the really appropriate reply is, In what profession can I do without philosophy? In addition to the ministry which, in a day of decline because of cultural lag and sectarian squabbles, offers especially great opportunity to high-calibre men with broadened vision. Both general education and educational administration provide increasing chances for profitable use of philosophical achievement. General education courses, such as the humanities, for example, are failures if not guided by some understandable and defensible philosophical aim. In days when academic administrators are drawn from teaching ranks, the narrower the specialization the less fitted does a teacher become, because of his specialized ability, for administrative positions. Statistically, a surprisingly large percentage of college deans are drafted from the ranks of philosophy teachers, doubtless because the demand for breadth both of understanding and appreciation of the essential need of each of the parts for the whole, which is typical of their outlook, makes specialists more willing to trust their fairness, for fairness rests upon insight as well as upon good will. However, when a philosopher is himself a specialist in some field or school of thought, he may be much less well-qualified than broad-minded persons in specialized fields, for to name something "philosophy" does not guarantee breadth. Junior colleges, requiring teachers to teach many different subjects, often find that one who is broadly trained is better able to adapt himself to new specialized courses than one with narrower training.

Finally, a word to those who would be writers. Too many who want to write, because they feel they have a message about the world's meanness or stupidity, fail because they understand neither the world, nor themselves, nor why anyone should want to listen to them, let alone pay for listening. Success as a writer is much more a matter of insight than of luck. Sale of creative writing is something one cannot do much of without some philosophical maturity. Pursuit of philosophical insight does not, however, necessarily require majoring in philosophy. Philosophy departmental requirements may be as narrowly misguided as any, though average practice allows better-than-average range of electives. Those who are undecided about vocational objectives may find philosophical generality of greater advantage than indecisive flip-flopping from one specialty into another. Those prospecting marriage as a career may find awareness of philosophical likenesses and differences of greater importance than money or looks in selecting a mate.

In closing, perhaps it should be pointed out that these few concluding remarks for majors should not mislead the reader to think that this book was primarily for them. Its aims were mainly to arouse some curiosity, to give some perspective of the problems and difficulties in philosophy, and to promote increased measures of tolerance and breadth in outlook. Whoever has achieved these has succeeded, regardless of his feelings of perturbation or the grade entered in the registrar's records; but he who fails to retain some doubts about his philosophical abilities has failed his introductory course.

Index